After the Berlin Wall

After the Berlin Wall
A History of the EBRD
Volume 1

Andrew Kilpatrick

Central European University Press
Budapest–New York

© European Bank for Reconstruction and Development
One Exchange Square
London EC2A 2JN
United Kingdom

Website: *ebrd.com*

Published in 2020 by
Central European University Press
Nádor utca 9, H-1051 Budapest, Hungary
Tel: +36-1-327-3138 or 327-3000
E-mail: ceupress@press.ceu.edu
Website: www.ceupress.com
224 West 57th Street, New York NY 10019, USA

This work is licensed under
a Creative Commons Attribution-NonCommercial-NoDerivatives 4.0 International License.

Terms and names used in this report to refer to geographical or other territories, political and economic groupings and units, do not constitute and should not be construed as constituting an express or implied position, endorsement, acceptance or expression of opinion by the European Bank for Reconstruction and Development or its members concerning the status of any country, territory, grouping and unit, or delimitation of its borders, or sovereignty.

ISBN 978 963 386 394 7 (hardback)
ISBN 978 963 386 384 8 (paperback)
ISBN 978 963 386 385 5 (ebook)

Library of Congress Control Number: 2020940681

Table of Contents

List of Abbreviations	VII
Acknowledgments	XI
Personal Foreword by Suma Chakrabarti	XV
Preface	1
PART I Post-Cold War Pioneer	3
Chapter 1 A New International Development Institution	5
Chapter 2 Creating the EBRD's DNA	43
Chapter 3 Difficult Early Years	73
Chapter 4 Restoring Credibility	109
PART II Transition Mode	131
Chapter 5 Scaling Up through Financial Institutions	133
Chapter 6 Supporting Privatisation and Restructuring	151
Chapter 7 Developing Local Services	185
Chapter 8 Environment Matters	221
Chapter 9 Nuclear Safety	249
Chapter 10 Embedding Impact in the Business Model	265
PART III Holding Course	291
Chapter 11 Russian Crisis	293
Chapter 12 Recovery, Growth and Graduation	311
Appendix	353
Index	359

List of Abbreviations

ADB – Asian Development Bank
AEB – Agreement Establishing the Bank
ARCO – Agency for Restructuring Credit Organisations
BCR – Banca Comercială Română
BCV – Board Consultation Visit
BOT – build-operate-transfer
BTC – Baku-Tbilisi-Ceyhan Pipeline Project
CBR – Central Bank of Russia
CEB – Central Europe and the Baltics
CFC – chlorofluorocarbon
CIS – Commonwealth of Independent States
Comecon – Council for Mutual Economic Assistance
COO – country of operations
CRR – Capital Resources Review
CSFR – Czech and Slovak Federative Republic
CSO – civil society organisation
CSOB – Československá Obchodní Bank
DABLAS – Danube Black Sea Task Force
DBO – design build and operate
DFI – Development Finance Institution
DfID – UK Department for International Development
DHEs – district-heating enterprises
EAP – Environmental Action Plan
EAU – Environmental Appraisal Unit
EC – European Community
EBRD – European Bank for Reconstruction and Development

ECB – European Central Bank
ECOFIN – Economic and Financial Affairs Council, of the European Union
EEC – European Economic Community
EIB – European Investment Bank
EMU – Economic and Monetary Union
ERA – Environmental Remediation Account
EMAS – Environmental Management and Audit Scheme
ETC – early transition country
ETCI – Early Transition Countries Initiative
EU – European Union
FDI – foreign direct investment
FIDP – Financial Institutions Development Programme
FOPC – Financial and Operations Policies Committee
FOPIP – financial and operational improvement programmes
FRY – Federal Republic of Yugoslavia
FSU – former Soviet Union
FVP – First Vice President
GDP – gross domestic product
GDR – German Democratic Republic
GNP – gross national product
H&S – health and safety
HELCOM – Helsinki Commission
IBCI – IntesaBCI
IBRD – International Bank for Reconstruction and Development
IEA – International Energy Agency
IFC – International Finance Corporation
IFI – international financial institution
IGC – Intergovernmental Conference
IMF – International Monetary Fund
IPO – initial public offering
ISB – international standard bank
ISF-2 – Interim Spent Fuel Facility
ISO – International Organisation for Standardisation
ISPA – Instrument for Structural Policies for Pre-Accession
KMB – Small Business Credit Bank
LNG – liquified natural gas
LRTP – Liquid Radioactive Waste Treatment Plant

LSE – London School of Economics
MDG – Millennium Development Goals
MEI – municipal and environment infrastructure
MELF – Municipal Environmental Loan Facility
MIS – management information system
MIT – Massachusetts Institute of Technology
MPP – Mass Privatisation Programme
MSA – municipal support agreement
MSEs – micro and small enterprises
MUDP – Municipal Utilities Development Programme
NBS – National Bank of Slovakia
NDEP – Northern Dimension Environmental Partnership
NGO – non-governmental organisation
NIB – Nordic Investment Bank
NIF – National Investment Fund
NPL – non-performing loan
NSA – Nuclear Safety Account
OCE – Office of the Chief Economist
OECD – Organisation for Economic Cooperation and Development
PED – Project Evaluation Department
PHARE – Poland/Hungary Assistance for Reconstruction of Economies
PBZ – Privredna Banka Zagreb
PMPP – Polish Mass Privatisation Programme
PPC – Project Preparation Committee
PPF – Post-Privatisation Fund
PPP – public-private partnership
PSA – Production Sharing Agreement / Project Support Agreement
PSC – public service contract
RPFB – Russian Project Finance Bank
RSBF – Russia Small Business Fund
RVCA – Russian Venture Capital Association
RVF – Regional Venture Fund
RZB – Raiffeisen Zentralbank Österreich
SBA – stand-by arrangement
SBI – Small Business Initiative
SSF – Shareholder Special Fund
SFRY – Socialist Federal Republic of Yugoslavia

SIP – Shelter Implementation Plan
SLA – subsidiary loan agreement
SMEs – small and medium-sized enterprises
SPF – State Property Fund (of Ukraine)
SPV – special purpose vehicle
SRP – Special Privatisation and Restructuring Programme
TACIS – Technical Aid to the Commonwealth of Independent States
TFP – Trade Facilitation Programme
TIMS – transition impact monitoring system
UK – United Kingdom
USSR – Union of Soviet Socialist Republics
UN – United Nations
UNCED – UN Conference on Environment and Development
WSE – Warsaw Stock Exchange
ZBB – zero-base budgeting
ZSNP – Zavod Slovenskeho Narodneho Povstania

Acknowledgements

The idea of this book came from Suma Chakrabarti, the EBRD's President, to whom I am immensely grateful for his encouragement and support.

As I began to research the origins and development of the EBRD early last year, I realised there was a great deal more to the Bank's history than I had imagined. That certainly made the project interesting, but also more daunting.

To make the task manageable I decided to address the EBRD's history in two volumes. This was not only convenient administratively, but also because the Bank's evolution itself divides neatly into two halves: an early period in which the focus was heavily on transforming the former socialist countries of central and eastern Europe into market-oriented economies, followed by a period of geographic expansion and promotion of broader needs to build sustainable markets and better-functioning economies.

The plan was to launch Volume 1 at the EBRD's Annual Meeting in London in May 2020. However, as with so many projects and events recently, the Covid-19 crisis blocked that path. With the Annual Meeting cancelled the suggestion was made to release an electronic version of Volume 1 as soon as the publisher could make this possible. CEU Press's forbearance and response to the difficult situation has been exemplary. I and others involved in the production of the book owe them, and especially Linda Kunos, a large debt of gratitude.

I could not have written this volume without the benefit of many valuable conversations and discussions—some brief, some long—with a wide range of distinguished and knowledgeable people and colleagues who have been involved with the EBRD, past and present. My warm thanks go to all those listed below and to many others not mentioned. The work of the Evaluation Department provided very useful insights in many areas. It was also a great help to consult the EBRD archives, nowadays a combination of paper and electronic records, where Joanna Conway and Emily Burningham provided excellent assistance.

I am especially grateful to the small production team who supported this project throughout, primarily Jonathan Charles, Jane Ross, Svitlana Pyrkalo and Anthony Williams, and to several people included below who provided very helpful comments and suggestions on various chapters.

Although this is a history of an institution, the EBRD, its experience reflects the contributions of the people in its countries of operations. Without their efforts the world would be a poorer place.

Finally, this volume has benefited enormously from the experienced editorial hand of Lucy Fitzgeorge-Parker of *Euromoney*, who kindly and painstakingly went through the manuscript, improving the text immeasurably. What follows is nonetheless my own responsibility.

Andrew Kilpatrick
London, 7 May 2020

Acknowledgements

The author would like to thank (in alphabetical order) the following for their help, insights and assistance:

Alex Allan, Gavin Anderson, Mahir Babayev, Leszek Balcerowicz, Chris Beauman, Vanora Bennett, Maureen Brown, Kevin Bortz, Alba Bozo, Emily Burningham, Roger Burston, Laetitia Camus, José Carbajo, Jonathan Charles, Alistair Clark, Alex Chirmiciu, Joanna Conway, Anne Cretal, Peter Curwen, Ralph de Haas, Friso de Jong, Claes de Neergaard, Milica Delevic, Noreen Doyle, Dermot Doorly, Tom Edmondston-Low, Joe Eichenberger, Elisabetta Falcetti, Tom Flemming, Anne Fossemalle, Charles Frank, Ron Freeman, Jorgen Frotzler, Lucy Fitzgeorge-Parker, Tea Gamtkitsulashvili, Susan Goeransson, Sergei Guriev, Bob Harada, Zsuzsa Hargitai, Kate Harrington, Janet Heckman, Adonai Herrara-Martinez, David Hexter, Suzanne Heywood, Matthew Jordan-Tank, Tina Hoy, Daud Ilyas, Istvan Ipper, Rika Ishii, Beata Javorcik, Stephane Jucobin, Ramon Juraboev, Fani Kallianou de Jong, Natasha Khanjenkova, Pawel Krasny, David Klingensmith, Zbigniew Kominek, George Krivicky, Libor Krkoska, Hans Peter Lankes, Oleg Levitin, Colm Lincoln, Balthasar Lindauer, Frederic Lucenet, Terry McCallion, Don McCutchen, Andrew McDonald, Thomas Maier, Francis Malige, Bojan Markovic, Emmanuel Maurice, Nik Milushev, Victoria Millis, Holger Muent, Doug Nevison, Gian Piero Nacci, Lucie Newman, Tanya Normak, Vince Novak, Dasha Novozhilkina, Lin O'Grady, Patrick O'Neill, Jonathan Ockenden, Tarek Osman, Nandita Parshad, Steve Petri, Craig Pickering, Alex Plekhanov, Irena Postlova, Charles Powell, Anne-Marie Pragnell, Dariusz Prasek, Svitlana Pyrkalo, Enzo Quattrociocche, Artur Radziwill, Simon Ray, Axel Reiserer, Mattia Romani, Jane Ross, Alan Rousso, Charlotte Ruhe, Cecilia Russell, Henry Russell, Peter Sanfey, Tracy Saunders, Christoph Sicking, Keith Simmons, Norbert Seiler, Josué Tanaka, John Taylor, Michelle Taylor, Mike Taylor, Philip ter Woort, Kjetil Tvedt, Christopher Upton-Hansen, Yvonne Vilhelmsen, Emily Walker, Sam Wallace, Peter Wanless, Bryan Whitford, Anthony Williams.

The EBRD as the Indispensable Multilateral Development Bank

Personal Foreword

Sir Suma Chakrabarti

It is a big claim to call the multilateral development bank that I have had the honour to lead for eight years "indispensable". I usually recoil when I hear words like "indispensable" or "unique" or "exceptional". But this volume, the first of two, a history of the European Bank for Reconstruction and Development, written by my former EBRD colleague, Andrew Kilpatrick, will, I trust, convince readers that this is not a fanciful claim.

The book is not an official history. It contains Andrew's views on the events and themes in the life of the European Bank for Reconstruction and Development (EBRD or the Bank) that, from my vantage point, show clearly how the Bank was a pioneer in the world of international development.

The book is timely. On 29 May 1990, only months after the fall of the Berlin Wall, the Agreement Establishing the European Bank for Reconstruction and Development was signed by its then 42 shareholders from around the world. As we mark the 30th anniversary of that historic day, it is worth reflecting on what made the EBRD so instrumental for the transformation of so many emerging markets, and what makes it vital for tackling today's global challenges.

This volume charts the history of the Bank from its very beginnings to the days before the global financial crisis, when it briefly seemed that EBRD's work was nearly done, at least in Central Europe. The second volume, covering the period from the crisis of 2007–2008 to more recent days, will be published ahead of the Bank's 30th anniversary since the start of operations in 1991—only one year after the international community agreed to its creation.

In this foreword, I give my personal take on why I believe the EBRD has been and continues to be the indispensable institution in the multilateral development bank (MDB) system. At its heart is a story of an MDB that seeks to move with the times, to climb the next peak and not just admire the one it scaled earlier. In short, to use its business model to be relevant to today's and tomorrow's challenges.

System Change

All other MDBs have the noble purpose of supporting the economic development of poorer nations. The EBRD, born at the end of the Cold War, has the unique mandate to foster system change: to support the transition of centrally planned countries to market economies, and to apply this purpose in countries that are committed to multi-party democracy and political pluralism. This is the most ideological statement in the founding articles of any MDB, a clear commitment by its owners that the EBRD should help bring about system change in the countries where it operates.

What did this transition to market economies mean? It meant, and still does mean, using the EBRD's investments to grow the private sector, which had been suppressed under central planning. It meant a focus on ensuring the Bank's investments helped make those economies more competitive.

Over time, the Bank realised that the narrow definition of the economic transition journey needed to change. Citizens now want much more from their markets than mere competitiveness. And the EBRD moved with the times. Today, the EBRD defines successful market economies as having six qualities: competitive, green, well-governed, inclusive, integrated and resilient. Each EBRD investment today must feature two of those six transition qualities. This modernisation of the concept of a market economy has impacted the debate and approach in the MDB system.

Because of its mandate, the Bank is about more than a change in an economic system. The commitment to pursue its purpose in countries committed to multi-party democracy and political pluralism required attention to the political trajectory in each of those nations. Assessments of how far each of the Bank's countries of operation have reached on that journey remain to this day a feature of the EBRD's work.

But, as with economics, so with politics, there has been a modernisation of the Bank's approach in four ways in recent years. First, there is now a more systematic approach to that assessment with the use of fourteen criteria to gauge where a country has reached on its democratic political journey. Second, the Bank has moved away from the binary and, frankly, inconsistent judgements of the past about whether a country passed the test of its commitment to the Bank's political mandate to a more honest and transparent description of what exactly is happening within the political system of each nation. Third, the Bank has placed much more emphasis in recent years on not just politics, but also on questions of political economy; for example, where does power reside and how do major decisions get made? And fourth, it has used this modernised political analysis to help shape its investments and policy work, at regional and national levels, and in its engagement with the leaders of the Bank's countries of operations. These considerations around a political system have sometimes led the Bank to modulate the volume and focus of its lending in some countries.

Such political analysis is invaluable to the work of the EBRD. It should be taken up by other MDBs to inform their work beyond the safe haven of economic governance.

System Change for What Purpose?

Over time, the EBRD recognised that economic system change alone—however important and historic—is not an outcome that is regarded by citizens today as valuable in its own right. So the EBRD recast the concept of a modern market economy at the time when many of the Bank's shareholders, in recipient and non-recipient countries, were questioning the utility of free markets and the associated globalisation of the world economy. To paraphrase the Monty Python joke about the Romans, many citizens asked: what has the market economy ever done for us? Governments increasingly realised: the modern market must deliver outcomes that are valuable to people today.

Cue the Sustainable Development Goals (SDGs), the COP21 agreement on climate change, and the 2030 Agenda for Development. The SDGs are, in my view, the best description of the outcomes that people of all nations want to see their economic and political systems deliver for them. In sharp contrast to the old Millennium Development Goals (MDGs), they go beyond a narrow set of outcomes to encompass the near totality of the characteristics of the development condition. And they define in each area the outcomes we should aim to achieve by 2030.

That is why the EBRD increasingly and more explicitly says that the modern market economies the Bank is seeking to create in its countries of operations should be geared to delivering the SDGs. In the language of the technician, the market economy is the output that must deliver the SDG outcomes if it is a system change that is to retain the support of the citizens of the Bank's countries of operations.

The What and the How

The clearest expression of what the EBRD does to achieve its mission is the investment project, whether through a loan or an equity stake. The investment operation has been the institution's successful unit of exchange for nearly thirty years. Each project has been assessed from the Bank's early days for its additionality (to be undertaken only if the market would not finance the same investment), its bankability (that the operation is structured in a way that is financially sound), and its impact on the transition to the market economy (now measured against the six transition qualities). Some things are eternal in the EBRD, even if the arguments continue to rage over the application of these concepts at project, sector, and regional levels.

But some very important aspects have changed over the years, or are beginning to do so, around the core investment operations of the Bank.

First, while the EBRD continues to aim for a market-based approach to loan pricing, the range of themes and countries with which the Bank is now involved means that grant financing is increasingly required alongside the loan. The grant-intensity of the EBRD's business model has increased. And the organisation has become very successful at attracting donor funds, including from some of its countries of operations, to provide more "blended" financing of its investments, and to support its growing policy work. This shift in themes and countries and the associated increase in donor funds has made the EBRD more of a "development" bank, albeit one that continues to focus on the private sector.

Second, the EBRD has emerged as the leading promoter among MDBs of local currency financing and the building of local capital markets. It understood early on that clients, particularly SMEs, needed local currency financing and the removal of foreign exchange risks in these vulnerable markets. And the Bank understood also the importance of building local capital markets, e.g. through the issuing of local currency bonds. Other MDBs know the importance of this, but the degree to which EBRD has followed through and increased its efforts in this area is striking, both in absolute and comparative terms, an indicator of its high risk appetite.

Third, there has been recognition in the Bank that operating through its vertical sectors—financial institutions, infrastructure, energy, natural resources, industry, commerce and agribusiness—alone and through clients of all sizes (from SMEs to corporate and state behemoths, as well as municipalities) would not cut it. The sectoral approach needed an overlay of increasingly important cross-cutting themes to be relevant in today's world.

The most well-known cross-cutting theme is the EBRD's contribution to the greening of its countries of operations, starting with the Sustainable Energy Initiative in 2006, which grew into the Sustainable Resource Initiative, and in 2015 became the ground-breaking Green Economy Transition (GET) approach. The GET approach established a target to invest 40 per cent of the Bank's annual business in the green economy by 2020. With 46 per cent of EBRD's investments in 2019 already in the green economy area, the EBRD has emerged as the leading player among the MDBs on delivery of the climate change agenda, most especially so in the private sector. The Bank is now gearing up to roll out a further modernised GET approach for the 2021–2025 period.

The Bank has also taken up other cross-cutting themes within its investment operations in recent years—gender, economic inclusion, support for refugees—although there is much further to go on these fronts. In each case, the EBRD has proved wrong those who doubted that these classic development themes could fit with its business model.

Fourth, the Bank has been a hothouse of product innovation over the years. Because of its client facing nature, the EBRD is a more demand-driven MDB than others. The EBRD is not a blue skies innovator; rather, it creates products that are useful for its clients but also meet its mandate. Some examples include credit lines to local banks to be on-lent to SMEs, including for energy efficiency improvements, small-scale renewables and women entrepreneurs; the long-standing and very successful Trade Facilitation Programme; the Bank's work on green, sustainability and climate resilience bonds; innovative risk products; sub-sovereign loans to municipalities and commercial finance to improve utilities and local services, including in more remote regions, and the increasingly acclaimed Green Cities programme; or the Equity Participation Fund, where institutional investors can co-invest alongside the EBRD. The Bank also has a unique expertise and mandate in nuclear safety and remediation, managing the Chernobyl New Safe Confinement on behalf of international community and helping decommission nuclear plants in other countries.

Fifth, a major development in recent years, has been the scaling up of the Bank's policy work. Until recently, the EBRD tended to make forays into policy making with its countries of operations based primarily on its investment operations needs.

That has now changed. The EBRD today has a more systematic approach to policy work at strategic levels (country, sectors, themes), based rightly on the knowledge gained from its many clusters of projects and from its clients. The Bank now actively pursues policy reform in its dialogue with leaders of countries of operations. And it has its own policy products, ranging from country diagnostic studies that precede country strategies to practical investment councils that bring governments together with the private sector to help create the right enabling environment for more investment. Of course, there is more to do on this front: in the best cases, a virtuous circle has been created between more reform leading to more investment, which then begets more reform.

And sixth, while the EBRD was an early believer in a matrix between an HQ (that contains sector teams, risk analysts, economists, and lawyers, among others) and Resident Offices in countries of operation, there has been a clear shift over recent years towards more senior boots on the ground. Some senior management posts and certain skills (such as economists, lawyers, portfolio managers) are now more prevalent in the Resident Offices than, say, a decade ago. This represents the growing need to be closer to the clients—private sector and sovereign—and the greater stress placed on policy dialogue.

Moreover, the EBRD is unusual among the MDBs in having offices in secondary cities as well as in the capitals. These offices outside capitals are focused on providing advisory services to SMEs and have grown very rapidly in number in recent years. They have proved their worth in good times and have been invaluable during the Covid-19 crisis in providing information about the impact on clients and how best to support them.

In short, the business model of the EBRD retains the original pillar of the investment operation at its heart but the foundations have been strengthened over the years to ensure the edifice is even more responsive to today's development challenges.

The All-Weather Bank

And the Bank has shown it can respond rapidly and successfully to changes of geo-political, financial, economic and pandemic storms.

As I write this, the EBRD is delivering its operational response to the economic crisis caused by the Covid-19 pandemic that has led to government mandated lock downs and a contraction of economic output. The latest economic forecasts for the Bank's countries of operations make depressing reading. Sharp recoveries are possible, provided lock downs are eased soon and economies (some of which are dependent on tourism and remittances, some on global value chains, and some on commodity prices) can return to some sense of a normalcy. For the EBRD, it has been imperative to deliver liquidity to clients, arrange payment deferrals and restructurings, increase trade finance, and ensure vital infrastructure and services are not disrupted. In short, the Bank's response is to help ensure a liquidity crisis does not become one of solvency for its clients. In true EBRD fashion, it was the first MDB to have its "Solidarity Package" approved by its shareholders and investment levels so far this year have outstripped all previous years. And it has done all this with staff working from home and managing their lockdown lives (such as providing home schooling and looking after elderly family members) alongside work.

That the EBRD has done so well in today's crisis—the most difficult the EBRD has ever had to face—is almost certainly because the Bank is no stranger to having to respond to crises over its thirty years. It responded fast and decisively to the break-up of countries (the USSR and Yugoslavia), geo-political tensions (for example, between Russia and Georgia and Russia and Ukraine), financial and economic crises (in Russia in the late 1990s), across its regions in 2007–2008 (which led the Bank to support the recovery of Greece and Cyprus), major regional political convulsions (following the Arab Spring), and after the refugee crisis caused by the war in Syria.

In all of these cases, the Bank has been able to flex its business model and make use of its matrix to respond rapidly and—very importantly—in a tailored way to the problem at hand. Rightly, the EBRD receives many plaudits from its countries of operations (that are of course best able to make comparisons with other MDBs) for its commitment, whatever the weather, and its ability to turn promises into reality very fast.

The Where

This adaptive, all-weather, successful business model has made the EBRD an attractive club. There has been growth of membership and of geographic scope in its operations. The EBRD is the only MDB today—other than the newest kid on the block, the Asian Infrastructure Investment Bank—that has a growing membership of both recipients and non-recipients. The EBRD started life with 42 shareholders, and the break-up of some of the original members added to this number, but more recently it has been its successful operational delivery that has attracted new members and turned some existing ones from non-recipients into recipients.

The EBRD is known as one of the four regional development banks. But it is the only one that has members that are countries of operations in Europe, Asia and Africa, so it is already pan-regional. And while the original intention of the Bank's shareholders was a temporary institution that would regard its job as done as soon as the former communist countries became market economies, the task has proven more long lasting and the business model relevant to nations that never had centrally planned economies. And the Bank has managed this operational expansion to new geographies with great success.

Today's EBRD attracts big new players as well as smaller countries. In recent years, China and India became non-recipient members of the EBRD, adding to the G20 contingent of the Bank. So, with the G7 and EU member states retaining a majority of the shareholding, the EBRD today—with 71 shareholders and more expected soon—can truly be called a "global institution with a European heart".

Future Opportunities and Challenges

That is my case for claiming the EBRD is the indispensable MDB for today and tomorrow. Indeed, the importance of the private sector focused business model to transition and economic development in different geographies, the shift from the narrow MDGs to the wider SDGs in the international system, and the acknowledged fact that the SDGs cannot be met without a ramping up of private finance and delivery, has led the EBRD to the centre stage in the MDB system.

How to keep it there? What makes an institution stay indispensable?

The first task of the future leadership of the EBRD must be to avoid any tendency to wallow in nostalgia. Indeed, put positively, it must be to seek out the opportunities where the EBRD can make a difference and seize them. And it must also identify challenges honestly and tackle them. That balance between seizing opportunities and tackling challenges gets harder as an organisation grows, when it moves from insurgent to establishment status. The Bank must retain its radical, innovative and agenda-setting character. This is the mind-set opportunity and challenge.

The second is to spot the coming issues and be ready with an EBRD relevant response. That means building on key strengths like the Bank's work on the green economy. It also means making a much improved offer on equality of opportunity, an area where the operational regions could easily go backwards after Covid-19. And it means tackling new areas which will impact the prospects of our countries of operations, such as the opportunities offered up by digital technology. All three of these themes will, I trust, be at the forefront of EBRD's 2021–2025 strategy. This is the thematic opportunity and challenge.

There is also the geographic opportunity and challenge. The EBRD has a lot more to offer in the neighbourhood regions of the EU and in Central Asia, and in the poorest EU countries of operations, all the markets where the "marginal euro" of investment and policy advice has the greatest impact. The Bank must scale up further in these countries. At the same time, the EBRD is now much less additional in the advanced EU countries of operations, for which there is plenty of finance available from the local banking systems, domestic public budgets, and from the European Investment Bank and the EU. The Bank's shareholders need to come together and accept this economic truth and work with management to create an approach and trajectory to graduation of these advanced countries of operations.

There is also a huge geographic opportunity for the EBRD beyond our current region of operations for all the right reasons: not because of the capital available, but to make a real difference to the creation of modern market economies to deliver the SDGs. Every one of EBRD's geographic expansions has been successful. It is no secret that I believe the Bank would be just as successful with its private sector model in sub-Saharan Africa. And all the analysis that has been done shows that too. Remember the SDGs will not be achieved without sharp progress in sub-Saharan Africa. It is high time to move from procrastination to decision on geographical expansion in the Bank's coming five-year strategy.

This is not a zero-sum game. The EBRD has the capital to achieve more than a limited and incremental expansion to sub-Saharan Africa and still scale up in its existing countries of operations. But it would also be good for the Bank, either alone or with other MDBs, to look now—five years on from the Financing for Development conference in Addis Ababa, perhaps at an "Addis 2"—how it can leverage its balance sheet to create additional firepower without requesting a capital increase. I believe in the next couple of decades that further expansion of the Bank's activities beyond even what is contemplated today will be inevitable and the right thing to pursue. Adding to the Bank's financing capacity over the next year would therefore be good to put on the table in the coming months.

This is a rich agenda for the future based on the EBRD's achievements over thirty years. But, in my claim for the EBRD's indispensability, I skated over one overarching issue: the role of shareholders.

Shareholders of MDBs can either accelerate or be a brake on change. The experience of the EBRD is instructive: the countries of operations, especially those outside the EU, have little voice in terms of shareholding but have consistently been the advocates of the Bank moving with the times; and the non-recipients have oscillated between periods of strong support for moving forward fast (for example, in founding the institution and providing the bulk of its capital, in pursuing four geographical operational expansions, and on the green agenda) and a reluctance in more recent times to face up squarely to and be decisive about compelling questions about the future.

If the EBRD is to move forward and retain the status of being an indispensable MDB, then thoroughgoing governance reform will have to come, to give greater voice to those who best understand today's problems of transition and development—the countries of operations themselves—and so can help the immensely talented management and staff ensure that the Bank remains match-fit for the future.

It has been a privilege to lead the EBRD for eight years. I leave the Bank knowing that it is a great institution. It has done so much to shape the transition and development landscape, to invest in supporting people to have better lives than would have been possible without the work of the Bank. And it is capable—with the right support from its shareholders—of doing so much more in the years ahead.

Sir Suma Chakrabarti
President of the EBRD,
3 July 2012 – 2 July 2020

Preface

Just before midnight on 9 November 1989 the wall that had separated West and East Berlin for 28 years was breached. The fall of the Berlin Wall came to symbolise the end of the Cold War and the era of Soviet-inspired communism.

Nine days later, at a special European Council, French President François Mitterrand persuaded his European Community (EC) colleagues to consider the creation of a "Modernisation and Development Bank for Europe", aimed at encouraging and supporting the nascent movement towards democracy and market economics that was flowing through central and eastern Europe.

Within 17 months of that Council meeting, the world would witness the birth of a brand new multilateral institution that was unique in the arena of international development. Owned by 42 shareholders from across five continents, and now named the European Bank for Reconstruction and Development (EBRD), this new institution opened its doors on 15 April 1991 in London.

The EBRD offered countries emerging from the wreckage of communist mismanagement and economic neglect a credible path towards sustainable prosperity as they embraced a democratic future. The new bank would be a pioneer in the promotion of sustainable market economies, putting a primary focus on private-sector development and bringing the skills of the private sector to the delivery of public services that improved the lives of millions across its regions. It would break new ground in the delivery of environmentally sustainable development in countries where energy waste and pollution were endemic.

The EBRD would be a partner in a journey of remarkable progress, even though that journey would last much longer than originally envisaged.

A robust balance between Anglo-Saxon and continental European perspectives would allow the EBRD to prosper through the many difficult times ahead. The success of its hands-on approach, and experience in transitioning countries towards well-functioning market democracies, would later take it well beyond its original geography of communist eastern Europe. The EBRD's business model would help it leverage the private sector to promote global public goods, such as more sustainable energy solutions to mitigate climate change, including in its original countries of operations. That development forms the subject of the second volume of this history of the EBRD. In this volume we look at how the new international institution emerged and used its public capital to support private-sector development in the former socialist countries of eastern Europe.

Part I

Post-Cold War Pioneer

Chapter 1
A New International Development Institution

Introduction

Mitterrand's original proposal for a new institution, the EBRD, to support the integration of central and eastern Europe into the European and global economy was endorsed in early December 1989 at the Strasbourg European Council by all 12 EC countries. The speed with which leaders decided to create a new international financial institution was unprecedented in European Council history and reflected the urgency of the situation. There was no doubt in the minds of the key actors about the potentially grave consequences for Europe of failing to support their eastern neighbours.

A variety of forces lay behind these events. The old certainties of the Cold War had begun to falter with the arrival of Mikhail Gorbachev as General Secretary of the Soviet Communist Party in the mid-1980s and his adoption of a reformist stance through *perestroika* and *glasnost* in the Soviet Union. This was followed by the visible abandonment of the Brezhnev doctrine and a new-found willingness to allow Soviet satellite states more independence, quickly built upon by populations eager to catch up with the West, as well as a more open approach to detente and relations with western leaders.

In western Europe too it was a moment of internal change. As envisaged under the Treaty of Rome, the EC was embarking on the next stage of integration and had begun to set out concrete steps to achieve economic and monetary union. Political union was also on the table, under which lay a schism with the United Kingdom which was to fester and undermine European unity. Despite this, there was full agreement that the adoption of sound market practices and democratic values was the right way forward and that the East should be encouraged to follow this path.

For Frenchman Jacques Attali, who was to become the first President of the EBRD, the circumstances offered a unique opportunity to create a unified Europe, which could include the Soviet Union and in which the common values of the different parts of the continent could be pooled and strengthened. If successful, the enlarged marketplace would provide a region to match the major global players of the day, the USA and Japan. At its centre could be a "Bank for Europe" with a remit to invest in projects that could bring benefits to both East and West. For other observers, the situation offered the possibility to instil ideas of market economics, the rule of law and multiparty democracy in a region where these qualities were absent and to populations brought up under communist rule. An international bank offered a convenient mechanism to achieve these goals.

The idea of the EBRD emerged at a time of momentous transformation and the pace of change would not slow over the coming months and years. Of the eight original beneficiary countries identified by the EBRD—Bulgaria, the Czech and Slovak Federative Republic (CSFR), the German Democratic Republic (GDR), Hungary, Poland, Romania, the Union of Soviet Socialist Republics (USSR), and the Socialist Federal Republic of Yugoslavia (SFRY)—East Germany would be absorbed into a unified Germany even before the EBRD's inauguration in 1991. The following years would see the division of the CSFR into two states, the dissolution of the Soviet Union and the violent breakup of Yugoslavia.

It would not be long before the EBRD was investing in more than 20 countries. But before all that could happen, and before the Bank could even take shape, there were to be many complex and sometimes tough negotiations.

This chapter looks at the background to the emergence of the EBRD, its establishment and early development and, in particular, the debates and arguments behind the work that led to the signing of the Agreement Establishing the Bank (AEB) on 29 May 1990.

1. The Historical Context: The 1980s in the West

During much of the 1980s, most advanced western countries enjoyed a period of steady economic expansion. This was in marked contrast to the previous decade, which had seen interrupted growth and high inflation. Once the shock therapy of the interest-rate hikes deployed by Federal Reserve Chairman Paul Volcker at the start of the decade had worked its way through the system, the countries of the Organisation for Economic Cooperation and Development (OECD) saw a strong expansion of output. Gross domestic product (GDP) grew at an annual average rate of 3.75 per cent between 1982 and 1989. The USA experienced its strongest period of growth for two decades, with GDP increases averaging almost 4.5 per cent per annum. Stock markets around the world reached peaks as the decade drew to a close.

These years represented the culmination of several trends that had emerged over the previous decade, including the relative decline of industry and the rise of services in western economies, a rebalancing of the state towards private enterprise, and in several countries a shift away from collective decision-making towards individual responsibility. The practical application of technological innovation dramatically reduced the cost of communications and shipping, increasing the ability of more mature economies to access cheap foreign labour and other resources. Meanwhile, the steady growth in incomes that these advances produced allowed citizens in the West to access an ever-expanding choice of consumer goods and services.

The decade had also seen fundamental developments towards market reform and the espousal of liberal democracy. In the USA the election of Ronald Reagan as President in 1980, a year after his British comrade-in-arms, Margaret Thatcher, was elected as prime minister of the UK, resulted in an ideological shift towards an anti-state, pro-enterprise culture. The "Reagan-Thatcher era", as it became known, marked a clear break with the immediate past.

The "Thatcher revolution" in the UK led to the privatisation of major state enterprises, a general rolling back of the state and significant labour-market reform, most notably in a reduction of trade-union power.

In the USA Ronald Reagan's presidency ushered in a period of radical deregulation, especially in the financial sector, which led to a spurt of restructuring and financial innovation. The rapid increases in lending and other financial products fuelled growth. This was echoed by the "Big Bang" financial reforms in the UK from the mid-1980s. The changes also helped to accelerate the global integration of financial markets and confirmed London and New York as the pre-eminent international financial centres. By the late 1980s, the Anglo-Saxon competitive financially-driven model appeared to reign supreme.

Developments in continental Europe were different, mainly focusing on intra-European trade and integration, but growth was also strong. Here, too, a path of opening up the state sector could be seen, with privatisations in France, Germany and later Italy. A steady low-inflation growth path also seemed to be universally in place in Europe, a welcome contrast compared with the 1970s.

The liberal market-based model seemed to be working well. By the end of the decade there had been no serious negative macroeconomic shock for several years. Indeed, there had even been a positive oil shock in the middle of the period. Oil prices dropped sharply in 1986, boosting growth.

By the end of the 1980s, the "Reagan-Thatcher era" had effectively come to a close. Reagan's presidency ended in January 1989 and Thatcher was ousted from the leadership of the Conservative Party, and as prime minister, in November of the following year. By the end of 1989, the political and economic ideas they had spawned were in many ways at their zenith in several leading western nations, but rapidly spreading across the globe—just as the EBRD was being conceived.

2. The Historical Context: The 1980s in the East

For countries behind the Iron Curtain in the East, and in Yugoslavia and Albania, life was nothing like as rosy, in either absolute or relative terms, during the 1980s. Direct comparisons between East and West were hampered by missing or unreliable data. However, most analysts of the Soviet economy conclude that growth rates were falling over time. One estimate puts the average gross national product (GNP) growth rate during the 1980s at 1.4 per cent, versus 2.7 per cent in the period 1971–80 and 5.1 per cent in 1961–70.[1] By the second half of the 1980s it was obvious that the centrally planned economies were failing to deliver rising living standards on any significant scale.

While the trends seen in the west in the 1980s were far more muted behind the Iron Curtain, some parts of eastern Europe[2] and Yugoslavia at least

---

[1] G. Turley and P. J. Luke, *Transition Economics: Two Decades On,* London: Routledge, 2011, Chapter 1.
[2] During this period 'eastern Europe' or 'central and eastern Europe' usually referred to the GDR, the CSFR, Hungary, Poland, Bulgaria, Romania and Yugoslavia (although Yugoslavia was treated separately on occasion). The USSR was also sometimes included in these groupings. When the EBRD started, the use of 'central and eastern European countries', as in the AEB, referred to the countries it sought to help, i.e. its 'countries of oper-

were not immune from these influences. Trade links with the West were improving and a number of joint ventures had been established involving western companies in countries such as Hungary and even in the Soviet Union. But if some of the advantages of market economics were being glimpsed in the Eastern Bloc, and enjoyed by some of its citizens, the same could not be said of political freedoms.

Political pressure was, however, building in the East. The vast majority of the population, whether silently or more vocally, sought a more open franchise and were demanding the right to strike, freedom of the media, freedom of movement and the formation of political parties. Above all, there was a desire to break away from what was increasingly seen as a failed political and economic system, whose leaders seemed increasingly remote from the realities of everyday life and who remained immune from the hardships facing the wider population.

Despite some earlier attempts to bring about reform behind the Iron Curtain and the emergence of Solidarity in Poland in 1980, relatively little progress had been made until Gorbachev took over as leader of the Soviet Union in 1985. He introduced policies of *perestroika* and *glasnost* in an effort to improve the situation while maintaining control through the Communist Party apparatus. Economic reforms were also introduced, mirroring to an extent the New Economic Policy adopted by Lenin in the early 1920s and the reforms of Deng Xiaoping in the early 1980s in the People's Republic of China.

Gorbachev also followed a more outward-looking approach in Soviet relations with the West, embarking on tours of western capitals and forging good relations with Reagan and Thatcher, in particular. Of great significance was his prominent rejection of the Brezhnev doctrine, which had already fallen into abeyance. Soviet satellite states were no longer required to bend unerringly to the will of Moscow and were allowed a greater degree of independence in relation to political reform.

As a result, domestic pressures for change grew, particularly among countries closest to western Europe. By 1989, real change was underway in central Europe, while difficulties at home meant Gorbachev became heavily focused on trying to manage internal strains within the Soviet Union.

---

ations'. Initially, these were the full set of countries mentioned above. The GDR disappeared with German reunification, while Albania became included (as a country of operations) by the end of 1991. Later nomenclature identified CEB (Central Europe and the Baltics) and CIS (Commonwealth of Independent States).

As people began to realise the new situation in the Eastern Bloc, momentum for reform built up throughout the year.

Among the first notable developments was Solidarity's landslide victory in the first round of Polish elections on 4 June 1989. The party won 92 out of 100 Senate seats and 160 out of 161 seats in the *Sejm*.

The election coincided with the events in Tiananmen Square in Beijing where the Chinese authorities, facing similar growing public restlessness over the lack of political freedoms, had decided to exert firm political control to prevent further sedition, resulting in many deaths.

There were serious concerns that a similar response by the Polish authorities might ensue. General Wojciech Jaruzelski, the Polish head of state, had imposed martial law in 1981 in response to the rise of Solidarity. This time, however, he accepted the situation, not least because Moscow was no longer ready to support a crackdown as it had in the past. The second-round election on 18 June confirmed Solidarity's success and the resulting government introduced a package of radical economic reforms early in the following year, known as the Balcerowicz Plan.

Poland was not alone in seeing an acceleration in demands for reform. On 16 June 1989, 200,000 people assembled in Heroes' Square in Budapest[3] to commemorate the reburial of Imre Nagy, a Hungarian reformer who had been executed for leading the uprising in 1956. On 23 October, a huge crowd heard the proclamation of a new Hungarian Republic outside parliament.

In September 1989 Miklos Nemeth,[4] the Prime Minister of Hungary, decided to open the border with Austria. This allowed citizens from the GDR to transit through the CSFR via Austria to West Germany, and by the end of October some 50,000 had left by this route. Separately, the West German Foreign Minister, Hans-Dietrich Genscher, negotiated with Moscow and East Berlin the transfer of thousands of GDR citizens, many of whom had taken refuge in West German embassies in central European countries, by train to the Federal Republic.

In the GDR itself, demonstrations grew during the year, albeit slowly, with numbers reaching around 70,000 by October. With the feared security service, the Stasi, still fully operational and the Communist Party leaders supportive of the Chinese authorities' response to the Tiananmen Square

---

3   Viktor Orban, the current Prime Minister of Hungary, was last to speak.
4   Miklos Nemeth became a Vice President of the EBRD in 1990, the first from a country of operations.

protests, a showdown was expected. However, when news emerged from Moscow that there should be no bloodshed, protesters came out in force, with some half a million gathering in Alexanderplatz in East Berlin on 4 November.

The decisive change came on 9 November when the regime announced, at a confused and sometimes rambling news conference, that GDR citizens could now travel to West Berlin and the Federal Republic of Germany. When East German official Guenter Schabowski explained that the new measures would take place with immediate effect, the response was electric. Spontaneous and euphoric celebrations began on both sides of the Berlin Wall.

East Germans arrived in their thousands to cross that most concrete symbol of the Iron Curtain dividing East and West. Border guards gave up all attempts to check documents, which were still needed even under the new rules. Crossing points opened. West Berliners were waiting with a welcome of flowers and sparkling wine.

West German Chancellor Helmut Kohl told a midnight news conference: "This is an historic moment. There is no doubt that world history is being written now. We Germans will rise to the challenge."[5]

In other Soviet satellites the change was less readily accepted by the communist authorities. In the CSFR, police attacked protesting students on 17 November. Nevertheless, the demonstrations continued and grew in strength. One week later, three-quarters of a million people gathered in Prague's Wenceslas Square. This was followed by a well-supported, two-day general strike. Government attempts to keep control by reshuffling the cabinet were unsuccessful. Members of the Civic Forum, a new party formed by dissident playwright Vaclav Havel, were appointed to the cabinet on 10 December. Less than three weeks later, the Federal Assembly voted unanimously to appoint Havel as president of the CSFR.

In Bulgaria, change was more gradual. Petar Mladenov, who in November 1989 succeeded long-standing leader Todor Zhivkov as Chairman of the State Council, was a Communist Party member. Nonetheless, Mladenov supported Gorbachev's reform programme. He implemented the separation of Party and state, and gave workers the right to strike. Following widespread protests, the State Council in December also announced plans to hold free elections.

---

5 Reuters Report, by Mark Heinrich. 10 November 1989.

Opposition to the communist authorities had built up in Romania too, but a particularly brutal and repressive regime held it back until late in 1989. Protests escalated after a blockade to prevent the deportation of a priest, and on 17 December several protesters were killed by shots fired into the crowd by the authorities. Nicolae Ceausescu, the Romanian leader, attempted to restore order by addressing a rally on 21 December but was booed by the crowd, which was again attacked by the army. A second address given from Communist Party headquarters the next day was so badly received that Ceausescu and his wife fled by helicopter. A short time later they were located and court-martialled, before being executed on Christmas Day.

The death of Ceaucescu marked the end to a tumultuous year. It would be another two years before the Soviet Union was dissolved but the tide was turning. In the words of Ian Kershaw, one of Britain's most eminent historians: "What happened between 1989 and 1991 was no less than a European revolution—and, amazingly, unlike earlier revolutions it was (largely) free of bloodshed."[6]

It now became the task of the EBRD to battle with the consequences of this revolution.

3. Ideological Issues: Market Economics and Liberal Democracy

The idea of the EBRD thus emerged against a backdrop of fundamental change. Before looking at the institution itself, it is useful to review briefly the ideological debates that prevailed at the time. Two were of direct importance to the formation of the EBRD: one concerned markets, the so-called "Washington Consensus"; and the other concerned democracy, the debate epitomised by the "End of History".

The economist John Williamson, who developed the concept of the Washington Consensus in the second half of 1989, defined it[7] as a 10-point list of policies then widely supported by policy actors such as US government agencies, notably US Treasury officials, and think-tanks.

---

6   I. Kershaw, *Roller-Coaster: Europe, 1950–2017*, Allen Lane, 2018, Chapter 9, 'Power of the People'.
7   J. Williamson, 'What Washington Means by Policy Reform', in John Williamson (ed.), *Latin American Adjustment: How Much Has Happened?*, Institute for International Economics, 1990, Chapter 2.

Several of the policy prescriptions, which were primarily aimed at development in Latin America, were macroeconomic ideas such as fiscal discipline, a competitive exchange rate, and tax and public-expenditure reform (for example, the introduction of a broad tax base, moderate marginal income-tax rates and a reduction in subsidies). Other suggestions concerned market liberalisation, such as trade and interest-rate liberalisation, privatisation, deregulation and openness to inward investment.

Williamson's list neatly summarised mainstream economic thinking in the USA and UK at the time. It chimed well with the views of supply-side adherents and the successful period of privatisation and deregulation that had been witnessed in the preceding period.

For senior officials dealing with international economic issues it provided a convenient template against which to assess policy. As such, it was a natural point of reference for those charged with establishing a new international financial institution (IFI), particularly one focused on transforming former state-controlled economies. As we will see, the precepts behind the Washington Consensus approach were influential in the design and operations of the EBRD.

Meanwhile, also in mid-1989, a little-known official in the policy-planning department of the US State Department published an article entitled "The End of History?" in a relatively obscure foreign policy journal.[8] The author, Francis Fukuyama, set out a Hegel-inspired assessment that history, viewed in terms of a dialectical ideological struggle for freedom, had reached a certain finality now that free elections were being held in former totalitarian states and their populations were embracing the ideology of the West.

Fukuyama summarised his argument as follows: "What we may be witnessing is not just the end of the Cold War, or the passing of a particular period of postwar history, but the end of history as such: the end point of mankind's ideological evolution and the universalization of Western liberal democracy as the final form of human government."[9]

This thesis proved hugely popular, to the extent that Fukuyama appeared in *Time* magazine within weeks of its publication. It appeared to validate the liberal market-democracy model as the victor in the battle of ideologi-

---

8 F. Fukuyama, 'The End of History?' *The National Interest*, no. 16, 1989.
9 Ibid.

cal ideas that had dominated political discourse since the Russian Revolution 72 years earlier.

Ironically, perhaps the most significant counter-argument to Fukuyama's thesis occurred at almost exactly the same moment he published it: the reassertion of political control by the China's Communist Party Politburo. History took a radical turn in 1989 but it clearly did not end.

These underlying themes influenced the design of the EBRD and lay behind a clash with those who did not readily or fully buy into the new liberal world order. Nonetheless, belief in the power of markets and liberal democracy was sufficiently widespread to support the emergence of central and eastern Europe from its Cold War hibernation and help these countries embrace the western model of political and economic development.

4. Central and Eastern Europe Reaches the International Stage: the 1989 Paris Summit

For the G7 and the 12 EC members, the events of 1989 posed significant challenges and uncertainties. How should the West respond to events? Who should lead and who should do what in this fast-moving game? Where was assistance best deployed? How could the Soviet Union be supported on a reform path when it remained a nuclear-armed adversary?

The key western actors in this drama—the USA, France, the UK and Germany—each had their own historical perspective and interpretation of the situation and how to deal with it. Many aspects of the complex geopolitical negotiations that were involved as the world order became reset spilled over into the debate on the creation of the EBRD.

Not only was 1989 a critical moment in central and eastern Europe, it was also a crucial point in the history of the European Union (EU). France was a key driving force trying to piece these elements together. The EBRD provided one piece of the jigsaw, while at the heart of both developments was the reunification of Germany. This was to be a key factor in what subsequently transpired.

That year, France was Chair of the G7 and preparing for the Heads of State Summit scheduled to be held in Paris on 15–16 July. These gatherings had become an annual showcase of multilateral solidarity and coordination among the leading nations, with each holder of the rotating Presidency keen to project an image of the world and its future as they would like to see it. The bicentenary of the French Revolution also fell in 1989, and to mark the occasion a huge celebration was arranged alongside the Summit.

For this Summit, Attali, a personal adviser to and confidant of Mitterrand, was the French Sherpa, one of the senior government officials who prepare for summits on behalf of the heads of state or government. It fell to Attali to send invitations to representatives of the EC to attend the celebrations, as well as to heads of state from developing countries, such as Egypt and India, so that a North-South element could be added to the G7 event.

As usual, the Sherpas had prepared the Heads' agenda a long way in advance. For that summer's Summit, this was shaping up to be a by-now traditional mix of international economic and global issues: the state of the world economy; increased coordination and surveillance, especially on exchange rates; trade (the next steps in the Uruguay Round); debt strategy towards the most highly indebted countries; combating drugs; tackling environmental issues, notably chlorofluorocarbons (CFCs) and the depletion of the ozone layer; and, following earlier devastating floods, assistance to Bangladesh.

Events in the communist countries could not, however, be ignored. Preparations therefore turned to the question of statements on Tiananmen Square and, by way of counterpoint, welcoming words and potential assistance for central and eastern Europe.

Shortly before the Summit George Bush, who had replaced Reagan as US President in January, had visited Poland and Hungary to show support for market reform and the steps being taken towards multiparty democracy. He was also under pressure from these countries' US diaspora to provide material assistance. Bush proposed a "consortium of the seven" to coordinate aid to Poland, reduce its external debt and initiate a publicly endowed US$ 100 million enterprise fund.[10]

Meanwhile Kohl, realising that funds for central and eastern Europe would be discussed at the Summit and wanting support that went beyond what the Federal Republic was already providing, had written to suggest that the G7 set up a mechanism to coordinate aid to Poland and Hungary.

As the main coordinator of the event, Attali was unhappy that the proposed consortium would in effect be under the control of the USA. He believed that it should be open to other European states to contribute and

---

10 G. W. Bush and B. Scowcroft, *A World Transformed,* Alfred A. Knopf, 1998, pp. 113–115.

should not be set up in a manner that appeared to be directly confrontational to the interests of the Soviet Union.[11] Furthermore, as host of the Paris Club, the group of creditor nations which dealt with official debt, France would have wanted any discussion of debt relief to be considered by the Club rather than the G7.

Gorbachev also saw an opportunity in the Summit. A few days before it began, he wrote to Mitterrand pushing for the involvement of the Soviet Union in these discussions to create a "multilateral economic partnership" and reach a "true equilibrium", rather than surging ahead with a West-centric solution and excluding the East from the decision-making process. He noted: "Multilateral East-West cooperation on global economic problems finds itself manifestly behind in comparison to the development of bilateral and regional ties ... which does not seem justified ... considering ... the responsibility [our States] have for the good of each country's citizens and of the world community in general."[12]

A G7 communiqué, entitled "Declaration on East-West relations", welcomed the move towards freedom and democracy in central and eastern Europe and encouraged the process of reform. It also pledged support to Poland and Hungary. Rather than placing the coordination of this support with the G7, the European Commission under its President, Jacques Delors, was invited to bring together "all interested countries"—thus not ruling out the Soviet Union—to develop an assistance package. The group of participants asked to assist was subsequently enlarged to include OECD member countries and became known as the G24.[13]

Requesting the Commission to coordinate activities was an unprecedented step for the G7. It appears that US Secretary of State James Baker had concluded, to no objections from others, that it would be advantageous to put the Commission in charge of this exercise, partly with a view to making the Commission more outward-looking in its general approach, but also to lock in European financial assistance should agreement be found to go ahead.[14]

---

11   Attali telephoned Brent Scowcroft, Bush's national security adviser, on 8 July to register his objections. Attali, *Verbatim III*, Fayard, 1995, p. 278.
12   Letter from Gorbachev to Mitterrand, 14 July 1989, G7/8 Summits, Munk School, University of Toronto
13   'Declaration on East-West Relations', 15 July 1989, G7/8 Summits, Munk School, University of Toronto
14   J. Baker III, *The Politics of Diplomacy: Revolution, War and Peace, 1989–1992*, G.P. Putnam's Sons, New York, 1995; and S. Weber, 'Origins of the European Bank for Reconstruction and Development', *International Organisation*, Vol 48, No 1, Winter 1994, MIT Press, p.10 and p.12.

Bush had also recently met Delors and knew that he had good contacts within the Catholic Church and with Solidarity.[15]

Attali was nonplussed that the Commission should be given this role, as this would normally fall to the relevant Presidency, in this case France. He protested to Mitterrand, urging him to intervene to reclaim the coordinating role, but was rebuffed. "The US prefers the Brussels imp to the French devil! A novel choice, more divisive than constructive. The President, to whom I speak to suggest, as host country, we reclaim the secretariat, refuses firmly: 'One can't have everything'."[16]

Mitterrand clearly did not want a row to cloud a successful summit or get in the way of the celebrations of two centuries of the French Republic. Attali, however, was determined not to be outmanoeuvred by the Commission.

5. The Looming Issue of German Reunification

The first follow-up aid coordination meeting took place the following month (August), with members of the OECD in attendance, and began to prepare a substantial programme of assistance. Significantly, this was to be made conditional on commitment to democratic reforms and liberalised markets. In parallel, the EC's own aid programme, PHARE (Poland/Hungary Assistance for Reconstruction of Economies), emerged from the discussions. This amounted in due course to billions of dollars in financial and other assistance.

Meanwhile in Germany events were moving quickly. With the exodus of people from the GDR growing by the day there was an increasing awareness of the possibility of German reunification. While this was still not expected in the short term, the key players nonetheless exchanged views in bilateral discussions on the potential consequences of such a development.

Kohl saw reunification as an historic opportunity for Germany. Gorbachev, Mitterrand and Thatcher were less enthusiastic. Gorbachev was worried about how Soviet troops stationed in the GDR might react if the desire for unity overwhelmed political control. Bush was more relaxed with the idea, seeing reunification as primarily a matter for German self-determi-

---

15 Attali, *Verbatim III*, p. 261.
16 Attali, *Verbatim III*, p. 284.

nation. He was more concerned with the consequences for NATO and US troops stationed in the Federal Republic.

Thatcher was uneasy at the prospect of a resurgent Germany dominating Europe and irritated by the approach adopted by Kohl, which she saw as overly eager. She believed it was vital to engage the Four Powers, the architects of post-war Germany, who still controlled Berlin and the eastern German border: the Soviet Union, the UK, the USA and France.[17] In her view, if care was not taken, "... all the fixed points in Europe would collapse: the NATO front line; the structure of NATO and the Warsaw Pact; Mr Gorbachev's hopes for reform."[18]

As part of the preparations for the December European Council, Mitterrand visited Thatcher at Chequers on 1 September. While politically they were poles apart, the meeting generated a rapport between them, notably through their common view on German reunification and NATO's stance. They shared an annoyance with Kohl's approach and were both concerned over Gorbachev's likely reaction.

Mitterrand, like Thatcher, was nervous at the prospect of a strong Germany.[19] He feared it could upset the balance in Europe and impact progress towards economic and political union. In due course, Kohl was able to allay these fears by committing fully to the single currency and the EU. But in 1989 the future of Germany, the EU, NATO, the Warsaw Pact, the Soviet Union and, more generally, the outlook for peace and stability in Europe was far from clear. Those most closely involved were acutely aware of this and of the need to ensure the continuity of the successful post-war period.

6. Attali's—and France's—Vision for Europe, Including the East

The summer of 1989 was also formative for Attali. Valuable though the OECD contribution to financing improvements in the East might prove to be, Attali felt it was insufficient. He believed what was needed was an institution that could provide a link between the "two halves of Europe", while

---

17 M. Thatcher, *The Downing Street Years*, HarperCollins, 1993, pp. 796–799.
18 C. Powell to S. Wall, 8 December 1989, National Archives, Kew, London.
19 C. Powell to S. Wall, 8 December 1989; Attali, *Verbatim III*, pp. 368–371.

ensuring no deflection from the course towards ever-closer union on which the EC was embarked.

Attali put his idea to Mitterrand at the beginning of September: "Why not create an institution which brings together all European countries, both East and West, including the USSR? ... This institution, to be credible, should not be solely an assembly or forum, but must be equipped with real resources. France ... could propose the creation of a bank which would finance projects of common interest. We could call it a 'Bank for Europe'."[20] Mitterrand, seeing potential in the idea, asked Attali to develop it further.

Initially, the proposal was greeted with scepticism, even in the French administration.[21] Many of Attali's colleagues believed that the World Bank, which was already active in Poland and Hungary, should remain the primary vehicle for development support. They also noted that Europe already had its own IFI, in the form of the European Investment Bank (EIB). Why create another institution which would inevitably be criticised as adding to the development bureaucracy and which in the end might not reflect fully the interests of the countries to be helped?

Attali's response was to position his proposal in a global context. He viewed the world at the time[22] as being dominated by the USA and Japan, then the major powerhouses of growth, productivity and innovation. He saw a need for Europe to improve its economic performance, along with its geopolitical standing. Integrating the two halves of Europe to create a market of more than 500 million people would, he argued, allow the region to match the major players in the global arena.

This perspective was not new. The French establishment had a long-held aversion to US dominance in many spheres: economic, political and cultural. Since the end of the Second World War they had seen the value of European unity, not only in keeping the peace and creating a large, protected market but also in giving ample room for French influence over the continent's future shape and direction.

An opportunity to strengthen France's position over Europe had arisen in April 1989 with the publication of a report by the Delors Commission on the measures required for the establishment of the Economic and Monetary

---

20   Attali, *Verbatim III*, p. 298.
21   Attali, *Verbatim III*, p. 315; Jacques Attali, *Europe(s)*, Fayard, 1994, p. 33.
22   Illustrated in a series of essays published in *Lignes d'Horizon* (1990).

Union (EMU). Discussion on how to deliver the three stages of EMU followed, with the Madrid European Council in late June affirming the EC's "determination to achieve EMU progressively".

The 12 European Community member states thus formally embarked on the final path towards one of the ultimate goals set out in the Treaty of Rome: establishing an economic and monetary union as part of an "ever closer union". The plan for EMU—a single currency and the creation of a European Central Bank—pooled sovereignty over monetary-policy decisions and thereby diluted the power of the Bundesbank, potentially increasing French influence.[23]

As part of the debate on EMU, a number of participants brought up the question of political union. Under Delors' leadership, there was pressure from Brussels to accelerate this discussion, although it only emerged formally at the Council level under the Irish Presidency in the first half of 1990.

7. The Launch of the Idea of a Bank for Europe

Behind the scenes, Mitterrand had lamented earlier that France lagged behind Germany on commercial ties with the East. He believed that promoting the "Bank for Europe" with a French imprimatur could benefit French companies wishing to exploit new opportunities in central and eastern European markets, including the Soviet Union.

With France holding the Presidency of the EC for the second half of 1989, there were further good reasons for launching a bold new French initiative. The central objective for the Strasbourg European Council (scheduled for 8–9 December) was to agree the timing of the Intergovernmental Conference (IGC) for EMU. But as the autumn progressed, it was clear that the EC's response to events in the East would have to feature. The launch of a "Bank for Europe" would be a political triumph for France, while if the proposal was rejected, it would still demonstrate commitment to the East, including the Soviet Union, and emphasise the French establishment's belief in European unity.

During September, Attali began to work up the idea more seriously, looking into the statutes of various international organisations and prepar-

---

23 The Bundesbank ultimately accepted the proposal but only, at the insistence of its President, on the basis that the future European Central Bank would be independent.

ing draft articles for the new institution. His efforts, which he discussed with Mitterrand towards the end of that month, were mainly based on legal texts that applied to the World Bank, the International Finance Corporation (IFC) and the Asian Development Bank (ADB). He was supported in his endeavours by Jean-Claude Trichet, then director of the Trésor, but found few other advocates.[24]

Events in eastern Europe by now were gaining momentum. Every day seemed to bring a new step on the escape route from communism and new proposals to help the liberated economies. At the Annual Meeting of the International Monetary Fund (IMF) and World Bank in Washington DC in September 1989, former French president Valéry Giscard d'Estaing proposed the establishment of a Euro-Polish bank (and a similar one for Hungary). At the same meeting Alfred Herrhausen, president of Deutsche Bank, argued in favour of an institute for the modernisation of Poland.[25] Then on 9 October European finance ministers agreed that the EIB should make loan finance available to Poland and Hungary from its own resources.[26]

None of these ideas met Attali's vision for the future financial architecture of a wider Europe. He remained sceptical of any solution based on the EIB, believing that would require bringing countries in the East into the Common Market—which at that point seemed a remote possibility.[27] Moreover, the EIB focused on public infrastructure rather than the private sector, where there was clearly a major need for support across the Communist Bloc. Mitterrand, speaking to the European Parliament later, was similarly dismissive of a role for the EIB.[28]

---

24 Attali, *Verbatim III*, p. 315.
25 Alfred Herrhausen was assassinated two months later on his way to work by a bomb detonated remotely by the Red Army Faction in Bad Homburg, outside Frankfurt.
26 It was agreed that the EC would guarantee the EIB against losses under loans for projects in Hungary and Poland. The EIB Board of Governors subsequently authorised loans of up to ECU 1 billion to these two countries, with the first loans made in July 1990: ECU 20 million to the Polish railways and ECU 15 million for power grid improvement in Hungary. *Source:* EIB Annual Reports, 1989, 1990.
27 Attali, *Europe(s),* p. 35. The EIB was an EC institution and provided funds on a large scale primarily to its members, who needed to be EC member states.
28 Mitterrand said "Simply this is not a role for the EIB. The task of the EIB is basically linked to the structural funds, it is oriented to another part of Europe; the EIB consists of only the twelve Community countries." Debates in the European Parliament, 22 November 1989, Bulletin, No 3-383/154. P. Menkveld in *Origin of the European Bank for Reconstruction and Development* (Springer, 1991, p. 38) argues ulterior motives may have been to secure assistance for the Soviet Union and to encourage a coming together of European states.

Nor did bilateral initiatives promise enough for Attali. Such arrangements had been in place during Cold War times and seemed too piecemeal to have much bite. Many of these arrangements took the form of export credits linked to western companies, with limited impact in the importing countries. Other ideas such as a parliament assembly seemed no advance on the Council of Europe, for which these countries were not yet ready given the democratic requirements of membership.

Attali believed any solution should be political as well as economic, involving genuine partnership and mutual commitments to development and democratic reform. He continued to think a new bank was the best vehicle to anchor western Europe with central and eastern Europe and the Soviet Union. His view that the bank should invest in projects of common interest harked back to Robert Schumann's call in 1951 for the creation of the European Coal and Steel Community: a view that multilateral ownership more than national sovereignty can achieve a common good more productively than on an individual basis, and one that lasts.

Without prior consultation with his EC counterparts, Mitterrand floated the development bank idea in an address to the European Parliament on 25 October, ahead of the Strasbourg Summit.

> For my country I have been thinking of a Franco-Polish investment promotion centre ... What can Europe do? So much more! Why not set up a Bank for Europe which, like the EIB, would finance major projects and have on its board of directors the twelve European countries. Not to mention the others, such as Poland and Hungary, and why not the Soviet Union and yet others? ... The creation of a Bank for Europe is a highly political decision.[29]

Marc Boudier, the adviser in charge of international economic issues at the Elysée, having received lukewarm reactions from other ministries to this section of Mitterrand's speech, had decided to cut out the section on the Bank for Europe and replace it with a vague reference to the Euro-Poland bank proposal. He told Attali: "No one in the administration believes in your idea!" Attali stood his ground and convinced Mitterrand to present his

---

29 Address by President Mitterrand on the 'Upheavals in Eastern Europe', 25 October 1989, Strasbourg. Bulletin of the European Community, 10–89, November 1989, pp. 79–86 and reproduced at cvce.org

suggestion noting: "for me, it will act as a bank for all Europeans, including the Soviets. And only Europeans."[30]

But there was a rationale for designing a multilateral institution, rather than a solely European one or one dominated by any single country. In terms of geography the problem being addressed was indeed primarily a European matter. Three EC members (Germany, Italy and Greece) and three other European nations (Austria, Finland and Norway) shared borders with Eastern Bloc countries. Moreover, while historical, ethnic, religious and cultural ties between these countries had been dormant or fractured over the decades of the Cold War, they remained close beneath the surface.

The gap between West and East, however, was not just a European problem, nor even simply an economic one. There were fundamental and ideological differences between western capitalist societies and eastern communist ones. Even more important from a global security perspective was the nuclear dimension of the Cold War. Collapse in the East could lead to unforeseen consequences for all countries, should the handling of nuclear weapons and the materials needed to manufacture them become uncontrolled. As proponents of a policy of containment, and with some 300,000 troops deployed in the Federal Republic, the USA had a direct interest in the situation in Europe and the future of nuclear weapons in particular. From the US administration's perspective, all options to influence outcomes in the East, especially when it came to the Soviet Union, were worth pursuing. Thus, despite Attali's vision of a European bank to deal with wider Europe's problems, the continent was never going to be able to "go it alone".

Finding a post-Cold War accommodation of East and West to ensure peace, growth and security required a global multi-dimensional effort, including in the political-economy sphere. Europe had the biggest economic interests in central and eastern Europe, but the USA still dominated the global financial architecture and was reluctant to cede or dilute this influence. A united front was also consistent with post-war cooperation in relation to the Eastern Bloc and through NATO. And all had a political interest in supporting markets and democracy. So aligning the political-economy approach to changes in the East through a multilateral, not just European, development bank made sense for both the West and the East.

---

30 Attali, *Verbatim III*, pp. 325; Attali, *Europe(s)*, p. 36.

8. Preparations for Strasbourg

With the idea of a Bank for Europe now formally in the public domain, time was of the essence to get wider buy-in to the idea before the European Council in six weeks' time. There had been passing interest in some capitals, but the general reaction to the new bank proposal was mostly lukewarm. Fortunately for Attali and Mitterrand events came to their assistance.

Two weeks after Mitterrand's speech to the European Parliament, the Berlin Wall fell. German reunification was no longer a distant prospect but an imminent possibility. Moreover, the Soviet economy, already in bad shape, continued to stagnate. Visible economic and political support to the East was looking essential to stave off outright collapse or the reversal of reforms.

As President of the EC, France called European leaders to a special European Council on 18 November to assess the situation. The meeting was designed to allow an early reflection on the momentous events taking place on western Europe's doorstep, ahead of what promised to be a heavy and difficult Council agenda dealing with the timing of the IGC for EMU.

Proceedings began with a dinner for Heads of State (plus Commission President Delors and French Foreign Minister Michel Rocard), hosted by Mitterrand at the Elysée. The French president outlined the situation in eastern Europe. Kohl followed with a 20-minute briefing on the German situation, which provoked a lengthy discussion on the question of German reunification.

At a parallel dinner for foreign ministers, Sherpas and lead foreign affairs, officials also considered the implications of German reunification. When discussion turned to the European Bank idea, it was not received with enthusiasm.[31] The rapidly evolving situation in the East and the lack of convincing alternatives, however, left sceptics with little room for manoeuvre. To publicly refuse the French President's initiative would have been politically and diplomatically embarrassing, as well as raising questions as to whether there were any viable alternatives to support communist countries seeking to tread a democratic path.

At the Elysée, Mitterrand introduced the subject of the Bank, now called the "Modernisation and Development Bank for Eastern Europe",[32] towards

---

31   Attali, *Europe(s)*, p. 40.
32   It had been renamed after German objections to the "Bank for Europe" as being reserved for the European Central Bank.

the end of dinner. After some initial mild support, Dutch Prime Minister Ruud Lubbers was the first to express opposition, arguing that plenty of institutions—including the Council of Europe—were available already. Thatcher echoed his objections. "It will be one more bureaucracy," she said.[33]

Nevertheless, Mitterrand wound up proceedings by suggesting that the Troika—the previous, current and future Presidencies (in this case Spain, France and Ireland)—plus the Commission, study the idea and report their findings to the Strasbourg Council in December. There were no formal objections but Thatcher stated pointedly that the Bank might be "something for the long term".[34]

In firming up the proposal ahead of the Strasbourg Council, there was a growing consensus that any such bank should focus on facilitating the transition of Eastern Bloc countries towards a market-oriented economy and accelerating the necessary structural adjustments. At this stage the shareholding of the institution was expected to comprise the 12 EC member states, the Commission, the EIB, other European countries including those in central and eastern Europe, and the Soviet Union. The supposition was that the EC 12, together with the Commission and the EIB, would hold a majority stake.

9. The 1989 Strasbourg European Council

The Strasbourg European Council took place on 8 and 9 December 1989. From the French point of view, the key goal was to set a firm date for the IGC and thus expedite preparations for stages two and three of EMU. The UK had the opposite objective and was keen to delay the decision on dates. The German position was uncertain, with the Bundesbank—and many Germans—unwilling to see an early end to its control of domestic monetary policy and the Deutsche Mark. Kohl was also preoccupied with reunification, on which he had wrong-footed everyone by announcing a 10-point plan a week or so earlier.

In the run-up to the meeting, Mitterrand had conducted a number of bilateral visits to capitals. His most recent journey, two days before the Stras-

---

33 Attali, *Verbatim III*, p. 344; Attali, *Europe(s)*, p. 39.
34 Her briefing indicated that the project could be emasculated by remitting the idea to the EC's Monetary Committee where officials could 'grind it to death'.

bourg Council, had been to Kyiv where he met Gorbachev. The Soviet leader had spoken harshly of Germany and Kohl's rapid pursuit of reunification. On the first day of the Council, Mitterrand held two bilateral discussions in the margins of the meeting with Thatcher and conveyed his concerns.

Thatcher was similarly worried about recent developments and stressed that under the post-war arrangements, the Four Powers—the USA, the UK, France and the Soviet Union—needed to be part of the decision on Germany's future. Taking a map from her handbag, she emphasised the importance of maintaining the post-war borders, notably the Oder-Neisse line under which some areas in the east, which used to be part of Germany, had been allocated to Poland. Mitterrand agreed that the reunification of Germany could not happen by diktat. "At moments of great danger in the past France had always established a special relationship with Britain. Such a time has come again," he said.[35]

That afternoon the G7 Heads discussed the draft paragraph on the Bank, prepared as a result of the Troika work. It did not start particularly well. Lubbers remained against and Thatcher sceptical, while Kohl was uncommitted. According to Attali, Mitterrand was preparing to concede defeat when Thatcher agreed to consent to the proposal, provided the communiqué stated that all OECD countries, not just the Europeans, could be admitted as shareholders.[36] Since all were ready to support the revised proposal, Mitterrand had little choice but to agree.[37]

It was Danish Prime Minister Poul Schlüter who suggested that the new institution should be called the European Bank for Reconstruction and Development, using the model of the World Bank's original name, the International Bank for Reconstruction and Development (IBRD).[38] The following day the Council conclusions were settled and published without further ado. The final communiqué of 9 December read:

"The European Council approved the creation of a European Bank for Reconstruction and Development [whose] aim will be to promote ... productive and competitive investment in the States of Central and Eastern Europe, to reduce ... any risks to financing their economies, to assist the

---

35   C. Powell to S. Wall, 8 December 1989, record of the Strasbourg European Council; Attali, *Verbatim III*, pp. 369–370; Thatcher, *The Downing Street Years*, p. 796.
36   Attali, *Verbatim III*, p. 370; Attali, *Europe(s)*, pp. 45–46.
37   At this point there was no specific mention of the Soviet Union as a member.
38   At present, the IBRD is an institution which forms part of the World Bank Group.

transition towards a more market-oriented economy and to speed up the necessary structural adjustments. The States of Central and Eastern Europe concerned will be able to participate in the capital and management of this Bank, in which the Member States, the Community and the European Investment Bank will have a majority holding. Other countries, and in particular the other members of the OECD, will be invited to participate."[39]

10. An International Institution and Not a Solely European One

The concept of a development bank to support the transition of socialist countries to market-oriented democracies was thus on the way to becoming a reality. Nonetheless, it was not altogether to Attali's liking, since the institution endorsed by the Council was no longer a purely European construct. Somewhat disheartened at the outcome he wrote in his diary: "the end of our dream of a strictly European institution. Under American influence the European Bank will become a development bank like the others."[40]

The collapse of communism in eastern Europe and the evolution of a new world order was not, however, just an issue for Europe. The Soviet Union had not yet disappeared and, although it was under strain, few were expecting its imminent dissolution. The USA still had a significant number of troops stationed in West Germany, as well as strategic concerns over the USSR's nuclear weapons. Bush's earlier economic initiative had also shown US desire to support the region, notably Poland and Hungary. Other non-EC countries such as Japan and South Korea were geographically far removed from central Europe, but close to the Soviet Union and its sphere of influence (and missiles).

Attali stated later that he had never been certain whether the outcome at Strasbourg was the result of a carefully planned coup by the British or simply a last-minute decision.[41] British diplomatic telegraphic traffic in advance of Strasbourg, however, records that Mitterrand was looking for agreement to the Bank for political reasons and that there would be no French objection to participation by the USA and Japan should it be raised.[42]

---

39 European Council, SN 441/2/89.
40 Attali, *Verbatim III*, p. 372.
41 Attali, *Europe(s)*, p. 46.
42 UK Ambassador to France, E. Fergusson, reporting telegram of an Elysée briefing by Mme Guigou and Msr Hennikine, 1 December 1989.

What is also evident from British records is that Thatcher was briefed by the Foreign Office and advised by the UK Treasury to resist the proposal but, if necessary, to ensure it included OECD countries.[43] The reporting note of the Council meeting by her private secretary, Charles Powell, on 9 December stated:

> There was some quite brief discussion of the Development Bank for Eastern Europe, with the emphasis on extending it beyond Europe, to draw on capital from Japan, South Korea and the US. Hence the need to have an institution in addition to the EIB. There was a general disposition to agree to it in principle, while remitting the details to ECOFIN [the Economic and Financial Affairs Council] to ensure that it was operated soundly and effectively. The Prime Minister did not contest this conclusion (having had to contest many others during the day).[44]

The communiqué did not however refer directly to any next steps.

In her memoirs, Thatcher notes in relation to the earlier meeting and Strasbourg:

> at the Special European Council [in November] … Mitterrand was pressing hard for the creation of an [EBRD] in order to channel investment and assistance to the emerging democracies. I was sceptical about whether such an institution was really necessary. The case had not been made that aid of this dimension had to go through a European institution, as opposed to national or wider international ones. I conceded the point in Strasbourg; but my wishes were eventually met because the EBRD now sensibly involves the Americans and Japanese, not just the Europeans.[45]

While Attali may have been disappointed with the outcome, it was nonetheless an extraordinary feat to have garnered support to create a new multilateral development bank in a mere three months. To a great extent it reflected the times: the rapid and accelerating pace of change in the East, the great uncertainties ahead, the high stakes and the pressure on all to act. It would not have happened without the strong French strategic perspective,

---

43 FCO briefing paper, Charles Powell's handwritten comments.
44 C. Powell to S. Wall, 9 December 1989.
45 Thatcher, *The Downing Street Years,* p. 759.

their good fortune in holding both the G7 and EC Presidencies at the right moment, the timing of the fall of the Berlin Wall, and the unexpected realisation that German reunification was just around the corner.

When push came to shove the key actors knew they had to do something visible to match the needs of the moment and signal a longer-term commitment to help rebuild central and eastern Europe. The EBRD fulfilled this purpose.

11. The Preparatory Conference Negotiations

With the EC 12 having signed up to establishing the EBRD, the next task was to seek agreement on its articles and modus operandi. Since the Bank was no longer a purely European body, this meant inviting all other interested parties to the table to negotiate its charter.

Before the year was over, Lubbers wrote to Mitterrand to suggest that his Finance Minister, Onno Ruding, should coordinate and lead the process of preparing the Agreement Establishing the Bank (AEB). His letter appears to have crossed with Mitterrand's invitation to ministers to a conference in Paris in January to start the negotiations.[46] Mitterrand's letter had been silent as to who would lead the discussions and coordinate the results. But the intention was clear that this would be in French hands and that Attali would hold the reins.

The G7's approach to the negotiations was one of the items on the agenda of the first Sherpas' meeting of the year in Key West in early January 1990. This marked the beginning of the US presidency and was a preparatory meeting for that year's Heads' meeting in Houston. Believing that negotiations on the EBRD's arrangements would get bogged down if all countries became fully involved, the G7 had expected to negotiate the main parameters among themselves first. According to Attali's account, they were shocked to learn not only that other European countries had already been invited to Paris but also that the Soviet Union had been included.[47]

Thirty-six delegations, headed by ministers or top officials, gathered at the Kleber Centre in Paris on the weekend of 15 January 1990. This was the first of what would become a series of high-level meetings over the follow-

---

46 According to Attali's account. See *Europe(s)*, pp. 51–52; *Verbatim III*, p. 379.
47 Attali, *Verbatim III*, p. 392.

ing months. The proceedings were introduced by Mitterrand and around the table for the first time were a large number of ministers and officials from West and East, including Soviet Central Bank Governor Viktor Gerashchenko, Polish Finance Minister Leszek Balcerowicz, and Vaclav Klaus, minister of finance for the CSFR. The atmosphere was one of excitement and curiosity, partly because the two sides of the Iron Curtain were meeting with the aim of working together to design a mechanism of mutual support rather than trying to undermine one another, but also simply because the information gap was so great that no one knew what to expect.[48]

The meeting itself focused on the proposed Articles of the AEB, taking them one by one. But behind the detail of the legal texts were fundamental questions about how the Bank should operate, including: the amount of initial capital that should be provided; the relative size of shareholdings; the number of Board Directors and their role; the place of qualified majority voting; currency concerns; and whether the Bank should finance only the private sector or include some public-sector investments as part of its operations.

One of the most difficult matters to resolve from the start was the status of the Soviet Union. The US delegation was led by the Treasury undersecretary for international affairs, the mid-western David Mulford, who strode purposefully ahead of his team into the room wearing his Stetson. He made it clear that Congress would not allow a nuclear-armed enemy of the USA to become a member of, and borrow from, a new international institution that was financed with US capital.[49] Gerashchenko was unfazed and referred to the rapid changes underway in the Soviet Union under Gorbachev's reforms. He advised the USA not to be "too hasty". The situation nonetheless became deadlocked and the atmosphere tense. In response, Mulford suggested that the Soviet Union might be admitted as an observer. The two-day negotiations concluded without agreement, however, with a follow-up meeting set for 10 and 11 March.

Another key item on the agenda was political conditionality. The mandate for the EBRD given by the European Council had been exclusively economic in nature. There had been no explicit reference to democracy or other

---

48 The intense experience was clearly cathartic in the case of one Hungarian delegation member and his Dutch counterpart. They married before the AEB was signed!
49 The Soviet Union, unlike Poland and Hungary, was not a member of the IMF or World Bank at the time.

political elements such as the rule of law or human rights, and to that point IFIs had avoided explicitly conflating economic and political objectives. Moreover, the 12 EC countries were long-standing members of the Council of Europe, which had dealt with such political concerns since the Second World War. However, the USA, Canada and Japan were neither members nor observers in the Council of Europe at that point.[50] Furthermore, the earlier G24 aid effort had linked funds to reform efforts. In this context, in which there was a desire to see political as well as economic change in central and eastern Europe, there was wide agreement that the EBRD mandate should include a political dimension.

For the US administration, an explicit reference to the pursuit of democracy helped persuade a sceptical Congress that the Bank could add value. Some EC member states also shared US concerns over the potential role of the Soviet Union as a borrower in the Bank[51] and it was by no means certain that the USSR would clear the political hurdle for membership. Importantly, in principle a reference to democracy in the mandate could provide a lever to hold back finance or even expel a member should they backtrack on their commitments to uphold democratic values, human rights or the rule of law.

Another topic that proved controversial at the January meeting was the amount of the EBRD's initial capital. France and Germany had suggested ECU 15 billion, whereas the USA argued for ECU 5 billion. A settlement was reached later on ECU 10 billion, a capital base considerably smaller than that of the World Bank and other regional development banks, and with a very conservative gearing ratio of 1:1. The Bank's lending capacity was a long way short of the "Marshall Plan" effort of which Attali had once dreamed.

Relative shareholdings and voting procedures were easier to reach preliminary agreements on, largely by following the rules and procedures of other multilateral development banks. With the prerequisite that the EC 12 plus the Commission and EIB should hold a majority, shares were allocated equally to the main players. France, the UK, Germany, the USA and Japan were each assigned 8.5 per cent, as were the Commission and the EIB. The remain-

---

50   The USA became an observer in 1995, and Canada and Japan in 1996.
51   For example, it was noted that the USSR was an 'AAA-rated' borrower and it was questioned whether it was appropriate for a development bank to lend to such a country. Italy made this point forcefully at EC coordinating meetings. The USA was concerned about lending to a long-standing military adversary.

ing shares were distributed roughly on the basis of GDP. The method allocated at the first stage 53 per cent to the EC blocking majority and 13 per cent to the borrowing community. The Soviet Union was pencilled in to receive half of the latter amount. Double-majority voting procedures[52] were agreed for the most serious matters, such as the admission of new members, an increase in capital or suspension of lending. Decisions in such cases would require the approval of two-thirds of Governors representing not less than three-quarters of total voting power. In the case of eligibility to borrow, three-quarters of Governors and 85 per cent of total voting power was required.

In the weeks following the conference events surrounding German reunification continued to develop. Gorbachev now acknowledged that reunification was inevitable and was prepared to accept it on the basis of the old Soviet ideal of a unified but neutral Germany.[53] However, at a meeting with Gorbachev in Moscow on 10 February, Kohl made it clear that neutrality was unacceptable. The impasse was critical. The Soviet economy was spiralling downwards, making western economic aid all the more attractive, and Gorbachev's control over the Soviet system was becoming more tenuous.[54]

This enhanced the appeal of the EBRD for the USSR. Membership of an international financial institution, for the first time in Soviet history since their withdrawal from the Bretton Woods institutions in the 1940s, could help pave the way towards membership of the IMF, which could bring with it potentially billions of dollars of essential support.

During February, various bilateral and multilateral discussions on the EBRD took place behind the scenes, although even among the EC 12 consensus could not be reached on many of the big issues. Despite their earlier scepticism, it was becoming clearer that the USA was more willing to participate actively.

The US team began to accept the inevitability of Soviet membership.[55] With support from the UK, Japan and some others, however, they insisted that the EBRD should not provide finance to the USSR beyond what it contributed to the Bank as a shareholder.

---

52   These procedures, which consist of a combination of simple-majority and weighted voting (according to capital contributions), are used in multilateral development banks, but not in the United Nations for example.
53   'Historical events in the European integration process (1945–2014)', University of Luxembourg, cvce.eu database.
54   According to the first EBRD *Transition Report* (2000). GDP in the Russian Federation (as an approximation for the Soviet Union) fell by an estimated 4 per cent in 1990.
55   Weber, 'Origins of the European Bank for Reconstruction and Development', p. 18.

This was an extraordinary condition, but in order to make headway the head of the Soviet delegation agreed that the USSR would borrow no more than its capital contribution in the first few years. Moscow would also limit its overall borrowing capacity to no more than 20 per cent of the institutional total so as not to crowd out smaller central European countries. The "Gerashchenko letter" outlining these commitments was annexed to the Treaty in due course.

Eleven of the 12 EC countries were prepared to accept this arrangement. But at a meeting in London in late February, the US, UK and Japanese representatives decided to reject the Soviet offer and demand instead that borrowing by the USSR be limited initially to its paid-in capital, then 20 per cent of the total (approximately US$ 150 million).[56] They also insisted that any move from one stage to another should require a supermajority of 85 per cent of voting power. In effect, this gave the USA with Japan, or with the UK, a veto on any borrowing by the Soviet Union.

As the date of the second conference approached, a number of new countries declared an interest in joining the EBRD. At Japan's request, South Korea applied for membership, while Morocco, Israel, Albania, Egypt, Mexico and Liechtenstein also expressed interest. With more countries involved than originally envisaged, the share calculations had to be reworked. Importantly, the USA now insisted that they should have a greater share (10 per cent) than any other member in recognition of their economic position. This reflected an about-turn in the US stance towards the EBRD, which was aired publicly by Secretary of State James Baker III. He told the Senate on 1 March: "the Europeans absolutely want us in this institution; and we want to show leadership."[57]

The Paris Conference in March, which was now made up of 42 delegations, once again involved a line-by-line negotiation of the draft Articles of the AEB. This time much quicker progress was made and by the end of the weekend 50 out of 58 Articles had been agreed in principle. Nevertheless, several points remained unresolved.

The Soviet Union took issue with the use of the term "multiparty democracy" in the preamble to the AEB[58] and "applying the principles" of the

---

56 The proportion of paid-in capital later became 30 per cent.
57 Testimony to the Senate Committee on Foreign Affairs, 1 March 1990.
58 EBRD archives. "Committed to the fundamental principles of multiparty democracy, the rule of law, respect for human rights and market economics", Preamble to the Articles of Agreement Establishing the Bank, EBRD.

same in Article 1.[59] Issues also arose over the currency denomination of the Bank's finances. The European side wanted to use the ECU. This would be a symbol of the European character of the institution and a means of building support for the single currency. The USA argued for the use of the dollar, on the basis of it being the most widely traded international currency, but also because use of the ECU would mean the value of their dollar contribution would fluctuate with exchange-rate movements. Similarly, Japan wanted to use Yen denomination.

There were also still disagreements over how to characterise the role of the USSR. These often turned on the debating point of whether or not the Soviet Union was a part of Europe, but more substantively on the question of its commitment to democracy. Under pressure to respond, the Soviets withdrew their objection to the preamble and Article 1 language on multiparty democracy. Three days later, changes in Moscow rendered the point moot. On 14 March, Article 6 of the Soviet Constitution, which assigned the "leading and guiding force of Soviet society" to the Communist Party, was amended, effectively removing the Party's absolute right to rule and opening the door to multiparty democracy. The last remaining impediment to full Soviet participation was now its borrowing capacity.

As part of the effort to resolve issues surrounding the USSR, the French hosts organised a private dinner with the US and Soviet delegations on the Saturday night of the two-day meeting. It was an unusual moment. Top finance officials from the three countries had not had much experience dealing with each other during the Cold War, let alone in an informal setting. According to Attali, who was present, the atmosphere was initially very tense. He recounts the following anecdote which helped to break the ice:

The Soviet Central Bank Governor describes how they are about to decide in the coming days whether to privatise parts of their economy. Mulford in a deadpan manner aims to put Gerashchenko on the spot over his claim that the USSR has changed, and asks:

'Suppose you privatise your oil sector tomorrow, what would happen?'
Gerashchenko exclaims: *'Ah no, that's impossible.'*
'There, you see!', says Mulford triumphantly, *'You'll achieve nothing if you won't privatise the oil industry.'*

---

59   "...committed to and applying the principles of multiparty democracy, pluralism and market economics", Article 1.

'*No*,' responded Gerashchenko with a big smile. '*No, it's not possible because tomorrow, it's Sunday!*'[60]

Nevertheless, it was not until May that the borrowing issue was finally resolved.

One of the major decisions remaining concerned the type of activities that the EBRD should pursue. The USA, Japan and the UK wanted to limit the Bank to supporting the private sector and privatisation. There was a strong aversion on their side to financing any state entities of former communist countries.[61] While the operational template for the EBRD envisaged investment in the private sector as a central feature, many of the Europeans present were concerned that establishing viable private enterprises would take time and would limit the amount of investment that could be undertaken initially. Equally important, they saw an urgent need to put in place the necessary infrastructure to allow the private sector to function effectively. They thus pushed for a role for the Bank in investing in public infrastructure.

The Europeans also wanted to provide balance-of-payments support and export finance, but this was rejected by the USA and others, again on the grounds of limiting the EBRD's involvement with the state. This ensured the Bank would not provide budgetary support or programme lending, unlike the World Bank and other regional development banks.

After very long discussions, a compromise was reached which would define the Bank's operational approach throughout its history. It was decided that investments in the state sector, in other words those involving public-sector entities and state infrastructure, should take up no more than 40 per cent of the EBRD's total business volume, initially over a two-year period and each year thereafter.[62] In other words, the Bank would be a private sector-led institution, but would not exclude some public-sector activities.

In another first for an IFI, it was also agreed that the EBRD would be able to offer a full range of financial instruments, including loans based on market rates, guarantees, and equity participations covering both private

---

60   "Everyone laughs and relaxes. The ice is broken." Attali, *Europe(s)*, p. 62, Attali, *Verbatim III*, p. 443.
61   An ODI Briefing Paper on the EBRD, published in September 1990, commmented: "the Bush administration initially opposed any EBRD funds going to the public sector, arguing this would amount to subsidising failed socialism." Thatcher's objections to state activities were well known, epitomised by her 'Bruges speech' in September 1988: "We have not successfully rolled back the frontiers of the state in Britain, only to see them reimposed at the European level." EBRD, ODI Briefing Paper, September 1990, p. 2.
62   Provision was also made that for any country no more than 40 per cent of commitments should be provided to the state sector over a period of five consecutive years.

and public sectors. In essence, it would combine the competences of a commercial bank with those of a development bank.

The primary objective of the EBRD, as expressed in the draft of Article 1, was mostly agreed. In its final form it would read: "the purpose of the Bank shall be to foster the transition towards open market-oriented economies and to promote private and entrepreneurial initiative in the Central and Eastern European countries committed to and applying the principles of multiparty democracy, pluralism and market economics."[63]

The Bank was also given a prominent role in protecting the environment. This featured in Article 2: "To promote in the full range of its activities environmentally sound and sustainable development." Concern over the environment was beginning to appear more frequently in G7 and other international agendas so it made sense to embed it as a permanent feature of this new institution.

There were other disagreements, mainly between the US and European participants.[64] The USA, for example, objected to the European Commission and the EIB becoming members, on the grounds that they were not sovereign states. They also wanted a resident Board of Directors, paid for by the Bank, to exercise control over management. This reflected the structure of institutions such as the World Bank over which the USA held considerable sway, including veto power. By contrast, most Europeans were happy with a non-resident Board, in line with the practice at the EIB, and agreed that it should be limited to 12 members. Despite the presence of the Commission representing the interests of the 12 EC member states, however, it was not possible to limit the number of European constituencies. After trying out many permutations for constituencies, the final number of resident Directors was settled at 23—one of the largest among IFIs—with single-constituency offices for the largest shareholders, namely the G7 countries, the EC and the EIB.

---

63 At this point the relevant section read: "To promote the transition towards open market-oriented economies and private initiative in Central and Eastern Economies engaged in applying the principles of multiparty democracy and market economics." Attali, *Verbatim III*, pp. 462–3.
64 Weber, 'Origins', pp. 16–19; Menkveld, *Origin*, pp. 63–65. Predictably one of the most fraught minor issues was over the official language for the internal documents of the Bank. It had already been agreed there would be four official languages: English, French, German and Russian. All the delegates apart from those from France and Germany, however, agreed that working documents should be distributed only in English. France tried to argue that using all four languages would be fair, but efficiency and economy won the day. *Source*: author interview with a senior Hungarian participant.

12. Sensitive Matters: The Location of the Bank and the Choice of its First President

The third constitutive conference, which was expected to be the last, was held on 8 and 9 April 1990. By now most elements were in place and thoughts were turning to a signing date for the AEB. To simplify matters, it was decided to aim for an OECD ministerial meeting in Paris on 29 May. Two important issues, however, had not yet been formally tabled: where the Bank's headquarters should be located and who should become its first President.

Many cities had offered to host the EBRD: Amsterdam, Berlin, Copenhagen, Dublin, London, Luxembourg, Milan, Prague, Vienna and Warsaw. In February, the UK had even produced a glossy brochure in three languages extolling the virtues of the City of London, which it claimed hosted more eastern European banks than any other western capital. Attali scouted a number of possible venues in Paris, alighting on an office in Boulevard Haussmann.

As with many such high-profile and politically sensitive decisions, the choice of the Bank's location would not be made in isolation. There were several other new institutions to locate at the time, including the European Trade Marks Office,[65] the European Environment Agency and the future European Central Bank (ECB).[66] Competition to become a winning city was fierce. Much later, Attali would describe the behind-the-scenes negotiations in a book of memoirs.

At the same time, among the international finance issues exercising the minds of senior officials was a long-running battle over IMF quotas. The ninth review of these quotas was long overdue and coming to a head for the IMF/World Bank Spring Meetings in late April 1990. The Japanese were arguing for a special quota increase to reflect the rise in their country's GDP. An adjustment on this basis would mean the UK's demotion from second to fourth place, behind both Japan and Germany. France was also insisting that, based on the size of its economy, it should be ahead of the UK.

There had been intense discussions for several months on how to resolve the impasse. British officials had put forward various solutions[67] but failed

---

65 This became the European Union Intellectual Property Office, located in Alicante, Spain.
66 The European Environment Agency went to Copenhagen and the ECB to Frankfurt.
67 J. M. Boughton, 'Tearing Down Walls: The International Monetary Fund 1990–1999', IMF, Washington DC, 2012, pp. 870–875. The key official at the time designing the possible solutions was Jeremy Heywood, later Lord Heywood of Whitehall and Cabinet Secretary to the UK government for many years.

to achieve consensus. The G7 finance deputies finally managed to agree a formula which they would try to sell to ministers in time for the IMF/World Bank Spring Meetings.

The proposal was that Japan and the Federal Republic of Germany should become second equal in the IMF, with the UK and France sharing equal fourth place through an unprecedented quota leaseback scheme.[68] In addition, the G7 would support London as the location for the headquarters of the EBRD, with a French President for a single non-renewable term and an American as First Vice President, or deputy to the President.[69]

Ahead of the final constitutive conference establishing the EBRD, the USA and the USSR also agreed the text limiting Soviet borrowing to ECU 180 million over three years before an increase could be considered.[70] The stage now seemed set for the signing ceremony of the AEB[71] to take place on 29 May.

However, despite the preliminary agreement achieved by the G7, proposals from other member countries—including a Dutch candidacy for President—remained in play. Typically, such agreements in the world of international affairs are reached by consensus, but at the constitutive conference between 9 and 10 May, no consensus emerged on either the location for the Bank or the nationality of its President. With less than three weeks before the signing ceremony, there was little option left other than to put it to a vote. The Secretariat duly informed the member countries that this would take place on 19 May, the last meeting to be held before the signing of the Treaty on 29 May.

In the end, the original G7 proposal was supported, despite concerns from smaller EC countries such as Belgium and the Netherlands that the powerful G7 nations—including other Europeans—had effectively called the shots. Attali was elected President with 32 votes out of 40. (The Commission and EIB abstained for reasons of conflict of interest, not wishing to

---

68 As the relative GDPs of France and the UK fluctuated, a lend-and-leaseback scheme of around 0.5 per cent of quota would ensure the quotas could remain equal in any subsequent review. Although the positions of France and the UK fell to fifth equal following quota reform and the rise of China, the agreement remains in place.
69 Confidential note from the UK Chancellor's Principal Private Secretary to Charles Powell, Thatcher's Foreign Affairs Private Secretary, dated 7 May 1990. National Archives; Bank of England Archives.
70 At the time an increase required a decision of not less than three-fourths of Governors representing at least 85 per cent of voting power. It was enshrined in Article 8, paragraph 4 and was linked to the "Gerashchenko letter" on the Soviet Union to the Chair of the Conference.
71 www.ebrd.com/news/publications/institutional-documents/basic-documents-of-the-ebrd.html.

choose sides between member states.) London was selected as the location. The tidying up of the rest of the AEB was done overnight.

It had been a momentous week, and not only for the Bank. On 18 May, the treaty bringing about monetary, economic and social union between West and East Germany was signed in Bonn. One week later, Gorbachev agreed that the enlarged Germany could join NATO in exchange for western financial assistance, including ECU 3 billion from the Federal Republic to pay for the repatriation of the 365,000 Soviet troops stationed in the GDR.

13. The Signing of the Agreement Establishing the Bank in Paris

The Treaty establishing the EBRD was signed on 29 May 1990 at the Elysée by the finance and foreign ministers of all 42 members. Ratification by national parliaments, two-thirds of which were required before the Bank could begin operations, was expected to take up to a year.

The signing ceremony had fired the starting gun for the creation of an institution that delivered a truly multinational response to a global challenge. Its shareholders comprised the entire EC and two European organisations, as well as other European states, including the eight prospective recipients of EBRD finance. Crucially, there was a hefty non-European presence including the G7 powerhouses of the USA (the largest individual shareholder), Japan and Canada, as well as Australia, New Zealand, South Korea, and also Mexico, Morocco and Egypt.

Reflecting on the result, Attali concluded that the EBRD at its birth was more Anglo-Saxon than European in its philosophy and design, but that the Americans and British had had to accept the membership of the Soviet Union and a French President. It was not the beginning which he had envisaged. For most other officials involved, it had been a remarkable feat to achieve consensus and to have built the core of a new institution to support central and eastern Europe inside six months. Politically at least it was a great success. Practically, there was a lot to do before the Bank could become operational.

After the Berlin Wall

Table 1.1.

The 42 signatories to the AEB included the eight recipient countries, the 12 EC members plus the European Economic Community (EEC) and the EIB, as well as 11 "other" European and nine non-European countries.

	Number of shares	Capital subscription (in million ECU)
A – European Communities		
(a)		
Belgium	22,800	228.00
Denmark	12,000	120.00
France	85,175	851.75
Germany, Federal Republic of	85,175	851.75
Greece	6,500	65.00
Ireland	3,000	30.00
Italy	85,175	851.75
Luxembourg	2,000	20.00
Netherlands	24,800	248.00
Portugal	4,200	42.00
Spain	34,000	340.00
United Kingdom	85,175	851.75
(b)		
European Economic Community	30,000	300.00
European Investment Bank	30,000	300.00
B - Other European countries		
Austria	22,800	228.00
Cyprus	1,000	10.00
Finland	12,500	125.00
Iceland	1,000	10.00
Israel	6,500	65.00
Liechtenstein	200	2.00
Malta	100	1.00
Norway	12,500	125.00
Sweden	22,800	228.00
Switzerland	22,800	228.00
Turkey	11,500	115.00
C – Recipient countries		
Bulgaria	7,900	79.00
Czechoslovakia	12,800	128.00

German Democratic Republic	15,500	155.00
Hungary	7,900	79.00
Poland	12,800	128.00
Romania	4,800	48.00
Union of Soviet Socialist Republics	60,000	600.00
Yugoslavia	12,800	128.00
D – Non-European countries		
Australia	10,000	100.00
Canada	34,000	340.00
Egypt	1,000	10.00
Japan	85,175	851.75
Korea, Republic of	6,500	65.00
Mexico	3,000	30.00
Morocco	1,000	10.00
New Zealand	1,000	10.00
United States of America	100,000	1,000.00
E - Non allocated shares	125	1.25
Total	1,000,000	10,000.00

SOURCE: *Basic documents of the European Bank for Reconstruction and Development,* EBRD, 1991, pp. 37–38.

Chapter 2

Creating the EBRD's DNA

1. Balancing the Governance of the New Institution

Against the odds and in record time for an international institution the EBRD had been established. This was the institution that would reach out to address the global challenge of a whole system that was disintegrating across a vast geographical area.

The challenge was global because the collapse of communist rule had immediate economic and social consequences, and was of a geopolitical relevance that spread far beyond the borders of its western European neighbours.

The response was also global. This was to be a bank whose shareholders stretched across five continents and whose owners included the countries it was created to support. It would have a unique business model that put a primary focus on the development of the private sector, while allowing for investment to flow to the public sector to help with immediate infrastructure demands and provide quality public services to improve the lives of millions across eastern Europe.

The EBRD would ultimately be designed to invest according to three criteria: i) it would support "transition", the transformation to functioning market economies; ii) it would be "additional" by investing only when the private sector either would not or could not; and iii) its investments would be "bankable", allowing it to make a profit and to continue investing on the basis of its income. It would also put a strong emphasis on environmental sustainability, a focus that would become even more significant in the EBRD's later years.

When the EBRD was being set up, Attali suggested it might take 20 years for the eastern European nations to catch up with their more prosperous western neighbours. While many of these countries indeed made remarkable progress over the next 20 years, that timetable turned out to be optimistic.

In 1990, however, the immediate challenge was to make the Bank operational as soon as possible. The key to successfully addressing this challenge lay in forging compromise and consensus among its broad sweep of more than 40 disparate shareholders.

Translating the common interests of the EBRD's founding members into operational reality was, of course, not straightforward. The West was in principle capitalist, with institutions based on the rule of law, but differences of interpretation existed, for example over the extent and role of the state, or between common law and civil law. However, debate among the members led to effective compromise.

Indeed, the fact that the creation of the Bank and its rules of operation was not dominated by any one country or institution meant that the parties *had* to work together. While the EC held a majority and, acting in concert, could exert an effective veto, this was not the same as the power vested in the USA at the World Bank and Inter-American Development Bank, or in Japan at the ADB.

Many differences in approach existed between EC member states. As with Brussels' European committees, compromises among individual country positions had to be found throughout the process. This contributed to a greater balance of interests across a wide spectrum of views—something that continued throughout the EBRD's history and became a unique institutional strength.

Common positions also had to be forged between shareholder countries and the new management of the EBRD. As a public institution, ultimately funded by taxpayers, the Bank needed to be accountable to the senior officials representing the shareholder countries. These officials were the appointed Governors of the institution, most of whom were finance ministers or central bank governors.

This was a time of vocal civil-society criticism of existing IFIs. The Governors were therefore keen to ensure that the new institution would have adequate oversight to prevent risky or unjustified decisions. Other development banks at the time were geared towards development impact, such as poverty reduction and lower mortality rates. A development bank which aimed to invest in and do business with the private sector was thus a very unusual creature.

At the same time, the EBRD was designed by its creators to make an adequate return on capital, meaning that the shareholder countries expected to see profitable operations. Hence, it needed to operate in many ways similar to a private bank. The management wanted the new institution to embody a private-sector ethos, have maximum flexibility and make investment decisions based on the fast-changing needs of the market, rather than seeking formal approvals for each move.

This chapter details the ways in which compromise was sought and achieved.

2. Maintaining Momentum and Developing an Ambitious Agenda

In setting up the EBRD there were many aspects to consider, from office location, staffing and administrative arrangements to the organisational structure, business plans and financing of operations. Moreover, while agreement on the AEB had set the key parameters defining the Bank, there was still a need to agree by-laws, rules of procedure for the Board of Governors and Board of Directors, and staff regulations. Not only would these texts need to meet formal legal requirements, they would also have to cover sensitive issues such as salaries, retirement plans, and the expenses and tax arrangements of Board Directors, the costs of which would be borne by the Bank's administrative budget. Then there was a Headquarters Agreement to be negotiated with the UK authorities to cement the EBRD's status as an international organisation under the United Nations (UN) system. In short, there was a daunting set of tasks ahead before the EBRD could be formally inaugurated and its operations begin.

In one respect, however, the EBRD was fortunate. It was not the first IFI to face many of these tasks. While none on this scale had been created since the ADB[1] more than 20 years earlier, and none with a mandate like that of the EBRD, there was much to glean from the legal documentation surrounding these institutions, as well as from the practices that had evolved over time to support their operability. Good use was made of these materials in marshalling the relevant building blocks quickly.

---

1 The ADB was inaugurated in 1966.

Creating a new IFI from scratch would present a major challenge, even for a President with a strong administrative and executive background. It was a particularly formidable task for Attali, an intellectual and adviser with no banking or managerial experience.

Undaunted, he approached the matter with characteristic energy and enthusiasm. He was particularly keen to ensure that the EBRD did not meekly slot in among the existing main multilateral players or become a means for the EC or Washington to pursue their own ends. He wanted the EBRD to push boundaries and develop an independent voice.

"I deliberately chose to make the European Bank [EBRD] a political as well as an economic institution, a spokesperson for the East, refusing to make it an annex of the Commission, as with the EIB, or of the World Bank as with the other regional development banks. I was aware that in doing so I would create an enemy a day."[2]

The major shareholders agreed that the EBRD was indeed something new and different from its predecessors. A multilateral public-sector organisation, it was to focus primarily on private-sector development. It would use innovative financial instruments to achieve its transformative mission of helping the newly democratising countries of central and eastern Europe on the difficult reform path forward.

From the operational perspective, however, there was an enormous amount of work to be done, barely any staff to do it and more than 40 countries and institutions to manage in the process.

3. Early Preparations and a Transitional Team

One of the first tasks was ensuring that all members ratified the Treaty signed in May so that the EBRD could begin investing in its target countries. Potential members had to submit legal documents confirming that they had completed the steps required by their domestic legislation to give legal effect to the immunities and privileges of the Bank. Ratification required the submission of these so-called instruments of approval by signatories representing two-thirds of total subscriptions, including at least two countries from central and eastern Europe.

---

2   Attali, *Europe(s)*, p. 82.

Since each tier of national government would be involved, it was clear that ratification would take time. This was reflected in the deadline of 31 March 1991 set in Article 62.

France was first off the mark, obtaining the necessary approvals in the National Assembly and the Senate by the end of June. After depositing the relevant instruments, it ratified before the summer break. The UK was next, meeting the requirements on 10 August, followed at the end of November with ratification by the two European institutions. Elsewhere progress was slow, but by the year-end nine members—including Germany, Bulgaria, Hungary and Romania—had ratified. Notably, it was a united Germany that had ratified, following the unification of East and West Germany on 3 October 1990. The USA made slower progress, partly because of a reluctance by Congress to countenance financial support for the Soviet Union.

At the same time, prospective shareholders were eager to finalise details concerning the governance of the institution, including a definition of the respective roles of the Board and management. This was a priority now the AEB had been signed. Everything had to be in place by the time of the EBRD's inauguration. Shareholders had also flagged the need for the Board of Directors to oversee the Bank's operational policies and procedures, including its structure and staffing.

Consideration of the principles guiding the Bank sought by shareholders did not stand in the way of Attali preparing the Bank for the start of its operations.

Under the AEB, the election of the President could only be made by the Board of Governors so formal confirmation of Attali's appointment had to wait until the Treaty was ratified. As President-designate, however, he began to assemble a small team. On 1 June 1990, he announced the appointment of Pierre Pissaloux[3] from the Trésor as his Directeur du Cabinet and Sylvia Jay[4] from the UK's Overseas Development Administration as Directeur du Cabinet Adjoint. Both had served as part of the Secretar-

---

3   Pissaloux, like Attali, was a *pied noir*, in his case born in Tunis (Attali was born in Algiers). He later became global head of MENA at HSBC private bank, manager of wealth management at Emirates NBD bank and founded Elyseum Capital Partners, based in Dubai.
4   After becoming director-general of the Food and Drink Federation of the UK, Lady Jay became chairman of L'Oreal UK, a director of Lazard Group and held director positions at Alcatel-Lucent and Saint-Gobain. She is currently High Sheriff of Oxford.

iat for the preparatory conferences. Pissaloux was the key point man for Attali,[5] while Jay served as the main link on the political mandate and with the British authorities.

At this stage, the embryonic Bank was being financed by the French and British governments. The EIB had also agreed to extend an ECU 10 million start-up loan for recruitment, rent and other initial expenses. A small office at 28 Avenue Hoche in Paris was made available by the French government. In London, the Bank of England provided space for EBRD staff before arrangements for temporary offices at 6 Broadgate in the City of London were in place. The team was thus split between Paris and London for a while.

Despite the high-level legal requirements of some of the agreements with shareholders, a large part of the work to be carried out in the near term was practical and administrative. There was a need for staff of all kinds, financial and operational arrangements, further temporary office space (since staff numbers were expected to outgrow the premises at 6 Broadgate before long), and forging contacts with governments and enterprises in the recipient countries.

The core work was put in the hands of the capable small team that had been assembled. They were to prepare papers describing the way forward, go on missions to the region and draft legal documents, while Attali focused on broader strategic questions and relationships with key players in the region. The President-designate continued to reside in Paris and remained Mitterrand's economic adviser. However, he became increasingly involved in the work of the EBRD, especially in the recruitment of senior staff. He also made a series of trips to central and eastern Europe and the Soviet Union.

Attali visited Gorbachev in Moscow in September. According to John Flemming, who was present at the meeting: "[Attali] spoke of the role of the Bank of Europe as an institution of which the USSR was a member—the first realisation perhaps of Mr Gorbachev's idea of a joint common European 'house'." Attali also offered to help in the training of Soviet specialists. "This seemed to strike a chord," Flemming commented.

Discussing the scope for the EBRD to participate in joint ventures, the President-designate asked Gorbachev: "What kind of projects would cap-

---

5 He had wanted Anne Le Lorier, an official from the Trésor who had acted as secretary to the preparatory conferences, but she turned him down.

ture the popular imagination? A TGV link from the West to Moscow? A communication satellite?" The Soviet leadership's demands were apparently more modest, as Flemming's summary records:

> The people had had their fill of grandiose schemes. What was needed was something to make the market mechanism, and its potential, intelligible to ordinary people, e.g. something to ensure regularity in the supply of meat. The area of distribution emerged as the most pressing...[6]

A little later, Attali toured Hungary, the CSFR and Poland to hold exploratory talks on the EBRD's role in helping eastern European countries make the transition from central planning to free-market economies. At a news conference in Budapest, he made clear that the job of bringing eastern Europe's economies up to the level of their western neighbours would require trillions of dollars in investment:

> If we want to see all the countries of Eastern Europe, including the Soviet Union, reach the level of France or Germany, you have to invest 2,000 billion ECUs (2,700 billion dollars). This will give you an idea of the task that has to be undertaken.[7]

4. The Soviet Study

The first Post-Signature Conference of prospective members was scheduled for mid-July 1990, six weeks after the signing of the AEB. However, just ahead of this was the annual G7 Heads meeting, which would mark the EBRD-in-waiting's first appearance on the international stage alongside the IMF, the World Bank and the OECD.

Throughout the first half of 1990, concerns over the future of the Soviet Union had been mounting. Its economy was not yet in freefall, but it was deteriorating rapidly. Export and tax revenues were weakening, as was production. The budget deficit, already at an estimated 8 per cent of GDP, was in-

---

6   Preliminary minutes of the meeting on 19 September 1990 between the President of the USSR and the President-designate of the Bank of Europe (EBRD), recorded by John Flemming, 20 September 1990.
7   'Trillions seen needed for East Europe investment'. *Reuters News*, 9 October 1990, Budapest.

creasing, and deteriorating supplies of goods and a huge monetary overhang meant that only rigid price controls were holding back inflation. Moves to switch to payments in hard currency among the members of the Council for Mutual Economic Assistance (Comecon) were also beginning to take their toll. Gorbachev was in even greater need of financial assistance. At home he was facing challenges to his programme from both hard-liners and the new Russian president, Boris Yeltsin, who was advocating faster reform.

Under the US Presidency, the G7 Summit was scheduled for early July in Houston. Gorbachev had indicated earlier to Bush his need for financial support, first at their meeting on the Soviet cruise ship *Maxim Gorky* off Malta towards the end of 1989, and then in his US visit in May 1990. Despite his plea, the USA remained reluctant to provide finance, citing the need to see reforms first. Bush was cautious about the chances of comprehensive reform given the uncertain Soviet political and economic outlook. While his Secretary of State James Baker was moderately optimistic, Secretary of Defence Dick Cheney and Deputy National Security Adviser Bob Gates were more hawkish.[8]

Most other G7 members were equally wary, not least as they perceived little clarity on how funds would be spent in delivering reform.[9] Like the USA, Japan and the UK were not prepared to go beyond technical assistance and pre-existing bilateral programmes for the Soviet Union. The EBRD was not in a position to offer funding, not only because it was not yet operational but also because of the restrictions that had been placed on lending to the USSR. Significant financial aid was therefore not forthcoming. Instead, the G7 decided to commission a study of the Soviet Union to assess its reform needs and make recommendations, including criteria for economic assistance in support of reform.[10]

The remit was handed to the IMF, in conjunction with the World Bank, the OECD and the EBRD. Being asked to be involved was a feather in the cap

---

8 Bush and Scowcroft, *A World Transformed*, p. 44, p. 154.
9 Kohl had offered to help Gorbachev (although specific amounts were not forthcoming until the following year), and Mitterrand was also urging colleagues to stump up large sums, without success. See Bush and Scowcroft, *A World Transformed*, p. 270; M. R. Beschloss and S. Talbott, *At the Highest Levels: The Inside Story of the End of the Cold War*, Little Brown, 1994, p.188, pp. 236–238; and W. Taubman, *Gorbachev: His Life and Times*, Simon & Schuster, 2017, pp. 569–570.
10 Asked at a press conference following the Houston Summit whether the study was a way of delaying a political decision on aid, Bush replied: "... it's not an effort to forestall anything, it's an effort to move forward ... and be helpful to the Soviet Union in terms of reform." 11 July 1990, G7/8 Summits, Munk School, University of Toronto.

of a new institution that had not even formally come into being. At the time, however, the Bank did not have the internal resources to cope with the task.[11]

Attali therefore recruited a team of external specialists, starting with Jean-Paul Fitoussi, a long-time friend and professor of economics at Sciences Po in Paris, and Philippe Aghion, back in Paris after a stint at the Massachusetts Institute of Technology (MIT) as assistant professor of economics. Fitoussi had been working closely with US economist Edmund Phelps on unemployment issues and brought him into the fold, along with Nobel laureate Kenneth Arrow from Stanford.[12]

As well as a team of economists, the head of each organisation involved in the Soviet Union study was asked to appoint a personal representative to manage the coordination process. Attali's first choice, Larry Summers, was about to take over as chief economist at the World Bank and was not interested.

Attali next turned to John Flemming, at the time the chief economist at the Bank of England, who was on holiday in the Pyrenees by the time Attali contacted him towards the end of July. After a series of messages left at a local post office, Flemming agreed to take on the role. The Bank of England was already providing administrative help to set up the EBRD and, as a guardian of the UK financial system, had an interest in ensuring the new Bank was a success.

The EBRD subsequently hired more consultants, including Paul Hare of Heriot-Watt University and Jacques Le Cacheux, an economist at the Observatoire Français des Conjectures Économiques and Sciences Po, as well as drawing on members of the expanding transitional team. The Bank was asked to lead the sectoral work, covering transportation, telecommunications, distribution and mining. In addition, the group led on the role of economic information and market behaviour and, with the OECD, foreign direct investment. A small team involving Hare was also associated with the World Bank's work on price reform, market structures, privatisation, decentralisation and financial markets.

---

11   A lack of staff did not prevent Attali from pushing for a more prominent role at the first coordination meeting of the four heads of institutions. His suggestion that the EBRD lead the study resulted in a clash with Michel Camdessus, the Managing Director of the IMF.

12   Arrow received his Nobel Prize (with John Hicks) for contributions to general equilibrium economics and welfare theory in 1972. Edmund Phelps would also receive a Nobel Prize in 2006 for his analysis of intertemporal trade-offs in macroeconomic policy.

The Soviet Study was substantial. It took up three volumes, amounting to well over 1,000 pages in total. The authors delved as deeply as they could into the state of the Soviet economy, travelling to Moscow to meet representatives of institutions including Gosplan, Gosbank, the ministry of finance, Vnesheconombank (Bank for Foreign Economic Affairs) and many others.

Phelps described the trip as "a wonderful experience".

> Our signature ... was the assortment of beat-up taxis from which six or seven of us would spill out in front of the ministry we were visiting, in the style of the old circus shtick, while the more venerable international agencies favoured their black limousines.[13]

He was also inspired by the "energy and zeal" of reformist Soviet policymakers:

> After you have met some of them you cannot but help feel confident—maybe unreasonably—that the drive for individual liberty and free markets is quite strong in Russia.

The study provided a comprehensive picture of the dire state of the Soviet system and concluded by noting the enormous challenge facing the authorities, including a need to decide on a division of responsibilities between the Union and the republics and the expectation that output and employment would fall as adjustment towards a market economy progressed. The four institutions urged the authorities to pursue a rapid path towards comprehensive price and trade liberalisation and to tackle the rapidly increasing general government deficit. The study described the need for the absorption of excess money holdings and, in the short run, for an incomes policy and social safety net. It advised unification of the exchange rate for current account transactions within a year. Establishment of private-ownership rights and elimination of controls was advocated along with the privatisation of smaller firms. For larger state-owned enterprises, commercialisation was seen as the first step, to be accompanied by the imposition of hard budget constraints.

---

13   E.S. Phelps, *A Life in Economics,* Columbia Education Press, 1993. Phelps and Arrow's assessment was subsequently published as 'Proposed reforms of the economic system of information and decision in the USSR: Commentary and Advice', *Rivista di Politica Economica*, 81, November 1991.

The Soviet Study did not put a figure on the appropriate degree of financial support for the reform process or what the West should provide, but recommended that funding should focus on technical assistance, along with some humanitarian aid. On the macro side, balance-of-payments finance was seen as useful, but only once "a comprehensive program of systemic reforms has begun to be implemented".[14] Some of the detailed analysis provided by the EBRD team, for example on sectoral needs, price signals and privatisation, was to provide a useful basis for operational considerations at a later stage.

The study was submitted to the G7 in early December and was well received. In its first task the EBRD had demonstrated that the organisation was up to the standards of leading global institutions and a significant player, intellectually at least, in the business of transition. The academic economists who had worked with the EBRD were to play a role in the Economics Advisory Committee which was set up shortly before the Bank's inauguration in 1991, helping to build its image as a thought leader on transition matters.

5. Deciding the Organisational Structure

One of the priorities ahead of the first Post-Signature Conference was the development of an organisational structure for the Bank. Emerging ideas were reflected in a draft paper of 23 June, which described the organisation and its context for members attending the conference. The aim was to decide on a structure that would best support the needs of the Bank's countries of operations and build linkages with investors interested in exploring opportunities in the new markets of the East, while at the same time developing an internal culture focused on transition and sound banking.

The paper noted the organisational implications of the fast-changing and unpredictable region in which the Bank would be operating: "a special character [of the] institution [will be] that [it] will have to adapt permanently to change" in order to "play a leading role in helping to establish the salient features of a market economy as well as changes in attitudes and institution building".

The need for a compact, unbureaucratic and flexible institution was emphasised. To support this, an adequate degree of delegation of authority was recommended, including from the Board.

---

14 'A Study of the Soviet Economy', IMF et al., 1991, p.2.

> Management should have the authority to approve investments and loans up to a certain financial threshold provided that the Board of Directors is informed of all agreements ... in order to ensure flexibility, efficiency and, where necessary, speed in Bank operations.

Emphasis was also laid on the catalytic role that the EBRD was expected to play by focusing on the private sector and putting less emphasis on sovereign-guaranteed lending to the state and other public institutions. This would mean mobilising domestic and foreign capital, as well as supplying management experience to a region that was sorely lacking such skills. The paper's authors also highlighted the need to develop well-functioning capital markets in the Bank's countries of operations and to provide advice on financial restructuring, privatisation, project preparation and policy frameworks affecting the private sector.

Within this context, the EBRD was expected to operate largely on a private-sector basis, supported by high-quality staff drawn from that sector. In order to attract top talent, the Bank introduced incentive systems similar to those used by investment banks and venture capital firms, including bonuses geared towards results. This was an innovative model and one which was more or less unheard of in the public sector at the time.

The suggested organisational structure, as depicted in a draft EBRD organigram, was nonetheless broadly conventional for a regional development bank. The main exception was the proposal for two Vice Presidents in the operational area. The Vice President in charge of Project Lending and Programmes was expected to formulate lending policy, develop country programmes, prepare economic and sector work, and oversee project lending. The Vice President for Corporate Finance, Privatisation and Investments was to be in charge of equity financing (including joint ventures), investments in state-owned companies slated for privatisation, and the provision of advice on financial techniques, especially restructuring and privatisation.

This division of areas of responsibility reflected the dual nature of the EBRD's remit. As well as private-sector investments, the Bank was permitted to make infrastructure and energy sector loans to public entities under the agreed 40:60 public-to-private ratio. As the Soviet Study had indicated, investment in basic infrastructure—including power, transport and telecommunications systems—was urgently needed to support the creation of a functioning private sector in the EBRD's countries of operations.

Such activities would require a high degree of interaction with the authorities on policy and regulatory issues, and would therefore be largely country-led. They would also involve relatively large sums of money and the use of sovereign guarantees where these were justified. Attali wanted a department that dealt with this area to sit alongside an investment banking unit covering the private sector, restructuring and privatisation.

Attali was also keen to separate the lending and equity investment functions of the Bank. He expected finance for public-sector projects to be predominantly sovereign and debt-based, whereas by contrast the private sector would involve equity as well as debt. Equity was also seen as a more complex product requiring specialist commercial expertise, particularly in relation to privatisations, while treating it separately from debt provided room (at least in theory) to avoid potential conflicts of interest.

A key reason for Attali's insistence on two Vice Presidents in Operations was political. During the establishment of the Bank, he had to accept a US citizen as his second-in-command. By creating a second Vice Presidency, and ensuring it was filled by a European, he hoped to limit US influence within the organisation.[15]

A wide range of skills was certainly needed to cover the broad variety of activities the EBRD planned to undertake. Furthermore, with programme lending to governments prohibited by shareholders, the focus was inevitably on bespoke deals in specific sectors, which placed more emphasis on the investment banking side. Sector knowledge was therefore essential.

At the top of this structure sat the Executive Committee, involving all senior management.[16] Its remit was clear: to deal with policy and institutional issues, plans and budgets, as well as be the final arbiter of difficult investment decisions. However, the responsibilities of the two other senior committees that were initially proposed, each chaired by the respective banking Vice President, were less well-defined. An Investment Committee, chaired by the Vice President Corporate Finance, had the task of deciding new investments and policy on equity participations, while a Lending Committee, chaired by the Vice President for Project Lending, was to be the forum for lending policy and operations. The overlap between the

---

15   Attali, *Europe(s)*, p. 86.
16   Attali's control of the organisation was nonetheless maintained effectively through his 'cabinet', especially via Pissaloux. A number of counsellors were also hired to advise the President on political matters and were managed by Jay.

two committees' responsibilities for the operational work of the Bank created confusion.

To add to the confusion, separate working groups were proposed to deal with the preparation of country assistance strategies, which would then be examined by one of the three committees depending on their relevance.

An attempt to marry two radically different cultures—development finance and investment banking—was never going to be straightforward. Many staff had worked at the World Bank, an institution known at the time for its bureaucratic procedures, while others had cut their teeth in deal-driven investment banks.

More positively, having analysed the experience of other development banks (particularly the IFC) and several large corporations, the EBRD's management foresaw clearly from the outset that a local presence would be essential to the success of the Bank. They recommended the establishment of branch offices in order to create efficient and effective ways of identifying investment opportunities and working closely with recipient countries in an advisory capacity.

The early organisational structure of the EBRD also envisaged the creation of a Business Advisory Panel, to be chaired by the President, which was expected to meet three times a year.[17] The aim was to bring together the chief executives of some 15 major industrial and banking firms to help the EBRD develop close relations with western investors interested in the markets opening up in central and eastern Europe. This could help the Bank learn about the pitfalls of investing in the region, as well as provide opportunities for co-investment and other forms of support, such as trade finance.

6. Efforts on High-Level Appointments

In the run-up to the first Post-Signature Conference in July, prospective members were naturally expecting to hear about progress in attracting senior staff. The US administration had proposed Ernie Stern[18], a Senior Vice

---

17 A parallel Economic Advisory Panel was established later. This comprised a number of leading academic economists and aimed to meet twice a year to discuss major topics of interest facing the transition economies. It spawned *Economics of Transition*, an academic journal co-managed by the EBRD's Office of the Chief Economist, but with an independent editorial board.
18 This was first put forward by Bush at a bilateral meeting with Mitterrand in Key Largo on 19 April, 1990. Attali, *Europe(s)*, p. 75.

President at the World Bank, for the number two position, which had been relabelled as the Vice President for Country Programmes and Lending. From July of that year, he began advising the EBRD from Washington DC while still at the World Bank.

As head of operations, Stern had effectively been number two at the World Bank for seven years before moving to the finance division in 1987. He was therefore ideally suited to help prepare operational and budget plans and financial projections for the EBRD, as well as to suggest knowledgeable consultants to do the hard graft. His involvement underlined the EBRD's status as a serious newcomer to the multilateral fold. Attali announced to members at the July Conference that an American would be the first of five Vice Presidents, although his intention to appoint Stern was not mentioned formally until the autumn.

Stern's credentials placed him firmly on the development side of operations. To complete the picture, a senior banker—or, in the City parlance of the time, a merchant banker—was required. Attali wanted a European to fill the role, "an Italian if possible".[19] Giulio Andreotti, the Italian Prime Minister, recommended Giuseppe Garofano. As president of Montedison and managing director of the Italian food and chemicals conglomerate Ferruzzi, Garofano was an industrialist rather than a banker. Nonetheless, Attali was keen to sign him up, impressed by his role in taking control of Enimont, a joint venture between Ferruzzi-Montedison and ENI, the Italian state energy company. Garofano did not take the job, however, and the position remained vacant for another year.[20]

7. The First Post-Signature Conference

Procedural issues were still being discussed as large delegations representing each of the EBRD's 42 prospective shareholders gathered for the Bank's first conference after the signing of the AEB. Many details still had to be thrashed out on diverse topics, ranging from the establishment of branch offices and arrangements for committee meetings to conditions of service for Governors and Directors and senior management. One key outstand-

---

19 Ibid., p. 86.
20 Garofano became embroiled in the 'Mani Puliti' affair.

ing element was the balance of responsibility between management and shareholders, whose interests would be represented by a London-based resident board.

The initial plans drawn up by the transitional team described fairly accurately the broad outlines under which the Bank subsequently operated. At the first Post-Signature Conference, however, concerns arose not only about Attali's style but also more importantly about the balance of power between the Bank's management and the Board of Directors who would represent the shareholders. The plans met with a hostile reception.

Attali turned up an hour late for this first meeting in London, keeping delegates waiting at the Queen Elizabeth II Centre next to Parliament Square. A lengthy speech focusing on how he intended to run the organisation raised the spectre of a presidential administration that would leave little scope for the Board to exert any influence.

A certain unease about how the EBRD was developing was reflected in a number of media reports at the time.

A report in *The Economist* magazine (28 July 1990) said:

> ...it is more than just the Attali style that bothered some of the people at the London meeting. They worry about what they see as his grab for power: too much of it for himself as president, too little for the board of directors. True, the bank's constitution ensures that any loans have to be approved by the board. But within such constraints, say the worriers, Mr Attali seems to want to make the bank as 'presidential' as possible; they see a risk of creating a monster that will be hard to control.

The US delegation was also irked that no precedence seemed to have been accorded to the American second-in-command.

On 30 July, a Reuters report[21] quoted US officials as saying Attali was being urged to revise his proposals to centralise power within the Presidency and set up an extensive branch network. Unless those changes were made, they said the Bush administration could have trouble winning congressional approval for US participation in the US$ 13 billion bank.

There remained discernible differences in expectations over how the Bank should be run. Most members had assumed that the EBRD would follow the

---

21 'U.S. seeks changes in East European Bank', *Reuters News*, 30 July 1990.

standard regional development model. In this set-up, a group of Vice Presidents from a range of (mostly major) countries would effectively run the key parts of the organisation—operations, policies and finance—and would report to the Board of Directors via the President. All policies, projects and major decisions would be discussed and signed off by the Board. When Attali's remarks suggested a different set-up, some shareholders saw in it a rejection of the established approach and a ploy to grab power by centralising control.

Three main areas of contention arose in the ensuing discussions: the use and extent of presidential powers; the proposed creation of resident offices; and the extent to which a resident Board was needed during the first phase and subsequently.

On the first issue, several shareholders felt the draft proposals[22] placed too much power in the hands of the President.[23]

A proposal to open branches of the EBRD in each borrowing country also proved controversial. Some delegates were wary of the potential cost of the initiative, given that seconding headquarters staff typically required generous allowances on top of already high salaries. There were also concerns that local offices would be able to agree financing with less oversight. The critics wanted to see a concrete, costed business plan before agreeing to the proposal.[24]

On the question of the resident board, US officials especially rejected any suggestion that it was not needed or that its creation could be put off for two years until the EBRD was properly up and running.

After turning up late for his own conference, Attali left shortly after the lunch break, a move not necessarily designed to bring the shareholders around to his way of thinking. Many delegates were less than happy. Nonetheless, in his absence during the rest of the meeting some progress was made, helped by effective management by a team led by Anne Le Lorier, the high-ranking official from the French Trésor, which formed the secretariat to the conference. This included a redressing of the balance in favour of the Board Directors.

---

22 In particular, there had been concerns over Section 8(b) of the By-Laws where an early draft had proposed: "The President shall have full authority to take all steps as may in his or her opinion be necessary or expedient for the efficient conduct of the business of the Bank." This subsequently became: "The President shall conduct, under the direction of the Board of Directors, the current business of the Bank. The Board of Directors shall establish conditions ... pursuant to which the President may submit various types of matters to it for consideration under an expedited procedure." By-Laws of the EBRD, Section 8(b).
23 *Institutional Investor*, September 1990.
24 *Financial Times*, 30 July, 1990.

8. Between Conferences: Gearing Up

The summer break allowed time to reassess the situation ahead of the next conference, which had been scheduled for October, and to renew efforts to put in place the building blocks for the EBRD to function effectively. Following a call to the EBRD's members for recommendations on potential recruits, the Bank's staff grew with progress made in the appointment of bankers and experts. Officials from Ireland and the UK provided personnel and administration support, while Guy de Selliers,[25] a Belgian banker from Lehman Brothers with earlier World Bank experience in metals and mining, led the banking side. He was soon joined by Thierry Baudon,[26] an infrastructure specialist from the World Bank, among others. Legal advice was provided by Dick Goodman, a senior counsel at the US Treasury, and externally by Adrian Montague[27] from Linklaters & Paines. The bankers were initially based in Paris while the London staff focused primarily on administrative aspects, including recruitment. They were helped by the accelerating availability of commercial bankers in the City as the UK economy entered recession. In August, the transitional team transferred fully to premises at 6 Broadgate. By the end of October, the team had grown to around 45 from less than 20 in July.

Two more Vice Presidents were lined up. Anders Ljungh, a Swedish banker at Svenska Handelsbanken, was put in charge of Finance. A little later the services of Miklos Nemeth, the former Hungarian prime minister who had played a pivotal role in the previous year's momentous events, were secured. Nemeth took charge of Administration, but the appointment was more significant than the title suggested. Not only did he represent a recipient country, becoming one of the first senior officials from the former Communist Bloc to hold a senior position in an IFI, but he also subsequently played an important role in opening doors for the EBRD in its countries of operations. Bart le Blanc, a Dutch former civil servant who had moved to the private sector as deputy chairman of F. van Lan-

---

25 Guy de Selliers de Moranville became a board member of Robert Fleming & Co, director of Ivanhoe Mines and president of corporate advisory firm HCF International Advisers.
26 Baudon became founder and chairman of Mid Europa, a private equity company specialising in central and eastern Europe.
27 Sir Adrian Montague became chief executive of the PFI Taskforce, chairman of British Energy and chairman of Aviva.

schot Bankiers, also joined. He would later become the Bank's first Secretary General. It was not until December that the Bank's first General Counsel, Andre Newburg, a New York attorney at Cleary, Gottlieb, Steen and Hamilton joined the Bank. Newburg, a German émigré from Berlin who had arrived in the US in 1939, was fluent in Russian, German, Dutch, French and English.

During this period thoughts turned to the image of the EBRD. A competition was launched to design a logo for the new organisation. Designers from the Bank's member states were invited to submit ideas on how best to visually depict the new institution. The judging panel included the Irish President Mary Robinson, CSFR President Havel, and Karl Otto Pöhl, President of the Bundesbank. The competition was won by a New Zealand designer, Bret de Their, whose symbol of two interlocking white flamingo-like shapes[28] against a blue background, one reflected by the other, symbolises the EBRD's role in bringing together West and East.

The search for a permanent headquarters building also got underway, with property consultants Frank Knight and Rutley winning a competitive tender to conduct the process and handle negotiations. The UK authorities wanted the EBRD to locate in Canary Wharf, a rundown former docklands area that had been redeveloped, but which had sunk into the doldrums with the downturn in activity in the financial sector. Attali had very different ideas. His first preference was Grand Buildings in Trafalgar Square, close to Parliament and the West End, but the deal fell through.

A number of other sites, including Billingsgate and the Midland Bank premises in Poultry, were considered before the final choice of One Exchange Square, where the Bank remains today.[29]

With the lease on 6 Broadgate due to run out towards the end of the year, another temporary location was sought. The EBRD moved to 122 Leadenhall Street in February 1991, sharing a building leased from stockbrokers Phillips and Drew (later part of UBS). It was here that the first Board meetings took place.

---

28 In some versions, thin metallic scythe-like shapes would be an alternative description.
29 In May 2019, the EBRD announced plans to relocate to Canary Wharf in 2022.

9. Developing a Business Plan and Operational Policies

As the team settled into the London offices, significant progress was made behind the scenes on more technical matters. In September, however, Attali again ruffled feathers at the IMF/World Bank Annual Meetings in Washington.

There was a long-standing convention that observers other than the European Commission were not admitted to IMF ministerial meetings. However, in what appears to have been a breach of protocol, Attali used his attendance as a member of the French delegation to present the outlines of the EBRD to a broad international audience and to promote the new institution he would ultimately lead. To make things worse he made continual reference to the "Bank of Europe" and "European Bank" rather than the EBRD.[30] This particularly annoyed the Germans, especially Bundesbank President Pöhl, who was concerned it would cause confusion with the soon-to-be-created ECB.

In an article from Washington entitled "Controversy over 'Bank of Europe' name", British newspaper *The Independent* wrote:

> Welcoming Jacques Attali, the new bank's president, to the British Embassy party, the UK Chancellor [of the Exchequer John Major] referred to the institution as "the European Bank". Perhaps he was merely shortening a cumbersome name, but it may be remembered that Theo Waigel, the German finance minister, and Karl Otto Pöhl, the Bundesbank president, were highly critical of Mr Attali's attempt to rename his bank. They fear it would come to be confused with Eurofed—the European central bank—which the Germans want located in Frankfurt. Whatever the Chancellor's motives, Mr Attali won't mind. He has instructed all his staff to answer their phones saying: "Bank of Europe".[31]

Despite these hiccups, the team at the EBRD pressed ahead with decisions on several substantive issues. Stern, as a First Vice President in-waiting, became increasingly engaged in discussions, feeding in ideas from Washington and helping to steer positions on a wide range of operational areas. With his input, papers were drawn up for the October conference covering,

---

30 Internal EBRD document, 'Annual Meeting News', September 1990.
31 *The Independent*, 1 October, 1990.

among other things, a business plan and possible EBRD activities, financial projections, initial policy guidelines for treasury activities and operations, and documents on compensation, benefits and information systems. Work was also undertaken on negotiations for a Headquarters Agreement, covering areas including tax and residency status for Directors and staff.

The proposed business plan[32] was ambitious. It began by noting the EBRD's aim of playing a leading role in the region to establish market-oriented economies and their integration into the international community. This was to be achieved by promoting a competitive private sector, especially through small and medium-sized enterprises (SMEs) and privatisations, as well as by facilitating a sound business climate, strengthened institutions and effective financial regulation.

In order to achieve this, the Bank would use "all the tools of modern finance", including equity and hybrid instruments as well as loans. It would also seek to develop a "unique niche" in its products and approach, and avoid duplication of efforts with other market players. Above all, an acknowledged need to be responsive to changes in the marketplace fitted well with the hope for the EBRD to become "a small, flexible, agile institution".

The business plan noted the challenges ahead, particularly the severe contraction likely to arise in former communist countries from stabilisation efforts and the closure of inefficient enterprises, the limited absorption capacity of corporates in the face of weak legal and accounting systems and inadequate financial intermediaries, the dearth of equity finance, non-existent capital markets and heavy external indebtedness. The tiny size of the private sector in central and eastern Europe—it was estimated that only 5 per cent of industrial value added in Poland was produced in the private sector, accounting for 2.5 per cent of the workforce—also drew attention to the time it would take to build up Bank business, especially given the requirement that at least 60 per cent of activity should be in the private sector. The paper's authors warned: "Progress is likely to be slow and jerky."

On the other hand, they noted the Bank's "comparative advantage relative to other multilateral institutions [and] private sector lenders and investors". It could respond quickly to market demand with tailored financial instruments to support growth. There were technical skills and entrepre-

---

32 Progress Report on Developing the Business Plan, staff paper for the Second Post-Signature Conference, 3 September 1990.

neurial potential in the region to draw on and, in the right environment, plenty of investment opportunities. Unlike the World Bank or IFC, the EBRD was well-positioned to act as both adviser and investor. It possessed sector expertise and would soon have strong and reliable country knowledge. As compared with private-sector investors, the Bank could take a longer-term perspective and, with its strong capital base and backing from the most advanced economies in the world, it could take on greater risk. Its preferred-creditor status and close links to relevant authorities were expected to increase investors' confidence in working alongside the Bank.[33]

The economic soundness of investments, and profit in the corporate sector in particular, was cited as a primary criterion for operations. The principle of sound banking, voiced for the first time here in the operational context, has remained one of the three key principles of the EBRD to this day. In terms of activities that the Bank was expected to undertake, infrastructure development, environmental rehabilitation, joint ventures, privatisation, venture capital and capital markets development were highlighted. Separately from investing in equity on its own account, the EBRD could also play a role as an advisor to private investors during privatisations of state-owned enterprises.

The institutional culture was regarded as an important factor in setting the tone for the EBRD. Management wanted the Bank not only to be sensitive to the broader, political nature of its mission but also to adopt a client-driven, flexible and responsive approach. A leading idea was to help bring foreign capital and expertise into the region by leveraging the Bank's unique characteristics and to combine this with a strong local presence based in regional offices. To do this effectively, the EBRD would be required to speak the same "banking language" as its partners, placing an emphasis on sector knowledge and expertise in the use of financial instruments and financial engineering.

Although a formal risk department had not yet been suggested, the high risks associated with the region were clear, necessitating close risk assessment of proposed investments. The legacy of state-run systems meant that most enterprises in central and eastern Europe were in poor financial

---

33 Preferred-creditor status means that the Bank is excluded from sovereign debt reschedulings where the borrower's inability to service their debt is due to a general foreign exchange shortage in their country. These legal privileges are also extended to other banks participating in EBRD loans, incentivising local investors to co-finance projects.

shape and needed substantial reorganisation before they could become viable banking propositions. Legal systems underpinning private-sector activity were also weak and capital markets rudimentary or non-existent.

The value of working with financial intermediaries, particularly to reach a wide range of smaller businesses quickly, was noted but there were some concerns. While acknowledging the efficiency of channelling funds through domestic financial intermediaries, significant dangers could be associated with lending to weak institutions in a distorted financial system.

As well as seeking investment opportunities and working with countries to establish a suitable policy framework to foster the growth of the private sector, the priorities identified included developing a well-functioning financial infrastructure, integrating central and eastern Europe and the Soviet Union into the world economy, supporting interregional initiatives related to transportation, telecommunications and environmental clean-up projects, and transferring resources from the military to civilian sector. An important emphasis was placed especially on urban renewal and improving the level of services in order to have an immediate impact on people's lives.

It was acknowledged that, in the first phase, reliance on co-financing opportunities with the World Bank and IFC would likely be necessary while an independent project pipeline was being built up, and that this might put pressure on meeting the private-public sector ratio within the required timeframe.

Overall, the Bank foresaw business volume of ECU 1½ –2¼ billion in its first two years of operations. Noting that this looked modest, especially in relation to the enormous needs of the region, the authors cited multiplier effects from co-financing and stimulatory impacts on local economies and supply chains. Using a multiplier of six, an estimated project value of ECU 9–14 billion was obtained.

A further paper for the October conference set out the operational challenges and priorities in more detail. This depicted the practical realities facing the Bank in starting up operations and made clear to delegates the magnitude of the tasks ahead. Meanwhile, a paper on operational policies[34] elaborated the criteria for Bank financing. Within an overall framework of country strategies and prudent risk management, all types of projects were

---

34 A more complete version of the Bank's Operations Policies, based on discussions with members, was circulated on 15 March, 1991 ahead of the first shadow Board meeting.

contemplated and in any sector. However, financing was not to be provided where participation would crowd out other investors or lenders willing to provide financing on suitable terms and conditions and at the same standards of quality. This was the additionality principle, the second key tenet of EBRD operations. The third tenet, "transition impact", was not adopted until much later.

Local costs of projects were assumed to be met by clients and profit potential was expected to be commensurate with the inherent risk. It was made clear that the EBRD would carry out a full economic and financial analysis of projects (including alternative designs and management or organisational needs), as well as assessments of their environmental impact. Procurement of goods and services financed by the Bank were to be on an arm's-length basis and subject (in general) to competitive bidding, open to both members and non-members of the Bank so as to achieve efficiency and value for money. The importance of monitoring projects was noted, as was their later evaluation, and loan agreements were expected to stipulate that borrowers should prepare an evaluation within a reasonable period. Projects designed to optimise balance sheets, support management reorganisations and seek board representation in equity cases were considered positively, as were recycling of equity funds and selling participations in loans.

Encouragement was given to co-financing as a means of providing additional sources of finance for clients as well as reducing the EBRD's exposure to obligors. Mobilisation of finance through the use of guarantees was also envisaged. In short, the paper provided prospective members with a comprehensive look at how the Bank intended to execute its operational activities once given the green light to do so.

In their preparations, the transitional team had drawn on long-established arrangements in other international financial institutions, especially the World Bank, ADB and IFC. There had been good collaboration with other international institutions, especially the EIB, Commission and the Nordic Investment Bank (NIB). The more novel aspects in the EBRD's version of activities concerned the private-sector focus[35] and the desire to operate as a fast and responsive client-oriented institution.

---

35   In this respect the EBRD was most like the IFC, something a number of shareholders had been keen to emulate when discussing the origin of the Bank. The EBRD, however, had a regional focus rather than a global reach and a very specific mandate.

10. The Second Post-Signature Conference

The second Post-Signature Conference took place in late October 1990 at Lancaster House, an impressive venue close to St James's Palace. The UK overseas development minister, Lynda Chalker, opened the proceedings.

The main thrust of the EBRD's approach papers, along with the texts of the four draft regulations—the By-Laws, rules of procedure for the Board of Governors and Board of Directors, and the staff regulations—were broadly agreed by members. Some tension remained over the business plan. The USA was adamant that negotiations on potential projects should not take place until the Board had endorsed the operational approach. Many other members focused on the terms and conditions of service of Directors, their alternates and staff.

Attali announced to the conference that he had offered Stern the position of First Vice President in charge of Country Programmes. However, by the end of the year, Stern had turned the offer down. According to the *Financial Times*: "No reasons were given for his decision not to accept Mr Attali's job offer."[36]

No replacement had been found for Garofano, so the decision by Stern to turn down the other Vice President position meant the search for operational leadership became an urgent issue. Fortunately Mario Sarcinelli, the head of the Italian Tesoro, who had been involved in the original conference meetings, was willing to take on a vice presidency role. Sarcinelli's background as a finance ministry official was best suited to the development side, so he was appointed Vice President of Country Programmes. This meant Attali would have to find an American to head Merchant Banking to meet the requirements for a US "number two".

The leadership gap in Merchant Banking continued to be filled by de Selliers, who was making good progress in recruiting bankers to build up that department. Despite the involvement of executive search firms, the role of First Vice President was not filled until the appointment of Ron Freeman from Salomon Brothers in the summer of 1991.

---

36 'World Bank executive turns down EBRD', *Financial Times*, 6 December, 1990.

11. Tying Things Up: The Final Post-Signature Conference and Shadow Board Meetings

By the turn of the year the EBRD's inauguration, now set for April, was looming and concluding the ratification process became a matter of urgency. Barely one-quarter of prospective members had completed the formalities by the time of the final Post-Signature Conference held at Lancaster House between 28 and 30 January 1991, where a further call for action was made. Delegates considered the substantive agenda for the first Board of Directors meeting, to be held after the inaugural ceremony, which would cover the action programme, technical assistance, operational and financial policies, the Bank's policies on human rights and the environment, its organisation, the Headquarters Agreement, and personnel issues such as housing allowances.

At this conference, members ruled that the Board would decide the EBRD's borrowing transactions in the start-up phase and emphasised the importance of evaluation, suggesting the establishment of an independent in-house capability to serve this function. Remaining details were concluded without much difficulty, although there was general pressure to hold back on negotiations with potential borrowers until the various policies, including individual country strategies, had been approved. The principal concern was over possible duplication of efforts with the World Bank—although this mainly related to policy advice rather than project operations—and private investors. There was a residual desire on the part of members to ensure a strong role for the Board of Directors and cost-efficiency in the establishment of field offices. Here management had provided a more detailed explanation of what was intended and offered reassurance that each case would be presented to the Board on its merits.

A report by McKinsey on the organisational structure, commissioned by the EBRD following the previous conference, was also presented. This simplified and clarified the earlier structure, particularly with regard to the two operational vice presidencies. The renamed Merchant Banking Vice Presidency was geared towards dealing with the bulk of operations, while the focus of the Country Programmes—now called Development Banking—Vice Presidency was to be country strategies, reform and the enhancement of public infrastructure and operations support, including the administration of technical assistance.

The number of internal committees was reduced to two: the Executive Committee, comprising the heads of departments, which would manage the EBRD as a whole; and an Operations Committee (OpsCom) responsible for country strategy execution and project management.

A shadow Board of Directors meeting was held on 25–26 March 1991 to sign off on the 14 Resolutions to be put to Governors at the Inaugural Meeting, as well as on the final drafts of the rules of procedure of the Board of Directors and staff regulations. The group was informed that more than two-thirds of members would have ratified the Agreement by the end of March. In addition, three members—the Republic of Korea, Malta and Romania—wanted to increase their shares, and Brazil, India and Venezuela had applied to become members of the Bank. (India in fact only joined the EBRD as a non-recipient member many years later—in 2018. Brazil and Venezuela never joined the Bank.)

Albania also expressed interest in membership and its representatives were invited to attend the Inaugural Meeting as guests of the Bank. Finally, it was announced that External Affairs would no longer be a separate vice presidency, but Evaluation would become a vice presidency.[37]

12. The Bank's Inauguration

The EBRD's inauguration was set for 15 April 1991, marking the successful launch of this brand new institution after months of sometimes painstaking preparation and the challenge of forging a common goal for more than 40 shareholders with sometimes very diverse views.

Crucially, it had brought the countries of eastern Europe into the international community, not only by reaching out to them with financial support but also by making them shareholders in the Bank that had been created to serve their interests.

It was all the more important now that the EBRD was moving towards its operational phase. West and East Germany had reunited, but the Soviet Union was on the brink of disintegration. An institution designed to bring former communist countries and western democracies together was

---

37 Dr Manfred Abelein, the chosen candidate for External Affairs, became Vice President in charge of Evaluation while External Affairs was effectively absorbed into the President's Office.

urgently needed. Finance and expertise was required to help drive through the economic reforms in eastern European countries that would underpin their path towards democracy.

The political and international importance of the endeavour was reflected in the high-level turnout for the 15 April inauguration. At the opening ceremony at the International Maritime Organisation (IMO),[38] UK Prime Minister John Major stood on the podium alongside Mitterrand and Attali, in front of more than two dozen heads of state and finance ministers. Also present were a large number of City grandees, international financiers including Salomon Brothers chief executive John Gutfreund, industrialists such as Gianni Agnelli of Fiat, several heads of IFIs—in particular the IMF's managing director Michel Camdessus—and top economists, including Phelps, Arrow and Janos Kornai. The ceremony concluded with a recital by Russian cellist Mstislav Rostropovich.

Major, opening the meeting, described the EBRD as "a unique institution ... special because it symbolises a new beginning for the countries of Eastern Europe". In his inaugural address, Mitterrand hailed it as "the first institution of the new Europe, the first concrete proof ... of the solidarity that unites us".[39]

In keynote speeches over the next two days, Governors reiterated their belief in the values and purpose of the EBRD: to support a well-functioning private sector, promote enterprise and innovation, and encourage democratic institutions in recipient countries. Wim Kok, deputy prime minister of the Netherlands and Chair of the Board of Governors, said: "The EBRD is distinctive in its private-sector focus, its commitment to environmental protection and its political orientation ... and ... eminently suited for its task" given that the "political transformation to achieve political and democratic institutions ... and the economic conversion towards a market-oriented system ... are closely linked ... and will have to take place simultaneously."

Among prominent statements by other Governors, Nicholas Brady, the US Treasury Secretary, emphasised the role of the private sector. "We believe strongly that the EBRD focus should be private sector development

---

38 This venue was chosen as it was the only UN-connected presence in London.
39 Governors speeches quoted here were published in Summary Proceedings of the Inaugural Meeting of the Board of Governors, EBRD, 1991.

and financing of infrastructure which directly supports private sector activity."[40]

His German and Italian counterparts, while agreeing with the importance of the private sector, also pointed to the political dimension of the new bank. "Not only must funds be raised ... but conditions must be created [for] the productive forces in the recipient countries themselves [to] develop. This is not a technocratic but a deeply political task," said Waigel. Guido Carli observed: "The Bank certainly has an important political role as a forum for East-West cooperation."

Havel summarised views from recipient countries: "We are glad to see that [the advanced countries of the world] understand how important it is for the political stability of the whole European continent to help our countries in their reforms in every possible way. The founding of the EBRD is proof of that understanding."

The following day, Attali was formally elected as first President of the EBRD, along with the Board of Directors. The Bank was now authorised and ready to begin operations.

The newly-elected Board of 23 Directors and 18 Alternates—who are empowered to act on a Director's behalf in their absence—began their tasks promptly on 18 April, starting with the appointment of Vice Presidents and the ratification of various administrative rules and procedures that had been discussed over the previous months. As well as an initial discussion of operational challenges, priorities and guidelines, the meeting set a budget for the Bank for the rest of the year of ECU 56.7 million and approved a paper on its financial policies. There was a general consensus that the operational papers were working documents to be improved as the EBRD's understanding of its countries of operations developed. It was also agreed to submit the relevant papers to rating agencies, since a triple-A rating would be essential to any future borrowing programme; and, in the case of the operational challenges and priorities paper, for it to be sent to the Economic Advisory Council.

One other significant move at the first Board meeting was the approval of a paper describing the EBRD's policy on environmental management.

---

40 Brady also made clear his view of the role of the Board: "The Directors, as personal representatives of the Governors must play a key role ... [in] guiding policy and approving operations. ... We do not view the activity of the Board as an advisory one, but instead a critical element of the Bank's operations."

This confirmed the Bank's intention to adopt sound environmental practices in all its activities. Its prominence reflected growing international concerns over environmental issues, and in particular the amendment to Article 130 of the Treaty of Rome under the Single European Act of 1987, which added a section on the environment.

Conclusion

In just under 18 months, the EBRD had gone from an idea tentatively put forward by Mitterrand to its first resident Board of Directors meeting. For a multilateral investment bank serving the interests of shareholders from 39 countries[41] and two European institutions this was unprecedented.

Also ground-breaking was the inclusion of the countries of central and eastern Europe and the Soviet Union in an IFI as equal members, in terms of voice and debate (and in certain votes). More generally, the Bank's prospective shareholders provided a robust check on the proposals of management, as well as on budget and financial projections. The official community helped to improve policy ideas and the drafting of relevant legal texts.

Given the differences between the public and private sector-oriented approaches, what is notable is that an accommodation of different interests was reached by all parties by the time of the inauguration and that the resulting structure has broadly held for nearly 30 years. Achieving this was at times a difficult, even painful, process. But because the different parties had to find a way to realise a goal that all agreed was significant and appropriate within a tight timeframe—where, as each day passed, the consequences of failure to find ways to support central and eastern European countries in the face of their collapsing systems became clearer—a compromise was reached.

Now operational with a full Board of resident Directors in situ and a growing staff, the EBRD was ready to find companies to support, make investments in central and eastern Europe and deliver on its mandate.

---

41 The number of shareholding countries was reduced by one after the Bank's inauguration with the dissolution of the GDR following the reunification of Germany on 3 October 1990. For more details on the evolution of EBRD's shareholding membership, from 1991 to the present day, see the Appendix.

Chapter 3
Difficult Early Years

Introduction

When the EBRD began operations in April 1991, it had 41 shareholders, seven countries of operations and the capacity to lend up to ECU 7 billion annually. At the same time, it had very few staff to do the lending and its region of operations was in a downward spiral of economic crisis. Three decades later, the number of shareholders has increased to more than 70 and the Bank operates in 38 markets. It has a portfolio of €44 billion, has supported hundreds of thousands of businesses and hundreds of municipalities, brought in foreign direct investment (FDI) from all corners of the world and invested more than €145 billion into the economies of its regions. Today, as a result of capital increases and reserve accumulation, the Bank's capacity to lend is up to €12 billion a year.

Turning a good idea into a thriving business takes time, a strong team, continuous support from sponsors, and a good dose of luck. In its challenging first few years of operations, the EBRD needed all of the above. Indeed, without strong shareholder commitment, a significant internal reorganisation and a fortuitous recovery in investment conditions, the EBRD could have withered before it had really got going. This chapter looks at the challenges, both internal and external, that the Bank had to overcome to find its feet.

The EBRD quickly established itself as an institution capable of developing robust policies and handling rapid change. Most policy questions concerning operations and financial requirements were resolved within six to nine months from the inception of the Bank, although these would be refined over time in the light of experience. Following the dissolution of the

Soviet Union at the end of 1991, the number of countries of operations expanded from seven to 22 within the space of a year.

By the end of 1993, this number had risen to 25, as parts of the former Yugoslavia came on board and Czechoslovakia split into the Czech and Slovak Republics. By then there were 12 EBRD regional offices, while staff numbers had increased to close to 700. Membership of the Bank had also increased from 40 to 59 countries (along with the two European institutions).[1]

The EBRD had also established itself at the forefront of intellectual debate on the transition from planned to market-based economies. It had done valuable work on complex issues such as trade, payments systems and currency convertibility, and had taken the lead in helping countries of operations improve their legal systems through a model law on secured transactions and advice on bankruptcy.[2] The Bank also promoted strongly the cause of environmental improvements and better management of energy and other natural resources, and had secured a prominent role in the field of nuclear safety.

In terms of business volume and profitability, the first years were challenging. By the end of 1992, 36 projects had been signed amounting to just under ECU 1 billion, although only ECU 0.1 billion had actually been disbursed. The EBRD made a small net loss in both its first two years. For a start-up operation working in a new and unpredictable environment this was not altogether surprising. While this was accepted by those who understood the situation, it gave ammunition to critics of the Bank's internal expenditure, particularly in relation to the fitting-out of its new headquarters.

Although relatively small, the EBRD had serious potential as a new IFI. It had a clear mandate: to help central and eastern Europe integrate with the western world and transition towards market-based economies. Its target countries were keenly looking for advice and financial help, its statutes were robust, it was located in a major financial centre, and its membership constituted a large part of the world economy.

There were nonetheless three major challenges. Successful business development needs skilled personnel, a predictable environment and conducive economic conditions. None of these was yet present. The EBRD had few

---

[1] As stated at the end of Chapter 2, membership numbered 40 countries when the AEB was signed in 1991, and then became 39 once the reunification of Germany had taken place. Membership then expanded towards the end of 1991 and early 1992 with the inclusion of Albania and the three Baltic states. For more detail on the evolution of EBRD's membership from 1991 to the present day, see Appendix.

[2] A dedicated legal transition team was created to extend this type of work in 1995.

staff and all were based in London. There were many uncertainties about the economic, political and institutional functioning of the countries the Bank was charged with operating in and even greater unknowns about the companies it was expected to invest in and support. Finally, the macroeconomic situation in emerging Europe was deteriorating rapidly.

At the start of operations, the EBRD had around 55 professional staff. Just over 20 were bankers, with the vast majority in the Development Banking department.[3] Total staff numbers were projected to more than treble by the end of the year and more than double again in the following year, with the sharpest acceleration expected on the Merchant Banking side. Managing such rapid growth, while at the same time developing a cohesive approach to the new business, was never going to be easy.

1. The Business Challenges of Central and Eastern Europe

At the start of business, the EBRD had seven countries of operations, reduced from the original eight following the reunification of East and West Germany in 1990.[4] These were Bulgaria, Czechoslovakia, Hungary, Poland, Romania, the Soviet Union and the Socialist Federal Republic of Yugoslavia.

Central and eastern European countries were emerging from a long period of state control. The absence of a market history and patterns of market pricing meant commercial and other project risks could not be easily assessed. A constantly changing and often opaque political scene added to the challenges. Lawyers regarded the legal basis for any transaction in the East as insecure. The EBRD's economists were also all too aware of the potential impact of macroeconomic risks on any transaction, which were especially large in relation to currency convertibility and trade arrangements.

The setting for the EBRD's activities was discussed at the first meeting of the Board. Those present saw four broad challenges to the Bank's business development: the "formidable array of complex problems in Central and Eastern European countries which need urgently to be tackled but which

---

3   De Selliers and a couple of other merchant bankers comprised the Merchant Banking department in April 1991.
4   The GDR was united with the Federal Republic on 3 October, 1990. Agreement was reached to transfer the GDR's shares to unallocated shares and that the EBRD would not invest in former East Germany (leaving this primarily to Germany itself and the EIB).

will take many years to overcome fully"; the immense scale of the problems facing enterprises; significant difficulties arising from poor infrastructure; and a legacy of environmental degradation and misuse of energy.

The EBRD's 1991 *Annual Report* described the year as "one of economic disappointment, or at least of hopes deferred". This was perhaps something of an understatement, given that GDP in central and eastern European countries (including the Baltic states) fell in 1991 by an average of 10.7 per cent.[5]

Exports to the West had exceeded expectations (although not universally). However, the timetables for new legislative programmes had slipped, and problems of property restitution were a particular challenge, with important implications for the timing of planned privatisations. Even when laws had been passed, for example on bankruptcy, this had not always led to implementation, partly reflecting understandable reluctance due to the potential for serious social implications.

Some progress had been made with smaller privatisations. The larger sales had been delayed because fewer businesses than expected were in fact profitable. Economic output and demand across the region had been affected by the introduction of stabilisation programmes. Output had fallen between 10 and 20 per cent from its previous peaks, and in most cases further falls of 25 per cent were expected before there was any recovery. Unemployment had started to rise towards levels typical of western Europe and showed no sign of stopping. An important factor contributing to the fall in output throughout the region in 1991 was the collapse in trade between the former Soviet Union and its erstwhile eastern European (Comecon) trading partners.

Management defined the challenge as: "… [creating] a new economic framework, whilst also changing the political system, behaviour, and even the attitudes of the people involved, without creating intolerable social conditions which would completely destroy their societies and endanger those nearby. There is no historical precedent for such restructuring."[6]

At the social and political level, there was a need for fundamental constitutional changes to prepare for a democratic future, including the recognition and exercise of basic civil and political rights and the protection of private property. At the economic level, the requirements included: price

---

[5] EBRD. *Transition Report* 1999.
[6] "Operational Challenges and Priorities"; the Initial Action Programme, April 1991.

liberalisation to clear the way for the elimination of shortages; currency convertibility and liberalisation of trade and payments regimes to reallocate resources and raise productivity and growth; stabilisation measures, notably tax reforms and the introduction of social safety nets, and steps to absorb excess liquidity and other measures to contain inflationary pressures; and a well-functioning banking and payments system which could mobilise savings and allocate investment funds efficiently. (In most of central and eastern Europe the financial sector lacked diversity and depth, notwithstanding the large number of banks in some countries, because under communism banks were mainly concerned with implementing and tabulating centralised decision-making rather than operating as genuine commercially oriented financial intermediaries.)

On the business side, privatisation and restructuring were at the core of enterprise reform. Privatisation would mean direct accountability, forcing companies to tackle deep-rooted problems and look to the longer-term. Restructuring was often expected to be a precursor to privatisation, not least since investors would be wary of getting involved until enterprises were on a sounder financial footing.

The magnitude of the problem at the enterprise level was huge. Estimates indicated there were 8,700 large state enterprises in Poland, 2,500 in the CSFR and 2,000 in Hungary. As in the West, the politics of privatisation was complicated. There was pressure to move quickly but also to avoid accusations of selling assets too cheaply, doing so without sufficient transparency, or concentrating their allocation in a few or foreign hands. Handling transactions was likely to be all the more difficult given the absence of the relevant skills and expertise to manage the process, as well as the poor management and financial skills of those running the enterprises.

These entities were in urgent need of modernisation and productivity improvements, implying a loss of jobs (and the associated political risks) in the short term. Many had accumulated significant debts, while workers' councils with ownership-like rights often complicated the picture, as did restitution issues. The absence of proper accounts made valuation of assets difficult and comparisons with competitors were equally problematic. With input and output prices changing rapidly, forecasting future revenues and making projections for business plans was similarly a "shot in the dark". A lack of underwriting capacity, a shortage of domestic institutional investors and poor liquidity undermined the ability of capital markets to operate effectively.

Restructuring allowed more time to deal with underlying problems but was no less daunting. Abolition of central planning meant management had to decentralise operational controls, organise debt and equity financing, understand effective balance-sheet management, and develop the notion of a cost of capital, in order to be able to judge the viability of investments. Other elements to grapple with included dealing with overcapacity in several sectors, making redundancies and incentivising remaining staff. At the government level, the removal of subsidies and the introduction of hard budget constraints, social safety nets and tax changes were needed to promote investment.

SMEs lacked associations of private entrepreneurs to lobby on their behalf and local banks were incapable of dealing with their needs. Entrepreneurship was not lacking, but few business owners had relevant expertise in areas such as finance, marketing or planning.

Two further limitations on operations in central and eastern Europe were the lack of modern communications and the need for more energy-efficient and environmentally sustainable economies. As the paper on challenges and priorities put it: "Roads, trains or air services; telephone or television services; the distribution of goods and services and the modern means of circulating money through bank transfers, credit cards or even cheques are either gravely insufficient or completely lacking … Yet despite this, the region uses a comparatively large amount of energy … in a way that is neither efficient or environmentally sound."[7]

Central and eastern Europe needed considerable capital to rehabilitate, modernise and expand its infrastructure. Traditional approaches would be hampered, however, by "several countries of operations suffering from limited sovereign borrowing capacity and severe budgetary restraints". This implied the need for "a massive input of technical assistance and advisory services [to help with] institutional strengthening, policy reforms and managerial support … in addition to direct financing … [and] innovative approaches to foster public/private partnerships in infrastructure financing and management". This would bring in "capital and managerial expertise from private operators on a long-term basis".[8]

On the environment side, the degradation of natural resources in the region was of such alarming proportions that access to uncontaminated water,

---

7   Ibid.
8   Ibid.

land and air could not be taken for granted. Pollution-related diseases, especially respiratory problems, and heavy-metal poisoning from food grown in contaminated areas impacted labour supply and economic growth. The EBRD's position was clear: "Major environmental policy improvements and direct restorative investments are prerequisites for the successful transition to a market-oriented economy. The Bank will therefore place environmental issues at the forefront of its efforts to promote sustainable economic growth in the region."

At the time, however, economic growth seemed a distant prospect. The countries of central and eastern Europe were seeing some of the worst economic indicators since just after the Second World War. Output had fallen sharply, while unemployment and inflation had risen. Bulgaria and the Soviet Union had introduced rationing in response to severe shortages of food and essential goods. Rising international interest rates and oil price increases put pressure on the already considerable costs of external debt service, while hard currency current account deficits increased in a number of countries. And in much of the region the situation was about to deteriorate still further.

Table 3.1 GDP Growth (% pa) in Central and Eastern Europe, 1989-1992

GDP growth	CEB	CIS	of which Russia
1989	0.1	0.6	0.0
1990	- 6.6	- 3.7	- 4.0
1991	- 10.7	- 6.0	- 5.0
1992	- 3.2	- 14.1	- 14.5

SOURCE: *Transition Report* 2000, p. 65.
CEB: Central Europe and the Baltics. CIS: Commonwealth of Independent States.

2. The Banking Teams' Early Responses

The operational issues discussed with the Board were supplemented by a set of guidelines covering issues such as the types of eligible projects, the uses of Bank financing, criteria for lending and the project cycle, as well as procedures for the evaluation of projects and co-financing. In due course, the banking and legal departments refined the guidelines to produce an Operations Manual which became an indispensable resource for the OpsCom secretariat.

The EBRD's remit permitted participation in more or less any sector that was of importance to a country's economic development. Even projects that involved the conversion of military complexes to industrial uses were not ruled out.

However, certain investments were prohibited, including defence-related activities, the tobacco industry, standalone gambling facilities, and selected alcoholic products (beer and wine were not included in the taboo list and support for Turkish breweries as they expanded especially into Central Asia was an early feature of the Bank's work). The EBRD would also not invest in products banned either by individual countries or by international convention, for example asbestos and other harmful substances.

It was clear that account needed to be taken of the activities of other organisations helping central and eastern Europe, most obviously in major infrastructure developments where the bulk of public funding was focused, and to avoid crowding out private finance. Given the scale of the needs in the region and the limited appetite of private investors, there was little risk that EBRD projects would deter or crowd out others. Co-financing with other entities was an option, for example with the World Bank or the ADB for infrastructure, or with foreign investors setting up new plants in the region (for example, in the automotive or agribusiness industries).

An initial emphasis was put on activities that would support the infrastructure necessary for private-sector development (notably energy, telecommunications and transport), as well as privatisation, the restructuring of industrial enterprises and banks, the development of SMEs, the creation of new financial institutions, the promotion of FDI and environmental rehabilitation. Municipal services were also identified as an area where the EBRD might take an active role since it attracted less support from other multilateral organisations and bilateral funding. Within this, urban development was seen a priority.

Teams were formed within the two banking departments to cover the ground and the number of employees to support operations expanded quickly. The pipeline began to grow more slowly. This reflected the newness of the organisation and the poor economic conditions in its countries of operations.

Bankers, particularly those from the private sector used to a performance-driven reward culture, were eager to make their mark by clinching deals. However, many were shocked at the situation they found when travelling to the region—not just the lack of viable enterprises but the difficulties in getting around to see prospective clients beyond capital cities, the inadequate telecommunications systems and the rudimentary state of hotels. Health and safety arrangements on visits to companies in the region were also very limited, particularly outside the main cities.

The EBRD teams also quickly discovered that the absence of a functioning private sector meant first and foremost dealing with the authorities. However, they were not the only parties making such visits. A number of western investors were familiar with the more advanced countries in the region and many of the most promising opportunities had already been targeted by others.

In addition, having a development banking department and a parallel merchant banking one pursuing similar goals did not make for internal cohesion and presented a difficult management challenge, as well as confusion on the ground.

What marked the EBRD out at that time though was the entrepreneurial spirit that ran through the whole organisation and was part of its attraction. At this stage almost any project was in some way novel, so closing a deal was particularly satisfying, especially if it had a demonstration effect on the sector as many early transactions did.

The crop of bankers who arrived on the EBRD's doorstep at the beginning was also strongly motivated by a desire to help the former communist countries in their struggle for freedom and a better way of life. One senior banker remembers: "We worked from eight in the morning until 10 or 11 at night to get things moving." Many at the EBRD at the time recall the sense of being part of history in the making.

Baudon was one of the first members of a working group established when ideas about the creation of a financial institution to support the systemic transition in central and eastern Europe were first floated. Joining the EBRD after its creation, he brought years of experience at the World Bank to address a very specific challenge. "Our objective was to apply the skillset of a development institution to foster the growth and strengthening of the private sector." It was a task that he and his colleagues took on with relish: "It was the only time in my professional life that I had a bed in my office."[9]

---

9   Axel Reiserer, '1989 and the aftermath: the role of the EBRD'. EBRD Press Release, 8 November 2019. https://www.ebrd.com/news/2019/1989-and-the-aftermath-the-role-of-the-ebrd.html

3. The Bank's First Operations in Central Europe and the Soviet Union

The first project to reach the Board for approval arrived on 25 June, less than two months after the EBRD's inauguration. This was a public-sector operation in Poland involving a US $50 million loan to Bank of Poznań (WBK), guaranteed by the Polish state, for a heat-supply restructuring and conservation project. The EBRD funds were to be used by WBK for on-lending to several heating enterprises and other enterprises with privatisation potential involved in the production and sale of heat and steam.

Although there was as yet no country strategy for Poland, which was seen as a prerequisite for framing the EBRD's activities in a country, the Board was prepared to make an exception given the early stage of operations.

This project aimed to support a comprehensive restructuring of the district-heating sector, extending the life of existing assets and encouraging energy conservation and reduced pollution. The credit line was to be co-financed by the World Bank, which was expected to implement five separate loans amounting to US$ 165 million to district-heating enterprises (DHEs) in major Polish cities, along with a US$ 75 million fast-disbursing balance-of-payments loan to cover increased energy costs.

The environmental benefits were clear but private-sector involvement in this sector was largely missing at the time, and the Board questioned the Bank's additionality. No doubt anticipating such criticism, the team proposed an innovative route for private investment by making room in the financing for an investment in a waste-to-energy incinerator in Gdynia and by suggesting a build-operate-transfer (BOT) model.

The credit line was slow to disburse mainly because the enterprises concerned were in very poor financial condition and undergoing restructuring and ownership changes which prevented them from borrowing. Conditions imposed on sub-project selection, such as the development of masterplans, cost-benefit analyses, procurement requirements, also proved onerous, given the clients' lack of experience in dealing with rigorous project appraisals. The legal system also gave insufficient security for lenders. As a result of the slow utilisation of the funds most of the line was cancelled in 1996.

Nevertheless, in its implementation report, the World Bank noted: "WBK indicated that their association with the EBRD and IBRD under this project provided their staff with an understanding of the modus operandi of the two institutions …WBK trained a team in project appraisal and evaluation, and actively marketed the line of credit to DHEs. Project proposals were received from about twelve DHEs and about US $19 million of the EBRD funds were committed ... This training was later utilised in implementing projects in association with EBRD including, inter alia, the privatisation of their own bank, financing small and medium enterprises, and financing of the dairy industry."[10]

While the EBRD component of the project had not developed as well as had been hoped, working alongside the World Bank offered important insights on the policy dimensions of engaging with the municipal sector and instilled a better understanding of lending to the sub-sovereign sector.

The loan would mark the start of a relationship between WBK and the EBRD that lasts to this day, and included the merger with Bank Zachodni and then the integration of the bank into Banco Santander. Under the name Santander Bank Polska, it is the second-largest bank in Poland.[11]

Paweł Kołodziński, one-time Head of EBRD's Corporate Development, remembers: "The 1990s were the breakthrough period for the Polish financial sector. At that time, the development of modern and mass banking was getting into full swing. It was 25 years ago that we issued our first payment card. The 1990s were times of great opportunities and great challenges. After the years of shortages inherited from the communist era, the demand on the Polish market was immense, and so was the potential for the development of new services and products."

The EBRD had relied heavily on the World Bank for its first operation but its second project involved private-sector players. A loan of DM 10 million to Petőfi Nyomda Rt., a recently privatised Hungarian packaging company, was proposed to the Board at the end of September. A Hungarian holding company majority-owned by Italy's De Benedetti Group owned 50 per cent of the firm, with 36 per cent held by three private Hungarian funds. The finance was part of an investment programme to improve quality and expand capacity in its fast-growing and competitive business. The company had made good progress post-privatisation (for example, by bringing in western-educated management) in a declining domestic market and was ready to build links to new western European clients by improving its product range and quality and exploiting lower labour costs relative to its western competi-

---

10 World Bank, 'WBK Implementation Report', 2000, pp. 6–7, 18
11 As of March 2020.

tors. With western multinationals increasing their investments in Hungary, the company was well-placed to capitalise on their packaging needs.

The two further investments approved at the Board in September also involved the private sector. One was a US$ 10 million equity investment in the Czechoslovakia Investment Corporation (CIC), a closed-end offshore investment fund to be listed on the London Stock Exchange which was being organised by British merchant bank Robert Fleming & Co. The Prague-based fund was set to invest in SMEs in the CSFR, helped by Fleming's strong relationship with Investiční Banka, the country's third-largest commercial bank. From the EBRD's point of view, this offered an efficient way to meet its mandate of supporting SMEs while managing risks (through working with quality investment managers) and earning an acceptable return.

The other project also focused on SMEs and joint ventures. This was a US$ 100 million Central Europe Agency Line with NMB, part of leading Dutch bank ING, which had recently moved into Poland and was opening branches and subsidiaries elsewhere in the region. The EBRD would be the lender of record and supply up to US$ 40 million, while NMB (and affiliates) would provide at least US$ 60 million. The project was facilitated by a Dutch central bank ruling that NMB participations would count as loans to a multilateral financial institution, thereby obviating the need for special provisions that were otherwise required for lending in central and eastern Europe.[12] The NMB was to act as the EBRD's local agent in loan screening, structuring, appraisal, execution and supervision, as well as conducting environmental audits. Loans would be jointly approved by the Bank and NMB.[13]

Within the first few months, the EBRD had set out its stall: a public-sector project focused on the municipal sector; a loan to a newly privatised manufacturing company; teaming up with a private equity fund to buy stakes in SMEs; and on-lending through a commercial bank to the small-business segment. A common aspect of all four projects was the attention to environmental issues, clearly articulated in each Board document. For example, in the case of the equity fund, agreement on environment guidelines

---

12 A similar structure was signed with IFC in December 1989 covering countries in south-east Asia and Latin America. Poland was added subsequently.
13 The Board welcomed the collaboration with an institution with a strong local presence. It was also interested in approving each loan but the decision was deferred to a later discussion on lending policy in general.

to be applied to its investments had been negotiated as a condition of disbursement of the EBRD's funds. Similar care was taken towards procurement arrangements. Moreover, the Board in its deliberations paid attention to the question of additionality.[14]

The EBRD's first projects in the USSR were approved in late November. Ironically, given earlier US misgivings about lending to the Soviet Union, both projects involved US sponsors. One was to finance the installation and operation of an enhanced international digital telecommunications system in the Moscow area by a joint venture between the Soviet government and Sovinet, a partnership between two US corporations.[15] It would mean a major advance in communications in Moscow's hotels and business centres, increasing the capacity of the system to allow up to 240 simultaneous conversations.

The other Soviet project was meant to be a first foray into the Russian oil and gas sector. The EBRD proposed to finance Parker Siberia, a wholly-owned subsidiary of Parker Drilling Company, to construct and operate three rigs under contract for a joint venture, White Nights. The latter was formed by Varyeganneftegaz, an independent enterprise established by the oil and gas ministry, which owned 50 per cent; Phibro Energy Inc, a leader in energy-related commodity trading; and Anglo-Suisse, a Houston-based oil and gas exploration company. The aim was to supply technologically up-to-date drilling rigs and training expertise, in order to increase oil production in western Siberia from 25,000 barrels per day to 150,000 barrels per day. The project also introduced to the Soviet Union the concept of a modern contract drilling industry, which (through the leasing arrangements) would free additional capital for the sponsor to make additional investments in future drilling projects in the country.

The impact was potentially significant in view of the very poor state of the Soviet oil and gas sector. Oil provided more than 60 per cent of the USSR's hard-currency earnings, yet the industry was being run on equipment similar to that used in the West in the early 1960s. Due to technical failures, almost half of Soviet-made rigs were not operational during the winter months. Moreover, due to a breakdown in ties between some ex-Soviet Republics and Russia, the supplies of oil-field equipment had been in-

---

14 Minutes on Petőfi and CIC record references to Article 13 (vii), for example.
15 An EBRD Evaluation Department study in February 1996 classified the operation as "Successful".

terrupted. Oil production in the USSR had fallen from 12.5 million barrels a day in 1988 to around 10.5 million in 1991.

As often happened, however, even with the most promising projects, the Parker Siberia transaction was interrupted by an unexpected event which impacted the economics of the project when the Russian government imposed an ECU 26 per tonne tax on the export of oil. The deal was cancelled less than six months later when the sponsors withdrew from the operation.

In terms of types and experiences, these first projects featured many times over in the EBRD's future operations. Although not all turned out to be successful, the selection was a promising start. They had come out of intensive discussions with market participants by bankers. In presenting the projects to the Board, there was limited clarity on financial remuneration (and even less on risks) and nothing at all on economic returns or, as required later, their "transition impact". Additionality, however, featured strongly in the Board's early deliberations. The overall approach towards the project work began to be driven during this period through a series of steering discussions between management and the Board around operational challenges and the development of operational guidelines, which subsequently became established in the Bank's Operations Manual.

4. Additional Operational Policy Issues

During its first year, the Board was preoccupied with formulating the EBRD's policies on a number of fronts. As well as the types of projects and the instruments to execute them, these policies also covered the Bank's approach to risk and environmental issues, and the interpretation of its political mandate.

Risk

Risk affected both sides of the EBRD's balance sheet: its ability to borrow and the limits on lending. Financial policies were agreed establishing the Bank's policy on interest-rate and foreign-exchange risk, liquidity management, eligible counterparties, financial reporting and accounting procedures. By adopting a robust and conservative approach, the EBRD was able to obtain a triple-A credit rating from Standard and Poor's in June 1991—

the Bank's first ever credit rating. This facilitated the placement of an inaugural ECU 500 million bond issue in October.[16]

A more detailed analysis was made of portfolio risk management and lending policies, which included exposure limits, terms of loans and equity investments, and guidelines on co-financing and the use of financial intermediaries. This provoked some debate among Board Directors. Key issues were the extent of exposure the Bank could take in any one country or sector or to individual borrowers.

Questions were raised over the disclosure to the Board of pricing on individual loans (it was accepted that specific pricing should not be disclosed), and whether the EBRD policy of price differentiation among state-sector loans on the basis of a country risk margin should be exchanged for a uniform margin across countries, as used by the World Bank and the EIB.

Although a seemingly small issue, this provoked considerable internal debate between the two banking departments and at Board level. Some argued that poorer countries needed access to cheap finance and thus supranational borrowers such as the EBRD should pass on to them the benefits of being able to borrow at below-Libor rates. A counter argument was that it was unfair to cross-subsidise countries in the region through those which were less poor (such as the CSFR, Slovenia or Hungary) by adopting a uniform pricing approach.

The private-sector differentiated approach prevailed at first, but eventually a fixed 1 per cent pricing margin was applied to sovereign loans on the basis that it would be difficult to obtain co-financing with the World Bank and other IFIs if a higher margin was applied. As the aim of the EBRD was primarily to finance the private sector, this was not a fundamental barrier, nor was it unduly disadvantageous from an income-generating perspective. Maintaining the principle of price differentiation according to risk, however, turned out to be important in relation to lending to sub-sovereign state entities such as municipalities.

Environment

The EBRD was the first IFI to be given a clear operational mandate on environmental protection and restoration in its founding charter. This reflect-

---

16 The initial funding programme was set at ECU 800 million (later revised to ECU 900 billion) to the end of 1992.

ed the increased global awareness of the environmental costs of economic growth and the importance of the environmental integrity of international institutions. It was obvious that ecological degradation in central and eastern Europe had damaged the fabric of society. Its origins lay in the distorted and inappropriate economic policies of the communist regimes. A combination of market-based signals supplemented by structural reforms was seen as the way forward, with the EBRD able to spearhead this approach through investment and policy advice.

The policy approach agreed by the Bank rested on four components. The first of these was the provision of technical assistance to help countries develop effective legal, regulatory and economic instruments, including adequate emissions and effluents standards, and the institutional capacity to monitor and enforce them. Important principles to be adopted included preventative action, the establishment of primary responsibility for environmental damage (the "polluter-pays" principle), and the involvement of local authorities and the general public.

Second, there was a desire to use the EBRD's financing to develop an environmental goods and services industry in its countries of operations. This could involve pollution-control technologies, technical and managerial consulting services, and environmental infrastructure with private-sector participation.

Third, special studies and programmes, including education and training, were seen as appropriate to address regional and national environmental challenges. This was partly prompted by the fact that many environmental problems in the region were transnational and affected western Europe as well as the former Communist Bloc. These included air pollution, acid rain, and pollution to the Danube River and Baltic Sea drainage basins.

The fourth, and operationally important, component was the adoption of thorough environmental assessment and monitoring procedures in the EBRD's own activities. Here a strong screening, review and evaluation process was advocated, based on a three-way categorisation of projects. Category 'A' projects were defined as those with diverse and significant impacts, and required a full environmental assessment. Category 'B' projects, where remedial measures could be prescribed relatively easily, required more limited analysis, while Category 'C' applied to projects with insignificant impacts where no assessment was needed (although opportunities to enhance environmental benefits were encouraged).

It was also made clear that local participation was essential to the process. The intention was to ensure project sponsors would provide adequate information to local communities, governments and NGOs on the environmental impact of projects. In addition, it was agreed to publish an annual report on the Bank's assessment of its environmental performance. Later, these assessments were supplemented by policies covering the disclosure of information to the public and a project-complaints mechanism.

Political mandate

A unique aspect of the EBRD was its political mandate, as set out in Article 1 of the AEB, and the commitment to fundamental principles of multiparty democracy, the rule of law and respect for human rights, and market economics as described in the preamble to the Articles. The first three paragraphs of Article 8, which defined the key rules on the use of Bank resources, made the link between finance and adherence to Article 1. Article 11 also instructed the Board to conduct an annual review to ensure that the Bank's strategy in each recipient country met the requirements in Articles 1 and 2. How to implement these aspects of the AEB, however, remained open to question.

The obvious way to ensure the critical link between economic and political objectives was to assess progress against these two dimensions in the country strategy process. One aspect that was clarified early on related to human rights, which were referenced in the Preamble to the AEB, but not in the Articles. The intention was to incorporate human rights into the EBRD's mandate, defining them as those rights which were pertinent to multiparty democracy, pluralism and market economics. Essentially this implied a focus on civil and political rights. Accordingly, the list of reference points for the political aspects of country assessments included free elections, representative government, duty to act in accordance with the constitution and law, availability of redress against decisions, separation of powers, independence of the judiciary, freedom of speech, association and peaceful assembly.

Should a country of operations fall short of the required political commitment, the EBRD's policy allowed for a variety of responses. It was left to the President to decide when to bring the matter to the attention of the Board of Directors, who in turn could call a meeting of the Board of Governors to consider their recommendations. These could range from fact-finding missions and warnings to the postponement of proposed operations in a country or, in the worst case, its suspension from access to Bank resources. A hierarchical approach was agreed, with public-sector projects to be curtailed ahead of private-sector operations and state infrastructure projects before local ones, while technical assistance would be continued for as long as possible. It was expected that any actions of this nature would also influence members' attitudes in other multilateral institutions in which they participated.

Country strategy

It was clear that the appropriate frame of reference for the EBRD's work should be the country strategy. Close engagement with the authorities was an important part of the process, and in the early days the leading members of the relevant government were invited to attend the discussion of the Bank's proposed strategy for their country. At that time most recipient country Governors did indeed do so. Another aspect of the process was what subsequently became known as Board Consultation Visits (BCVs). Prior to consideration of a strategy for a country of operations, a group of Board members would travel to the relevant country to meet representatives of the government, commercial banks and enterprises undergoing the process of restructuring. This helped deepen understanding on all sides.

Beginning with Hungary in June 1991, the Board had approved country strategies for the CSFR, Poland, Romania and Bulgaria by the end of the year. The intention had been to cover the Soviet Union and SFRY as well, but this proved impossible due to rapidly changing political circumstances in those countries.

5. Advisory Councils

To underpin the EBRD's early development, three Advisory Councils were established covering economics, business and the environment. The intention was to provide intellectual input, leadership and guidance, and access to external expertise in areas which the Bank was unable to provide alone.

The Economic Advisory Council first met in February 1991, before the EBRD was inaugurated, with the second meeting at the Inauguration itself.

A third meeting was held in November. The cast list of nine eminent economists—including three who were already, or would be in the future, Nobel laureates—was impressive;[17] however, its contribution to the work of the Bank is unclear. (No records of the discussions appear to have been circulated or kept.) Some members participated in a conference at the Bank's headquarters on the 'Economics of Transition' held just before the London Heads Summit on 13 and 14 July. Although the Council failed to continue beyond 1992, its intellectual legacy lived on in *Economics of Transition*, an academic journal sponsored by the EBRD, which was founded the following year.[18]

The Business Advisory Council, set up to provide advice on the transfer of private-sector capital, technology and expertise to central and eastern Europe, included the heads of a clutch of major industrial and financial groups.[19] A first meeting with four Board Directors present was held in September 1991 (although no record appears to have been kept); the second was scheduled for 1992, and no further meetings took place. However, many of the members' companies were involved with the Bank in subsequent operations in the region.

The Environment Advisory Council was set up to advise the President on all aspects of environmental protection and natural resources management. It comprised a group of experts including representatives of NGOs, trade unions, and local and regional governments. The last Council to be established, it met for the first time in September 1991 and again at the Bank's first Annual Meeting in Budapest in April 1992. The formation of this Council was an important development since it presaged a more open interaction between the Bank and the public on issues of environmental policy. Unlike its two companions, the Environment Advisory Council survived and developed in importance, later becoming the Environment and Social Advisory Council.

---

17 The members were: Arrow* (Stanford), Jean-Paul Fitoussi (OFCE), Ryutaro Komiya (MITI), Janos Kornai (Budapest), Assar Lindbeck (Stockholm), Ed Phelps* (Columbia), Robert Solow* (MIT), Luigi Spaventa (Rome) and Carl Christian von Weizsäcker (Cologne) (*Nobel Laureate).

18 The journal's editorial team was (and remains) mostly outside the EBRD, to ensure independence and academic rigour in deciding which articles should be accepted for publication.

19 On the industrial side, it included Giovanni Agnelli (President of Fiat), Pehr Gyllenhammar (Executive Chairman, Volvo), Karlheinz Kaske (President of Siemens), Helmut Maucher (Chairman of Nestle), Takuma Yamamoto (Chairman of Fujitsu), and, on the financial side, Gutfreund of Salomon Brothers, Jean-Yves Haberer (President of Credit Lyonnais), Yusuke Kashiwagi (Chairman of Bank of Tokyo), Lord Richardson (former Governor of the Bank of England and Managing Director, Morgan Stanley) and Hans-Joerg Rudloff (Chairman, Credit Suisse First Boston).

6. The Bank's, and Attali's, Strategy towards the Soviet Union

From his earliest thinking about the EBRD, Attali had included the Soviet Union in his grand vision of a reunited Europe. Its size, natural resources and international influence made it central to the future of the region and of great strategic importance to the Bank. The Soviet Union thus commanded a good deal of attention among the EBRD's management, especially the President and Flemming, the Chief Economist.

Although the EBRD's ability to lend to the Soviet Union was initially constrained, it was widely assumed that in the longer run the country would become the largest source of operations.

The previous year the Bank had already studied the problems of the USSR closely in its work with the IMF and others in the Study of the Soviet Economy[20], so preparation of a country strategy proceeded quickly. Arrangements for a Board consultation visit were scheduled for August, shortly after the G7 Economic Summit, which on this occasion was to be held in London under the auspices of the UK's Presidency. Attali saw an opportunity to strengthen the Bank's hand by supporting Gorbachev, who was facing increasing challenges at home.[21] A paper advocating a meeting between the G7 and Gorbachev was prepared by the EBRD in June for circulation on a confidential basis to the Sherpas.

The Soviet economy, already in poor shape in 1990, had deteriorated steadily during early 1991, and the political pressure on Gorbachev was increasing on all fronts. Towards the start of the year the three Baltic States and Georgia had held referendums on independence, voting overwhelmingly in favour. A referendum on the future of the Soviet Union in March supported its continuation, but only nine Republics voted in favour, with the Baltic States, Georgia, Armenia and Moldova abstaining. In April, Georgia unilaterally declared independence. Nonetheless, the Novo-Ogaryovo pro-

---

20 IMF et al., *A Study of the Soviet Economy*, 1991. This three-volume study of the Soviet economy is discussed in Chapter 2.
21 In an article published in *The Washington Post* just ahead of the Summit on 9 July, 1991, Henry Kissinger wrote: "A joint study group has been propagating a 'grand bargain' according to which the Soviet Union over seven years would move toward market economics, democracy and disarmament in return for an aid package reported at anywhere from $25 billion to $35 billion a year. The energetic head of the European Development Bank, Jacques Attali, triggered a stampede to have Gorbachev invited to the annual meeting of the heads of state of the industrial democracies and, in frequent consultation with Gorbachev, is drafting his own version of a long-term aid package."

cess of negotiations with the Republics, and thus some delegation of powers ahead of a proposed Union Treaty, led to the signing of the 9+1 Agreement in April. The restructuring of the political party systems continued and in June came the dissolution of the Warsaw Pact and the appointment of Boris Yeltsin as the first democratically elected President of the Russian Republic. Political developments had advanced, making it easier for the Board to begin the country strategy discussion.

It was undeniable though that big uncertainties remained. Major problems still existed between the centre and the Republics, with some Republics refusing to sign the Union Treaty. (Issues such as agreeing a federal tax to cover defence spending, for example, were unresolved.) The Communist Party, still with 14 million members despite mass resignations, was divided between the pro-Gorbachev reformers and "Bolshevik conservatives". The allegiances of the armed forces and KGB were unclear. Gorbachev's rejection of the radical "500 days" plan a year earlier, in favour of a more gradual approach under the "Guidelines for Stabilisation of the Economy and the Transition to a Market System", had resulted in failure, having been interrupted by the deterioration of the economy and the need for an anti-crisis programme. Increasing tension between Gorbachev and Yeltsin complicated the picture. Many aspects of the way forward—such as trade, currency and debt relationships between the Republics and the centre—remained ambiguous as the country drifted closer towards a breakdown of the Union.

Reformers such as Yeltsin were pushing for faster change, while the military leadership and others were unhappy with the direction of travel. Gorbachev was seeking aid from the West to shore up his position. In March he had written to Bush to request US$ 1.5 billion in grain credits under US agricultural programmes. Bush noted: "While I wanted to help, Soviet behaviour over CFE [*conventional forces in Europe*] and START [*the Strategic Arms Reduction Treaty*], and the crackdown in the Baltics, made the case very difficult. I was also pessimistic about the Soviet economy and the commitment to the reforms needed to foster a market economy."[22]

Other G7 Heads were also wary about the extent of support that should be offered. Gorbachev wanted to attend the Summit in July to obtain immediate assistance and win support for full membership of the IMF and World Bank (and thereby access to significant finance). Large-scale economic aid and IMF

---

22 Bush and Scowcroft, *A World Transformed*, p. 503.

membership for the USSR were unlikely to be agreed at the meeting. At the same time, the G7 Heads were aware of the risk of misinterpretation of their intentions towards Gorbachev, and the reform process, if they refused him.

Attali highlighted the danger of a breakdown in political order across this vast country with its many different states and ethnic populations and, above all, the risks associated with the nuclear weapons which were distributed among them.[23] He reiterated his view that the G7 should invite Gorbachev to the Summit to help reinforce his authority in the Soviet Union.[24]

Given the need to manage expectations carefully ahead of the Summit, the suggestion was not welcomed in Washington or London. Attali nonetheless decided to invite Gorbachev to London in his capacity as President of the EBRD. "Naturally, I explained to John Major, if the G7 also invite him to their summit, in the same city, on the same date, it will be even better."[25]

Gorbachev accepted the invitation. However, Downing Street, Bonn and Washington felt that this cut across the delicate handling of a situation where Gorbachev's expectations were likely to be disappointed and which could play into the hands of those working against him in Moscow. According to Attali, after a phone conversation with Major, the UK Prime Minister, Gorbachev's visit to the Bank was cancelled.

Instead, the G7 invited Gorbachev to meet the heads of government in a special session outside the formal Summit discussions. A few days before, the Soviet leader sent a remarkably frank letter to Major setting out his reform stall. Over 23 pages, it listed ongoing and planned reforms, including the introduction of market-friendly legislation, the conversion of defence industries, preparations for privatisations, an anti-crisis programme and budget-deficit reduction. It even included detailed annexes on the comparative advantages of Soviet industries and draft legislation to bring it into line with Western standards. Gorbachev wrote:

> I am pinning high hopes on the upcoming meeting in London..., it may mark a turning point in the efforts to bring about the Soviet Union's organic integration into the world economy ... [While] through our joint ef-

---

23   Attali's plan to exchange Soviet nuclear warheads for a write-off of US$ 60 billion of foreign debt became public after relevant documents were released by the UK's National Archives. See *Financial Times*, 29 December 2017. https://www.ft.com/content/c81f433a-e1ac-11e7-8f9f-de1c2175f5ce.
24   Attali, *Europe(s)*.
25   Ibid., p. 107.

forts we have succeeded in making a radical shift away from confrontation to understanding ... in extinguishing the flash points of a number of international conflicts and armed clashes [and] the process of disarmament has got off to an effective start ... the sphere of economic relations has seen no noticeable change.[26]

Major's reply thanked Gorbachev for his approach to economic change and agreed with the objective of working together to integrate the Soviet Union into the world economy. This sentiment was echoed by a G7 communiqué at the conclusion of the Summit, which cited the Soviet Study by global IFIs as a template for economic success.[27] The Chairman's Press Statement, however, made clear the continued reluctance of leaders to provide economic aid:

> We also agreed that our help would not have a lasting effect unless there was a clear political will in the Soviet Union to create the right environment for change ... outside assistance can make a contribution, it can help catalyse the process, but it is the Soviet Union itself that must mobilise its resources. The primary contribution should come from inward private investment, the key is to create an environment, legal, political, economic, social, in which investment would be attracted and could flourish.[28]

The G7 agreed, however, to continue the dialogue and grant the Soviet Union special association with the IMF and the World Bank that would allow both to offer advice, although not funding. International institutions, including the EBRD, were encouraged to work closely together and intensify their efforts to support the Soviet Union. This motivated the EBRD to push ahead with the development of a country strategy for the USSR. Although investment on any scale was ruled out, recommendations for action could be made as long as they were couched in terms of technical assistance. These ranged from providing advice on privatisation—an area where the Bank was already working with the Moscow authorities—to conversion

---

26 Personal Message from President Gorbachev to G7 Heads, 12 July 1991, Munk School, University of Toronto.
27 "This study sets out many of the elements necessary for successful economic reforms, which include fiscal and monetary discipline and creating the framework of a market economy." 'Economic Declaration: Building World Partnership', G7 Heads Economic Summit, 17 July 1991, Munk School (ibid.).
28 John Major's Press Statement, G7 London Summit, 17 July 1991, ibid.

7. The Moscow Coup and the Bank's Revised Approach Towards the Soviet Union

The Bank distributed its first country strategy for the Soviet Union on 1 August 1991, for discussion by the Board after the summer break early in September. Some Directors had left early for their summer holidays in order to return in time to participate in a consultation visit to meet officials in Moscow and Kyiv, scheduled for 4-10 August. The group included five G7 Directors (USA, Japan, Germany, Italy and Canada), the Director for the EC and the Director for Finland/Norway, as well as the Director for the USSR. The management side was led by the Secretary General, le Blanc, and included the Head of Soviet Affairs for Merchant Banking, Boris Fedorov (who two years later became Finance Minister of the Russian Federation), two development bankers, a lawyer and a political counsellor.

The team's report[29] of 15 August made clear that the situation was in flux, ahead of the planned signing of the Union Treaty on 20 August. In more or less every sphere of the reform plans mentioned in the report—including taxation, external debt, convertibility, conversion of defence industries, and property rights—it was obvious that major disagreements existed between the Soviet leadership and the Republics, and while there was agreement on the need for privatisation, there was no common definition or approach. The Directors came away convinced that "the need for [technical] assistance is immense" but "opportunities for financial operations seem to be limited at this stage".

Their report was filed four days before an attempted coup by senior Politburo and Soviet army figures on Monday, 19 August. Following a dramatic confrontation outside the White House parliamentary building in Moscow between the military and Yeltsin and his supporters, the constitutional government was restored on 21 August.

Attali, as the EBRD's President, wrote on 20 August to express support to Gorbachev, Yeltsin, and the Mayors of Moscow and Leningrad. A special

---

29 'Report on the Information Visit to the Soviet Union on 4-10 August 1991'.

meeting of the Board was called for 22 August and a press statement was issued "welcoming the return to legitimacy in the Soviet Union". It stated that the EBRD would "continue to assist the USSR and its Republics in their transition to a free market economy" and would consider its strategy for the country, as planned, at its next meeting.

By the time the Board met on 3 September, the break-up of the Soviet Union was already well underway. On 20 August, Estonia declared independence and Latvia followed suit the next day. Three days later, after Ukraine also declared itself an independent country, Gorbachev dissolved the Central Committee of the Communist Party of the Soviet Union (CPSU) and resigned as the Party's General Secretary. By the end of the month, Moldova had also declared independence and the CPSU had suspended all activity in the Soviet Union.

On 2 September, Gorbachev and the leaders of 10 Republics announced their intention to create a federation in which each republic would define its participation independently.[30] Four days later, the Soviet Union recognised the independence of the three Baltic states.

Under the circumstances, it was clear that a full country strategy for the USSR could not be endorsed by the Board. Instead, it was agreed to pursue an Action Plan in the short term, which could monitor developments and offer support where appropriate. This included a continued search for private-sector projects but concentrated on advisory assistance, particularly for privatisation. The Bank was already lead adviser for the Moscow City Municipality privatisation programme and was in discussions about a similar role in St. Petersburg, as Leningrad had been renamed.[31] Other target areas included training programmes (particularly in the financial sector), mobilising private-sector investment in sectors such as agricultural distribution, and the oil and gas industry, especially the introduction of energy-efficient and safer technologies. Funds from the EC and Japan were made available to help.

The Action Plan noted that the strengthened resolve of some Republics to seek full independence from the Union meant that the single economic space within the USSR could not be assured. Nevertheless the Board endorsed the proposed approach and approved the establishment of a resi-

---

30 EBRD, *Annual Report* 1991, p. 104.
31 The agreement was signed on 22 October.

dent office in Moscow. The President also advised that he had written to the heads of the IMF, the World Bank, the OECD and the European Commission proposing a coordination meeting within the following two weeks.

Representatives of the heads of the five institutions, including Flemming for the EBRD, met with G7 Deputies in Dresden on 14 September. Massimo Russo, the IMF representative, arrived directly from Moscow, where he had been negotiating a Special Association Agreement for the Soviet Union. This was due to be put to the IMF Board soon, even though there were uncertainties over whether it might be signed by the Republics and, if so, how this might be handled. Russo brought with him copies of a draft treaty prepared by Russian economist Grigory Yavlinsky for a new economic union to replace the USSR, which had been endorsed by Yeltsin and Gorbachev.

The meeting discussed technical assistance (mainly training), coordination among IFIs (the EBRD was seen as having a clear role on privatisation and capital markets), and food aid. The Soviet Union's grain harvest was expected to be down by 25 per cent in 1991 and Gorbachev had made an urgent request to the EC for assistance worth US$ 5–6 billion.

Shortly after the coordination meeting, which became known as the CORUSS group,[32] the agreed text was put to the State Council (an advisory body to the Russian head of state) for final approval on 30 September, allowing the Special Association between the USSR and the IMF to be signed by Camdessus and Gorbachev on 5 October. This provided the first framework for the IMF to offer technical assistance to the Soviet Union and advice for the development of a reform plan without economic assistance in the form of loans (which would require full membership).[33] The formal involvement of the IMF, with which the EBRD had a good relationship,[34] helped to strengthen the Bank's efforts on structural reform.

Meanwhile, events in the Soviet Union continued to move fast. Gorbachev's attempts to keep the remaining Republics together were doomed

---

32 Coordination USSR.
33 The association idea had been first mooted by Bush some nine months earlier, and was then pursued by the Fund after Gorbachev's formal application for IMF membership at the July Summit. Following the coup, France, Germany and Italy became more favourable towards full membership so 'special association' status became a useful compromise for Bush and Major, who remained reluctant to go the whole distance fearing backsliding on reform and with uncertainty over the future of the Union.
34 In particular, John Odling-Smee, head of the IMF division dealing with the Soviet Union/Russia, and John Flemming were long-standing close associates from when in the 1980s Odling-Smee was in charge of macroeconomic policy at the HM Treasury and Flemming was similarly involved at the Bank of England.

when, on 1 December 1991, Ukraine held a referendum in which more than 92 per cent of voters approved the declaration of independence.

On 8 December, the leaders of Russia, Ukraine, and Belarus agreed to the Belovezha Accords, dissolving the Soviet Union and forming the Commonwealth of Independent States (CIS). On 21 December, Armenia, Azerbaijan, Kazakhstan, the Kyrgyz Republic, Moldova, Tajikistan, Turkmenistan, and Uzbekistan joined them in signing the Alma-Ata Protocols, which constituted the founding declarations and principles of the CIS. Gorbachev resigned as President of the Soviet Union four days later, and on 26 December the Supreme Soviet formally dissolved the USSR.

8. Breakdown of Trade Flows

One of the biggest risks posed by the break-up of the Soviet Union was to regional trade, as noted by Attali in a keynote speech to the Royal Institute of International Affairs on 22 October. While technical assistance could help, he concluded the need for an inter-republic trade and finance clearing system was vitally important.

The EBRD's economists had already spent some time looking into trade issues and trade financing in particular. Since 1 January 1991, when Comecon members had begun trading on a hard-currency basis rather than in (inconvertible) roubles, intra-regional flows had more than halved. The new settlement system shifted the terms of trade radically in favour of the USSR, relative to its former Comecon partners.[35] However, falling oil output, a drop in world oil prices and the fact that around 50 per cent of hard-currency earnings were required for debt service limited the benefits to the USSR of dismantling the previous structure. The impact had been especially hard on the countries of central Europe, which were heavily dependent on the USSR for energy and also as a destination for exports. In Poland, it was estimated that some 60 per cent of exports were produced in enterprises specialised in dealing with the USSR. With most factories obsolete and unable to compete with cheaper products now available from south-east Asia, the impact was significant.

---

35 Comecon was disbanded in September 1991, following the last council session in Budapest in June.

The combined effect of three simultaneous shocks that resulted—demand (loss of markets), supply (price realignment) and structural (a lack of technological substitution to meet the loss of essential imports and the dismantling of trade links)—was severe. The EBRD had been working on ways to tackle the problem and had been involved in bilateral discussions between both Hungary and Poland and the USSR concerning trade guarantee schemes and other steps that might be taken on a path towards full convertibility (the ability to conduct trade and services in roubles freely).

In the context of the complex problem of trade, including between the Republics, management presented an issues note to the Board, which was discussed around the same time as Attali's speech was delivered. Directors agreed that it was important for the EBRD to continue its public advocacy of freer trade among its countries of operations and that it should be involved in research efforts on trade issues to underpin this stance.

9. Dealing with New Members: Albania and the Baltic States

The dissolution of the Soviet Union raised the prospect of a rapid expansion of the EBRD's membership. Fortunately, the Bank already had experience of approving a new recipient country member. In July 1991, Albania's application to become a member of the Bank had been accepted.

The process helped clarify the conditions for membership. It required first of all an assessment by staff of the readiness of the country for EBRD operations. This was based on a review of economic and political conditions, notably the extent of reform and progress on constitutional change, elections and legislation enabling market-based activities. In principle, this allowed the exclusion of countries that would be unable to make the required political commitments or make use of the EBRD's capacity to leverage private-sector finance.

Consideration had been given to including Albania among the original central and eastern European members identified in 1990, but the country was judged not to meet the political standards for membership. By the end of the year, however, the Communist Party government was starting to relax its 45-year grip on power, as well as its isolationist stance. In March 1991, Albania held its first multiparty elections and in June, after a four-week general strike, a coalition government took power under the leadership of Ylli Bufi.

A Bank fact-finding mission to the country in the early summer of 1991 reported an improvement in conditions, and in September Directors recommended that Albania be admitted as a member. Shares for new members were to be taken from the unallocated portion. This amounted to only 125 shares under the AEB, but the absorption of the GDR into a larger Germany had allowed its 15,500 shares to be added to the unallocated pool. Albania was thus allocated 1,000 shares, based roughly on the size of its GDP and population, and Poland and Bulgaria took it into their constituency at the Board of Directors.

The Board of Governors supported Albania's membership unanimously in October. There was little doubt that the country was in need of assistance. Albania was one of the poorest countries in Europe, with a GDP per capita (not adjusted for purchasing power parity) of just US$ 346.[36]

An initial strategy had therefore been prepared on an accelerated timetable. The Board decided to proceed with the strategy and was able to endorse it at their last meeting of the year on 16–18 December, conditional on Albania fulfilling the membership procedures (which were completed on 18 December).

The main focus was technical assistance and support for the Albanian government in developing strategies in priority areas. Some Directors felt uncertainties facing Albania meant that the initial strategy should be revisited in a year's time. Recognising the limited value in the extra work, the President suggested regular updates might be given on all strategies (three or four times a year was suggested) and revisions made if major changes were required. This met with the Board's approval.

The decision on membership of the three Baltic states, following shortly after the decision on Albania, was again agreed unanimously by the Board of Governors, in this case in November. The three countries—Estonia, Latvia and Lithuania—had applied for membership in September, immediately after the recognition of independence by the Soviet Union. They became members of the EBRD early in 1992, subscribing to 1,000 shares each.

In approving the applications, the Governors emphasised the fact that the Baltic states' independence had been *restored*. This ensured decisions on membership could proceed without creating a precedent for future applications, notably from other former Soviet territories.

---

36 EBRD, *Transition Report* 1999.

10. The Implications for the Bank of the Dissolution of the USSR

By the end of 1991, the USSR had broken up into 15 independent successor states. It would not be long before the CSFR too would lose its federal status. Meanwhile Yugoslavia was in the throes of a bloody break-up. The speed of change and disintegration of the old world order was remarkable. The path to the East's integration into the new world order was far less obvious and its likely pace was orders of magnitude different.

For the EBRD there were immediate consequences. A decision had to be made as to the legal status of successor states and it was rapidly agreed with the Board that the imperative was to ensure operations were not unnecessarily halted or hindered by membership issues. There was also no desire to reopen the matter of the Bank's capital, so the 6 per cent of shares held by the former USSR remained unchanged. The question was how to distribute them among its successor states. It was decided that all such states should be eligible to access the Bank's ordinary resources on two conditions: that the relevant governments confirm they wished to be a member of the Bank, and would meet the financial and institutional conditions of membership; and that they would adhere to the AEB and be committed to the Bank's purpose, as defined in Article 1.

A further important consideration involved Article 8, paragraph 4, and Article 13 (iv). The former defined the restriction on borrowing by the Soviet Union; the latter was a more general rule on avoiding disproportionate use of resources by any one member. The General Counsel opined that since the USSR no longer existed the letter from Gerashchenko attached to the AEB, which in effect activated Article 8, paragraph 4, was otiose. The general limitation on the disproportionate allocation of Bank resources was reaffirmed.

It was also agreed that for the purposes of the AEB the remaining relevant countries (Armenia, Azerbaijan, Belarus, Georgia, Kazakhstan, the Kyrgyz Republic, Moldova, Russia, Tajikistan, Turkmenistan, Ukraine and Uzbekistan) would each be deemed to be a central and eastern European recipient country. This ensured former Soviet states in Central Asia and the Caucasus would not be excluded from the Bank. Under the General Counsel's guidance the Board agreed there was sufficient flexibility in the Articles to avoid reopening the AEB, and that a simple Resolution by Governors would suffice.

The 12 newly independent states quickly applied for membership, and in early 1992 the Board of Directors agreed that the 60,000 shares in the EBRD previously held by the USSR should be divided among them.[37] By the end of the year, all 12 countries had completed the procedures to make their membership in the Bank effective.

The Board also agreed in early 1992 to relax the limitation on the EBRD's operations in the USSR. However, in order to preserve the geographic distribution of the Bank's activities, the Governors passed a Resolution to ensure that during its first three years of operations (until the end of 1994) at least 60 per cent of commitments would be to 10 countries: Albania, Bulgaria, the CSFR, Estonia, Hungary, Latvia, Lithuania, Poland, Romania and the SFRY.

11. The Problem of Yugoslavia

Meanwhile, Yugoslavia had seen steadily worsening civil conflict since the independence declarations of the republics of Croatia and Slovenia in June 1991 despite the efforts of the EC, and then the UN, to mediate. The Serbian province of Kosovo voted overwhelmingly for independence in an unofficial referendum in September 1991. The Yugoslav Republic of Macedonia, which was not directly involved in the conflict, declared independence on 25 September.

The worsening political situation was matched by economic collapse. Industrial production halved in 1991 and inflation soared. The EBRD President called a Board meeting on 8 November to discuss the situation. Referring to Article 8, he noted that it was not clear who had governmental power in the SFRY and thus "to what extent Yugoslavia … can be regarded as implementing policies inconsistent with Article 1 of this Agreement. It is my judgement … that force rather than democracy holds sway in parts of Yugoslavia."[38]

The Board strongly endorsed the view that activities should only be conducted with parties able to contribute to "the resolution of the current conflict by peaceful means and procedures".[39] Within the scope of that decision,

---

[37] The initial allocation was: Armenia, 500; Azerbaijan, 1,000; Belarus, 2,000; Georgia, 1,000; Kazakhstan, 2,300; Kyrgyz Republic, 1,000; Moldova, 600; Russia, 40,000; Tajikistan, 1,000; Turkmenistan, 100; Ukraine, 4,000; Uzbekistan, 2,100; unallocated, 4,400. (*Source*: EBRD, *Annual Report 1992*.)
[38] Memo to the Board from the President, 6 November 1991.
[39] EBRD press release, 8 November 1991.

the Bank in 1991 provided technical cooperation to help with privatisation plans in Macedonia, and held discussions with Slovenia on future assistance.[40]

In July 1992, the Board of Directors again reviewed the situation in Yugoslavia. They concluded that the SFRY no longer existed and that there was no sole successor to its membership in the EBRD. In September, the Board recommended that, pending a definitive reallocation of the SFRY's shareholding in the Bank by the Board of Governors, each of the countries previously forming part of Yugoslavia that were admitted to membership should be given an initial allocation of 100 shares.

In October, the Governors agreed—on the recommendation of the Board of Directors—to admit Slovenia to membership in the EBRD. Slovenia completed the procedures to make its membership effective by the end of 1992. In December, the Directors recommended that Croatia should also be admitted.[41] Macedonia became a member, as Former Yugoslav Republic of Macedonia, in April 1993. Bosnia and Herzegovina had to wait a further four years to join the EBRD, while the rump Federal Republic of Yugoslavia—comprising Serbia and Montenegro—was not approved for membership until December 2000.

12. The First Annual Meeting

The EBRD's first Annual Meeting took place in Budapest on 13–14 April 1992 and was well attended by Governors, including representatives from the Republics of the former Soviet Union, and by the business community. It was the first major event on the territory of the former Eastern Bloc to bring together a large number of actors from the international community, the West and the East, to discuss market reforms and private-sector development. The format of roundtables, workshops and a closed-session discussion for Governors provided a template for future EBRD Annual Meetings.

The main points of substance that emerged came from the closed-session discussion of a paper on privatisation, restructuring and defence conversion. The President also suggested that the Bank undertake a Special Restructuring Programme targeting large industrial enterprises, including military conversion projects. The programme was launched in 1993.

---

40 EBRD, *Annual Report* 1991, p. 112.
41 EBRD, *Annual Report* 1992, p. 8.

As the Annual Meeting in Budapest was underway, an event near the EBRD's London headquarters was recorded in history for very different reasons. On 10 April, the day after the re-election of Major's Conservative Party in UK parliamentary elections, the Provisional IRA detonated a massive (one tonne) car bomb, which largely destroyed the Baltic Exchange at St Mary Axe in the heart of the City. Three lives were lost and 91 people were injured. The force of the blast was so great that the EBRD's offices in Leadenhall Street were also affected with the windows blown out (no Bank staff were injured). As the East recovered from decades under communism, this was a reminder that the West had its own battles to fight.

13. The Bank's Nuclear Safety Remit

Attali's persistence on nuclear safety matters was finally rewarded later in 1992 at the G7 meeting in Munich under the German Presidency. There the G7 Heads, concerned about the varying capacity of Soviet successor states to deal with operational and technical safety demands, agreed to set up a multilateral fund for nuclear safety, to be established through donor contributions and coordinated by the EBRD in conjunction with the G24.

The President's press release showed his delight at the EBRD being asked to take on this role: "This wise decision is the first step in pulling the world back from the potential nuclear catastrophe posed by deadly nuclear reactors scattered within breathing distance of the heart of Europe."[42]

It was a significant moment in the history of the EBRD. It led to the final safe confinement of Chernobyl, proper management of spent nuclear fuel and waste throughout the region, and efforts to shut down high-risk, Soviet-designed nuclear reactors.[43]

14. A Permanent Headquarters and the Departure of the First President

In November 1991, the Board of Directors had approved Attali's proposal of One Exchange Square for the EBRD's new home. Designed by Chicago-

---

42 EBRD Press Notice, 1992.
43 Nuclear safety is discussed Chapter 9.

based architects Skidmore, Owings and Merrill, the 12-storey building on Bishopsgate covered 38,000 square metres over 12 floors. Attali hired French architectural design company Berthet Pochy and a British design company, run by Ron Sidell and Paul Gibson, to undertake a lavish redesign of the building's interior. It was formally opened by Prince Charles in late 1992 and the Bank moved in over the Christmas and New Year break.

The fit-out of One Exchange Square included removing the original travertine decoration from the entrance hall and replacing it with high-quality Carrara marble. The grandiose reliefs, rough on one end and gradually turning into polished surfaces, were meant to tell the story of eastern Europe's transition. But that was not the story that came out.

On 13 April 1993, a week before the EBRD's second Annual Meeting was due to be held in London, the *Financial Times* published a front-page piece under the heading: "EBRD spends more on itself than on loans to Eastern Europe". On its inside pages it gave details of the costs of the marble and chartered flights, in particular. The story was picked up by other publications the following day. *The Sun* reported that the headquarters building featured "nine dining rooms" with "French chefs serving haute cuisine". A few days later, *The Guardian* added fuel to the fire by detailing internal rifts at the EBRD between the two banking divisions.

Attali denied any wrongdoing, but his rebuttal in *The Times* failed to allay concerns. Directors wrote to the President on 15 April requesting that steps be taken to strengthen the Bank's budgetary process. The Audit Committee was also asked to conduct a special inquiry into the fit-out of One Exchange Square and other expenditures.

At an EBRD press conference on 22 April 1993, Attali said: "With the benefit of hindsight it is clear that we should have done certain things differently. The replacement of some of the original marble clearly falls into this category. Our other main concern now is to learn from this experience: we intend to put in place new measures to strengthen our internal procedures and our cost effectiveness."[44]

The writing was on the wall for Attali, however, from the Bank's Annual Meeting in April, where key Governors spoke of the need for greater accountability and efficiency. Attali also planned an internal reorganisation to

---

44   Colin Narbrough, 'Apologetic Attali will not resign over EBRD costs'. *The Times*, 23 April 1993.

deal with the duplication and lack of coordination between the two banking departments.[45]

According to an account in *Institutional Investor*,[46] Attali's idea of internal reorganisation was broadly accepted at a G7 Deputies' meeting in early June. However, the new Chair of the Board of Governors, Swedish Finance Minister Anne Wibble, was adamant that no reorganisation should take place until the Audit Report was completed.

The crunch came on 24 June, when the *Financial Times* rang Attali's office to ask for comment on a story they planned to run the following morning concerning a $30,000 payment he had allegedly received for a speech in Tokyo and allegations that he had been reimbursed twice for his first-class fare.[47]

Attali called a Board meeting for the next day, 25 June, and read a short resignation statement to the 23 Directors blaming the press. He concluded: "I know of no action that I have taken that in any way could be worthy of reproach." He announced his intention to leave the EBRD in the autumn once a successor had been found.

At midnight on 15 July, the Audit Committee presented its findings. *The Independent* newspaper later wrote that the Audit Report did not see any evidence of fraud and did not recommend any disciplinary action. However, the newspaper pointed out that the report was critical of the marble and a number of other expenditures.[48] Attali left abruptly on 16 July, saying that it was in the best interests of the EBRD. Ron Freeman, his deputy as First Vice President, took over as Acting President.

By the following week, when the process closed, four candidates had put their names forward to replace Attali, but three of them—former Italian Prime Minister Giuliano Amato, former Polish Finance Minister Leszek Balcerowicz, and top European Community economics official Henning Christophersen—withdrew their candidacies before the vote. This left only Jacques de Larosière, who was due to step down soon as head of the Banque

---

45   Various efforts at reorganisation of the banking departments had been made in the course of the previous year to improve their functioning, but overlaps and tensions remained.
46   'The last days of Jacques Attali' by Kevin Muehring, Institutional Investor, August 1993.
47   'Attali quits after damning report' *Financial Times*, 17 July 1993.
48   'Attali makes sudden exit after audit report', *The Independent*, 17 July 1993. https://www.independent.co.uk/news/business/attali-makes-sudden-exit-after-audit-report-ebrd-president-and-board-criticised-over-spending-1485283.html.

de France. On 19 August 1993, de Larosière was elected as the EBRD's second President and formally took office in September.

Attali continued to be a writer and a thinker. Many years later, he said about the EBRD:

> ...the vision was and is to build the first pan-European institution, in order to make totally irreversible the end of the split of the European continent in two... We could have thought about a confederation, about political institutions. But today the main problem is finance... The EC was not built up through the ideas of European political union—although that was useful—but through the first institutions having money.[49]

---

[49] Quoted in Robert Bideleux and Ian Jeffries, *A History of Eastern Europe: Crisis and Change*, Routledge, 1998, p. 625.

Chapter 4
Restoring Credibility

1. A New President Takes the Helm

The EBRD's second President, Jacques de Larosière, came to the Bank with an impeccable pedigree. He had served four years as Director of the French Trésor in the 1970s before being appointed to head up the IMF in 1978. After two successful terms at the Fund, de Larosière moved back to Paris in 1987 to take charge of the Banque de France.[1] His time there coincided with a succession of currency crises as the ERM, the precursor to monetary union, came under speculative attack. After six years in the role, the EBRD presented a challenge of a different kind. "When I arrived in Bishopsgate, London alone … one day in October 1993, I found a bank in complete disarray," de Larosière wrote later, "the public perception of the EBRD needed to be changed completely and immediately."[2]

EBRD staff were anxiously awaiting the arrival of the new President. After the period of internal confusion, the media storm and Attali's abrupt departure, bankers did not know quite what to expect of their new boss. He did not keep them guessing for long. On his first day at the Bank, de Larosière addressed a full staff meeting in the auditorium. According to one witness:

> His opening salvo was along the following lines: "To those of you in this room who believe that the issues of this Bank are limited to its marble, let me tell you they aren't. There are three main issues confronting the organisation: a lack of strategy; resources out of control; a terrible public image".[3]

---

[1] De Larosière swapped roles with Michel Camdessus.
[2] J. de Larosière, *50 Years of Financial Crises*, Odile Jacob, 2018, pp. 174–175.
[3] Interview with senior EBRD official.

On the same day, he signalled his intent by ordering the closure of the Bank's gourmet restaurant and abandoning the huge presidential office "to join my colleagues in rooms similar to their own".

More substantive cost-cutting measures followed. At the initial meeting of all Bank staff, de Larosière announced that flights would henceforth be reimbursed only at economy rates, hiring would be frozen and some redundancies would be made. Office space would be freed up to allow the subletting of some floors and provide savings on the expensive rent. Salary increases would be held back and managed within a "zero growth" budget for the following year (despite an expected increase in the volume of business) and Attali's cabinet—and with it its "political activities"—would be wound up.

2. Reorganisation

A tough approach to managing costs was not the only measure de Larosière took to restore the Bank to a more even keel. Even more important was a reorganisation and simplification of the management structure.

The existing structure had serious weaknesses that had become more evident as business developed. A key area of concern was the dual system whereby public-sector bankers operated independently of private-sector bankers, each seeking to build their own portfolios. An organising principle was needed that would allow them to work together. De Larosière saw this as being the country context, no doubt influenced by his years at the IMF where individual country programmes were run by mission chiefs, supported by specialist teams covering areas such as tax administration or monetary arrangements.

The IMF model could not be lifted wholesale for a project-based institution such as the EBRD, but a country-led approach, focused on clients' needs, could help to align the operations of the public and private-sector sides.[4] The goal was to create good deals without reliance on 'soft' money or sovereign guarantees. Sector teams were also rearranged on regional lines. A North-

---

4   The abolition of the divide between private and public sector teams forced a convergence of thinking and appreciation of different approaches. As a result, projects were more easily facilitated through private sector structures and financial instruments combined with technical advice and policy dialogue.

South divide was adopted initially, with responsibility for the regions assigned to Ron Freeman and Mario Sarcinelli, respectively. Russia was allocated to the North, and the Caucasus and Central Asia to the South.

Sarcinelli subsequently left the EBRD in April 1994,[5] and the Banking Department was consolidated under Freeman as sole First Vice President (FVP). The FVP was fully in charge of the Banking Department, chaired OpsCom and was the senior executive responsible to the Board for operational activities. Three deputies and a similar number of advisers formed the FVP's front office. The rest of the FVP's office essentially looked after the running of the Department. As a mark of the importance of operational business, and deal-making in particular, the country and sector team leaders reported directly to the FVP. All projects needed dual sign-offs by the relevant country and sector team leaders, improving coordination and understanding between banking teams.

First announced in November 1993, the country focus and flat matrix organisation—with sector teams providing transactional expertise while country teams fronted the handling of the authorities and government contacts—had bedded in when Freeman reported on the new structure to the Board in May 1994. In essence, the changes made then have lasted to the present day.

At the apex of the project decision-making process was OpsCom. The project cycle started with exploratory transactions at the operation-leader level which, if agreed with their team director, would then move to the concept stage. This required a written memorandum and appraisal for OpsCom, whose members included a full range of senior departmental representatives. If a project passed Concept Review it would progress to a Structure Review and then Final Review before being sent to the Board for approval. The fact of Board approval was no guarantee of a project's signing, which depended on the client and often the speed with which the project was processed through the internal cycle of approval.

OpsCom included senior lawyers and risk managers, in line with established practice in commercial banks. Membership was extended to the EBRD's Chief Economist to ensure that each project achieved transition impact and complied with the notion of additionality. Representatives of

---

5 'EBRD in line for another round of reorganisation: Bank may abolish regional divisions'. *Independent*, 21 February 1994. https://www.independent.co.uk/news/business/ebrd-in-line-for-another-round-of-reorganisation-bank-may-abolish-regional-divisions-1395565.html.

the environmental department also attended. Freeman ensured every interested party was represented around the table:

> The key to success was to get every constituency involved in ensuring the various criteria which the Articles set forth were present in each project. So I made it a collegial, open forum in which every constituency was equal. Everyone had a vote. Unless we had unanimity a project wouldn't pass [though] we'd try to fix what was missing. We ran it openly and collegially and on an equal basis. People recognised that and responded to it, as people do when treated respectfully. That basically carried forward.[6]

Intense scrutiny was applied at the concept stage to wean out dud transactions and offer clear guidance on how to structure projects. Early scrutiny also provided clients with clarity on what was needed for the project to go forward. This contrasted with other development finance institutions (DFIs), where the announcement of new requirements in the end stages of a transaction (reflecting late interventions by senior officials) caused clients significant problems. The EBRD was not immune to this, particularly in bigger and more contentious cases, but in general the early input of senior management helped to smooth the process. Bankers' presence on the ground, and their readiness to listen and adjust to local circumstances, was another positive factor. As a result, clients' confidence in dealing with the Bank grew.

Another advantage of the arrangements was that it was open and gave junior staff members direct access to the FVP. At this point, relatively few deals were going through the system so they all went to OpsCom, which would discuss three or four projects a week at the regular Friday morning slot. Junior bankers gained exposure to the thinking at the top, either through having to defend their projects in front of the Committee or by attending sessions where similar or related operations were being scrutinised. This provided a vital training ground on how to develop and manage transactions. It was also good preparation for cross-examination by the Board.

Freeman and de Larosière were perfect complements for one another in their different roles and got on extremely well. As a Salomon-trained US banker with a legal background,[7] Freeman was an ideal foil for the experi-

---

6   Conversation with the author.
7   Freeman was a graduate of Columbia Law School and a member of the New York State bar.

enced French international finance manager and civil servant. It helped that Freeman's mother was French and he had spent several years working in Paris. He preferred to converse with de Larosière in French.

A consummate manager, de Larosière also took care to ensure that the roles and responsibilities of the Bank's senior executives were clear and distinct. He saw no reason to interfere with the management of the Bank's operations when it was in the hands of someone with obvious capability in that field who commanded the respect of his staff. The EBRD was a bank with a focus on the private sector and earnings, and Freeman was the top executive of the banking division. This meant de Larosière was able to focus on running the organisation and acting as Chairman of the Board. (Formally, the President of the EBRD is both in charge of the management and chairs the Board.) In particular, it left him free to drive the strategic direction of the Bank and secure its proper place in the international arena among other IFIs.

3. The Task Force on Operational Priorities

Shortly after taking up office, in the autumn of 1993, the new President announced the creation of a Task Force to determine the operational priorities of the Bank. De Larosière wanted to carry on his predecessor's efforts to foster change in the East but within a more precise strategic purview. The remit given to the Task Force was quite broad and included the suggestion of soliciting the views of stakeholders to gain an inclusive assessment of the future direction of the Bank. This turned out to be the start of a more formal series of planning exercises which lasted well beyond de Larosière's time as President.

The Task Force was led by Nick Stern, whose appointment as EBRD's Chief Economist,[8] was announced in June 1993, in anticipation of Flemming's departure to Wadham College, Oxford, and following Michael Bruno's decision to move to the World Bank.[9] The objective was to generate a clearer focus for the EBRD and lay the grounds for a medium-term strate-

---

8   See the list of current and past EBRD Chief Economists at: https://www.ebrd.com/who-we-are/senior-management/beata-javorcik.
9   Bruno was appointed Chief Economist in March 1993 to take up the position in October that year, but he did not do so. Stern acted in an advisory capacity before taking up his appointment as EBRD Chief Economist formally in early 1994.

gy. The setting, as the Report put it, was to ensure that the Bank's priorities matched the process of growth and transition, and leveraged its comparative advantage relative to private-sector financial institutions and other IFIs. It involved a rapid but comprehensive assessment of the views of stakeholders in the Bank's business, from bankers and clients to shareholders and other IFIs. Some 250 people were interviewed within a month and a half and the Task Force submitted its report to the President in mid-December 1993.

The Board and IFI interviewees believed that the first priority of the Bank, and its comparative advantage, was the development of a competitive private sector. The EBRD's ability to participate in private-sector projects was not something the World Bank or the EIB were designed for, and the IFC, while similar to the EBRD in this respect, was not very visible in central and eastern Europe. Further advantages of the EBRD were its relatively fast and flexible processes, its ability to combine policy work with projects ("having the IBRD and IFC under one roof"), and the range of instruments at its disposal.

The Board also added some important insights which the Task Force included in its final Report. One was that the Bank should ensure that support was provided to all of its countries of operations. More than half of Board-approved projects to that point had been in just three countries: Hungary, Poland and Russia. Adding the Czech Republic and Romania brought this up to three-quarters of the total. The Bank still had no signed commitments in seven of its 25 countries of operations, and no private-sector signings in a further three.

Second, the EBRD should be seen as a wholesale rather than a retail organisation. This meant working much more through financial intermediaries instead of via direct investments, particularly in trying to reach SMEs. The SMEs were viewed as the backbone of a successful market economy and needed help which could be best leveraged by deploying Bank funds through intermediaries.

Third, there was a desire to see an increased use of equity, which at that point comprised 12 per cent of the investment portfolio. This was seen as a valuable way of driving improvements in the performance of companies, and especially in their corporate governance.

Fourth, while infrastructure investment to support private-sector development remained acceptable, Board members felt it could be more selective—public infrastructure projects accounted for 44 per cent of the portfolio—and better designed to address problems facing the private sector. At the same time, the need for a commercially oriented approach with identification of revenue streams was emphasised. The Board made clear that it was for other IFIs to do the majority of large sovereign infrastructure loans.

The Board also advised selectivity on privatisation and restructuring operations and clarified that the primary focus of technical assistance should be project-related. A final recommendation was that the EBRD should move towards developing the private sector based on indigenous companies and away from joint ventures with foreign sponsors. At that point, foreign joint ventures had accounted for 46 out of 52 corporate investments. The corollary was a need to move operational staff closer to clients in the countries and employ more local staff.

Officials, clients and the business community in countries of operations agreed with the need for more local input and increased activity in the financial sector, including in venture funds.

The Task Force's conclusions essentially defined the path for the EBRD over the coming years. By February 1994, they had been turned into a paper which fed into the Governors' discussions at the Bank's Annual Meeting. After the summer break, the material was used to define the strategic priorities for the Bank going forward and how they would be implemented. An internal paper on 'Institutional Priorities and Medium-Term Scenarios' framed the Bank's operational intentions against the transition backdrop and provided for the first time a comprehensive plan for the future which was fully costed and budgeted for, including details on planning assumptions and upside and downside scenarios. By looking several years ahead, it became possible to understand better where management's priorities stood and what resources and reallocations, might be necessary to achieve them.

De Larosière's approach was beginning to bear fruit. With a comprehensive reorganisation of the core banking department delivered, costs under control, and a proper planning and budgeting system in place the EBRD was taking shape as a more mature institution.

4. Setting a Path Forward

De Larosière was conscious of the vital task of supporting the still nascent private sector in most countries of operations. Creating a competitive and efficient private sector could only be achieved through increased support for smaller businesses and entrepreneurs, along with improved infrastructure to promote private-sector development. The Bank needed to scale up its activities in these areas and, as laid out by the Board, increase its local presence. To do that a number of further changes were needed.

The Task Force and the strategic papers that followed had pulled the threads of the organisation together and the internal restructuring had oriented the Bank for the future. A business model was beginning to emerge which could be strengthened by scaling up the impact of the Bank's activities through greater use of intermediaries and greater local input.

Chief among the vehicles to be used were financial intermediaries and depository banks, in particular. By providing credit lines to these institutions and requiring that the funds be on-lent to SMEs, the multiplier factor associated with Bank funds could be vastly increased. This would make longer-term funds available to a wider range of private businesses and at the same time support the performance of commercial banks. There were some downsides from potentially smaller margins and less direct control but these could be off-set though strict covenants limiting the size and type of loans on-lent, and the categories of firms eligible to borrow. As banks began to realise that this new business could be highly profitable, the hope was that lending to SMEs would continue to grow without the EBRD's help.

Strengthening activity in the financial sector through credit lines had the additional advantage of helping the EBRD achieve its 60:40 ratio of private-to-public financing. Before de Larosière's appointment, the Board had expressed its frustration at the management's slow progress in bringing the portfolio ratio into line with the Article 11 requirement. Fortunately, the AEB had been crafted to ensure it was the ultimate beneficiary that provided the test for a private-sector classification rather than the intermediary through which the Bank's funds passed. This meant that SME credit lines to state-owned banks counted as private-sector transactions in relation to the 60:40 ratio. (Transactions with state-owned companies being privatised or on a path to privatisation were also classified as private-sector deals.)[10]

Other intermediaries targeted by the EBRD included equity funds. Equity was in very short supply in the region and provided greater leverage over companies than debt financing. The AEB ruled out majority control—another reason why equity funds provided a valuable alternative—but the abil-

---

10 Article 11, paragraph iii.

ity to appoint nominee directors to boards and committees gave the Bank the opportunity to steer business plans, improve practices and introduce good corporate governance.

A further idea to reap economies of scale was the use of multi-product facilities for western industrial companies looking to invest in several countries in the region. Improvement in the mobilisation of additional funds for projects through syndication activities and other funding mechanisms, such as parallel and club loans, was also seen as a means to extend the Bank's influence.

Scaling up, however, meant higher costs, which in turn could delay a shift to sustainable profitability. Plans to boost business activity were therefore matched by an increased focus on productivity and cost-control. Productivity of bankers as measured by average signed commitments per staff month had been falling. Credit lines and other ideas being floated had the advantage that they could be relatively large in volume, given that the funding needs of banks were generally greater than those of individual companies. They also offered economies of scale in processing. It was estimated that financial intermediary operations took 30 per cent less staff time to reach signing than average operations. Facilities, or frameworks, offered efficiencies in processing terms.

The second strand of thinking, a greater degree of localisation, had been brewing for a while. The number of countries of operations had expanded dramatically since the EBRD's launch in 1991. The Bank was now active in 25 markets, which were very diverse in their degree of development and needs. More advanced countries were relatively accessible and could be managed through limited interactions with bankers, but countries at an early stage of transition needed much closer attention.

5. Increased Local Presence: Strengthening Regional Offices

The EBRD had been developing a network of regional offices from the outset. Both management and the Board saw the advantages of having a local presence, while countries welcomed the visibility of the Bank in their capitals and the recognition of their importance to the international community.

The main benefit, however, was as a focal point for communication. Bank officials could explain what the EBRD was designed to do and what it could offer, while local companies and entrepreneurs knew where to go for much-needed finance. The Resident Office also provided a reporting link with headquarters, so that the latest developments in the country were always close to decision-makers back in London. In many cases this was essential given language and media barriers, including state-controlled reporting restrictions.

The first Resident Office was opened in Warsaw in January 1992. By the end of the year, a further six had been opened—in Budapest, Sofia, Prague, Moscow, Tirana and Kyiv—and by the start of 1994 the total had risen to 12. Not all had finalised the legal Host Country Agreements necessary to ensure the Bank's rights and immunities would be respected, but the rapid pace of deployment indicated the emphasis placed on a local presence.

In this period, a typical Resident Office was very small, comprising two professionals and two support staff. There was a total of 19 expatriate staff in Resident Offices by the end of 1993. Few were professional bankers and their remit was limited. Essentially, their function was to promote the Bank's services, undertake some reporting duties, and host senior management visits and missions. They also provided useful input in the preparation of country strategies. There was a growing feeling, however, particularly in the Merchant Banking Division, that they could do more to help.

The 1993 Task Force concurred with the view that Resident Offices were an underutilised resource and poorly integrated into the main business activities of the Bank. It concluded that much more localisation was appropriate for the EBRD to be successful in its transformative mission. Private-sector development required the input of experienced practitioners on the ground and accelerating the Bank's investment activity would be enhanced by able bankers who knew how to find and screen project opportunities.

The Board paper on guidelines for the medium term, which built on the Task Force conclusions, made clear that "stronger local presence was ... one of the key priorities of the Bank". Following the reorganisation towards a more country-focused structure, Resident Offices became an integral part of the Country Teams that now had operational responsibilities within a single Banking Department. A paper on "Stronger Local Presence", circulated in October 1994 following discussions with the Board and Resident Offices, noted the management's view that the EBRD would gain effectiveness and local profile through strengthening its local presence: "The new approach is operationally driven, breaking with the past where offices were mainly representational."

The approach was consistent with the Bank's other efforts to build a local presence, particularly through financial intermediaries. Local investors were being reached through investment funds, direct loans to banks and for on-lending to local companies, and co-financing. Establishing and managing client relationships effectively, however, whether private or public, required a professional presence on the ground. Not only would it encourage better marketing of the Bank's services and a stronger flow of projects, but also demonstrate the EBRD's complementarity with other international banks and IFIs, and reinforce its separate identity.

There were other good reasons for strengthening the role of Resident Offices. London was too remote to be of much help with smaller projects. As markets developed, and with them financial intermediation, the operational emphasis turned towards assisting companies unable to access finance. Many were SMEs and local entrepreneurs, dealing with whom involved a higher degree of risk and required a greater depth of local knowledge.

Local presence was important too for managing complex privatisation and restructuring cases, which involved extensive preparation and regular follow-up. An increasing number of technical cooperation projects required more time in situ by relevant experts. As the Bank's portfolio grew, implementation and monitoring of the stock of projects was also an increasing challenge. Field supervision, explanation and chasing of covenants, watching financial developments, sitting on company boards and diligence work were time-consuming and better performed on location. It was also believed that increased investment in the Resident Office network would strengthen the corporate culture of the EBRD as a "transition bank".

The next few years saw a significant increase in local capacity. By mid-1999, the Bank had Resident Offices in 30 locations with a total of 255 staff. Secondments from headquarters comprised about one-quarter of the professional headcount, with the remainder recruited locally. In addition, as part of its efforts to strengthen financial intermediaries in less developed countries and regions, a number of secondments were made directly to local commercial banks and other institutions.

A review in 1999, as part of a medium-term strategic assessment under Horst Köhler's Presidency, concluded that the effort to develop a local presence was working well but could be reinforced in some areas. Suggestions included: providing leadership for the development of business start-ups and SMEs; exploring restructuring of large enterprises where close day-to-day involvement with clients was essential (as had been shown in several complex privatisation and restructuring projects in Poland and Hungary); taking an active approach to equity investment, where again regular interaction with the management and owners of companies was essential for success; and promoting better institutions and a stronger investment climate. The report clarified further Resident Office staff's membership of project teams and their role in originating and screening project opportunities, particularly where they were best-placed to understand the nature of the risks faced. The significantly increased presence of operational bankers on the ground and the linking of the Resident Offices more fully into the Banking Department's operational planning processes strengthened considerably the EBRD's relationships with clients, country authorities and business associations, and gave it much greater visibility where it was most needed. Frequent visits by heads of Resident Offices to London to support and defend projects based in their countries helped them understand the wider political context of the Bank's work, and provided Board Directors with a clearer appreciation of the operating context for the Bank's investments and its engagements with authorities.

6. Preparations for a Capital Increase

By 1994, the EBRD was finding its feet in terms of its business operations. Annual commitments in the previous year had reached ECU 1.5 billion, with the private sector beginning to feature strongly. The portfolio ratio, which had been the subject of close attention during the previous two years, was still only at 50:50 but the direction of travel was clear. Reaching the 60:40 private-public goal was now simply a matter of time, at least in aggregate. There remained work to do to achieve this ratio in many markets, notably in early-stage transition countries, but the Board had recognised this challenge and allowed some leeway.[11]

From de Larosière's perspective, the banking side of business was not the key problem, particularly now that it was under one roof and fully in the capable hands of Freeman. Two different concerns presented themselves. The first was that the EBRD had yet to prove it could become a profitable or-

---

[11] A five-year period was set, with provision for a timetable and targets for achieving the ratio to be set at the end of the period if necessary. See 'Portfolio Ratio: Individual Countries of Operations', EBRD, 1995.

ganisation. Two years passed before the Bank started making profit; meanwhile some small losses resulted from the early investments. The Bank started making money in 1993, but only just. At ECU 4.1 million, profits after provisions did not even cover the previous year's losses.[12] With assets of over ECU 7 billion and members' equity of ECU 3 billion, the Bank knew it should start earning more. It was still, of course, early days for the new institution. Productivity, in terms of commitments and income generated relative to administrative expenses, had to improve markedly over the coming years if sustainable profitability was to be achieved.

De Larosière's introduction of a tough budgetary regime was part of a focus on longer-term financial sustainability. General administrative expenses had increased almost threefold between 1991 and 1993. Net income was growing strongly but an increase in the stock of commitments in higher-risk countries meant provisions for loan losses were growing faster still.

The effect of his approach had been immediate, stopping the growth of administration expenses in its tracks. So strict was budgetary control during de Larosière's time as President that general administration expenses were the same in 1997 as they had been in 1993.[13] As he commented in his farewell remarks to the Board in 1998:

> Keeping a tight rein on the budget is not a mania that I have developed. It is indispensable. Look at the figures. Suppose we had, like many institutions do, increased our budget in nominal terms by 5 per cent a year which, after all, with an inflation of 2 to 3 per cent and with a portfolio that has increased by significantly more than 20 per cent a year, might have been envisaged by some. With such a scenario, we would have ended up with five consecutive years in the red with losses of over ECU 20 million a year: the Bank would be in shambles, our capital would not have been doubled and I would not be talking to you today... Experience shows us that the best performers in the financial sector are the ones who keep to the cost cutting line.[14]

---

12 Losses in 1991 and 1992 were ECU 7.1 million and ECU 6.1 million, respectively.
13 General administration expenses were recorded as ECU 137.3 million in 1993 and ECU 137.1 million in 1997. Meanwhile operating income grew from ECU 191.3 million to ECU 346 million. A rapid expansion in provisions for losses however from ECU 39.4 million to ECU 177.7 million meant that profits only increased by a small amount to ECU 16.1 million by 1997.
14 'Letter to Governors – Farewell Statement from the President', 4 February 1998.

Losses and weak profitability also restricted the growth of reserves. In turn, this constrained the scope for growth of the Bank given the statutory requirement in Article 12.1, which limited total commitments to the sum of unimpaired capital, reserves and surpluses. De Larosière could see a further constraint looming in the coming years: the need to pursue more equity and growth in less advanced countries. This was the right strategy for the organisation but it would mean taking greater risks and invoke higher provisions. A greater financial cushion was going to be needed to ensure the steady growth of business and its diversification.[15]

This fed into the question of whether to push for a capital increase. Article 5.3 of the AEB required a review of the Bank's capital stock "at intervals of not more than five years". Following the EBRD's inauguration in 1991, a decision would have to be taken by the 1996 Annual Meeting.

De Larosière was clear that a capital increase would be required sooner rather than later if his plan to expand business was to be realised. With commitments increasing at a rate of ECU 1.5 billion to ECU 2 billion a year, headroom—the difference between statutory capital and outstanding commitments—would shrink fast. The "trigger" for headroom, which was set at 90 per cent of the statutory limit to allow for volatility in exchange rates, would be breached before the decade was out at this rate of business growth. De Larosière had no desire to alter the gearing ratio. "The financial integrity of the Bank does not allow tinkering with this," he commented.

From his experience with Quota Reviews at the IMF, de Larosière was aware that discussions with shareholders on matters of capital frequently took a long time to resolve. He therefore determined that demand assessments, technical scenarios and other material should be developed in time for Governors to approve a proposal at their 1995 Annual Meeting for a formal study on capital resources. A draft proposal on a capital increase would then be presented by the Board of Directors to Governors as a Resolution to be voted on at the 1996 EBRD Annual Meeting in Sofia.

Success depended on convincing the Board, and Governors, that the EBRD was likely to continue to grow fast, was having an impact on the transition process, and that failure to grant a capital increase would jeopardise its

---

15   This was especially true as the income from the EBRD's Treasury operations provided critical support to the Bank's financial performance.

role. It was here that Chief Economist Nick Stern and his team, and others drawn from the Project Evaluation Department and Banking, made a substantial contribution. They provided a frame of reference through which progress in transition could be understood, and with it the challenges ahead and how the EBRD could address them through its operational activities, business and operational model, financial instruments and business tools, delivery capacity and financial situation.

To help, in 1994 Stern introduced the first *Transition Report*, which became EBRD's flagship annual economic publication. Notably, the report introduced a series of transition indicators that measured progress in structural reform across countries in areas such as privatisation, enterprise restructuring or trade liberalisation.[16] These indicators were backdated to 1989. Together with the effort on operational priorities, which included "guidelines for the medium term", started soon after de Larosière's arrival, this work set the tone for the strategic review ahead.

Combined with analyses of institutional priorities, medium-term scenarios and financial considerations undertaken over the following year, the material fed into the final Capital Resources Review in November 1995, which set out all the relevant information covering the period ahead (1996–1999) for Governors at their meeting in Sofia. The approach was repeated subsequently at each five-year interval dictated by Article 5.3, with a five-year (rather than four-year) planning timeframe and the addition of more detailed reviews of the Bank's contribution to transition impact.

One aspect of the analysis that would become a prominent feature of the debate between the Board and the management was the assessment of the way the transition process was evolving and its implications for Bank resources. More advanced countries such as Hungary and the Czech Republic were moving rapidly towards functioning market economies, while several CIS countries still had a long way to go. Where reform-mindedness was weak, demand for EBRD activities was poor and the risks associated with operations were high. Conversely, the Bank could contribute successfully where serious reforms were being undertaken. However, in the latter case, the EBRD's additionality and the set of transition targets were likely to narrow over time, reducing demand for the Bank's services. This suggested an S-shaped path towards demand for EBRD investment as countries pro-

---

16 The measurement of transition is discussed in more detail in Chapter 10.

gressed along the transition path. It implied weaker demand at early and advanced stages of transition than at the intermediate stage. In 1995, the Bank argued that the majority of countries were in the intermediate zone. Demand remained strong even in more advanced countries where, for example, an influx of foreign direct investors and increasingly domestic investors were keen on obtaining EBRD support. Given the scale of the region's investment needs, it was not difficult to construct scenarios even on moderate business volume growth—after allowing for efforts to sell-down loans and equity, and recirculate capital—which showed a need for more capital by the end of the projection period (1999).

On the basis of the main projection, described as a "manageable growth" scenario, management argued for a 100 per cent increase in the capital stock. With annual business volume assumed to increase steadily from ECU 2 billion in 1996[17] to ECU 2.5 billion in 1999 (and 5 per cent per annum in nominal terms thereafter), the projections showed headroom would disappear in 1998, forcing an immediate drop in business volume to around 10 per cent of its annual level to be consistent with long-term financial sustainability. A 50 per cent capital increase would extend the time before a similar effect occurred to 2000, while a doubling of the capital stock suggested there would be no need for "additional capital in the foreseeable future".[18]

Management also argued for the paid-in portion to be 30 per cent, as had been applied to the EBRD's original stock. The chief argument used was the intention to increase the proportion of equity in the Bank's portfolio, but a build-up of reserves was also suggested as a reason. Article 12.3 limited equity commitments to the sum of paid-in capital, reserves and surpluses so this acted as a constraint but was not as severe as the overall one, even in higher equity growth scenarios.

At the Annual Meeting in April 1996, the Governors accepted the Bank's analysis and unanimously agreed to a doubling of the Bank's capital from ECU 10 billion to ECU 20 billion. However, for budgetary and other reasons they restricted the paid-in amount to 22.5 per cent rather than the 30 per cent sought by the management. Three countries—Mexico, New Zealand and Morocco—decided not subscribe to the increase.

---

17 Estimates for 1995 showed ECU 1.9 billion, up from ECU 1.74 billion in 1994 and ECU 1.5 billion in 1993.
18 The projection indicated that the 90 per cent 'trigger' threshold would be reached around 2004 though a more proactive portfolio turnover could extend this further (just as faster volume growth would bring it forward).

7. The Matter of 'Graduation'

EBRD Governors had agreed to secure the Bank's future and role in fostering the transition of its countries of operations on the basis of management's arguments and the political context of wanting to show continuing support for the region's reorientation towards market democracy. The new capital would help some of the more advanced countries accede to the European Union, which now loomed on the horizon, and there was work to do to encourage less advanced reformist countries in their transition.

It was clear that in granting a doubling of the EBRD's capital stock Governors saw it as a one-off decision. There could be no repeat for the foreseeable future. Nor would it be appropriate for the Bank to consider any relaxation of cost controls. Indeed, a view developed among Board Directors in the aftermath of the discussion that a root and branch review of productivity and operating practices would be appropriate to ensure the best use of capital going forward. In response, management introduced a zero-base budgeting (ZBB) exercise soon afterwards.[19]

One issue however, which had become a focal point for debate in the discussions leading up to the capital increase, was 'graduation', shorthand for when a country would no longer be in need of EBRD finance and resources. The AEB had not provided a definition of what was meant by a market economy or criteria by which to judge when the transition was complete. With fast improvements being seen in the market development of some central European countries several Board members felt that the time was right to clarify the issue. In their Report to Governors on the Capital Resources Review, the Directors thus recommended a commitment be made to prepare a policy on graduation before the end of the year, which was agreed by Governors at the Sofia meeting.

Preparatory work[20] had made clear that graduation could be considered only with reference to the Bank's own operating principles—additionality, transition impact and sound banking[21]—rather than to per capita income levels or other measures of advancement used in most development

---

19 Ideas were discussed in 1996 during the debate on the 1997 budget and a ZBB Initiative was launched in January 1997.
20 'The Bank's Role in Countries at More Advanced Stages of Transition', 20 October 1995.
21 Reference to environmental factors was added later in view of Article 2 and the legacy of environmental problems in the region.

banks.²² What mattered was whether there remained profitable operations which advanced transition and where similar finance on reasonable terms and conditions could not be obtained from elsewhere. The key test was the Bank's additionality. In the limit, the Bank's finance would be unnecessary, or even counterproductive, and the country would manage its own affairs through the presence of effective financial institutions and an efficient capital market.

As a project-oriented institution, a 'bottom-up' test could be applied to every project. But this was not sufficient for a complete understanding of graduation. The market level, or a 'top-down' perspective, was relevant, too. Where markets and institutions had reached an advanced stage, that is where they were open and competitive and functioning well, the EBRD was unlikely to fulfil the additionality criterion. The combination of 'bottom-up' and 'top-down' approaches meant there was scope for sectoral analysis and judgements over which activities and instruments might no longer be relevant to the achievement of the Bank's goals.

As transition advanced, therefore, it was expected that the EBRD would move away from certain areas of activity. Analysis of the product mix showed this was already happening to some degree. The Bank had for example moved away from sovereign infrastructure projects and other state loans towards private loans and equity in advanced countries. The pattern of FDI and the Bank's involvement with it was also changing with domestic investors in the most advanced countries scaling up and foreign investors more comfortable with local market conditions.²³

The transition indicators too, which had been developed in part to assist with the graduation debate, brought the 'top-down' perspective into sharper relief by showing that Hungary, the Czech Republic and Poland were well ahead of other countries of operations with the Slovak Republic, Slovenia and Estonia not far behind.²⁴

---

22   Graduation from IDA, the fully concessional arm of the World Bank Group, is based on GDP per capita for example.
23   In the early years the EBRD had been a significant catalyst for foreign investment in the region, providing finance for projects that represented "more than 5 per cent of total investment taking place in the Bank's countries of operations" (Capital Resources Review 1995) with the share of FDI in countries of operations "surpass[ing] 15 per cent each year before 1995." (Capital Resources Review 2001) As the second half of the 1990s began, these percentages began to diminish.
24   See Table 10.1 in Chapter 10 which shows the relative positions of countries of operations as measured by the transition indicators at the time, 1995.

Management presented their conclusions in a final policy paper on graduation in November 1996:

> The Bank will have achieved its objective when it is no longer additional. That will be a measure of the success of the transition and of the Bank. In countries which are very advanced in transition [graduation] will *de facto* start to occur ... when the areas of Bank additionality have decreased to such an extent that demand for EBRD services has withered away. At that point a country of operations may indicate a wish to graduate.[25]

Nonetheless, the paper noted "even the most advanced countries of the region are some distance away from meeting the standards of a well-functioning market economy."

Among the areas that were expected to continue to develop were the environment, commercial infrastructure, banking and financial development (including for SMEs), enterprise restructuring and investments to help countries respond to intensified competition and trade reorientation. There was no suggestion that any country of operations was close to the point of graduation.

The Board agreed that graduation could not be mechanistic or deterministic and cautioned against seeing transition as a linear process. Instead, the Bank could shift its product mix according to demand, dropping back from areas where it was no longer additional but responding to new demands and opportunities, especially in more risky areas, even in the most advanced countries. Eventually, countries of operations would rely on their own resources and capital markets to provide finance and risk-taking capacity. But in their view that point, the end of the transition, was not yet in sight since there was still significant demand for the Bank's financing in areas in which it could be additional and a strong wish on the part of the countries concerned that the EBRD remain active in their markets. Graduation was not seen as an imminent prospect.

Shareholders also took the view that geographic shifts in EBRD operations should take place only gradually to maintain portfolio balance, credit quality and profitability.

---

25 'A Policy on Graduation of EBRD Operations', 11 November 1996.

As far as the legal position was concerned, the General Counsel, John Taylor, reassured the Board that the policy fell squarely within the scope of the AEB and Article 29.3[26], since the policy would result in graduation of a country only through the natural consequence of the application of the Bank's basic operating principles and, importantly, only with the concurrence of the country itself.[27] Alternative routes through numerical scores, indicators or force majeure were regarded as legally complex and requiring a Board of Governors' decision.

The agreed policy decision was that the application of the Bank's principles throughout the project cycle would determine graduation at the project and sub-sector level. At the country level, the transition indicators provided guidance but would need to be supplemented at the time in country strategy reports with up-to-date information on the availability of domestic and external finance for sovereign and corporate borrowers, credit agency ratings and terms and conditions of borrowing.

Conclusion

In line with the Governors' request at Sofia, the issue of graduation had been resolved by the end of the year with a policy clarified and agreed. The conclusion that no country of operations was yet ready to embark on a graduation path was helpful in attenuating the debate and preventing distractions when there was clearly still much to do. There was advantage in reaching an early policy conclusion in an era when the issue was less contentious than it would be a decade or so later.[28]

The Governors' decision to go ahead with a capital increase meant de Larosière, and his successors, could embark on a programme of rapid expansion to deliver the transition results shareholders hoped for. It was a vote of confidence in the EBRD and de Larosière, in particular. His strategy of re-organising the Bank and focusing on what was needed for steady growth had paid off. As he later wrote:

---

26 With a two-thirds of voting power majority.
27 'Memorandum on Legal Aspects of the Proposed Policy on Graduation of EBRD Operations', 13 November 1996.
28 See Chapter 12.

[The decision to double the capital was] a significant acknowledgement of the fact that the now profitable institution was operating in the interests of both the countries of operation and the shareholders ... The decision ... really marked the end of the crisis: the EBRD was no longer a subject of debate, mockery and controversy. It had gotten its credibility back. After that, no one dared to challenge its usefulness and merits.[29]

---

29   de Larosière, *50 Years of Financial Crises*, p. 179.

Part II

Transition Mode

Chapter 5
Scaling Up through Financial Institutions

Introduction

One key development from the revamp of the EBRD's strategy under de Larosière was an emphasis on the Bank acting as a wholesale institution as the most efficient way to leverage its capital, particularly with regard to SMEs. There remained plenty of scope for larger-sized transactions aimed at significant local companies and strategic players but these took time to develop and were not easily scalable. The great majority of resources was taken up with small deals in the range ECU 5 million–15 million. Continuing along this path would make it difficult to expand quickly and maximise the potential of the Bank to help as wide a range of clients as possible. Utilisation of available capital was low in these early years. De Larosière did not see the solution to expanding business volume and the Bank's reach in terms of adding more bankers but rather in terms of increasing their efficiency.

An obvious way to achieve the desired wider impact was to develop relationships with financial intermediaries and through them expand the Bank's impact. The primary route for this approach was to provide loans and equity to depository credit institutions. Non-bank financial institutions, such as insurers, were also targeted but the weakness of local financial markets and the lack of savings intermediaries such as pension funds precluded quick progress in this direction. Here more fundamental efforts were made through legal and technical work to improve the functioning of capital markets in many countries. However, one area that proved successful for leveraging the EBRD's financing capacity was on the equity side through venture capital and private equity funds.

1. The Role of Financial Institutions

The starting point for the 'wholesale approach' was based on the supply of credit lines to carefully selected financial institutions which had the capability of reaching a broad range of businesses in need of finance.

This approach was hampered at the beginning, however, by the virtual absence in the EBRD's region of banks run along the lines of their western equivalents. In most countries the level of financial sector development was very low: financial institutions were largely state-owned and centralised, and many were burdened by bad debts. Regulatory and supervisory institutions were also in their infancy and appropriate policy frameworks had yet to be developed.

The first strategic document on financial sector operations, issued in 1991, listed helping to establish market-oriented financial institutions as the EBRD's main objective. This was to be done through the creation of new intermediaries (often with the help of strategic investors), and support for bank privatisations in advanced transition countries. An additional route suggested for the least developed countries was the use of Apex credit lines which funnelled EBRD finance through the central bank, with a sovereign guarantee, and on to banks which could lend to businesses.

As markets and rudimentary regulatory institutions began to develop in the Bank's countries of operations, and with them a variety of private banks, the opportunity to expand business in this area increased. Provision of credit lines to banks for on-lending to private businesses became a feasible stream of EBRD business activity.

There were several advantages to the approach. The EBRD's ability to provide longer-tenor finance than was available in the market meant partner banks could use the funds to offer a new product to their clients—three or five-year loans instead of the more typical six to 12-month facilities, which required regular reviews and rollovers. The additional finance, to begin with, was provided in foreign currency, which gave new partner banks a valuable source of scarce foreign exchange. This was useful for their treasury operations and balance-sheet management. Although some larger clients of these banks who were involved in external trade were given access to foreign currency, the great majority of on-lending was made in local currency at the Bank's insistence, as most sub-borrowers were unable to hedge the foreign-exchange risk.

From a development perspective, it was crucial to ensure that the sub-loans reached business segments previously underserved by the banks. Among the most notable recipients here were small and micro-businesses and those outside the main cities or in more remote regions.

Financial partners were eager to tap the EBRD for funds on a regular basis in the absence of longer-term deposits and effective local capital markets. As well as offering the opportunity to increase business volume, this allowed the EBRD to be selective in choosing local partners and work closely with them to improve functionality, which in turn enabled an accurate assessment of the success of their on-lending activities. An additional, crucial part of the process involved capacity and institution-building. Alongside the loans, technical assistance was provided to support improvements in key areas such as credit-risk management, accounting and management information systems (MISs). In some cases, comprehensive institution-building programmes to upgrade management standards, corporate governance and business practices could be introduced.

Board Directors revisited the question of financial institutions in 1995, before agreeing on a new operations policy for the sector the following July. They endorsed a shift in focus to financing the real sector through intermediation and on institution-building at the project level. This meant more credit lines, including in the least advanced countries, some of which were still backed by sovereign guarantees. The importance of the sector to the EBRD's work and its influence on transition was clear.

> The [Financial and Operations Policies] Committee strongly endorsed the statement [that] "the financial sector is … essential for the success of the transition process" … and the vital role of the Bank's financial sector operations in addressing the key strategic priorities of the Bank. These included support for the private sector and developing private enterprise; reaching and supporting the SME sector; and strengthening local financial institutions in CoOs to encourage the more effective mobilisation of domestic savings for investment purposes.[1]

---

1 Report of the Chairman of the Financial and Operations Policies Committee (FOPC) on the Financial Sector Operations Policy, 19 July 1996.

A number of facilities aimed specifically at financial institutions were launched around this time. One of them was the EBRD's very successful Trade Facilitation Programme (TFP), which was first piloted in 1994 and, after a series of country level programmes, promoted as a regional programme in 1999. Another was the Russia Small Business Fund (RSBF). Ahead of these programmes was one developed with the World Bank, the Financial Institutions Development Programme (FIDP).

The Financial Institutions Development Programme

Shortly after Russia became a member of the World Bank, on 16 June 1992,[2] a World Bank country study[3] focused on key problems in the financial sector. At the time, this was largely unreformed and geared towards a command rather than a market economy. Loans were being made to enterprises that were not creditworthy. A high proportion of loans were also made to the companies and cooperatives that owned the banks. Political pressures and public policy incentives exacerbated the problems, as did weak legal, accounting and supervisory arrangements.

The study suggested a programme with the Russian authorities to develop a separate tier of banks, known as international standard banks (ISBs), which met certain conditions, such as greater capitalisation, better practices and closer supervision. Becoming an ISB would be voluntary, so the study suggested offering benefits to banks meeting the standards. At the time there were more than 1,700 commercial banks in Russia, of which 1,000 had been created after 1990. The rest were mainly spin-offs of former Soviet specialised entities. Most were "pocket banks" designed to finance enterprises owned by their shareholders and served to perpetuate the practice of connected and insider lending.

The concept was refined in 1993 to allow for the gradual introduction of higher standards. A decision was also taken to focus on 20 to 30 leading commercial banks with the potential to form relationships with foreign banks and integrate into international capital markets. The project became known as the FIDP, and the EBRD was invited by the G7 and the Russian government to participate. In May 1994, the Bank's Board approved a US

---

2   It became a member of the IFC in April 1993.
3   *Russia: The Banking System during Transition*. The World Bank. Washington DC, 1993.

$100 million participation in an overall US $300 million sovereign loan to the Russian government.

The World Bank's role in the project was to support the Central Bank of Russia (CBR) on bank supervision, regulation, accounting and auditing. The EBRD's funding was intended to promote institutional development by strengthening the management and operational and strategic processes of participating banks, and modernising their IT systems.

By the end of 1997, 39 banks covering more than 50 per cent of banking assets in Russia (excluding the state-owned giant Sberbank) had been accredited under the programme.

In several areas, however, the FIDP failed to achieve the desired impact. An Evaluation Study from 2002[4] noted that the influence exerted by the two IFIs was limited. The CBR, which should have played a significant role, showed little commitment and a lack of enthusiasm for systemic reform. Many banks used the public nature of the FIDP accreditation as a badge of approval for promotion purposes but failed to address the underlying problems adequately.

A Task Force set up to review the programme failed to monitor progress or take action quickly against banks facing deteriorating performance. In 1996, an examination of nine of the accredited banks found that none of them was financially sound. The institutional development component was also lacking in the majority of the accredited banks, partly due to a reluctance to share information. The system modernisation component fared better, with 25 banks taking up funds to improve IT systems.

Disbursements under the FIDP ceased shortly after the Russian banking crisis erupted in August 1998. The remaining amounts under the programme were cancelled at the Russian government's request in 2000.

Russia Small Business Fund

In the early years of the Yeltsin administration, the authorities repeatedly asked the EBRD for help financing small businesses as these companies found it hard to obtain credit from banks. The development of a healthy small-business sector was seen as essential to the government's economic reforms. The Bank and its shareholders agreed that this was a key component

---

4   'Financial Institutions Development Project', Project Evaluation Department, August 2002.

of the successful transition to a well-functioning market economy and saw political value in creating a new class of entrepreneurs able to represent the interests of small business and shareholders.

By 1993, Yeltsin was facing serious domestic pressures from conservative opponents and the main players among the G7 realised that he needed support, lest progress in reform slip away. In early March, President Bill Clinton and François Mitterrand mooted the idea of an emergency G7 meeting to discuss aid to Russia and eastern Europe. Fedorov, now the Russian deputy prime minister, was dispatched to a meeting in Hong Kong to brief G7 Sherpas on the Russian situation and to seek assistance for Yeltsin's reform programme.

It was Japan's turn to host that year's G7 Summit. Japanese Prime Minister Kiichi Miyazawa called an emergency G7 meeting for 14 and 15 April (ahead of a key national referendum on Russia's leadership and reform programme on 25 April), and invited Yeltsin to the Tokyo Summit in July.[5]

The Summit led to proposals for a package of measures for Russia, some of which related to privatisation and enterprise restructuring and called for the EBRD's involvement. Another proposal that involved the Bank explicitly concerned the establishment of a facility for micro and small-business finance, the Small and Medium-Sized Enterprise Fund.

The fact that the G7 had turned to the EBRD for help was a vote of confidence in the institution. The challenge for the Bank was that any such fund could quickly become depleted at a time of high inflation in Russia and inadequate financial infrastructure. It would also take time to develop better financial mechanisms, such as risk assessment and collateral requirements, and to obtain reliable data on the performance of relevant companies.

The G7 was keen to get the Fund off the ground, however, and offered to match the US $150 million that the EBRD was prepared to finance from its own resources. The financing, to which other donors were invited to contribute, together with EBRD's funds met the US $300 million objective announced in Tokyo.

The programme—which later became known as the Russia Small Business Fund (RSBF)—had two key aims: to bring previously unbanked micro and small enterprises (MSEs) into the formal financial system, and to contribute to institution-building and capacity-strengthening in the banking

---

5   See Hugo Dobson, *Japan and the G7/8: 1975–2002*, Routledge Curzon, 2004, pp. 98–99.

sector. To this end, the EBRD provided training to partner banks in areas including credit analysis for MSE financing. It also helped them expand and diversify their client bases.[6] RSBF donor contributions were split into two Special Funds, one for debt co-financing and the other for technical assistance (mostly consisting of training programmes).

Implementation of the RSBF began in 1994 with a pilot phase conducted in Tula, Nizhniy Novgorod and Tomsk, which were chosen because they had previously been closed or military zones. The idea was to stimulate entrepreneurship and provide finance for cities in decline.[7]

The RSBF began with the idea of providing loans, small investments in equity and business advisory services. Funds provided by G7 countries and Switzerland provided support through two windows, one a first loss cover for investments, the other for technical assistance. A small enterprise equity fund was tried out in two regions but the main thrust of the programme was bank-to-bank lending for local currency on-lending to small and micro enterprises and risk-sharing of sub-loans, along with capacity building in partner institutions.

After the pilot phase, it was rolled out across Russia and proved to be one of the most successful EBRD programmes, bringing new financing opportunities to a wide array of small businesses. By the time it was formally wound up at the end of 2017, more than 874,000 loans worth over US$ 17 billion had been issued to small businesses. More than 40 partner banks received institutional support, helping to create the structures that were necessary to support lending to SMEs throughout Russia.

Of equal importance was the wide geographic spread of the loans, with more than 90 per cent made outside Moscow and St. Petersburg, including strong representation in the Urals and Siberia through regional banks. It was a highly visible programme that created a strong brand for the EBRD and a lasting legacy, with many alumni of the programme's training component going on to occupy important positions in some of the top banks in Russia.[8]

---

6   Russian Small Business Fund Strategic Review, 2011, p. 6.
7   The EBRD used consultants from South Shore Bank, Chicago, a specialist institution that had successfully built lending programmes in ghetto districts in the USA.
8   Russian Small Business Fund Strategic Review, 2011, see p. 4, 6, 8, 10–11. The Bank replicated the model in Moldova, Kazakhstan and Bosnia and Herzegovina.

Trade Finance

Another area that fitted well with de Larosière's ambitions to scale up operations was the facilitation of trade. In keeping with an intensified focus on wholesale activities, from 1994 the EBRD introduced a trade-facilitation product aimed at financial intermediaries rather than individual exporters and importers. This involved providing guarantees to cover the payment risks of banks in countries of operations which were providing letters of credit on behalf of local companies.

The EBRD had the advantage of being well-known among potential correspondent banks in the West—such as ABN Amro, Raiffeisen Zentralbank Österreich (RZB) and Bank of America—which were interested in developing relationships with banks in the East. It could play an intermediating role by helping the more reliable and better-managed local financial institutions to develop their capacity to conduct trade-finance transactions and build up their reputation in this aspect of bank business. The EBRD's hope was that trade could become more robust and that the lack of available finance for this purpose, particularly for smaller or less well-known local companies, would no longer be an impediment to growth.

There were, however, initial obstacles to rolling out a trade finance programme. The EBRD's articles stated: "The Bank shall not issue guarantees for export credits nor undertake insurance activities." This was intended to prevent the Bank from replicating the work of national export credit agencies. As a result, Directors insisted on a legal opinion before committing to offer EBRD guarantees in support of trade. Early in 1994, General Counsel Andre Newburg set out the Bank's legal position in the context of a proposal for a pilot trade facilitation programme with Komercijalna Banka in FYR Macedonia.

Newburg argued that there was a distinction between guarantees relating to the payment risks associated with banks facilitating trade and guarantees covering risks to export credits linked to transactions made by exporters or importers. Under this interpretation, the EBRD would guarantee that the relevant bank, in this case Komercijalna Banka, would honour its financial obligations to the foreign bank. The EBRD would thus assume the general credit risk of Komercijalna Banka rather than the credit risk of the exporter or importer as in the case of credit guarantees. The Board accepted the General Counsel's reasoning.

Mechanisms to support banks and their role in promoting trade in Russia and eastern Europe at that time were much needed. In the years since the late 1980s, after the switch to hard-currency convertibility and international market prices, external trade had suffered a precipitous drop, particularly among former Comecon partners and between the Republics of the former Soviet Union (FSU).

By mid-1994, the EBRD estimated Eastern European[9] exports to Russia were 32 per cent of their 1988 level,[10] with the corresponding figure for intra-Eastern European trade 46 per cent; Russia's exports to Eastern Europe were estimated to be 23 per cent of their 1988 levels.

Although trade with the West had improved, led by the "fast-reformers" of central Europe, it was insufficient to compensate for the decline elsewhere. Moreover, with the downturn in trade came a considerable breakdown of commercial links between countries. This had negative consequences for growth in the region and put a spotlight on factors holding trade back. Many fundamental obstacles and institutional weaknesses were to blame (as well as macroeconomic policies), but the failure of the financial sector to intermediate trade also played a significant role.

Management argued that supporting trade was one of the main objectives of the EBRD and that commercially oriented trade finance, which was fundamental to the facilitation of trade in western economies, could be developed in countries of operations with the Bank's help. The aim was to stimulate trade by increasing the availability of finance and by lowering transaction costs. The Bank was able to do this to good effect by supplying funding and through its ability to manage and assume risks and its information advantage. It was able to enhance markets and create track records and transaction experience. To assist with the latter, institution-building was improved through the use of technical co-operation funds, which were also used to strengthen local legislation and regulation.

The Board took a while to accept the idea. This was partly due to a feeling that short-term trade finance was not "proper investment" and thus a questionable use of the EBRD's resources. However, once it was explained

---

9 'Regional: Trade Facilitation Strategy', p. 7. Eastern Europe in this definition included Albania, Bulgaria, the Czech and Slovak Republics, Hungary, Poland, Romania, former Yugoslavia and the German Democratic Republic through 1990. Data excluded new foreign trade (i.e. trade among the successor states of the CSFR and Yugoslavia).
10 Former Soviet Union, rather than Russian Federation.

how trade finance worked and that each transaction would be signed off by Bank staff (with arms, tobacco and other prohibited transactions excluded), Directors became more relaxed about the idea and the proposal was finally endorsed.

Once under way, the TFP accelerated quickly. It became one of the largest and longest-running programmes offered by the EBRD and continues to this day to help with trade in the least advanced countries. Up until the start of 2020 since it became a regional programme in 1999, the TFP had supported 25,350 transactions for €20.5 billion in trade in partnership with 218 partner banks across 31 EBRD countries of operations.

2. Post-Privatisation Programmes and Private Equity

An early effort to create a Special Restructuring Programme (SRP)[11] to assist countries that had been slow to implement privatisation programmes ran into trouble. The aim had been to provide equity to troubled enterprises where it was thought they could be made viable once stabilised and restructured.[12] Part of the attraction was that many were larger state-owned enterprises which might ultimately be privatised. However, the scale of potential job losses, political factors and misaligned interests between the many parties involved resulted in little visible progress.

Much more successful—and in keeping with the wholesale 'leveraged' approach—were efforts to stimulate post-privatisation company improvements with the use of fund managers. A number of Post-Privatisation Funds (PPFs) were launched from late 1995 onwards. Similar to SRPs they differed in one important respect: the SRPs involved a partnership with sovereign states and government agencies (and state-owned banks), whereas the PPFs targeted privatised firms whose owners could negotiate more straightforward shareholder agreements (and realistic entry valuations) with the Bank and its fund managers. Their precursor was the Regional Venture Funds (RVFs) programme in Russia.

---

11 SRPs were approved for Poland (1994), Slovenia (1994), Latvia (1996) and Hungary (1996). The concept was also used to explore the conversion of a number of military enterprises in Russia in 1992.
12 According to one Bank participant, the programme was partly modelled on the experience of British Steel which had been successfully restructured and privatised in the 1980s.

Regional Venture Funds

In 1993, the political situation in Russia was hindering the progress of democratic and economic reforms. The economic situation was extremely poor, with GDP projected to decline by 10–15 per cent after an estimated drop of 19 per cent in 1992 and a fall of 9 per cent in 1991.[13] Progress on privatisation was one of the few bright spots, with more than 50,000 small-scale businesses having been transferred into private hands. The restructuring and privatisation of medium-sized enterprises had lagged behind, however, and the situation with very large state-owned enterprises was even worse.

The 25 April 1993 referendum, which lent support to Yeltsin's reform policy, and the appointment of well-known reformer Yegor Gaidar as first deputy prime minister in September, improved the operating environment and gave new impetus to the EBRD's operations in Russia. It was decided that the Bank's privatisation work should shift from the implementation of state asset sales towards the provision of post-privatisation support.[14] This approach was supported by Deputy Prime Minister Anatoly Chubais, who was in charge of the GKI, Russia's privatisation ministry. Chubais wanted a fund to help finance enterprise post-privatisation restructuring as a principal means for encouraging and demonstrating the value of privatisation and to reinforce the efforts of the reformers.[15]

It was in the run-up to the Tokyo G7 summit, where support for Yeltsin was already on the table, that the EBRD proposed the idea of the RVF Programme as its contribution to supporting Russian privatisation.[16] This fitted well with G7 and EU plans and became incorporated in a new initiative, the Special Privatisation and Restructuring Programme (SPRP).[17]

---

13 After later revisions, outturns for 1991 and 1992 respectively were -5.0 per cent and -14.5 per cent. The outturn for 1993 was -8.7 per cent (followed by a fall of 12.6 per cent the following year). Source: World Bank.
14 This was a more general conclusion that applied to the EBRD's countries of operations as a whole and not just to Russia.
15 Mid-Term Review of the Regional Venture Funds Programme (Russian Federation), Appendix 2.
16 The Bank proposed US $125 million equity be invested in Russian privatised enterprises through RVFs, provided matching grant finance was available.
17 The relevant section of the Economic Declaration of 9 July 1993 read: "Recognizing that privatization and enterprise reform are at the heart of Russia's transformation into a market economy, we agree to create a Special Privatization and Restructuring Program, in cooperation with international financial institutions, consisting of enterprise restructuring support, technical assistance and oblast support, focusing on an initial period to the end of 1994. In total, this program is expected to mobilize $3 billion. In addition, we are ready to encourage our private sectors to assist in this process, sharing with their Russian counterparts methods and techniques to increase productivity."

The rapid transfer of ownership to the private sector meant that few enterprises had had the opportunity prior to privatisation to make the changes necessary to adapt to the commercial realities of the private sector. Effective corporate governance was largely absent, as were modern management techniques. There was also a severe shortage of risk capital to finance the growth of privatised companies.

When the RVF Programme was being drawn up, the EBRD already had some experience of investing in private-equity funds, mostly in central Europe. Such funds were seen as an effective way for the Bank to supply relatively small amounts of capital and know-how to a wide range of enterprises, with a portfolio approach helping to spread the very high risks involved. The private-equity template provided the basis for setting up funds to invest proactively in local companies and fitted under the restructuring umbrella of the SPRP approach.

The main objectives of the RVF Programme were to create a demonstration effect across Russia of the value of private capital and entrepreneurial behaviour and to develop an infrastructure for private-equity investments in medium-sized private companies in Russian regions. The hope was that this would demonstrate the viability of private-equity investing in Russia and in the process attract more private-equity investors to the country. The dearth of equity in the Bank's countries of operations, and especially in the Russian regions, meant the initiative was warmly welcomed by the Board.[18]

It was nonetheless a challenging proposition for the Bank, given the risks involved in investing in companies that needed considerable financial and managerial help, in a market that remained vulnerable to macroeconomic shocks. There was also a lack of private-equity fund managers with early-stage investing experience in Russian regions, and most owners of companies had little understanding of the concept of private equity or experience of working with the sector. Donor funds were needed to provide cover for the extra risks involved and to help with the high cost of the delivery mechanism. Technical co-operation finance was used to pay the expenses of the fund managers and for due diligence on potential investee companies on the one hand and post-investment consulting support on the other. This was expected to form a high share (40 per cent) of the costs of the programme, split

---

18   The first RVF, for Smolensk, was approved by the Board on 25 January 1994. It was seen as an "important initiative" and a "particularly innovative instrument".

roughly half and half between the two components.[19] The largest donor was the EU, followed by Germany, the USA, Japan, the Nordic countries, Italy and France.

Between 1994 and 1997, 11 RVFs were set up, each run by a separate fund manager. Apart from a pilot project in Smolensk, each received a US $30 million capital commitment from the Bank for investing in target companies, together with an allocation of US $20 million of donor grants. Investments were expected to be in a range of US $300,000 to US $3 million and designed to support the rationalisation, modernisation and expansion of productive capacity. At least 75 per cent of the voting shares of a target company had to be held by private shareholders prior to the RVF investment. The funds covered the sweep of Russia's regions and, like the SRPs, were managed funds with each individual investment by a RVF held on the EBRD's balance sheet.[20] Experienced private-equity fund managers were sought to run each of the RVFs. In aiming to create an infrastructure for private-equity investments, the programme sought to establish a successful network of fund managers with strong track records of investing in medium-sized private companies that would encourage other investors to follow suit.

Considerable operational difficulties were faced initially, mainly as a result of the differing degrees of commitment by the various fund managers. Progress at the start of the programme was slow. By mid-1997, only 22 investments had been signed for a total value of US $33 million, accounting for just 11 per cent of the capital committed. Donor commitments were also lower than expected. Given there was no precedent for such a programme in the regions of Russia, it was not wholly surprising that it took time for portfolios to build up. A bigger issue was the variation in quality of the fund managers, the inefficiency of small deals and the limited size of some funds. A review in 1998 led to the consolidation of some funds and the removal of several fund managers.[21] As a result, with the exception of the two funds covering the far east and southern Russia, most funds completed their cap-

---

19 The external consultant component turned out to be about half as expensive as anticipated, making the TC/EBRD capital ratio nearer 30:70 than 40:60 as originally expected.
20 Russian legislative constraints precluded setting up the funds in Russia. There was no apparent benefit in incorporating them as offshore venture capital funds given that the EBRD was the sole investor (at least in the start-up phase). The managed-account approach also had the advantage of retaining the Bank's immunities and privileges, including tax exemptions.
21 Some fund managers agreed to take over existing portfolios of underperforming investments which required intensive workout efforts and detracted from their fund's overall performance.

ital investment within the following five years. Five fund managers proved to be particularly successful and only one fund out of the seven remaining after consolidation failed to earn a positive return. Moreover, four independently created follow-on funds.

The RVF experience contained some important lessons for the EBRD. Some of these were technical, such as ensuring that funds had sufficient capital to achieve a critical mass of investments and that estimates were made of the optimal and minimum deal size for the particular context. Others were more general. For example, it became apparent that raising of capital for follow-on funds required time and separate resources, which needed to be managed in a way that did not detract from maximising the value of existing investments and exits.

Most instructive was the realisation that identifying strong and committed managers was essential. The experience of using "fly-in" senior managers supplemented by local staff had not proved effective. Successful managers were those who were prepared to commit to the region and devote hands-on support to investee companies to help them realise their potential and prepare them for exit and the next stage of their development. This also meant the introduction of managers who were not merely financial engineers but possessed a range of managerial skills. Typically, these were people who were able to motivate multidisciplinary teams of expatriates and local specialists. The establishment of management teams based in Russia added to the cohesion of the programme and facilitated the monitoring of investments and the negotiation and completion of exits.[22]

The EBRD's early review of the RVFs, which was made all the more urgent by the 1998 Russian crisis, was instrumental in ensuring the success of the programme. While the measures taken did not ensure the success of every fund, they allowed many to reach a more efficient size and to be run by high-quality management teams. A skills transfer was also evident as experience grew in the surviving RVFs and as local staff trained in these funds moved in due course to other positions in competing funds. Nurturing the funds also required a major and time-consuming effort on the part of the EBRD's staff, from active participation on the supervisory boards and investment committees of the management companies to portfolio monitoring. The managed account approach, which had been deemed necessary in

---

22 This section draws on an Evaluation Department Special Study of the RVF Programme (Russia).

the absence of fund managers with a track record in Russia, was seen in retrospect as overly burdensome. It was far more efficient to rely on fund managers with expertise in equity investing and local contacts to deploy the EBRD's capital at the micro level, rather than have the Bank in effect duplicate the monitoring of individual investments in the sub-portfolios of funds.

Russian Venture Capital Association

Another notable outcome of the RVF Programme was the setting up of the Russian Venture Capital Association (RVCA). The idea came from a seminar for RVF managers held in St. Petersburg in December 1996. The RVCA was created the following year, with several Bank funds becoming founder-members. The aim was to promote best industry practice, with members required to adhere to the RVCA Code of Conduct. This was modelled on the standards of the European Venture Capital Association, which the RVCA joined as an associate member in 1997. The founding of the RVCA helped to ensure a lasting impact of the EBRD's initial efforts in supporting equity funds.

Post-Privatisation Funds

The RVF programme was followed by a broader-based Post-Privatisation Funds (PPF) initiative, through which the Bank began to invest in medium-sized enterprises in a range of countries from 1995 onwards. While many private investment funds existed by this time focused on the more advanced countries in the EBRD's region, there were few dedicated country funds. Most equity funds were regional with a broad focus, with limited investments in EBRD countries of operation and targeting the best companies or, occasionally, start-up situations. The PPFs targeted higher-risk privatised and private medium-sized companies (typically with 100 to 2000 employees) in which other financiers would not invest. This helped to fill a gap and assured the Bank's additionality.

The first PPF was approved for the Slovak Republic[23] in November 1995 and was followed soon after by PPFs for the Baltics[24] and Kazakhstan (Feb-

---

23 Although the fund was approved in November 1995, it was not signed until April 1996 and its first investment was not made until over a year later.
24 This began as a PPF in Lithuania and an SRP in Latvia, but the latter attracted no investments and was cancelled in early 1998. Its capital was transferred to the Lithuanian PPF, which was renamed the Baltic PPF.

ruary 1996) and Romania (June 1996). PPFs for Ukraine and Bulgaria were approved in December 1997.[25] The PPFs were designed to provide local private-sector financing in the absence of a banking sector able to supply medium-term funds and to instil better management practices in newly privatised enterprises. Many companies had been dependent on state subsidies or cheap loans, which were being withdrawn, and needed new sources of funds. Few among the new class of shareholders had money to invest, nor did they have much idea of how to deliver effective governance for their enterprises.

As with the RVFs, the best-performing PPFs were those with competent and committed expatriate managers with stable and dedicated local teams. Investments by the funds in terms of deployment of available capital and returns were good in the Baltic, Romanian and Ukrainian funds, while returns across the whole set of PPFs were generally satisfactory, even after taking the costs of technical co-operation into account. Not only did the EBRD help create new sources of equity financing for SMEs in the region but, through the fund managers, is was also able to introduce corporate-governance improvements, such as the introduction of supervisory boards and improved transparency and disclosure (audit and IAS statements for example).

Private Equity Funds

Equity funds also offered a way to deliver the wholesale approach. Placing EBRD capital with experienced equity fund managers to help them invest in a range of companies multiplied the impact the Bank could have on supporting and driving businesses forward. Moreover, as these funds were able to take majority stakes, unlike the Bank, and with their general partners having 'skin in the game' they could exert control over companies and their future direction as well as improve their corporate governance. This sent a strong signal to the market about best commercial practices and effective management.

EBRD investments in these funds began to accelerate with the expansion of business during de Larosière's Presidency. Indeed, in the years from

---

25   PPFs were also approved for the Czech Republic and Uzbekistan. The Uzbek fund was cancelled before any disbursement took place, while the Czech fund was restructured in 1997 as the Czech Direct Equity Fund with enhanced sponsorship.

1993 to 1997, more than 50 equity fund projects were signed, amounting to half the total signed between 1991 and 2007. This matched the desire to increase equity activity that had been identified as an important objective in the operations policy review, and was helped by improving economic conditions across much of the region at that time.

A similar pattern was seen in equity investments in banks, with about one-third of the total for this period made in 1993 through 1997. This reflected the Bank's efforts on privatisation, including post-privatisation support. The number of deals involving lending to banks was also around one-third of the total.

After an initial wave of enthusiasm on the part of foreign sponsors seeking equity opportunities in the newly-opened countries of the East, many withdrew as they came to realise quick returns would not be forthcoming and that long-term active support would be needed. Many major private equity investors soon designated the region as non-core. This allowed the EBRD to assist those more intrepid investors who were prepared to make a longer term commitment. The Bank became a catalyst for private equity in the region, in many ways providing the linchpin for its development. The EBRD was very widely consulted as new funds emerged and as successful funds launched second or third generation funds. The Bank was sought after by fund managers for its expertise and understanding of the region and for its consistent ability to supply new capital, including through co-investments.[26]

Within ten years of starting operations the EBRD had committed €1.5 billion in private equity funds with a joint capital of over €5 billion. Around half the commitments were in expansion or buy-out funds which targeted larger companies, while just under a fifth (though more in terms of number) were venture capital type funds. The rest were donor-supported first generation funds, mostly in less advanced transition countries, and second generation funds. Among the most successful were the Polish Private Equity and Enterprise Funds and Baring Vostok in Russia. Strong managers with a clear strategic focus and direction once again played an important part in success in conjunction with the EBRD's partnership role.

---

26   During the 1990s, three single-fund co-investment facilities were established. These were replaced in 2000 with a region-wide Private Equity Funds Co-Investment Facility, which was a more successful vehicle for this activity.

By the turn of the decade and into the 2000s, the EBRD was the leading private equity fund investor in the region—the biggest by far—and making good returns from the successful funds it had backed. The use of experienced fund managers leveraged the Bank's capacity to improve the performance of the corporate sector. The Bank played a unique role in supporting an industry that helped to fill a major transition gap—by addressing the lack of an equity culture and instilling good corporate governance.

Chapter 6
Supporting Privatisation and Restructuring

1. Early Thinking

With its unique ability to work with both the public and private sectors using a range of financial instruments, the EBRD was well-placed to support enterprise restructuring and privatisation in central and eastern Europe. Its resident Board, which included the relevant countries of operations as well as countries with recent experience of privatisation such as the UK and Mexico,[1] was also able to contribute to the task. The Bank lost no time in preparing the ground for this business, which for many was a core task of the new institution.

From the outset there was much debate about the speed with which liberalisation should be pursued in former socialist countries. Poland, for example, had already embarked on a rapid programme of reform under Finance Minister and Deputy Prime Minister, Leszek Balcerowicz.

Academics such as Jeffrey Sachs of Harvard University and David Lipton of the World Institute for Development Economics Research[2] argued that freeing up prices and trade (including currency convertibility) as quickly as possible—combined with reduced restrictions on private economic activity, improved discipline in the state sector and macroeconomic stabili-

---

1 A conference co-sponsored by the Mexican government was held at the Bank in November 1992.
2 See, for example, D. Lipton and J. Sachs, 'Privatisation in Eastern Europe: the Case of Poland', *Brookings Papers on Economic Activity*, Vol 1990, No. 2; and D. Lipton and J. Sachs, 'Creating a Market Economy in Eastern Europe: the Case of Poland', *Brookings Papers on Economic Activity*, Vol 1990, No. 1. Also D. Lipton and J. Sachs, 'Prospects for Russia's Economic Reforms', *Brookings Papers on Economic Activity*, Vol 1992, No. 2.

ty—would start the reallocation of resources and create an environment conducive to growth and entrepreneurship. As Sachs explained in an article in *The Economist* in January 1990:

> The economic and political complexities of the transition to a market economy argue strongly for a decisive and comprehensive approach, such as the new Polish economic programme.[3]

Sachs' vision for the reform process in eastern Europe extolled the virtues of the Balcerowicz Plan, despite the risks of a political backlash.

As well as helping to establish a private sector and embed the concept of private ownership, privatisation of state enterprises was expected to provide the opportunity for entrepreneurs to exploit efficiency gains by restructuring these companies. Profits would then be invested in new technology and in industries where latent demand was strong. According to this view, "shock therapy" would quickly establish functioning markets, force existing enterprises to restructure and create the conditions for new business start-ups.[4] This in turn would create demand for supportive institutions that would reinforce the path towards a properly functioning market system.

Others were sceptical of this "big bang" approach, believing that rapid liberalisation in politically fluid and weak institutional environments posed a number of risks.[5] One was that more jobs would be lost through the downsizing of inefficient enterprises than were created by new businesses, causing unemployment to rise. Another was that pushing through privatisation before enterprises had been restructured could result in many failures and a consequent loss of support for market-based solutions.

The alternative was a "gradualist approach" to liberalisation and privatisation. In principle, this would allow state enterprises to adjust their operations and workforce more slowly, allow time for the development of new business models, and enable new private-sector companies to expand at the same rate as the decline of the state sector. The risk with this strategy was

---

[3] He continued "Poland's goal is to establish the economic, legal and institutional basis for a private sector market economy in just one year." *The Economist*, 13 January 1990.
[4] EBRD, Transition Report 1999, p. 27.
[5] Larry Summers, a future US Treasury Secretary, was one of those who took a less sanguine view on the speed of privatisation. See *Brookings Papers* (1990).

that a partially reformed economy might allow rent-seeking and vested interests to block further reforms.[6]

2. The Bank's Approach

When the EBRD was inaugurated in 1991, there was little doubt among its economists of the need for rapid price liberalisation, the introduction of competition and the removal of the soft or non-existent budget constraints of state enterprises that had bedevilled the socialist economies. In central Europe, the process was already underway. Further to the east and south, however, it was only just beginning.

Not all privatisations were challenging or controversial. At the lower end of the scale, the process largely involved transferring the ownership of shops, hotels and other small businesses to private-sector owners, usually those who already ran them. Individual profits, control and impact on the wider economy were limited. Poland, the CSFR and Hungary had scored early successes with this type of small-asset privatisation. In the CSFR, for example, some 20,000 small enterprises were privatised by the end of 1991.

The privatisation and restructuring of medium-sized and especially larger enterprises presented more of a challenge. Here much bigger issues were at stake: the livelihoods of large numbers of workers, the control of monopolies, and the management of strategic industries and crucial financial infrastructure. In this context, the EBRD was eager to help develop the right conditions for successful privatisations, a process that in some countries was going to need intensive policy dialogue and technical assistance ahead of investment.

Management was also aware that privatisation and restructuring were closely linked, in that both were designed to enable enterprises to succeed in a competitive environment. Restructuring was inevitable: decisions on privatisation determined when it should be carried out and by whom. State and private actors had very different incentives. The former had to respond to voter concerns about job losses and the returns on the sale of state assets, while private-sector buyers were responsible to shareholders seeking good financial returns.

---

6   EBRD, *Transition Report* 1999, p. 29.

This tension was reflected in interventions by the EBRD in many privatisations and related restructurings, especially in cases where the state wanted to retain a stake in the enterprise. The Bank in general took a selective, pragmatic case-by-case stance on privatisation. Its position was set out in a paper on 'The Bank's Policy Approach to Privatisation Advice', which nevertheless stressed:

> Although it is too early in the overall privatisation process for the Bank to endorse a particular doctrine, some conclusions may be drawn ... most categories of enterprises should be privatised speedily through a fair and transparent process, by following simple rules.[7]

For the majority of state enterprises, privatisation without undue delay was the Bank's recommended route. Simple and transparent administrative and commercial rules to effect a rapid wide-scale transfer of assets and enterprises to new owners were suggested, with programmes aimed at providing equality of opportunity to different classes of investors.

For larger enterprises, many of which were unviable, the situation was more complicated. Significant funding would be required, as well as large-scale restructuring, and their importance to the economy made the process politically sensitive. The state would often seek to maintain a significant stake for strategic and other reasons. Sales would require diligent preparation and marketing and most likely follow a staged approach, which would allow the EBRD to deploy a degree of selectivity in its interventions.

More enlightened local policymakers were aware that the restructuring and privatisation of state behemoths was necessary to improve their performance and that of the wider economy. They also understood the need for a sound legal, financial and institutional framework to exert discipline on enterprises that had market clout or close political connections.

The 1992 paper noted several different techniques for achieving privatisation, from public offerings to private sales by negotiation or tender to strategic investors (including foreign investors), free mass privatisation "voucher" distribution schemes, management and employee buy-outs, and asset sales through liquidations. The method depended on local circumstances—for example, initial public offerings (IPOs) would only work in countries where capital markets were sufficiently developed.

---

7 'The Bank's Policy Approach to Privatisation Advice', 1992, p. 3.

For some enterprises, privatisation was not appropriate without the adoption of a regulatory framework to protect the public interest. With natural monopolies such as the supply of water and other utilities, for example, and dominant enterprises in a sector or companies able to exploit high barriers to entry, market-oriented outcomes through privatisation required adequate safeguards to be in place to ensure effective competition.

Military conversion

One area requiring radical reform and deep restructuring concerned enterprises involved in military production. With the Cold War over, there was an additional reason to reorient these military-industrial complexes beyond the task of developing the private sector. The significant spending on defence of the Soviet era was no longer needed or affordable. This presented a formidable challenge. The closure of factories and the break-up of large organisations as procurement orders declined would have social and regional consequences, due to the concentration of many military-related enterprises in specific—and often remote—areas.[8] The secretive character of the sector, combined with its privileged status, lack of cost-consciousness and conservative attitudes to change among both management and workers, meant defence conversion was expected to be especially challenging. Nevertheless, management believed the EBRD could play a role in the process.

Military conversion was not unprecedented: it had taken place on a large scale in Japan, Europe and the USA after the Second World War. There, however, it had been largely a matter of converting civilian facilities that had been requisitioned for the war effort back to their original use. In the former Soviet Union, thousands of enterprises had been built specifically for military production with no preceding management culture based on civilian production. The scale of the problem was significant: the armaments industry in Russia alone involved some 1,500 to 2,000 enterprises and more than 10 million employees, while up to 50 per cent of industrial output was defence-related.[9]

---

8   The EBRD, based on discussions with western experts, estimated the productivity of the best military establishments at 30 per cent to 40 per cent of similar foreign ones.
9   Estimates for the former Soviet Union were 2,000 to 3,000 enterprises, with Ukraine the second-ranked republic after Russia.

Banks

Another priority for the EBRD was the privatisation of banks. Modernising the banking system of transition economies was key to achieving a more efficient allocation of resources and supporting SMEs.

In central and eastern Europe, the state banking systems inherited from communist times were problematic. Opportunities for privatisation would remain limited until the substantial unrecoverable loans from state enterprises on banks' books had been dealt with and capital injected to permit portfolio write-downs. For example, even in Poland it was estimated that substandard loans in the banking system amounted to at least 15–20 per cent of total assets, while in Bulgaria as much as 60 per cent of banks' loan portfolios were non-performing. Administrative and management skills—such as credit assessment, loan monitoring and payments systems—were also notoriously deficient.

Large enterprises

Many large enterprises were also unattractive to private-sector, and especially foreign, investors. Years of non-market pricing, lavish subsidies, lack of proper accounting and cosy relationships between managers and their political masters made assessing the enterprise value of state-owned firms extremely challenging. In more strategic areas, especially those offering the prospect of large profits, local relationships were difficult for outsiders to navigate. Restructuring in many cases was needed before private investment would be forthcoming.

The Governors' first roundtable discussion

At the EBRD's first Annual Meeting in Budapest in April 1992, there was general agreement that the Bank's aim with regard to privatisation was "to work sensitively and cooperatively with its members from countries of operations, to help them make choices… and to help them deal with the consequences of those choices". In countries just starting on a privatisation path, the Bank sought to provide advice based on pilot projects, mostly through technical assistance funds. Where the institutional framework was reasonably well-developed, it could play a more operational role through lending and equity investments and by supporting enterprises seeking new, especially foreign, investors.

When it came to the restructuring of large state enterprises, the EBRD was prepared to consider the provision of loan financing where long-term viability was likely. Equity investment was deemed too risky at the restructuring stage. Defence conversion looked financially unattractive for similar reasons. Instead, the Bank advocated the provision of enhanced technical assistance and proposed setting up a Special Restructuring Facility to deal with problematic, larger state enterprises. Because financial institutions were seen as fundamental to the economic transformation of command economies, advising on and participating in the restructuring and eventual privatisation of state-owned banks was seen as a priority.[10]

While agreeing on the importance of speed in the privatisation process, the Governors concluded that restructuring should be taken on a case-by-case basis, depending on the size and nature of the enterprise. They noted that, for large enterprises, "operational and financial restructuring will require enormous resources, innovative approaches and will take much time".[11]

3. Advice on Privatisation Programmes

Despite a cautious view on large-scale privatisation, there was agreement on the urgent need to find ways to develop the private sector which the Bank and the Board could support. Close cooperation with the authorities was an important strategic move in this direction. Being aware of transactions in the pipeline, as well as gaining a better understanding of the associated political and financial risks, enabled the Bank to choose which privatisations and restructurings to participate in when the time came.

The EBRD provided advice to governments on privatisation programmes, organising and reviewing key recommendations and discussing with authorities. It also advised on specific transactions, helping to identify bottlenecks, set precedents and provide "sell-side" expertise.

---

10   First Annual Meeting Paper for the Closed Session of the Board of Governors, Privatisation, Restructuring and Defence Conversion.
11   Chairman's Report to Governors, 14 April 1992.

Moscow City

One of the Bank's first advisory assignments was with Moscow City.[12] Here three 'pilot transactions' were looked at, including a consumer plastics manufacturer, a stone processing factory and a gelatine manufacturer. The experience of providing advice gave insights into the problems facing investors in privatisation in Russia and led to some important conclusions.

Moscow City owned around 17,000 enterprises of which the vast majority—more than 95 per cent—had fewer than 200 employees and non-real estate assets of under US$ 20,000. They were over-manned, by factors of up to 500 per cent, and the general state of their industrial plant and equipment was very poor. The technology was mostly obsolete and the cannibalisation of machines to keep others working was endemic. Confusingly, there was a proliferation of agencies competing for authority over the privatisation process. In the case of the Moscow State Property Agency (MKI), which the Bank worked with as it was the most obvious lead authority, EBRD bankers recalled a lack of administrative capacity and an unwillingness at all levels to make judgements and take decisions. Furthermore, while the Russian privatisation law had imported concepts and approaches developed elsewhere, they had not yet been tested in Russia. Workers' collectives also complicated the picture. Many claimed historic rights to take over the enterprises, but had little knowledge of what was needed to improve performance and survive in the new market economy. Furthermore, insiders and political connections served to undermine the process.

The Bank concluded that privatisation in Moscow—and in Russia more generally—faced three main problems: a huge managerial task of privatising a large number of low-value enterprises in a short time with market forces likely to bankrupt many, if not most, of them; a unique shortage of entrepreneurs and managers willing and capable of transforming privatised entities into viable and successful businesses (central Europe had lost two generations of entrepreneurs, whereas Russia had lost at least four); and widespread problems of legal interpretation and corruption. The EBRD concluded: "The present setting is not conducive to efficient, fair and transparent priva-

---

12 The advisory programme ran from 1991. A similar programme was carried out in St. Petersburg where, as in Moscow, three pilot transactions—in this case involving a consumer products manufacturer, a confectionery manufacturer and a chain of department stores—were considered for the city's privatisation programme. EBRD, *Annual Report* 1991, p. 44.

tisation." It advised that radical changes to establish a consistent legal basis, a single independent professional privatisation agency, standard valuation procedures and legal documentation were needed.[13]

Russia's Mass Privatisation Programme

Early on under Yeltsin's Presidency, the Gaidar/Chubais[14] government decided to go for rapid privatisation despite the risks in order to create an irreversible move towards the private sector. Small enterprises were sold through auctions and tenders organised by municipalities, while larger non-strategic enterprises were allocated to a Mass Privatisation Programme (MPP). The EBRD joined forces with the World Bank in providing advice to the Russian government on the Mass Privatisation Programme, which was announced in January 1992. The MPP covered around 6,000 large enterprises employing 30 million workers and involved issuing vouchers free (with a nominal value of 10,000 roubles, worth approximately US $22 at the time) to every member of Russia's population. Almost 150 million citizens were eligible.

To support the process, a Privatisation Advisory Programme for the Russian Federation (PAPRF) was discussed with the Russian authorities from early 1992 on and came into operation that summer. It built on the EBRD's experience in Moscow and a similar project in St. Petersburg, and was far larger in scale than anything the Bank had attempted before.

The PAPRF gathered momentum throughout 1992 and into 1993. A significant part of the initial cost was financed by the EC's TACIS,[15] which provided ECU 5.3 million. The technical assistance programme covered design and project management, the voucher scheme, financial instruments, legal advice and accounting. It was jointly prepared by the State Committee for the Management of State Property (GKI), the World Bank and the EBRD using a consortium of consultants.

The programme was supplemented and expanded through a large sovereign loan in December 1992. The EBRD provided US $44 million, while

---

13 'Moscow City Privatisation', Annex 4, 'Privatisation, Restructuring and Defence Conversion', 24 March 1992.
14 Yegor Gaidar, finance minister from November 1991. Anatoly Chubais joined Yeltsin's cabinet in November 1991 as head of the Committee for the Management of State Property.
15 TACIS, 'Technical Assistance to the Commonwealth of Independent States', was a programme of the European Community that began in 1991. The EBRD became a significant implementing agency for the EC in its countries of operations.

the World Bank's contribution was US $90 million. Although the loan was essentially for technical assistance (and thus not remunerated by commercial returns), it had been agreed earlier that this could be allowed.[16]

Small company privatisations got underway quickly. By April 1993, the State Statistics Committee estimated that more than 60,000 enterprises had been privatised, as much as half of all small enterprises.[17] The MPP also accelerated through 1993.

The first example of the effort by the Bank to assist the MPP process was a model transaction involving the Bolshevik Biscuit Factory and was carried out at a rapid pace.

Bolshevik Biscuit Factory

The EBRD's role in the privatisation process included preparing state companies for corporatisation and organising and monitoring auctions. In 1993, the Bank designed a pilot voucher auction for the Bolshevik Biscuit Factory, a medium-sized company of around 2,000 employees. As with many privatisations, the assumption had been that strategic investors would take responsibility for improving enterprise performance after privatisation. However, while Alpha Capital, an investment fund, acquired just over 25 per cent of the company's shares, some 55 per cent remained in the hands of management and employees. When the Bolshevik Biscuit Factory convened its first shareholders' meeting in April 1993, the three to four board seats which had been earmarked for external investors were reduced to one, while the other six board directorships were given to the factory's senior management.

As western press reported at the time, enterprises which were being privatised were subject to campaigns to "discourage" non-company shareholders from participating in the elections. The reasons given reflected common concerns at the time: external investors would not be familiar with the company's problems; their investors' livelihoods were not directly affected and they would not have workers' interests at heart; and they would have no interest in participating in board meetings.[18] This reflected widespread igno-

---

16 The Bank's Approach to 'Technical Assistance, Training and Advisory Services', 21 July 1991.
17 ITAR-TASS News Agency, Moscow, 4 June 1993 quoted in Appendix 5, OPER on 'Privatisation Advisory Programme in the Russian Federation', 18 August 1995.
18 *The Economist* reported growing complaints against highly-paid western consultants funded by EU's TACIS programme, who were criticised for spending more time on feasibility studies than on capital invest-

rance of how privatisation was meant to work, as well as the exploitation of workers' fears by insiders. This tendency was compounded by the failure to enforce regulations associated with the privatisation process and a lack of clarity over valuation stemming from unfamiliarity with proper accounting methods, inadequate audits, unharmonised company laws, weak company organisational structures and governance, and poor planning and business forecasting. The Bolshevik Biscuit Factory exhibited the hallmarks of this wider malaise.

This compendium of problems ultimately created barriers to the EBRD's participation in privatisation of some larger, more strategic and financially valuable enterprises. However, against the odds and despite its name, the Bolshevik Biscuit Factory was ultimately privatised. In late 1994, France's Groupe Danone acquired control of the company through the purchase of shares from investors in the 1992 privatisation and injected new equity. Three years later, the EBRD took around 30 per cent of the company (renamed AOOT Bolshevik), under a multi-product facility with Danone to support the infusion of new management and capital to assist the company's modernisation, product rationalisation and expansion. Danone later sold its stake to Kraft Foods (in 2007) as part of the divestment of its global biscuit business and the Bank eventually exited in 2010.

Some difficulties

The drive for rapid privatisation in Russia through the MPP suffered from two key problems. First, external voucher-holders were offered shares for "purchase" (that is, in exchange for free vouchers) whose real value could not be properly assessed, particularly by ordinary citizens. For small businesses with assets of limited value, such as shops, this was not a major concern. For larger companies, however, it was more important and many of these were significantly undervalued. Unlike in the earlier Czechoslovak mass privatisation programme, which started in November 1991, in Russia vouchers could be sold for cash. This created a liquid market on many newly-formed "commodity exchanges", allowing richer Russians to purchase extra vouchers. As a result, former managers gained control of many companies and

---

ments. It gave an example of how ex-communists created bureaucratic and other hurdles (such as stealing equipment) to prevent a foreign entrant's success. *The Economist*, 10 April 1993.

were subject to little external shareholder pressure. Well-connected owners were also able to exploit weak valuations and anomalies between domestic and world prices.

An Evaluation Report of the Bank's Privatisation Advisory Programme highlighted several deficiencies in newly privatised entities. Many featured unchanged management, administration and production structures. Inconsistencies in legal and regulatory frameworks adversely affected day-to-day operations, combined with deficiencies in law enforceability. The financial status of most of the entities was unclear and underdeveloped capital market structures and financial instruments weakened discipline. Although the study rated the EBRD's operation as "generally successful", it concluded:

> Post-privatisation problems are immense, accumulate steadily and hence contain considerable political, social and economic tensions that appear not to have been fully anticipated and appreciated...[19, 20]

Ukraine's Privatisation Advisory Programme

In mid-1992, shortly after Ukraine became a member of the EBRD, its government began formulating a privatisation policy. The Bank launched the Ukraine Privatisation Advisory Programme. This was designed to help the State Property Fund (SPF) prepare a privatisation strategy, develop appropriate procedures and carry out pilot privatisations. Consultants were employed using almost ECU 3 million technical cooperation funds supplied by the EC under TACIS and by Japan.

The political environment in Ukraine was challenging. A long public debate over privatisation resulted in a temporary moratorium on state asset sales following the election of Leonid Kuchma as President in July 1994.[21] Work with the SPF on the privatisation strategy also ran into cultural and legislative hurdles. The EBRD instead focused on a handful of pilot projects as a way of demonstrating the viability of privatisation in Ukraine.

The Bank's first mandate was for the sale of Ukrrichflot, a state-owned sea and river transportation company. Supported by Japanese funding, sev-

---

19 OPER on 'Privatisation Advisory Programme in the Russian Federation', 18 August 1995.
20 Post-privatisation issues are discussed in Chapter 5.
21 Yuri I. Yekhahurov, 'The Progress of Privatisation', *Eastern European Economics*, Vol. 38, No. 1, Jan–Feb. 2000.

eral consultant firms worked on the identification of assets, valuation issues, and legal complexities. Ukrrichflot was successfully privatised in 1994 and, after further work to improve accounting and control systems, the EBRD supported the company with a post-privatisation loan in 1995. The other main pilot privatisation was of Kiev Dairy No. 2, which was also sold in 1994. Of the four smaller companies piloted, two—Kispo, a sports shoe manufacturer, and Gostomel, a glass container company—were also successfully privatised.[22]

Poland's Mass Privatisation Programme

Other countries also found privatisation harder than anticipated. The Polish Mass Privatisation Programme (PMPP) was originally conceived in 1991, but was delayed for political and other reasons over the following three years. Alternative routes to privatisation, such as strategic trade sales and IPOs on the Warsaw Stock Exchange (WSE), also made little progress during this period. In late 1994, the government therefore sought the EBRD's help in launching the PMPP. By engaging with the Bank, the authorities hoped to overcome scepticism towards the programme. Former Deputy Prime Minister Leszek Balcerowicz noted "We wanted … to attract capital from abroad. We welcomed the support of projects by the EBRD. The main role was in helping with privatisation. Having the EBRD made it easier and helped legitimise the process."[23]

For its part, the EBRD believed that by making a series of equity investments during the early stage of the programme it would not only support the programme itself, but also provide a valuable demonstration effect to investors and a riposte to critics of privatisation.

In May 1995, the Board approved a US $50 million equity facility to support the PMPP, targeting up to eight investments of US $3 million to US $10 million under a delegated procedure to ensure a swift response to opportunities as they arose. The structure of the programme involved 15 National Investment Funds (NIFs)[24], each of which would hold a 33 per cent stake in 28 out of the total number of 420 companies to be privatised, with the remaining 14 NIFs holding a 2 per cent stake each. However, delays and im-

---

22   The EBRD subsequently provided a loan, part of which was convertible (and was converted) into equity, to Gostomel in 2002 and a further loan in 2004.
23   Interview with author, December 2019.
24   The Bank also provided a sovereign-guaranteed loan to assist with the start-up of the NIFs.

plementation problems meant that only three EBRD operations had been approved by 1997, the last of which involved a fully subscribed IPO on the Warsaw Stock Exchange in which the Bank did not take any shares (for additionality reasons), although it received a fee as a guarantor of the transaction.[25] The Bank's hoped-for demonstration impact through its equity facility was unfortunately not achieved in the case of the PMPP. More success was found in two other areas: participation case-by-case in large-scale privatisations, and developing a private equity industry in the region.[26]

4. Large-Scale Privatisations and Restructurings

Large-scale privatisations presented specific challenges. Many of the biggest enterprises were utilities or dominant players in their sector, which meant proper regulatory arrangements needed to be in place, in particular transparent tariff-setting rules and adequate social safety nets. The path from state ownership to a fully functioning private entity was not only complicated technically at the enterprise and sector level but also highly political. Many governments found the EBRD's sectoral knowledge, practical experience and independent viewpoint of great help in this process. But equally, the Bank often became caught between different factions seeking control of significant state assets.

A review of some examples of high-profile privatisations and restructurings in which the EBRD participated illustrates the range of issues and complexities involved, and the Bank's role in the process.

Industrial sectors

Among the most commercially attractive areas for early privatisation were large chemical and pharmaceutical companies and oil-refining businesses. Necessarily large to obtain economies of scale, these enterprises typically held a substantial share of the domestic market and were thus of interest to strategic investors. In these cases, the EBRD was able to play a significant

---

25 Lentex, a manufacturer of PVC floor coverings, non-woven interlinings and waddings, was considered by NIF as one of its best assets in its portfolio of companies and a natural choice for the first ever floatation of an MPP company on the WSE. Had it not been fully subscribed, the Bank would have taken an up to 12.5 per cent stake. Poland Mass Privatisation Equity Facility, 18 March 1997.
26 The Bank's influence in the development of private equity in the region is discussed in Chapter 5.

role in shaping the privatisation process and reassuring private, especially foreign, investors. Egis in Hungary, Pliva in Croatia, Sodi in Bulgaria and Petrom in Romania are examples of successful interventions by the Bank in industrial companies, while Kamaz in Russia illustrates some of the difficulties that could be encountered.

Egis, Hungary

The pharmaceutical industry had been regarded as a key sector for privatisation in Hungary due to the high local scientific skills base, but early attempts at asset sales proved unsuccessful. Shortly after the creation of the Hungarian privatisation agency AV Rt in 1992, the EBRD was asked by the authorities to evaluate a list of 10 companies that might help break the impasse. Egis was selected as the first target for a transaction likely to meet the Bank's criteria as well as furthering the AV Rt's objectives for privatisation and restructuring. As the first industrial privatisation undertaken by the EBRD with the AV Rt, it was a test of the Bank's ability to assist in the programme.

Egis was a leading pharmaceutical company in central and eastern Europe. In 1993, it employed around 3,500 workers, most of whom were highly skilled and earned wages some 60 per cent above the Hungarian average. It was owned by the Hungarian state (84 per cent), Egis's employees (around 10 per cent) and some municipalities (around 6 per cent).

The AV Rt was initially required by government decree to maintain a shareholding of 25 per cent plus one share in any privatised company. In the case of Egis's privatisation, a strategy was agreed whereby the EBRD would purchase a 30 per cent stake in the company and within a year the AV Rt would sell shares to private investors through a public offering on the Budapest Stock Exchange (BSE), or via private placement such that their holding would drop to 44 per cent or less. After that, the company would seek a strategic partner to further reduce the AV Rt's holding.

Like several other Hungarian pharmaceutical companies, Egis had been seeking to sell a majority stake to foreign investors for some time. The new strategy involving the EBRD envisaged a financial strengthening of the company to increase its attractiveness ahead of an IPO or trade sale, as well as the provision of support to Egis's management ahead of a public capital market appearance. It was hoped that the presence of the EBRD would reassure potential investors that the company was run on a commercial basis, while a successful transaction would provide a strong signal to the market on the diminishing level of state control in Hungary and on the growth possibilities of the pharmaceutical sector.

The EBRD subscribed for 30 per cent of Egis' shares in December 1993. Following the purchase, the Bank had three representatives on the board of Egis (two of whom were pharmaceutical experts), and was well-placed to help prepare the company for an IPO. The AV Rt held to its side of the bargain by selling a 30 per cent stake in the IPO on the BSE in July 1994. The transparent offering was very successful, helping to both legitimise the privatisation and develop the Hungarian stock market. It introduced a broad base of domestic and international shareholders to the company and set the course for the search for a strategic investor.

In 1995, the Privatisation Law was changed to allow the state to reduce its holdings to nil if required and Egis was removed from the list of companies where the state intended to keep a long-term holding. In August that year, the government sold its remaining shares to the UK's NatWest Securities Ltd via a competitive tender involving a number of financial institutions. The EBRD, NatWest Securities and Egis conducted a search for a strategic partner. After negotiations with several potential suitors, they settled on Servier, a French pharmaceutical company. In December 1995, the Bank sold its entire holding of Egis shares to Servier, which in parallel bought a 21 per cent share from NatWest Securities. Servier thereby acquired 51 per cent of Egis shares and control of the company. It also undertook to maintain Egis's research and development (R&D) function and the manufacture of generics and other pharmaceuticals in Hungary.

In this case, the role of the EBRD had been to provide a launch pad for a large industrial privatisation that had stalled. The Bank's intervention helped in two key ways. First, by strengthening Egis's financial credentials through a sizeable capital increase and preparing it for an IPO; and secondly, by finding a strong strategic investor, which reassured the authorities that the skilled jobs Egis offered would remain based in Hungary. Peter Reiniger, an EBRD banker, became Chairman of the Board of Egis in 1995 and led the successful work with the management team and their advisers in the search for a strategic investor. This took time, extensive market knowledge, good contacts and excellent negotiating skills. The transaction showed that the Bank could provide vital strategic links to foreign investors. The Evaluation Department rated the operation as "highly successful", its top accolade.

Pliva, Croatia

Another prime candidate for privatisation was Croatia's Pliva, the largest pharmaceutical firm in former Yugoslavia. Based in Zagreb, the company had around 5,600 employees, a strong R&D function and a diverse product line, while assets included the patent to azithromycin, an important antibiotic. By 1992, however, its export-based business had been badly affected by the dissolution of trading agreements within the former Comecon countries and the war in Yugoslavia.[27] State ownership hampered reform and Pliva was losing skilled professionals to private-sector companies.

In 1993, Pliva was restructured and became a joint stock company. At the same time, the Croatian government reduced its shareholding to 84 per cent and increased the holding of employees and other individuals from 11 to 16 per cent. The following year, the company was selected for privatisation and the government announced plans to achieve majority private ownership by the end of 1995. A wholesale review of the business had emphasised the need to transform Pliva from a production-driven organisation to a more demand-led, sales and marketing outfit and to rationalise the large product mix in order to concentrate on profitable products.[28] In mid-1995, the EBRD agreed to provide long-term debt (to be co-financed by a local bank) to construct a new production plant that would more than double the capacity for the production of azithromycin and a much larger convertible loan for a set of priority projects to help with restructuring ahead of privatisation.

The privatisation did not meet the timetable originally set but a highly successful IPO on the London and Zagreb Stock Exchanges took place in April 1996, reducing the government's holding to 42 per cent. Conversion of the EBRD's loan gave it an 11 per cent stake in the company. Following a series of sell-downs, the Bank finally exited in 2006 when a successful takeover bid was made for Pliva by Barr Pharmaceuticals, a US company.

The main objective of the operation had been to bring about Pliva's privatisation. This was very successfully achieved and was beneficial to the company. It was highly visible in Croatia and, through its London listing, created a central and eastern European "blue chip" stock. This gave credibility to

---

27 Sales fell by 30 per cent between 1990 and 1992.
28 The review was supported by a study by consultants Arthur D. Little commissioned by the EBRD.

Croatia's first Eurobond issuances in 1997.[29] The operation also boosted the profile and liquidity of the Zagreb Stock Exchange.

Sodi, Bulgaria

Poor economic performance, a lack of political support and public distrust had delayed structural reforms in the early 1990s in Bulgaria. By the middle of the decade, however, the legal and licencing framework for privatisation had been completed and in 1996 the state privatisation agency launched the first round of mass-voucher privatisation. At the same time, the government put up for sale 15 major industrial companies including Sodi, owner of one of the world's largest synthetic soda ash plants.

Following three rounds of bidding, a tender to acquire 60 per cent of Sodi was won in early 1997 by Solvay, a multinational chemical and pharmaceutical company headquartered in Belgium. The deal, which was signed in April 1997, was the first cash privatisation in Bulgaria. The remaining stakes were to be sold to employees (15 per cent) and through mass (voucher) privatisation (25 per cent). Solvay had sought a strategic tie-up with Şişecam, a Turkish regional soda ash producer and global supplier of glass[30], in part to defray the costs of the acquisition but also to secure an off-take and access to a new market. Key for both companies was the prospect of expanding production capacity without having to invest in a new plant. For Sodi and the Bulgarian government, the deal meant an influx of FDI and expertise, as well as an opportunity for renewed export growth after the earlier collapse in demand from former Comecon countries.[31]

The competitive advantages of Sodi were clear: low production costs and good proximity to core markets. It was one of the lowest-cost producers in Europe and its regional competitors were either too remote (Russia), or still state-owned and in dire need of modernisation (Romania). However, Solvay had paid a significant cash sum for their share of the company and needed to invest in new lines of production. The EBRD refinanced around a quarter of the acquisition costs in exchange for a 14.5 per cent stake in Sodi. The key

---

29 The pace of follow-on privatisations of large state-owned companies was relatively slow however.
30 Soda ash is an important ingredient in the manufacture of glass.
31 Anti-dumping duties had been imposed on cheaper US natural soda ash since 1984, and similarly against eastern European (including Bulgarian) soda ash. The lifting of duties meant easier access for soda ash from Bulgaria to the European market but also, because it was cost-competitive, made it a valuable source against the increased competition now coming from the USA.

advantage of bringing the Bank into the transaction, however, was to mitigate country and political risks, which were perceived to be very high. The presence of the EBRD was also helpful to the government in legitimising the process and reassuring the public that the sale was fair.

This was an example of the third-party "honest broker" role that the EBRD played in a number of similar cases. It was not a matter of adding expertise, or seeking a turnaround and major improvement in performance[32], but rather of helping to bring together two sides with different goals and expectations.

Petrom, Romania

The government of Romania first tried to privatise Petrom, central and eastern Europe's largest oil company, in 2000. The attempt failed, and the government, which in 2001 owned 93 per cent of the enterprise through the ministry of industry and resources, realised that significant organisational restructuring and financial improvements were needed before a successful privatisation could take place. A revised strategy based on targeting strategic investors was devised in 2002 with the help of an international privatisation adviser, in consultation with the EBRD and the World Bank.

In addition to support with the pre-privatisation programme, the EBRD organised a pre-privatisation syndicated loan of US $150 million, of which US $50 million was lent by the EBRD itself and US $100 million was provided by a mix of commercial and development banks. The World Bank, meanwhile, provided a structural adjustment loan for Romania in 2002[33], which also supported privatisation of state-owned banks and industrial enterprises.

In 2004, the Romanian government privatised Petrom by selling a large stake alongside a simultaneous capital increase to enable the selected strategic investor, the Austrian integrated oil and gas group OMV, to reach a 51 per cent majority holding. In the process, the EBRD converted its outstanding pre-privatisation loan into a small equity stake of around 2 per cent, which it finally divested in 2013.

The privatisation of the largest oil company in the region to a strategic investor was a landmark transaction and attracted a number of reputable

---

32 High returns were not expected from this operation and the IRR was fairly modest.
33 http://documents.worldbank.org/curated/en/932801468095991902/Romania-Second-Private-Sector-Adjustment-Loan-Project.

international oil and gas investors. The process was successful and generated wide international interest and praise for its transparent and market-based approach. The operation also helped create a new financial product for the region in the form of a non-sovereign unsecured long-term syndicated loan. In this case, the EBRD had worked alongside the World Bank and the IMF to develop sector conditions conducive to greater commercial success for Petrom, enhanced by the Bank's financial and operational restructuring and corporate governance interventions.

Kamaz, Russian Federation

The EBRD's privatisation and restructuring work was not always successful. Large-scale failures included an attempted restructuring of Kamaz in Russia.[34]

Kamaz was one of the largest truck and diesel engine manufacturers in the world, a strong brand name in its market segment and one of the first industrial companies to be privatised in Russia. Like many Russian enterprises of the time, it managed the manufacturing process from beginning to end, in this case from foundry and forging to stamping, engine production and assembly. Based in the semi-autonomous Republic of Tatarstan, its 18 plants covered 22 square miles. The company was a major local employer with 130,000 direct or indirect employees.

Kamaz was owned by the governments of Tatarstan and Russia, its employees and management, and other shareholders including a consortium, the Kamaz International Management Company (KIMCO), led by US leveraged buyout specialist KKR. KIMCO provided strategic advice by acting as a "shadow management" and had options to buy nearly half the company.

The deterioration in the Russian economy had already hit Kamaz hard when, in 1993, a fire destroyed its uninsured engine production facility. By 1995, falling sales and the cost of a partial restoration had created a liquidity crisis. At this point, the EBRD offered significant loan funding to help the company restructure its finances, rebuild production and increase the level of private ownership.

---

34   A comprehensive review of the Bank's experience in privatisations of large state-owned enterprises, including other failures such as Slovnaft in the Slovak Republic, can be found in 'Insights into the Privatisation of Large State-Owned Enterprises', S. Slavova, EBRD, December 2016.

The project was approved by the Board but several Directors voiced concerns at the risks involved, given the enterprise's lack of profitability, the absence of a western strategic industrial investor, and the working capital and refinancing nature of the loan. Their scepticism proved justified. The restructuring plan failed and Kamaz's debts rose to US $1 billion within two years. The company became insolvent and defaulted on its debt obligations, including the EBRD's loan, in August 1997. The Tatarstan government tried and failed to take control and conflicts arose with the lenders. After lengthy negotiations, a financial restructuring plan involving the conversion of debt into equity was effected in 2001, giving the EBRD a 6.8 per cent shareholding. By then, however, the state along with the financial asset management company Troika Dialog had majority ownership and control.[35] Although the Bank recovered some money when it sold its equity stake to Troika Dialog in 2005, the investment was effectively written off.

Kamaz had been a painful experience for the EBRD. It learned that a highly reputable financial management company was insufficient to tackle deep-rooted industrial problems, particularly in a "one company" town and was not the right vehicle to lead a turnaround requiring a strong commitment over a long period. Nonetheless, armed with knowledge from this experience the Bank did not completely turn its back on the company. In 2010, another strategic investor, Daimler AG, was found. The EBRD invested alongside Daimler to facilitate its entry into the Russian (and CIS) market and re-doubled efforts to finally implement the environmental and social mitigation measures identified back in 1995.[36]

Regulated sectors: Utilities

For some regulated sectors, such as power and energy, privatisation was inextricably linked to sector and regulatory reform, and therefore took some time to emerge in the EBRD's countries of operations. Others were more easily transferred to the private sector. In telecommunications, for example, the move away from fixed-line technology towards mobile and broadband communications reduced the state's ability to maintain control over the sector. Commercial niches were also found for former state transport entities

---

35   Troika Dialog was acquired by Sberbank, Russia's state-owned and largest bank, in 2011.
36   https://www.ebrd.com/work-with-us/projects/psd/kamaz-equity.html.

through unbundling segments such as rail rolling stock and shipping operations. The Bank played a leading role in many of these transactions.

Telecoms

HTC, Hungary

One of the Bank's earliest privatisation projects involved Matav, the Hungarian Telecommunications Company (HTC). The company was fully owned by the AV Rt, which intended to sell a 30 per cent stake plus management control to a strategic investor while retaining 50 per cent plus one share. The remaining 20 per cent was to go to employees and municipalities in exchange for land used for HTC facilities.

The EBRD had already provided HTC with a large sovereign-guaranteed loan in 1992 following the separation of telecommunications from Hungary's postal and broadcasting services. Bankers concluded, however, that equity rather than more debt was required for HTC's next stage of development. This chimed with the government's plans for privatisation, since considerable further investment was required to improve the digital backbone network and quality of service.

As HTC was then a monopolistic supplier, reforms to the sector were needed prior to privatisation and had been taking place in parallel. A new Telecommunications Law establishing the liberalisation of the sector was enacted in late 1992 and a Policy Statement on the new regulatory framework, including open tendering for licenses and other concessions, was issued in 1993.

Bids were invited from pre-qualified candidates by the AV Rt, with the aim of completing the sale by the end of 1993 and the EBRD subscribed to convertible preference shares in November of that year.

The AV Rt sold its 30 per cent stake in December 1993 to a strategic investor, MagyarCom, a consortium comprising Deutsche Telecom and Ameritech. The EBRD received close to 2 per cent of ordinary shares on conversion. MagyarCom's holding subsequently increased to 67 per cent in 1995, when the AV Rt reduced its stake to just over 25 per cent.

The privatisation of HTC was the largest in central and eastern Europe at the time. Careful early preparation by the EBRD, IFC, World Bank and EIB, working alongside the authorities to prepare the sector and the company, was key to its success. A transparent political commitment had been given ahead of the tender and a reasonable degree of "regulatory certainty" had been signalled to investors through improvements in the legal and regulatory environment. Further, in the first phase, the proceeds of privatisation benefitted the utility.

The deal again demonstrated the EBRD's catalytic role in helping the authorities prepare for privatisation. The Bank's earlier loan helped HTC improve performance in the first phase of its restructuring and modernisation programme, while the presence of two commercially oriented IFIs as shareholders prior to the privatisation gave confidence to potential investors and helped the company access international credit markets.

Power sector

One of the most important areas of Bank activity on the infrastructure side was in providing finance for the development of the power and energy sector. A reliable supply of power is vital to any business operation and essential for industrial production. In Soviet times, large vertically integrated state entities fully controlled by ministries were in charge of power and energy supply. The technologies used were largely outdated owing to the weak incentives to invest in and maintain plant and equipment. Equally significant problems lay in the efficiency of supply of energy, its pricing and use for political ends.

In many countries of operations, the energy sector was a tool by which subsidies and favours could be doled out as part of the system of political control. With several countries in possession of plentiful supplies of the natural resources used in electricity generation (coal, gas and hydropower), the influence of the state in the sector was extensive and hard to change. Citizens had become accustomed to cheap electricity and gas and businesses were able to survive despite using inappropriate and inefficient technologies. For CIS countries without indigenous supplies of energy resources, dependence on external suppliers—especially Russia—also limited power-sector reform. Even in the more advanced economies, private-sector participation took time to build up and required considerable changes to markets and regulation.

There were a few privatisation opportunities in the power sector in the early 1990s in more advanced countries such as the Czech Republic, Hungary and Poland. However, in these cases private finance was forthcoming so the EBRD lacked additionality and did not engage. Outside central Europe, moves towards private-sector involvement were slow, hampered by the severe and persistent economic downturn in much of the region during the 1990s, which interrupted reform progress and reduced the demand for energy.[37]

Against this backdrop, the Bank was more closely involved in trying to create markets and in providing long-term debt facilities to state electricity utilities for rehabilitation, repair and improvements to power-generation plants and transmission systems. Environmental and energy-efficiency objectives were also important, as was strengthening implementation capacity. Significant involvement with the private sector did not come until the 2000s. However, the EBRD played a valuable role in supporting the unbundling of the sector and the introduction of wholesale, capacity and day-ahead markets and other market mechanisms.

ZSE, Slovak Republic

One of the first successful cases of privatisation support by the Bank in the power sector was for ZSE, one of three regional electricity distribution companies owned by the Slovak Republic. In November 2001, the Slovak government tendered 49 per cent of its shares in each of the three companies (at the time the state was legally required to maintain a majority stake). The EBRD had been advising the Slovak government on the privatisation process and was invited to offer support to interested bidders. Three international energy firms—France's EDF and Germany's RWE and E.ON—bought stakes. E.ON took up the Bank's offer and the EBRD paid for a 9 per cent stake in ZSE.[38] The Bank's additionality lay in providing a safeguard for E.ON against political and regulatory risks in Slovakia. The Evaluation Department assessed the performance of the project as "successful". The partial privatisation of these assets helped the turnaround process and the presence of experienced private-sector strategic investors led in due course to significant improvements in the Slovak electricity sector.

---

37 Electricity consumption in Russia fell by 25 per cent between 1991 and 1998, p.2. 'Market Liberalisation and decarbonisation of the Russian Electricity Industry', A. Khokhlov and Y. Melnikov, Oxford Institute for Energy Studies, May 2018, p. 2.
38 The form of the EBRD's investment was a "portage equity investment", which meant upside gains were limited (allowing E.ON to benefit in the event of success), but with a put option to minimise the risks to the Bank.

RAO UES, OGK-5, Russia

The power sector in Russia was owned and controlled by the Ministry of Power and Electrification (Minenergo) until RAO UES (Unified Energy System of Russia) was established as a state holding company and sold as part of the voucher privatisation programme in 1992. The state retained a 52 per cent holding, with the majority state-owned Gazprom owning 12 per cent and the remaining shares mainly distributed among various Russian groups. RAO UES was effectively a state monopoly[39] that controlled two-thirds of generating capacity and over 95 per cent of transmission and distribution.

Liberalisation and privatisation of the power sector was a relatively novel concept in the 1990s. Falling demand for energy, a very poor financial performance by RAO UES and a fractious political environment stalled reform until Anatoly Chubais became Chairman of the Board of RAO UES in 1998. That prompted a push for the break-up of the state electricity monopoly and market reform, and the path towards privatisation began in earnest. An energy-sector reform plan was approved by the early 2000s and was followed by the unbundling of RAO UES which separated generation from transmission and distribution. The Bank engaged with the authorities and established a restructuring working group, which was made open to minority shareholders, and signed a memorandum of understanding (MoU) with RAO UES. In 2001, the EBRD provided a €100 million loan to help RAO UES restructure its balance sheet and finance priority investments in transmission and despatch in preparation for privatisation. The Bank's involvement helped to convince investors that reform was fully under way. In the following years, several of the six unbundled large generation companies (OGKs) were privatised, as well as the 14 regional generating companies (TGKs).

The EBRD supported one of the first OGK sales by participating in a public offering of its shares in October 2006. OGK-5 was one of the main thermal wholesale generating companies with installed capacity of some 8.7 GW, equivalent to 4 per cent of total generating capacity in Russia. The Bank participated to assist the public offering ahead of the sale of a further 25 per cent of the company to a strategic investor. The proceeds of the public offering were allocated to priority investment needs, in particular the rehabilitation of OGK-5's four power stations. The public offering reduced RAO

---

39 There were four regions that it did not control, while nuclear power was managed by Rosatom.

UES's stake in the company to around 75 per cent. The Bank's investment was intended to send a signal to the market about the privatisation process, as well as offering the opportunity to improve corporate governance standards and protect the interests of minority shareholders.

In June 2007, Italian energy company ENEL won an open tender for a 25 per cent plus one share stake in OGK-5, in the first deal in Russia to involve a major international energy utility. ENEL subsequently increased its stake to 37 per cent and triggered a mandatory buyout offer, as a result of which it obtained clear majority control. In April 2008, the EBRD bought around 4 per cent of OGK-5's shares from ENEL as part of a strategic partnership designed to enhance the firm's political clout in an evolving but uncertain market. From the Bank's perspective, the main objective was to establish a strong presence in the sector from which to advocate for liberalisation and reform.

As a conclusion of the Bank's policy dialogue on the Russian power sector throughout the 2000s, the privatisation of OGK-5 was a significant success. The goal of initiating transparent, commercially-driven privatisation of the generating companies was achieved. Between 2006 and 2008, 19 thermal generating companies were sold and RAO UES was replaced by independent market participants. However, the only other foreign strategic investors to obtain shares in the generating companies were E.ON and Fortum of Finland, and subsequent reversals in energy sector policy led to the resumption of state control of the majority of generating capacity in Russia.[40, 41]

The Bank's close involvement in the Russian power sector in the 2000s through a large number of debt transactions and technical assistance for regulatory reform, as well as its support for privatisation and entry of strong strategic investors, was largely successful. According to an Evaluation Department report in 2010: "The Bank was closely involved [in the process of reform] and played a pivotal role, unmatched by any other IFI, both with high level institutional and policy dialogue and with targeted investments at critical junctures in the evolution of the reform."[42]

---

40 Gazprom and InterRAO (majority-owned by state entities) own significant stakes in many of the OGKs and TGKs.
41 Further information, including on privatisation of electricity distribution companies in Bulgaria and Romania, can be found in Stefka Slavova, 'Privatising Electricity Companies; Insights from the EBRD Experience', EBRD, December 2016.
42 Country Level Evaluation: Russia Power and Energy Sector Special Study, July 2010. See also Special Study Power and Energy Sector Review, October 2011.

Banking sector

The Bank's ability to act as an intermediary between governments or privatisation agencies and foreign strategic investors proved particularly useful in the banking sector, especially in the late 1990s and early 2000s when mainly European banks acquired subsidiaries in central Europe in anticipation of European Union (EU) expansion. In the earlier part of the 1990s, the privatisation of banks had been hampered by high non-performing loan (NPL) levels, opposition from vested interests (mainly managers and employees), weak appetite for foreign ownership, and a lack of clarity on sectoral laws and regulations. There were also significant gaps in management capabilities and corporate governance after a long period of directed lending. It took some time before it was accepted that an infusion of capital and expertise was needed to underpin banking systems in central and eastern Europe and that an influx of foreign investors was the best way to achieve this goal. The Bank's advice and support during this period, along with particularly the IFC, was an important influence on the eventual approach towards privatisation in many countries.

BCR, Romania

The EBRD's support for the privatisation of Banca Comercială Română (BCR) was one of the most successful transactions in the Bank's history and an example of how it turned round the fortunes of a company by taking a calculated risk.

BCR had been established in 1990 and took on the National Bank of Romania's portfolio of corporate loans as a two-tier banking system was created. During the 1990s, while under state ownership, it expanded its range of customers and acquired the foreign trade activities of Bancorex, the Romanian Bank for Foreign Trade.

In 2002, the Government of Romania tried to privatise BCR by selling more than 50 per cent of shares to a strategic investor. Two rounds of tendering failed, however, in part because of the significant investment required. The authorities wanted to continue with the privatisation and revised their approach. They decided to sell 25 per cent plus two shares directly, and equally, to the EBRD and the IFC as a first step, to be followed by a sale of 8 per cent to employees. The sale to a strategic investor was set to be completed by the end of 2006. The process was helped by setting the privatisation as a milestone for completion of Romania's IMF programme and as a condition of a World Bank Public Sector Assistance Loan (PSAL 2).

As part of the shareholders' agreement with the two IFIs, BCR undertook an institution-building plan (IBP) to prepare for privatisation. This laid the foundations for improvements in corporate governance, organisational restructuring, risk management, and IT and accounting systems. The EBRD and IFC were each represented on the supervisory board and other committees, enabling the two institutions to exert strong oversight over developments, including providing a transparent distinction between shareholder rights and management powers. Changes in the decision-making structure of BCR were also influenced by a new banking law in line with EU directives.

The operation was a good example of an investment made in a context of considerable uncertainty and designed to facilitate the transfer of a major state entity to the private sector. It was backed by strong conditionality and prepared BCR for private ownership by reviewing and upgrading its key business and control functions through a tailored plan. It signalled confidence in the Romanian banking sector ahead of the country's accession to the EU.

The EBRD signed a share purchase agreement in late 2003 and subscribed for its 12.5 per cent holding in June 2004. It was a major investment for the Bank. The sale to a strategic investor began in May 2005 with a competitive tender for the shares owned by the state, the EBRD and IFC. Several reputable financial institutions put forward binding offers for the almost 62 per cent holding on offer. After narrowing down to two final bids, the stake was sold to Erste Bank of Austria. The EBRD exited by signing a sale agreement in late 2005 and received payment in October 2006.

Bank Pekao, Poland

Group Pekao was formed in 1996 by the merger of Bank Pekao, historically Poland's foreign currency savings bank, and three regional banks. The merger was undertaken as part of the consolidation of the banking sector and as a prelude to privatisation. In June 1998, the Polish government decided to start the privatisation process by selling 15 per cent of Pekao via an IPO on the Warsaw Stock Exchange (WSE). The bank was in need of restructuring and capital support before privatisation, so the EBRD agreed to make a large US $100 million equity investment as part of a capital increase at the same time as the public offering. The authorities committed to sell a further

35 per cent of stock to a strategic investor acceptable to the Bank at a later stage. The EBRD thus acquired just over 5 per cent of Pekao in September 1998 and obtained seats on the Supervisory Council.[43] After the IPO and sale to a strategic investor, the State Treasury was expected to hold less than 30 per cent of Pekao.[44]

In June 1999, a consortium of UniCredit and Allianz purchased a controlling stake in Pekao of 50 per cent and 2 per cent of shares respectively. As part of the deal, the strategic investors agreed to inject Zl 1 billion of capital within two years. The EBRD subscribed to a capital increase in October 2000 and purchased additional shares from Bank Handlowy, lifting the Bank's stake to more than 6.5 per cent. The EBRD sold most of its shares via an accelerated book-build in late 2003 and a block trade in mid-2005, finally exiting in mid-2009.[45] By the end of that year, the state treasury's holding was less than 1 per cent and UniCredit, with an almost 60 per cent stake, was in full control of the bank.

The EBRD successfully assisted Pekao in the privatisation process by providing senior capital to improve leverage pre-IPO, gave confidence to investors and to the share placement on the WSE and helped to attract quality strategic investors in the full privatisation. It also contributed to strengthening management and corporate governance in Pekao, providing a demonstration effect to other Polish banks.

CSOB, Czech Republic

Československá Obchodní Banka (CSOB) was originally the CSFR's foreign trade bank. On the dissolution of the CSFR in January 1993, it was divided between the Czech and Slovak states, with around 66 per cent going to Czech government agencies. By the time privatisation was initiated in 1998, it was the fourth-largest Czech bank by assets and the largest by equity.

The EBRD was asked to participate in the privatisation by purchasing shares held by the National Bank of Slovakia (NBS). The Bank was seen as a neutral body that could facilitate resolution of political differences between the Czech and Slovak governments, and help assuage the political concerns of potential investors. However, elections in 1998 and a breakdown in com-

---

43 At the start of the process the 11 member Supervisory Council comprised nine state representatives and two academics, and was chaired by the Treasury Secretary of State.
44 Other main owners were management and employees at 15 per cent.
45 The investment returns for the Bank were above average.

munications between the two governments meant the transaction did not proceed. Instead, the Czech government offered their holding in a privatisation tender in June 1999, which resulted in a sale to KBC, a Belgian bank. The IFC also took a stake of just over 4 per cent via a sale of treasury shares.

Prior to the offer, the NBS announced plans to sell its share too. The EBRD agreed to participate in the process and did so alongside KBC. By the end of 1999, the Bank had acquired around 7.5 per cent of CSOB. In due course, CSOB was fully privatised and the EBRD sold its shares to KBC in 2006.

Having been closely involved from the start of the privatisation process, the Bank was able to offer comfort to all sides as the privatisation moved forward. It helped normalise CSOB's governance structure and resolve a long-standing ownership dispute between the Czech and Slovak national banks, removed concerns over the Slovak government's involvement in the capital of the bank, and enabled a foreign sponsor to improve the quality of banking services and products in both the Czech and Slovak Republics.

PBZ, Croatia

In December 1999, the Croatian government began the process of privatising Privredna Banka Zagreb (PBZ), the country's second-largest lender, through its bank rehabilitation agency (DAB). A 66.3 per cent stake was sold to Banca Commerciale Italiana (BCI), which shortly afterwards merged with Banca Intesa to form IntesaBCI (IBCI). IBCI had the option of buying the remaining 25 per cent from the government but both sides asked the EBRD to participate. Policymakers were keen for the Bank to support the privatisation and the development of the Croatian capital market, while IBCI saw value in the Bank's expertise in bank restructuring and privatisation and its knowledge of the Croatian financial sector.

The sale of the government stake in 2002 completed the privatisation, with 15 per cent going to the EBRD and 10 per cent to IBCI, and triggered a mandatory take-over offer by IBCI for the 8.7 per cent of minority shares. The EBRD agreed with IBCI to take shares tendered up to 7 per cent. The Bank thus obtained in due course a near 21 per cent holding in PBZ. Taking into account a participation in a capital increase in 2006, this was one of the largest equity investments by the Bank.[46]

---

46 The EBRD invested a total of €167 million.

As part of the deal, IBCI agreed to sell some of its shares in an IPO within six years, allowing PBZ to raise its profile and tap into a new investor base. It also provided a route for the Bank to exit. However, the IPO did not happen and in 2015 the EBRD exercised a put option to exit, leaving Intesa Sanpaolo (the successor to IBCI) holding almost the entire stock.

The Bank's involvement supported the full privatisation of PBZ to a strategic investor and helped with its restructuring from a bank serving state-owned companies to a universal bank targeting retail, private corporate and SME borrowers. It also led to an improvement in corporate governance standards.

5. Lessons from the Bank's Experience of Privatisation and Restructuring

At the start of its existence the EBRD embraced privatisation with enthusiasm, tempered by the knowledge that the business and policy environment in which it was to take place was challenging and volatile. Privatisation was already a sensitive subject in the West, with political parties often differing on its merits, and this division was reflected in the East. While the Bank's Board covered the full spectrum of these views, it was nonetheless supportive of privatisation as a key means to help build the private sector in former command economies.

The need for open, transparent processes in privatisation was clear to all members and the EBRD made efforts to promote this perspective. The Bank was, however, cautious and selective in its approach to privatisation. There was little appetite for involvement in small-scale asset sales, which in most cases progressed rapidly without the need for external intervention. Their size, prospective profitability and costs of assessment also made them unappealing for the EBRD.

Larger privatisations were more appropriate but had their own problems. The inefficiency of large state-owned enterprises meant future profits could be made but extracting value required effective managers, significant investment and potentially large-scale redundancies. Many countries had no tradition of or training for modern management practices, while weak financial sectors and even weaker capital markets meant a dearth of long-term financing to support what the EBRD might be able to provide. Strong commitments to privatisation by the authorities were needed to overcome the political risks associated with layoffs and other turnaround measures. Here, political changes frequently slowed the evolution of privatisation. The effectiveness of competition, the legal underpinnings of privatisation and the fluency of regulation and related factors such as tariff-setting also varied considerably, making investments something of a lottery without careful prior scrutiny. Rudimentary accounting methods and valuation procedures added to the uncertainties.

The Bank therefore began by advising on privatisation processes and sales rather than by making multiple large investments. This also had the advantage of giving bankers a better understanding of the preparedness and financial soundness of companies to be sold, the attitudes of political parties towards privatisation, the political economy of sales and their methods, and the evolving legal and regulatory landscape. When the Bank did participate in privatisations, which began to take off from the late 1990s, it was well-prepared and made relatively few significant losses from its investments in privatised companies.

When it came to restructurings, the EBRD found more could be achieved once enterprises were under private-sector control. The Bank was successful in helping privatised companies improve performance by raising management standards as well as providing financing for much-needed capital expenditure programmes through equity injections and long-term loans. Persistent efforts to improve corporate governance within privatised enterprises by bringing to bear clearer lines of responsibilities between owners and managers and greater scrutiny of performance also paid off. This function was enhanced where the Bank had sufficient stakes in a business to enable its nominee director to be appointed to company boards and committees.

Restructuring state-controlled companies in the hope of subsequent privatisation was more difficult, largely due to the power of vested interests. Where the political authorities were clearly committed to a path for privatisation, the Bank's interventions were more successful. Sometimes initial barriers to privatisation were overcome when authorities recognised that the cost of maintaining inefficient state enterprises was unsustainable, particularly when fiscal pressures were prevalent. In other cases, notably in the utilities sector, investments aimed at restructuring state enterprises proved valuable where undertaken in conjunction with policy dialogue to improve regulation. In the case of banks, efforts to provision for or write off bad loans and strengthen capital adequacy towards international standards were additionally valuable. Such restructuring efforts helped companies become more realistic targets for strategic investors.

Of great importance was the EBRD's role as a reliable intermediary between private sponsors looking to invest in new markets and public authorities seeking to sell assets to improve the performance of their economies and raise fiscal revenues. As an "honest broker" between parties with different cultural and business backgrounds, as an investor taking "skin in the game" and demonstrating the viability of the deal, and as a source of political comfort to investors, the Bank was able to act as a conduit for successful privatisation as well as enhance its status as a long-term financier. By supporting a number of high-profile western industrial and financial investors making their first forays into central and eastern Europe, the EBRD helped to connect East and West, fostering trade and investment linkages and the transfer of skills.

Chapter 7

Developing Local Services

Introduction

The early post-communist years in central and eastern Europe saw a dramatic change in the role of the state. One element countries in the region had in common was a desire on the part of their populations for greater local autonomy and democratisation. This meant having a say not only in who governed the country but also in decisions over local services. As a result, all countries began a process of devolution of economic and social decision-making. While many aspects of the vertical structures of the communist economic system were slow to be dismantled, the move towards decentralisation was rapid. The everyday life of citizens depended on local services—the supply of housing, heat, water and wastewater, local transport—that were inefficiently managed from the centre. It made sense to shift the burden towards municipalities and local districts.

The EBRD was established with a political as well as an economic mandate. The notion of multiparty democracy and pluralism applied to the local and regional level as well as the central level. In this respect, the Bank had a valid interest in supporting the democratic changes that were emerging across the region. The wider point, however, was an economic and institutional one relating to improvements in living standards. Simply put, the inefficiencies of central state control meant there were immediate gains to be made by organising the provision of local services in a better fashion. Decades of underinvestment could begin to be rectified under a properly functioning municipal utilities system.

The Bank saw the opportunity to bring in new structures and western expertise to help remedy the situation and it developed an important model early on to meet these needs. The groundbreaking work that followed resulted in the EBRD becoming the front runner among IFIs to develop and implement sub-sovereign lending operations, a novel non-sovereign product that proved to be highly resilient and well regarded by municipalities in the years ahead. This chapter looks at the background to these developments.

1. Early Efforts on Decentralisation in Central and Eastern Europe

In Europe in the 1980s, interest grew in devolution and methods of enhancing local democratisation. Near the end of the decade, in September 1988, the Council of Europe's European Charter of Local Self-Government, which defined the concept of local autonomous self-government as a fundamental right, came into force. This was the first international treaty to lay down the principle of subsidiarity, which allows for the transfer of power to the level closest to the citizen. Articles 2 and 3 of the Charter required that local self-government be recognised in domestic legislation and that local governments manage public affairs under their own responsibility in the interests of the local population as exercised by councils or assemblies, whose members should be freely elected by secret ballot under universal suffrage. This legitimised a transfer of competences to local communities and with it some transfer of financial resources. The Charter established a number of safeguards to protect the rights of local communities, for example that local authority boundaries could not be changed without agreement of the community and that the supervision of the activities of local authorities should be defined by law, with the possibility of recourse to a court.[1]

When Hungary became the first former Eastern Bloc country to join the Council of Europe at the end of 1990, many western European countries had recently ratified the treaty and several others were in the process of doing so. The Charter's principles became important in guiding governmental reforms and the establishment of devolved legal and administrative structures in central and eastern Europe at the time. Poland, which became a member of the Council of Europe in November 1991, became the first former socialist country to ratify the treaty (in November

---

[1] 'The Charter of Local Self-Government', Congress of Local and Regional Authorities of the Council of Europe, October 2015.

1993) followed by Hungary in March 1994. By the time Russia ratified the agreement in February 1996, all the EBRD's countries of operations in the Baltics and central, south-eastern and eastern Europe had already done so, with the exception of Belarus and the country which at the time had the provisional name of "Former Yugoslav Republic of Macedonia" (now North Macedonia).

Laws introducing decentralisation and local autonomy were set in motion across the region between 1990 and 1992, with local elections held in several central European countries during this time. However, the extent of devolution varied considerably, as did the financing arrangements. In most cases, greater local responsibility with elected representation was introduced, and with it a weakening of central administration branches at local level as elected municipal councils became empowered. At the same time, there was a lack of provision at the regional level, where elections were not introduced, and the number of local authorities multiplied substantially in some countries. The result was a large increase in the number of local government units and considerable fragmentation spatially and institutionally. This resulted in a loss of coordination and diseconomies of scale.

Fragmentation was particularly dramatic in the Czech and Slovak Republics, where respectively some 4,000 and 3,000 elected local authorities were created to represent 10 million and five million citizens. In Hungary, more than 3,000 local authorities were created for a population of 10 million.[2] With an average of 2,500 to 3,000 citizens to each local authority (less than 2,000 in the Slovak Republic), efficiency was clearly limited, particularly in small rural or suburban contexts where some level of aggregation was necessary to provide services and deal with environmental problems effectively. Similarly, district governments with a high degree of autonomy could frustrate infrastructure improvement and urban development in major cities within their jurisdiction.

Further complications arose over the question of financial support. There was a wide range of arrangements in sharing finance between central and local governments across the region. Poland, for example, relied heavily on local resources (around 40 per cent of funding, with another 40 per cent from shared taxes), whereas some 85 per cent of local funds in the Czech Republic came from transfers from the central government.

---

2   Figures quoted in 'Municipal Development Operations Policy Background Paper', September 1992.

There were many arguments about the appropriate balance between raising local revenues and sharing centrally collected taxes, as well as over the degree of transfers for social and other reasons. But the bigger problem for most countries in the early transition years was the poor state of the economy, with high inflation rates and chronic fiscal problems. This limited the scope and willingness to transfer resources from the centre, and difficulties in raising and collecting taxes made changes to this situation unlikely. The only realistic solutions were to increase efficiency in the use of existing resources and charge users more realistic rates for services. In other words, more market-oriented solutions. It was in this context that a role for the EBRD would emerge.

A combination of factors led the Bank to develop a sub-sovereign lending model built around carefully constructed economic and legal checks and balances that applied to the relevant parties: municipalities, their utilities and central authorities. The result was that the EBRD early on introduced a unique approach to the financing of local services in the context of the wider IFI landscape.

2. The Bank's Role

The thrust of the Bank's approach was to support the effective decentralisation of the funding and provision of municipal services and infrastructure. Alongside the privatisation of industry and production capital, the decentralisation of public services was regarded as one of the defining characteristics of the transition process. Decentralisation could improve the efficiency of public-resource allocation and bring investment decisions closer to the needs and preferences of users of local services, as well as supporting democratisation processes.

The price signal that acted as the mechanism for the efficient matching of needs with resources in a competitive market could not immediately be adopted to solve the problems facing municipalities, particularly given the complex institutional structures surrounding the financing and provision of services and the importance of meeting social needs. But the adoption of more sustainable funding mechanisms and regulatory procedures, improved institutional structures and new ways of financing would allow price signals and a more transparent financial performance to penetrate the system and improve its efficiency and investment capacity. The EBRD saw the promotion of "capital efficiency, commercialisation of municipal services, involvement of the private sector in the funding and provision of public services, municipal credit strengthening, and accountability towards local constituencies" at the heart of its municipal operations.[3]

The Bank's engagement with the authorities in its countries of operations and its presence on the ground in major cities meant it was quickly able to establish a dialogue with local and national governments and with other organisations involved in urban and municipal development matters. A number of EBRD development bankers came from the World Bank and had experience of dealing with local infrastructure issues in other regions. The EBRD also believed it could add value by supporting the development of municipal infrastructure as an important element in the evolution of the local private sector—both by making it easier for small enterprises to grow and thrive but also potentially by creating direct business opportunities in the provision of services—and in environmental improvement.

Where substantial progress in establishing decentralised local government institutional and financial frameworks was feasible, the aim was to assist municipalities' financing, particularly by increasing their borrowing capacity. This could lead to project preparation and specific investment projects in large and small municipalities financed on a sovereign, limited recourse or even non-recourse basis. In the many cases where local government financial frameworks were ill-defined, the EBRD undertook to help with design issues, such as effective grant allocation and analysis of local taxes and tax bases, while indicating potential investment projects in major cities once financing issues were settled. Elsewhere, the scope for action beyond general policy advice was limited.

In September 1992, after surveying the state of municipal affairs as far as it could, management put forward an operations policy paper on municipal development which described how the EBRD could improve the situation.[4] The underlying analysis showed significant municipal infrastructure gaps existed in terms of rehabilitation and extension, as well as a need for improvements in efficiency.

---

[3] 'Policy Issues Arising from the St. Petersburg Municipal Support Project', 13 June 1997.
[4] 'Municipal Development Operations Policy', 4 September 1992.

A number of options were presented on the Bank's role. Its involvement could "directly support on-going political, administrative and economic decentralisation and the transition away from central planning". With urbanisation rates in most CEE countries above 50 per cent, a focus on the efficiency of urban centres could provide employment opportunities and help "national and local economic development". The transfer of assets from central to local levels of government presented privatisation and efficiency opportunities as well as in developing new instruments of "public-private partnership". The EBRD also believed it could help with infrastructure requirements necessary to support private and entrepreneurial initiative, promote environmental improvement and contribute to a "more democratic and participatory society" in line with its political mandate.[5]

The Bank was in a strong position to address local government and urban development given the mix of private sector and public management issues and the close long-term partnerships involved. Responding to local needs in a visible way also presented a good opportunity to build a strong image for the EBRD across its countries of operations.

Immediate obstacles to progress

There were nonetheless a large number of obstacles to overcome, even in areas where central-local relationships were close to being settled. For one thing, there were imbalances between large and small municipalities and cities, with many of those most in need being remote, both geographically and in understanding, from the main centres.

More problematic, however, was a lack of clarity over responsibilities and financial arrangements, as well as weak capabilities in carrying them out. Assets had been transferred to local authorities, but there was limited capacity and often only moderate appetite on the part of local managers to take over deteriorating assets and the responsibilities of underperforming service providers. Many assets involved high maintenance costs and were not revenue-earning, yet equivalent budgetary transfers had not been made to cover the gaps. The determination of the share of proceeds of sales was also often unclear, and in some instances proceedings were complicated by

---

[5] 'Municipal Development Operations Policy', 1992.

issues of restitution. Implementation of local autonomy was also hindered by legislative gaps and the lack of clear financial frameworks.

Local governments faced financial pressure as their ability to raise revenues was low and lagging behind the transfer of responsibilities and expenditure functions. The squeeze on operating budgets left little room for investment and the limited creditworthiness of municipalities ruled out borrowing, which was in any case difficult given the underdevelopment of local financial markets. In contrast to some other sectors, FDI was not forthcoming since revenue potential was based on local currency rather than foreign exchange. Risks were perceived by foreign investors as being exceptionally high except in the most advanced and creditworthy cities. Lastly, a lack of stability in local government teams as regular elections resulted in changes of personnel, as well as the difficulties experienced by staff in adjusting to the introduction of new concepts and demands under the revised institutional arrangements, made investment a difficult and sporadic job.

In this context, the EBRD saw its role as developing its infrastructure lending in parallel with capacity-building activities, particularly to enhance local management capacity and authorities' ability to enforce an appropriate regulatory and tariff framework. Here it could act as a catalyst for investment and provide technical assistance, for example in training local elected officials and managers in budgeting, project preparation and financial management. It also had the capacity to serve as a promoter of private-sector involvement and a broker of international experience in municipal services, with the aim of creating specific showcase operations to strengthen local authorities and generate interest in new approaches.

The Bank chose to focus its main initial operational activities on project preparation and the development of environmental infrastructure, particularly water supply and wastewater treatment, the rehabilitation and financing of urban transport in capitals and large cities, and district-heating supplies. Given the fluidity of the situation relating to the development of local autonomy in many countries, the EBRD did not expect to achieve high investment volumes quickly. It believed that most of its early activities would be in central Europe and those parts of eastern Europe where legal, administrative and financial arrangements at local level were more advanced.

3. The Main Starting Point: Romania's Municipal Utilities Development Programme

The EBRD's operational programme gradually took off. In the first four years after the adoption of the municipal operations policy, only five projects were formally approved. However, by mid-1995 it was clear that municipal authorities were emerging as an important client group and that a pipeline of viable projects was building. This prompted the creation of a municipal and environment infrastructure (MEI) team within the EBRD. Early projects in Estonia and particularly in Romania were influential in its development. The Romanian Municipal Utilities Development Programme (MUDP) is a good illustration of the way in which the EBRD established a successful mode of sub-sovereign operations in this field.

The Ceausescu legacy for Romanian infrastructure was especially disastrous. In contrast to other Eastern Bloc countries, he had insisted throughout the 1980s that Romania fully repay its foreign debts. As a result, investment in public services and infrastructure had been severely curtailed, causing major damage to the economy and people's livelihoods. The post-communist authorities were therefore desperate to find ways to show genuine progress in raising living standards for their citizens.

Legal reforms in Romania in 1991 had provided for the devolution of infrastructure and municipal services to the local level, including autonomy of financial management and expenditure decisions. This had not, however, been accompanied by a commensurate transfer of financial and human resources. In 1993 the Romanian government asked the EBRD to help with the preparation of an investment programme in 12 municipalities as part of its efforts to reform public services and their financing. The Bank welcomed the opportunity to help and to develop municipal business but it was a risky area and one which the finance department was wary of. The focus of activities under the MUDP—which was described as a pilot—thus became narrowed down to water supply, sewerage and wastewater treatment services provided by water utilities. The requirements of the programme suggested a two-stage approach was most appropriate. A first stage covering five cities[6] could help inform the second stage for the remaining seven municipalities. If successful, the initiative could be extended further.

---

6   Brasov, Craiova, Iasi, Timişoara and Tirgu Mures.

There was no doubt that the system needed a radical overhaul. The quality and supply of water in Romania was inadequate. Supply was provided for only part of the day in many places and was below the government's own health standards.[7] Pressure was so low in distribution systems that consumers living on the top floors of apartment blocks frequently received no services at all. Wastewater collection and treatment was well below adequate effluent standards and sewer collectors leaking into water distribution networks presented serious health hazards. Estimates of water losses ranged from 40 to 60 per cent of water produced.

The poor quality of water services and wastewater treatment, which were deteriorating in many places, was mostly due to lack of investment and chronic long-term underspending on asset maintenance. Expenditure on municipal services and infrastructure investments had reached a low of US$ 3 per capita in 1992 against an estimated requirement of US$ 75 to US$ 100 per capita to prevent further decline.[8] At the same time there was considerable inefficiency in the provision of services with a need to improve operational and financial performance and generate revenues. Cost-recovery and a move towards credit and loan-financed capital spending were required to move away from the unsustainable practice of funding investment via government grants. Centralisation had put more emphasis on the technical or engineering aspects of investments rather than their financial viability. Inefficient pricing, which in economic terms was too low, combined with an absence of effective metering and significant leakage in water distribution networks meant water consumption was two to three times higher than in western Europe.

Although provision was now decentralised, the central government retained control over financial operations and tariffs. The approval of capital expenditures also remained centralised, meaning that investment by water utilities effectively depended on government capital subsidies. In 1993, for example, it was estimated that some 70 per cent of capital expenditure on local services and infrastructure was funded from the central budget. The government saw the EBRD as a useful ally in helping to implement what was at

---

7   One of the first bankers to arrive in Romania to negotiate the programme in Timișoara had to find the way to his hotel on the first evening through streets in complete darkness. In the morning, he took a shower before leaving for a meeting with the Mayor only to find after having soaped himself and shampooed his hair that the water stopped. In those days bankers had to be resourceful!
8   Figures quoted in 'Romania: Municipal Utilities Development Programme', 18 November 1994.

that point a radical shake-up of the sector and providing a model that could be used in other cities.

An audit commissioned by the Bank confirmed major issues with financial and accounting practices and, more generally, in operational practices and the lack of investment. Financial planning, programming and budgeting were rudimentary. There was no proper economic appraisal of investment projects, and internal cash generation for asset rehabilitation and renewal was virtually non-existent. Overstaffing, frequent breakdowns requiring yet more additional staff and reliance on cheap electricity—when power prices were likely to rise towards world market levels—resulted in cost inefficiencies. Meanwhile, low tariffs and charges based on a flat per capita rate rather than on the amount consumed meant that revenues barely met operating costs.

The MUDP, which involved a loan of US$ 28 million, was approved by the Board in November 1994 and signed the following year. It involved three components: investments in rehabilitation and improvements to the asset base; programmes to enhance the operational and financial performance of the five water utilities; and technical assistance to strengthen management capacities at central and local levels. Investments were chosen on the basis of their impact on net cash flows and on the ability of water utilities to service their debts. The main investments in water were in meter installations, upgrading of pipes and pumping equipment, while elsewhere critical parts of the sewer network and wastewater treatment plants were upgraded.

To improve productivity and efficiency, the EBRD appointed a team of operational and financial managers from a privatised UK water utility to work closely with the senior management of the MUDP. Specific measures, actions and timetables using performance indicators and project milestones were set to improve performance and move towards cost-recovery levels and corporatisation of the utilities. Each party to the programme—the municipalities, the utilities and the ministries of finance and of public works—was involved before agreement was reached. The novelty for Romania was a series of agreements to incentivise each party to work together towards the collective goal of a more efficient and productive water sector better designed to meet consumers' needs.

The EBRD's finance was a sovereign loan to the government of Romania. This was on-lent via a subsidiary loan to the utilities by the ministry of finance which, together with central government grants and own local funds via the municipalities, financed the investments. The utilities were required to repay the interest and principal on the subsidiary loan through operational income from user charges. The municipalities guaranteed the subsidiary loans.

As well as the loan agreement between Romania and the EBRD there were project agreements between the Bank and each of the five utilities and their municipalities. These agreements defined the obligations on performance and set conditionalities such as achievements to be made before the loan could become effective, before procurement could be carried out and before loan disbursements.

The loan agreement between the EBRD and Romania required the borrower to ensure the municipalities and the water utilities complied with the terms of the project agreements. This was important as the ministry of finance had to approve the tariff increases. The agreement also provided for the suspension of disbursements should a municipality or water utility fail to meet its obligations.

Disbursements of the Bank's loan to the ministry of finance and from there to the water utilities depended on the actual implementation of tariff increases and satisfactory progress in performance and revenue targets. Further financing and a second programme also depended on performance.

The final part of the contractual structure concerned the subsidiary loans, where a subsidiary loan agreement (SLA) tied together the ministry of finance as lender, the utilities as borrowers and the municipalities as guarantors. It included financial and project covenants and implementation arrangements.

Agreement was reached to facilitate compliance with debt obligations by defining steps by which tariff increases in real terms—of between 80 per cent and 150 per cent over 16 months—would be made (to enable the SLA debt to be serviced) and a set of actions by the utilities to reduce operating costs. The SLA stipulated that the municipality would indemnify the water utility for any loss of revenue arising from the local authority failing to approve tariff increases in a timely manner and as agreed in the project agreements.

The set of measures represented a considerable tightening and advance on previous procedures. It anticipated future arrangements across the MEI sector whereby public service contract (PSCs) and project support agreements (PSAs) became commonplace tools for effecting reforms and sector progress using EBRD finance and legal expertise. PSCs and PSAs will be explored in more detail later in this chapter.

The rationale behind the Bank's approach was not only to begin to address the investment gap in water and wastewater service provision, but also to restructure the financing and management of municipal utilities to improve their efficiency and bring them towards self-financing. Higher operational and financial performance meant that in future, instead of being secured by state guarantee, loans could be made directly by the Bank to municipalities that were sufficiently creditworthy and, in due course, by commercial lenders in the market.

The EBRD was uniquely placed to effect direct lending to municipalities and their utilities, and transformation in the creditworthiness of municipal service enterprises and municipalities represented a major contribution to the transition process. Where successful, municipalities would be able to assume their responsibilities and be accountable to local electorates rather than central bureaucracies, and utilities would provide quality services to local consumers.

The municipal finance system introduced in Romania with the Bank's help proved to be significant for the five cities involved. After the initial success it was followed a few years later by a second programme covering a further 10 cities.[9] The MUDP introduced the notion of long-term debt finance for the provision of municipal services, which was a new concept at both central and local levels. It encouraged discipline in investment decisions and financial management, full cost-recovery (including the capital costs of the loan)—despite local resistance to charging the economic costs of services—and the introduction of demand management through metering and economic pricing to reduce overconsumption of water. Asset maintenance improved and development reserves were established in each utility. Meanwhile, their corporatisation progressed towards self-financing capacity through the improvement of operational and financial performance.

A mid-term review by the Evaluation Department, which was undertaken as preparations were being made under the second programme, concluded that the pilot MUDP had begun very successfully:

---

9   'Romania: Municipal Utilities Development Programme II', 27 June 1997.

The Project (in close conjunction with the preparation work for MUDP II) can be assessed as already having influenced changes in the legal, fiscal and administrative procedures in Romania regarding local government finances, provision of municipal services and ownership of municipal property, assets and land.[10]

The report also praised other aspects of the project:

There is clear evidence that the Project has already impacted extensively on the water utilities themselves, in all aspects of their financial and operating performance. Project design effectively institutionalised their corporatisation ... The Project (in conjunction with MUDP II) appears to have affected changing perceptions and operating practices of water and wastewater provision across the entire country ... and is clearly much appreciated by the Romanian authorities at central and local levels.[11]

MUDP II followed the principles adopted in MUDP I. Given the scale of problems to be addressed, it was clear that local governments and municipal utilities could not be forever dependent on IFI financing. There was thus increased emphasis on strengthening their underlying creditworthiness and rationalising the provision of credit by the central government. The EBRD pushed for a Romanian bank to act as administrator of government loans. With technical support to raise its capacity, Banca Comercială Română was given the task of appraising the creditworthiness of municipal borrowers. However, the small size and poor skills of most municipalities (around 70 per cent had less than 5,000 inhabitants), the large number of regional and local utilities (almost 1,000 in the water and wastewater sector) and limited regulatory arrangements meant commercial borrowing arrangements were slow to materialise.

In fact, domestic currency loans to local governments were non-existent before the 2000s but annual new lending rose from RON 3.6 million (US$ 1.2 million) in 2001 to RON 1.4 billion by 2006. Domestic currency bonds issued by local authorities were similarly limited in 2001 (RON 2.3 million) and rose, though only to a very low level, to RON 33 million of new issuance

---

10 'Mid-Term Review of Municipal Utilities Development Programme, Romania', March 1999, p. 6.
11 Ibid., p. 7, p. 10.

in 2006. Bonds issued by utilities were rare even at the later date. Most loan and bond deals that emerged came from bigger municipalities.[12]

4. Developing the Municipal Sector

A number of water and wastewater projects followed the Romanian programme, particularly in the Baltic States. Similar multi-city programmes were introduced across a number of cities in Croatia[13] and Estonia.[14] A major effort was also made to support the municipality of St. Petersburg, with two projects signed in 1997. Gradually the efforts to support decentralisation and improve local services began to gain traction, with around seven projects a year being initiated in the second half of the 1990s, of which well over half were in the water sector.[15]

Initial experience was that the financial and operational improvement programmes (FOPIPs) worked well. Corporate partnerships encouraged by the Bank through the twinning of water companies with experienced western water utilities led to improved practices, and compliance with tariff increases was good. Actual project implementation was more difficult. This reflected the lack of experience of local authorities with IFI procurement procedures, the fragmented nature of rehabilitation projects (which involved a multitude of sub-projects) and more general weaknesses in preparation capacity.

Small and challenging projects compared with other sectors

Most projects were small. The average size was around €16 million and around half involved less than €10 million of EBRD finance. This was a mixed blessing. On the one hand, it meant that the Bank was directly reaching the local level and a wide range of populations across regions and countries, bringing in new practices from the bottom up and providing unique

---

12 Figures from statistical annex of 'Romania Municipal Finance Policy Note', World Bank Report 38357-RO, 3 June 2008.
13 'Croatia Municipal Environmental Infrastructure Investment Programme', 28 October 1996. This covered six cities on the Adriatic coast which were important for the tourism industry.
14 'Estonia: Small Municipalities Environment Project', 5 June 1995.
15 About one quarter were district-heating projects.

(for an IFI) services. On the other hand, it was very labour-intensive, often involving long trips with poor communications and due diligence on many unknown parties. It was partly for these reasons that the majority of activity during the early phase of the Bank's municipal work was in bigger cities and in more advanced transition countries.

The planning and implementation stages of projects often took a long time due to changes of national or local governments, revised budgets, land disputes, permit and tendering delays, and many other case-specific problems, with delays in one area feeding delays elsewhere. These issues were particularly acute early on, when implementation capacity was especially weak among local authority clients. As a result disbursements were very slow, with well over half of the portfolio undrawn in 2000. This improved over time as familiarity with the processes increased, supported by the rise in the number of Bank projects, related policy dialogue and technical help, and more robust systems of local budgetary finance.

Sub-sovereign lending

The EBRD's work with municipalities evolved over time. At the beginning, projects consisted almost entirely of sovereign or sovereign-guaranteed loans. This was less than ideal for a bank designed to promote private-sector participation, but at the time offered the only viable way of supporting decentralisation. Despite overarching pressures from the Board relating to the Bank's 60:40 private-public portfolio requirement, in the early years it was clear that the transition goal of supporting local autonomy and service-efficiency was of paramount importance. This was emphasised by taking account of realistic financial returns to the Bank once the full resource costs were included. Although returns were low in absolute terms, or possibly negative in some instances, the principle of "sound banking" could be maintained since sovereign lending was remunerated at a fixed margin to any country regardless of risk.

The Bank's strategy in the sector, however, was to take steps towards sub-sovereign lending, commercialisation and private-sector involvement. These materialised in due course. Although the number of sovereign-guaranteed deals remained broadly steady at around three or four a year, their proportion in the total dropped significantly as direct loans to municipalities and municipal companies without a sovereign guarantee (and eventually to private entities operating in the sector) increased. From more than 70 per cent by number in the portfolio at end-1996, the proportion of sovereign-guaranteed projects fell below 40 per cent by the end of 2003 and to around 10 to 15 per cent of new deals. In value terms, the decline was even faster.

Moving away from sovereign and sovereign-guaranteed lending, however, changed the risk profile and introduced the need for risk-based pricing consistent with the Bank's approach to non-sovereign loans elsewhere. While a portfolio approach afforded some room for manoeuvre in relation to particular projects of high transition and strategic importance, projects needed to be soundly financed and properly priced for risk. Persuading municipalities and their utilities to take on what they perceived as expensive loans was a challenge. It could be mitigated, however, by bringing down the risk profile of projects through improvements to financial and operational performance, as well as clear and precise contracts between the relevant parties. Working with reform-minded mayors who wanted to effect change in their communities also helped. This was why the EBRD's unique structuring and partnership approach made such an important contribution to altering municipal finance.

Municipal projects in less advanced countries and smaller municipalities

The EBRD moved away from sovereign-guaranteed lending as the introduction of PSCs and PSAs and the commercialisation of municipal companies moved forward. This happened first in the EU accession countries. The initiative got under way in major cities, such as Belgrade in Serbia and Sofia in Bulgaria, but also included Baku in Azerbaijan, Chisinau in Moldova and Tashkent in Uzbekistan and, as mentioned earlier, St. Petersburg in Russia. In successive MEI strategies the Bank also made efforts to increase the number of projects in Russia and the early and intermediate transition countries.

The range of municipalities receiving EBRD advice and finance began to expand fairly rapidly. In Russia, projects were signed as far afield as Surgut in Western Siberia (2002), Arkhangelsk (2003), Komi (2004) and Sakha (Yakutia, 2006). Early recipients among early transition countries (ETCs) also included Tajikistan (2004) and Georgia (2005), while intermediate countries included Ukraine (1999), FYR Macedonia (now North Macedonia) (2000) and Albania (2006).

The move was consistent with wider efforts by the Bank to move "south and east" and tackle more difficult transition challenges. Difficulties with ETC projects were legion: distance, unfamiliarity with processes and standards, the need for extensive dialogue, very limited availability of local finance, non-creditworthy municipalities and utilities, substantially longer project-development times and serious questions of affordability over tariff increases and how to compensate losers. The Bank's local presence helped, however, as the bankers in situ were able to make the case for pursuing municipal deals on their doorstep and had a good understanding of local political conditions and regulatory issues.

As the EBRD developed its MEI business, more effort was also made to reach smaller municipalities. This became a specific objective in the 2004 MEI operations policy[16] and fitted with the more general intention at the time to tackle harder transition tasks. One solution was to work with local banks to persuade them to provide long-term facilities to more stable local municipalities and public utilities. Another approach to the issue was to develop regional and multi-municipality project structures.

Wholesale financing through domestic financial intermediaries could be successful and achieve economies of scale where banks had a clear strategic focus on the municipal market. It was dependent, however, on those institutions knowing how to choose and monitor projects effectively. Where this did not happen, it imposed resource burdens on the EBRD to assist with monitoring. This was often the case in the early stages of implementation.[17]

Opportunities to work with financial intermediaries in the sector turned out to be fairly small.[18] The EBRD did nonetheless reach many small municipalities via direct transactions, either individually or through multi-municipality facilities. Some frameworks, like the Municipal Environmental Loan Facility (MELF), involved lending to water companies with a local authority guarantee. This allowed the Bank to finance eight companies in second-tier cities in Romania. Direct projects in Serbia were signed from 2002 on in Novi Sad, Nis, Kragujevac and Subotica, whose populations ranged

---

16 'Municipal and Environmental Infrastructure Operations Policy', 20 October 2004, p. 9.
17 'Municipal and Environmental Infrastructure Operations Policy Review' (2010), Evaluation Department, Appendix 5, p. 15, 20, 32.
18 One example was a risk-sharing arrangement with Dexia Banka Slovensco in 2004. The EBRD participated in loans made by Dexia to small and medium-sized municipalities (populations below 100,000) and municipal companies in Slovakia, bearing the risk of non-payment by municipalities.

from 100,000 to 200,000. Projects in Croatia covered Rijeka, Pula and Dubrovnik, where populations were smaller (50,000 to 150,000). In Montenegro, water-supply projects were successfully implemented in coastal towns with even smaller populations. Projects in solid waste management and water services lent themselves more easily to economies of scale through the connection of several small towns in a region. For example, a project to create the first regional operating company providing water and wastewater services along a river basin in Romania in 2005 brought together a set of small water companies covering one city and seven towns with very small populations to invest in metering and water pipes in the counties of Cluj and Salaj.[19]

Demonstration effects: the case of Tajikistan

Another approach that proved effective involved demonstrating the feasibility of the EBRD's approach in a more prominent city and then applying it to smaller centres. Improvements to tariff-setting processes, which in many public services were driven by national authorities with whom the EBRD engaged in policy dialogue, also gave impetus to municipalities to pursue follow-through investments involving the EBRD. In the earliest days the Bank focused on the capitals of central European countries before branching out. The same approach was taken in Russia. By the 2000s, with national-local government arrangements largely settled across the region and with the need for improvements to local services especially acute in ETCs, the Bank sought to tackle municipality-service reform in more difficult countries and regions. A good example of how it worked is provided by Tajikistan.

In 2004, an operation to improve the water supply in Khujand (population 160,000) in northern Tajikistan was launched as a demonstration project. The initiative was then extended to three much smaller cities in southern Tajikistan: Danghara, Kulob and Bokhtar (formerly known as Kurgan-Tube), with populations of 21,000 to 85,000. Subsequently, several other Tajik cities received EBRD investments targeted at improving water supplies. Such projects were already complex in terms of their components—technical aspects, procurement, tariffs, PSCs and corporatisation—and had to be conducted in difficult environments. This required strong resident office input, especially in these relatively inaccessible parts of the world.

---

19 'Romania: Regional Operating Company (ROC) Apa Somes', 2005.

Affordability

Municipal projects in the poorer countries had a significant impact on transition and in improving living standards through better access to clean water, lower pollution and better services in such areas as transport, solid waste management and energy supply. But conducting projects in poorer areas raised the issue of affordability, particularly when increases in tariffs were necessary to improve the financial performance of utilities supplying local services. In countries such as Tajikistan there were two dimensions to affordability that required donor support.

First, loans needed to be large enough to ensure that improvements to services were significant and effective. Tangible results also helped to encourage people to pay the fees (non-payments of municipal tariffs reached very high levels in some cases), which helped utility companies move towards financial sustainability. However, many smaller cities, especially at the start of a programme, had very little borrowing capacity. In the case of highly indebted countries with limited earning capacity, such as Tajikistan, non-concessional loans as normally provided by the EBRD via sovereign-guaranteed finance were also restricted under IMF programme rules on international borrowing and required proportionately large grant co-financing.[20]

Second, the EBRD assessed the impact of tariff increases against specific indicators of affordability. These were based on the proportion of household income paid for municipal services and were considered for all household deciles, although they were mostly relevant to the most vulnerable groups.

For these two reasons, many projects in the municipal sector in less developed regions required a significant share of grants. Grant funding helped make investments more affordable for municipalities and minimised the impact on poorer households of tariff increases ("communal tariffs" on services like electricity or water were often heavily subsidised, resulting in large financial losses for utility companies). The share of grants in the cost of a project could reach 50 per cent or even more. Donor funds have remained an invaluable tool for municipal financing in the poorer countries.

---

20 In such cases a grant element of at least 35 per cent was required. See 'IDA Countries and Non-Concessional Debt', 19 June 2006, World Bank 36563. SECO (Swiss) and SIDA (Swedish) funds were important contributors to these needs.

As projects in smaller municipalities began to grow, particularly in ETCs—something the Board encouraged—so too did the need for donor finance. For the EBRD, these projects were not especially profitable. While their value to the population was unquestionable, low profitability could be an issue, as the Bank was still expected to show a return on each investment. This issue was resolved when a "portfolio approach"—the balancing of risk, returns and transition impact across the Bank's portfolio—was introduced in 1999.

5. Core Sectors

Despite some efforts to extend municipal and environmental lending to include areas such as housing and business parks, the portfolio during this period remained dominated by water supply and wastewater treatment projects, with some operations in district heating, urban transport and solid waste management. The number of urban transport projects rose quickly from the 2000s, in part due to growing urban populations and increasing congestion and pollution. The following section describes the key challenges in each sub-sector.

Water and wastewater treatment

By the end of the first decade of transition, more than half of the municipal projects financed by the EBRD were in the water and wastewater treatment sector. The Bank cooperated in the development of projects at the early stages of preparation and helped to structure them in order to reduce operating costs and enhance cashflow generation. This also supported commercialisation through strengthened public service contracts, cost-recovery tariffs, improved collections, better accounting practices and preparation for outsourcing for future private-sector participation. Policy dialogue was focused on regulatory reform, and the Bank's legal transition team was heavily involved in work related to concessions and frameworks for private financing, such as PPP legislation in Poland.

The main parameters of decentralisation had largely been achieved during the 1990s (other than in some ETCs). Some public utilities had been privatised. Nonetheless there was further to go. In Bulgaria, for example, the state remained the majority owner in 29 out of 49 water enterprises in the early 2000s.²¹ Moreover, the quality of water and wastewater treatment services was still far from adequate.

Water and wastewater treatment services were mostly organised throughout the region by municipal departments or municipal enterprises. Private-sector involvement emerged mainly in advanced countries such as the Czech Republic, Hungary and Poland and in a few major cities such as Bucharest and Sofia. Regulatory arrangements were mostly in the hands of local or regional authorities, who set tariffs on the basis of advice by the water enterprises. This created conflicts of interest between cities in their role as regulators and as shareholders in the companies. Independent regulators were a long time in coming and service contracts between the local government and operators were of variable quality. There was also a need to set service targets and monitor performance.

Pricing reform was much needed in ETCs, where tariffs typically covered between 30 per cent and 80 per cent of operating costs, with the remaining funding provided from the public purse. In Georgia and Armenia, the figure was as low as 15 per cent in 2002. Collection was also poor and took a long time, averaging 10 to 14 months in Ukraine and Moldova, compared with one to three months in OECD and Baltic states.²² In an EBRD survey of utility companies in Russia in 2002, no investment was reported during the previous five years. Cross-subsidisation between industrial and domestic consumers was common, although attempts were made to phase it out. Metering at that time was a long way behind OECD levels of near 100 per cent, with fewer than 30 per cent of the population having meters in Russia, Moldova and Ukraine.²³

The quality of services varied across the region. By the early 2000s, the proportion of the population with a water connection in some parts of the region was still well below western norms. Rural communities in Ukraine and Georgia were particularly poorly served, with just 26 per cent and 35 per cent connected, respectively. In Romania, only 58 per cent had connectivity. Sewerage was not much better and wastewater treatment coverage was notably low in the Balkans and Lithuania. In the CIS-7 (Armenia, Azerbaijan, Belarus, Georgia, the Kyrgyz Republic, Moldova and Tajikistan), it

---

21 'Municipal and Environmental Infrastructure Operations Policy', 2004, Annex 1, p. 6.
22 'Urban Water Reform in Eastern Europe, Caucasus and Central Asia', OECD, 2003, p. 39.
23 'Municipal and Environmental Infrastructure Operations Policy', 2004, Annex 1, p. 7.

was estimated that 30 per cent of the population was drinking water below adequate standards. A National Environmental Action Plan for Moldova concluded that between 950 and 1,850 premature deaths arose annually from unsafe drinking water. Moreover, road accident rates in the region were vastly higher than in OECD countries, with between two and 10 accidents per network kilometre in the CIS-7 against 0.2 to 0.3 per kilometre in OECD countries.[24]

International attention on the water sector was boosted in 2000 with the publication of the Millennium Development Goals (MDGs), which included a commitment to halve the proportion of people without sustainable access to safe drinking water by 2015. At the Johannesburg Earth Summit of 2002[25] this was extended to basic sanitation.[26] A report led by Camdessus, the former IMF managing director, for the World Water Forum in Kyoto 2003[27] recommended that donors and MDBs raise investment volumes and make use of financing instruments, notably sub-sovereign and private-sector financing, to improve water governance. The EBRD's work was already in keeping with these aims and unlike other MDBs it had no limitation on lending without a sovereign guarantee. The Bank already had considerable experience with financing at the sub-sovereign level without such guarantees, as well as in lending to the private sector.

Urban transport

Urbanisation in the EBRD's countries of operations, while lower than in the EU, was significant and rising. Nearly half of Poland's population at the turn of the millennium lived in 250 towns and cities. In Russia, urbanisation was even higher at 73 per cent. Car ownership also increased rapidly after the end of communism, growing by more than 10 per cent a year throughout the 1990s in many cities including Prague, Brno and Budapest. This led to traffic congestion and the need for off-street parking. Congestion not only increased air and noise pollution, but also lengthened travel times and the costs of doing business.

---

24 'Municipal and Environmental Infrastructure Operations Policy', 2004, Annex 1, p. 3.
25 UN World Summit on Sustainable Development, Johannesburg, 2002.
26 UN Millennium Development Goal 7c.
27 'Financing Water for All', report of the World Panel on Financing Water Infrastructure, M. Camdessus and J. Winpenny, March 2003.

With rapid increases in urban motorisation came falls in usage of public transport. With countries starting from a very high base, however, passenger trips by public transport remained significant. In the early 2000s, the proportion of journeys by public transport in Bucharest at 51 per cent and Prague at 48 per cent were still far higher than in Berlin and Paris (28 per cent and 19 per cent, respectively).[28]

These trends put increasing pressures on cities and municipalities to find solutions to urban transport problems. With its deep knowledge of urban systems and access to authorities and public transport utilities in OECD countries, the EBRD was a natural partner to help. The MEI portfolio began to show a higher share of urban transport projects from around 2001.

Most cities lacked coherent and sustainable transport strategies and frequent use of "pay-as-you-go" budgetary arrangements detracted from multi-annual planning and long-term funding methods for investment. Maintenance depots had mostly not been modernised since the 1960s and 1970s and ticketing systems were still based on cash and coin. Poor procurement practices added to costs and, while decentralisation had taken place, financial arrangements took a long time to follow suit. Managements had very limited business orientation and focused on technical aspects of transport rather than the quality of customer service, while large numbers of low-paid staff had little incentive to drive improvements. Governments took decisions on investment (but not maintenance) and defined a wide range of low or non-paying customers (up to 50 categories in some cases, including war heroes, teachers and so forth), but without directly compensating transport operators. This had a deleterious effect on the financial situation of operators, leading to a degradation of service quality.

In a number of countries, the drop in public funding following the collapse of central planning resulted in low-quality, low-capacity minibuses (known in the former USSR countries as "marshrutkas") filling the gap. This commercialisation of transport witnessed self-employed entrepreneurs building a market for minibus services, helped in part by weak reg-

---

28 'Municipal and Environmental Infrastructure Operations Policy', 2004, Annex 2, p. 2. Eurostat figures for passenger kilometres travelled by transport mode (passenger cars, trains, motor coaches, buses and trolley buses) in 2001 show more than twice the proportion of journeys by trains, coaches and buses (public transport) in several central European countries compared with their main EU counterparts: the proportion in Romania, the Czech Republic, Poland, Slovakia, Hungary and Bulgaria with Czech Republic and Romania ranged from 28–39 per cent, while for the UK, France, Germany and Italy the range was 12–17 per cent.

ulation. Although this was a valid response to customers' needs—especially for those unable to afford car ownership—it brought with it problems of uncontrolled development, as well as health and safety issues. Rather than a "competition for the market" in public transport ridership using a system of well-regulated concession contracts, competition consisted of minibus services literally racing to pick up passengers in an uncontrolled manner.

Commercialisation of standard bus services, trams and trolleybuses occurred relatively slowly, even in advanced transition economies such as Hungary and Poland. To some extent this also reflected long-standing social attitudes to the private sector and its profit-orientation encroaching on important social services. In Russia, for example, public transport in the early 2000s was provided by some 350 municipal and public operators versus more than 1,500 private and 35,000 self-employed operators, yet public enterprises reportedly continued to hold around 85 per cent of the market.[29]

The EBRD's interventions were designed to transform the transport entities into modern companies with proper business plans and accounts, appropriate PSCs and tariffs (with payment for non-economic services), full responsibility for investment decisions, auditing and recognisable corporate governance. Twinning arrangements with experienced operating companies with good practices helped to shift attitudes and behaviour towards western market norms.

Solid waste management

The handling of waste arising from consumption (municipal waste) and industrial production (mining, metallurgy, fertilisers, glass, cement, etc.) was a concern in all EBRD countries of operations, particularly when it involved hazardous materials such as household solvents, discarded medicines, asbestos, spent oils and other contaminating substances. Waste management—which involved storage, collection, transport, processing and final disposal—was important most of all from an environmental and sustainable development point of view. This was relevant to the EBRD's mandate, and the Bank was well placed to help improve arrangements by which waste disposal was managed. The modernisation of the sector accelerated in countries seeking EU accession by their adoption and transposition of EU

---

29 'Municipal and Environmental Infrastructure Operations Policy', 2004, Annex 2, pp. 9–10.

Directives under the Waste Acquis, in particular the Landfill Directive introduced in 1999.

Landfill was the major disposal for waste in countries of operations, amounting to some 84 per cent of the total in 1999. This was far higher than in western Europe, where comparable figures were 45 per cent in 2000. The difference was largely accounted for by incineration, energy recovery and recycling. The latter—which involved organics (food waste, etc.), paper and cardboard, glass, metals, plastics and textiles—was low in central and eastern Europe at 9 per cent, compared with 26 per cent in western Europe.[30] Waste-to-heat recovery arrangements were similarly a long way behind major European countries.

Some landfills took both municipal and industrial waste, including in several cases co-disposal of industrial and hazardous waste. Most sites were overloaded and not designed or operated to meet modern public health standards. Only a very small number of landfill sites met EU standards, for example. In less advanced transition countries such as Russia and other CIS countries there was no system for integrated waste management nor any body of law relating to waste (although technical norms and sanitary rules did exist). Dumping of waste at unauthorised sites in rural areas was common.

Tipping fees, where charged, were low and non-compliance charges were infrequently applied. When strengthened without proper regulation and oversight, this simply encouraged illegal disposals. Nonetheless, the increasing quantities of waste being generated, the requirement for greater investment and treatment costs (particularly in EU aspirant countries) and rising public expectations led to more serious consideration of the issue among countries of operations and their municipalities.

In advanced countries following EU environmental policies, a new instrument—"extended producer responsibility"—was introduced in the early 2000s. This transferred responsibility for the final disposal of products after consumption from the public sector (that is, municipalities) to producers. This helped municipalities raise revenues to pay for waste treatment and disposal infrastructure, for which demand was on a steep rising curve. The Slovak Republic was one of the first EBRD countries to apply the procedure for substances including batteries, waste oils, paper and packaging and glass. Compliance demands grew and with them the need for new in-

---

30 'Municipal and Environmental Infrastructure Operations Policy', 2004, Annex 3.

vestment, which increased the attraction of outsourcing to private providers. This helped local businesses and competition for contracts became more intense, leading to some consolidation. Waste management was also aided by the development of regional and inter-municipality arrangements among small and medium-sized municipalities (in the Baltic States, for instance). All of this helped the EBRD develop this side of its municipal business.

District heating

Urban areas with concentrated populations were common in many countries of operations as a result of central planning, with heat supplied by district-heating systems owned by the state. In Russia and Latvia, the market share of district heating in 2003 was 70 per cent, while in the other Baltic States, Poland and Belarus it was more than 50 per cent.[31] Decentralisation had shifted ownership to municipalities but there was little private provision outside the Czech Republic and Estonia. Low incomes meant that energy, most of which was used for space heating, took up a high proportion of household incomes and made price increases a sensitive and politicised topic. Getting the balance right between improved service provision and higher district heating charges to pay for better services was a delicate business. Nonetheless, gross inefficiencies in most systems meant there were at least some easier wins to be made early on. According to the World Energy Council, energy losses in generation, transportation, distribution and end-use ranged from 35 per cent to more than 75 per cent in the EBRD's countries of operations due to stretched networks using old and poorly maintained equipment and technology.

Heat tariffs in most countries remained regulated to keep them affordable for consumers and rarely took into account the costs of depreciation and of financing investment. There was also considerable variation in heat tariffs, both within and between countries, in part reflecting different heat sources and the condition of distribution systems. On the demand side, consumers had little incentive to rationalise consumption and in large apartment blocks had no control over supplies. Over time there was a trend away from district heating towards natural gas distribution networks, allowing consumers to install autonomous heating systems. This was particularly the

---

31 World Energy Council, 2003.

case where district heating was not the least-cost option—as in many less built-up and rural areas —and where reliability of supply was poor. In Moldova, for example, it was estimated that by 2000 up to 20 per cent of flat-owners in multi-storey buildings had installed autonomous boilers, while demand for district heating in Poland and Hungary had fallen by 15 per cent and 30 per cent over the decade.

These conditions put pressure on district-heating companies to improve physical efficiency by reducing heat losses, both to save costs and increase reliability, as well as enhancing overall performance to remain competitive as alternative sources of supply emerged. The EBRD was able to assist with instruments such as FOPIPs, finance for new (and more energy-efficient) equipment, technical assistance and and municipal support agreements (MSAs). After water and wastewater treatment operations, district-heating projects were the second-biggest part of MEI business, accounting for around one-quarter of volume by the mid-2000s.

6. PSCs and PSAs

The EBRD successfully improved the water and urban transport sectors through sub-sovereign direct lending underpinned by solid funding arrangements and financial and institutional instruments designed to improve creditworthiness within an off-balance sheet project funding structure. Contract incentives were strengthened by PSCs and PSAs or MSAs, the latter being used in urban transport projects.

The non-sovereign nature of the Bank's business model was in contrast to other IFIs, where sovereign lending was the norm. Among its advantages was that greater efficiency and commercialisation were needed before the EBRD or commercial co-financiers were prepared to lend. This process forced improvements in revenues and greater cost-discipline, allowing companies to leverage finance for higher investment and better service quality. An analysis of a representative sample of EBRD municipal infrastructure projects showed that revenues were on average 90 per cent higher in real terms 10 years after full implementation.[32] The objectives of the Bank

---

32 'Accelerating Infrastructure Delivery: New Evidence from International Financial Institutions', paper submitted to the World Economic Forum, April 2014, p. 9.

focused on building a sustainable financing and operating model, one that would ultimately lead to self-reliance for investments.

The PSC was a key component of this successful approach and used widely across the EBRD region. Some 50 per cent of all PSC-based projects were carried out in non-EU countries of operations, from Russia to Central Asia and the Caucasus and elsewhere, where they were adjusted for local legal and administrative requirements and national budget codes. The PSC defined the contractual arrangement between the service provider and the municipality as owner. It clarified the commitments, rights and obligations of all parties and, properly written, included well-defined long-term operational, technical and financial performance targets. The owner's rights covered approval of business and investment plans and tariff adjustments (with agreement not to interfere in short-term operational issues), while the company's rights and obligations involved the implementation of the business plan, annual statements of progress and delivery of targets such as water supply, metering, billing and payment collection.

PSAs (and MSAs) formed the other core component of the EBRD's approach in municipal projects. These were contractual agreements between the EBRD and the relevant authorities, for example the municipal owners of the water companies, who were borrowers from the Bank. Agreements included a general commitment to support and cooperate with the project and to facilitate key decisions such as tariff adjustments. An important component was an obligation to provide financial backing to the company to cover all economically justified costs not covered by tariffs. If the tariff was insufficient to meet the full costs of operations or if the municipality was unwilling to raise tariffs sufficiently for political or social reasons, the company would be compensated. Equally, the owner was not obliged to pay for non-economically justified costs or, for example, a failure to collect payments from users. The PSA discouraged the owners from having to pay for inefficiencies by the company not related to the proper cost of operations. The PSA did not entail any guarantee by the municipality to repay the EBRD but acted as a strong risk mitigator that helped to lower the risk profile of the project. It was an effective and robust credit enhancement tool.

The PSC and PSA approach formed an important new way of managing project finance risks in the municipal context. It also helped to persuade the Bank's finance department (and later the risk department) that this type of sub-sovereign lending was acceptable when combined with technical support and operational and financial reform by the utility companies. Despite the high risks involved in dealing with municipal projects, default rates were remarkably low, helped by the careful selection of reform-minded cities as partners. In fact, the EBRD has never had a payment default on its sub-sovereign portfolio.

The credit enhancement approach also made it easier to attract commercial finance. Several European commercial bank groups—including Dexia (Belgian), RZB (Austrian) and Swedbank (Swedish)—became B lenders in EBRD-led syndications in water and wastewater treatment operations. They also obtained comfort from the EBRD's preferred creditor status. The financial multiplier from the successful application of the overall approach was substantial. In the case of Romania, where the Bank engaged with 20 cities directly between 1994 and 2011, it was estimated that revenues increased more than fourfold in real terms, from US$ 300 million to US$ 1.4 billion.[33] A similar pattern was seen in urban transport. For example, a project in Kaunas, Lithuania based on the cost control exerted through a PSC reduced real operating expenditures by more than one-third between 2004 and 2010, and increased the fare-box recovery ratio[34] from 30 per cent to more than 80 per cent.[35]

7. Private-Sector Participation

Private-sector solutions

In a number of projects the EBRD sought private-sector solutions and involved international private companies, for example in design, build and operate (DBO) arrangements in wastewater treatment plants (as in Zagreb)[36] or in the privatisation of municipal companies. This was not an easy exercise and in more complex cases was very resource-intensive. Foreign investors were concerned about the risks involved, for example relating to tendering processes (and whether they were open and transparent), the need for clearly specified contracts, the robustness of payment streams (which were linked to tariff-setting and fee collection) and the ability to reap economies of scale

---

33 'Accelerating Infrastructure Delivery', 2014, p. 12.
34 The proportion of operating costs covered by ticketing revenues.
35 'Accelerating Infrastructure Delivery', 2014, p. 15.
36 'Zagreb Wastewater Treatment Plant', 3 September 2001.

(which required larger or multi-city contracts). They also often sought guarantees against political risk.

At the same time, successful private-sector involvement depended on the capacity of local administrations and their commitment. For example, the role of a local administration as a client in a PPP deal required efficiency in planning, tendering, contract negotiations and contract monitoring. Commitment to using the private sector and long contracts for service provision, typically up to 10 to 15 years, also required adequate and predictable tariffs to attract private-sector operators.

However, the scale of the tariff increases required to reach economic viability, combined with the profit element for private companies, frequently incited controversy and political pressure to avoid making changes. Privatisation of municipal companies was even more difficult since few were prepared to take the risks of restructuring unviable entities, while in cases where companies were economically more efficient, there was less need for municipalities to sell them off. A further requirement for successful private-sector participation—which was only properly met in advanced countries towards the end of the 1990s and early 2000s—was a stable and effective regulatory system.[37]

PPPs were an area in which the private sector engaged with municipal and city investments, often in public transport, parking and water and wastewater treatment projects, and usually in cases where grant funding for public investment in infrastructure was unavailable. In some cases, PPP financing was related to the construction and management of city infrastructure, as in the effort to improve the central section of the St. Petersburg western high-speed diameter road. Onerous legal structures in environments where the institutional setting was weak and volatile and where political interference was similarly frequent and unpredictable, however, meant PPPs had a more chequered history than the EBRD hoped for. More positively, services outsourced to the private sector using performance-based contracts allowed entities to mobilise private-sector expertise and share risk while avoiding the legal complexity of fully-fledged concessions and the political hurdles involved in public asset transfers.[38]

---

37 This section draws on 'Municipal and Environmental Infrastructure Operations Policy Review', Evaluation Department, May 2010.
38 'Municipal and Environmental Infrastructure Sector Strategy', 28 June 2012, p. 39.

A number of major international players who had entered the market in the 1990s—such as Suez Environment and Veolia (both French-owned) and International Water Limited, which was jointly owned by Bechtel's Italian subsidiary and Edison—consolidated and retreated from the region in the 2000s, preferring developed countries and faster-growing and larger emerging markets such as Brazil and China.[39] Smaller players such as Berlinwasser International took up some of the vacant space, but PPPs were limited and confined mainly to the Czech Republic, Hungary and Poland. Here, there were a few PPP district-heating projects but most activity was in the water sector and focused on less risky structures such as shorter-term leasing and operation and management contracts, which required less capital investment. The availability of EU pre-accession and post-accession grants served to disrupt the private sector participation (PSP) market in advanced transition countries, while a lack of adequate PPP legislation in less advanced countries, as well as the caution of international investors, limited its development.[40]

In all its work with the private sector the EBRD was keen to ensure that high standards were achieved. This was made easier by the use of technical cooperation funds but required vigilance to ensure competition, fair contracts and the avoidance of corruption, especially given the lack of experience of most municipality staff in these areas. Inevitably, compliance with best practice and the intensive dialogue required to put in place legal conditions for private-sector participation resulted in long lead times and was burdensome financially and in terms of resources.

Although the EBRD had high hopes for eventual private-sector participation in the MEI sector, expecting it to offer value for money and better allocation of risk, the outcome was generally disappointing during the Bank's first 15 years. Long-term leases or concessions to private operators (up to 25 years) in principle offered an appropriate longer-term commercial approach to project development and problem-solving, as compared with public-sector managers trying to cope with short-term pressures and adapt to pressing political goals. An EBRD Legal Indicator Survey in 2000, however, found that three-quarters of the Bank's countries of operations had "barely adequate" or "detrimental" concession laws. Such arrangements needed legal and regula-

---

39 'Municipal and Environmental Infrastructure Operations Policy', 2004, Annex 5.
40 See 'Private Sector Participation in MEI Projects', Evaluation Department, 2014.

tory certainty to work well and this was often lacking: seemingly stable regulations were too frequently interrupted by political developments.

Access to private financial capital markets

Another area the EBRD supported was increasing access by municipalities and municipal companies to commercial finance and capital markets. This had been an aspiration from the beginning, albeit a long-term one. The main success was seen in the promotion of commercial bank co-financing through the Bank's syndication capacity and in the use of partial guarantees for other lenders' exposure to municipalities. In some cases, forms of quasi-equity or mezzanine capital were used to expand access of the municipal sector to long-term capital, while equity finance was provided in a few cases to service providers. EBRD support for revenue bonds (as in the Bydgoszcz Water Revenue Bond Project in Poland in 2005) also promoted the expansion of the market for local government investment beyond commercial banks to institutional and individual investors looking for long-term investments.

Bringing municipalities' performance to a level where they were able to access private financial capital markets, even with the Bank's help, was not an easy task. Larger and more advanced cities provided the most suitable cases but even here local commercial banks' lack of experience of municipal lending made them less interested in participating. They were also often unwilling to provide waivers, which resulted in significant delays to projects and increased wariness on all sides.

Local currency finance

A particular factor in the municipal sector was that municipalities and providers of municipal services received the bulk of their revenues in local currency. The EBRD strove to provide its clients with local currency finance, which became easier in later years as sources of funding began to develop with improvements in capital markets in more advanced transition countries. In Russia, after the 1998 financial crisis, restrictions on foreign borrowing by municipalities also forced the EBRD to source roubles in order to lend, which it did through its treasury department via marketable rouble financial instruments.

Providing local currency finance remained difficult in many countries where the Bank was active in supporting the development of municipal services. The only realistic alternative was to use risk-sharing mechanisms to help local financial institutions provide local currency finance. While local currency finance mitigated foreign exchange risks, municipal clients faced local interest rate risks. In weak economies, local currency interest rates were usually high and volatile, increasing the reluctance of clients to take on such loans. Given the variety of risks involved and the EBRD's commitment to sound banking, local currency lending to municipalities took time to develop beyond central Europe.

Commercial bank and DFI co-finance

Commercial bank financing of the municipal sector began to grow from the late 1990s onward and the EBRD successfully syndicated several loans, usually in dollars or euros, using its A-loan/B-loan structure. There were also projects involving parallel finance by local commercial banks. Several municipal transactions in advanced transition countries undertaken by the EBRD during the mid-2000s involved co-financing with western European banks such as Dexia, RZB and Société Générale. By late 2007, the amount of commercial co-finance facilitated by the EBRD had more than doubled compared with the early years of the decade. Indeed, commercial financing of municipal enterprises in Poland and other advanced countries, and even in Romania, was expanding fast with margins falling sharply. Better terms were beginning to be offered by the market than by the EBRD. The Bank was being priced out of the market and its offer was no longer financially additional. In the words of one senior EBRD manager: "We could see the end of the line in Romania and Poland already."[41]

This judgement, however, proved to be premature. Commercial finance and co-finance for municipalities and municipal companies came to an abrupt halt with the onset of the financial crisis in 2008. Pending the revival of the commercial market, IFI co-financing expanded considerably. This involved institutions such as the World Bank, IFC, EIB, ADB and NIB, as well as national development financial institutions such as the Agence Française de Développement (AfD), Germany's KfW, the Millennium Challenge Corporation (USA) and Vnesheconombank (Russia).

---

41   Interview with author, January 2020.

Conclusion

The EBRD's policy towards municipalities was based consistently on three themes: decentralisation, commercialisation and environmental improvement. These were fully in keeping with the objectives from the start of encouraging greater autonomy from the state, decentralisation and devolved decision-making, and financial self-sustainability. An Evaluation Department study in 2010, after consulting a wide range of municipalities and municipal companies that worked with the EBRD, concluded that several municipal companies had "changed from a weak state with no autonomy and poor services that rely on subsidies to be sustained, to a commercialised company with decision-making powers, high accountability, and providing high standards of services".[42]

For the Bank's projects to be successful it was first necessary to ensure the city administration was fully committed to improving municipal services and to build capacity and make the municipalities creditworthy. Use of technical cooperation funds was an essential part of the process of commercialisation, as was the development of tariff policies that improved cost-recovery and gave more certainty over future revenues and the ability to plan investment programmes. Once municipal utilities were able to operate freely within a proper financing structure and manage those activities for which they were responsible, progress could be made. Particularly successful projects tended to be associated with very strong management skills and experience in municipal companies.

The development and signing of PSCs and PSAs were a vital part of the process of helping municipalities improve institutional structures and services. By adding clarity to the relationship between the city administration and municipal companies through the specification of roles and responsibilities, tariffs and subsidies, PSCs and PSAs cleared a path towards commercialisation and ultimately private-sector participation. Urban transport—where private companies in many cases took over the running of metro, bus, tram, trolley and light rail routes—was a successful example of the value of adopting PSCs (and MSAs).

The EBRD's track record in pioneering a sub-sovereign approach to municipal finance and implementing a very large number of projects with PSC,

---

[42] Municipal and Environmental Infrastructure Operations Policy Review', Evaluation Department, 2010, p. 47.

PSA or MSA structures in many cities, large and small, was unparalleled. To implement a novel method without a full default is all the more remarkable given the commercial pricing approach and the often very high risk levels involved. Longer-term viability was enhanced by targeting reform-oriented municipalities, especially those with supportive mayors and authorities. Careful integrity checks and the pursuit of high standards (with support from the EU) also helped.

An improvement that strengthened commercialisation, particularly among local public transport companies, was the increased collection of data and its greater reliability. Electronic ticketing systems that could record and forecast passenger usage, including for those with subsidised fares such as pensioners and students, were valuable for planning routes and tariffs. Similarly, metering of water and heating supplies, weighing of solid waste landfill deliveries, registration of vehicles for fees, and recording of properties and the number of residents for tariff-payment purposes brought modernisation and progress to areas long left behind. Specific fees, charges and taxes on citizens by local authorities also brought greater visibility and accountability for service quality and helped to strengthen local democracy.

One area that took longer to bed in was procurement. The EBRD's procedures, which were very thorough and designed to eliminate anti-competitive practices and corruption, required competitive and transparent tendering. These were poorly understood at first and disrupted previous practices. Once the process resulted in savings of investment costs, however, awareness of commercial benefits helped to persuade clients of its value.

Commercialisation brought greater private-sector involvement. A number of international companies—Veolia in water and solid waste, for example—took advantage of concessions available in larger cities and regions to develop investment programmes. Usually these were cases where tariff-setting was designed to meet full cost-recovery, political risks were relatively low—mitigated by working with the EBRD—and there was room for privatisation. There were some successful PPPs but municipalities were less committed here and many projects were small and not appropriate for the complexities involved.

Establishing a successful, broad and enduring municipal lending model was largely the result of EBRD's unique approach. Internally, integrated project teams – comprising bankers, sector and environmental experts and procurement and technical assistance specialists – all reported to a single banking director to work cohesively, creating a clear and consistent direction in non-sovereign municipal work and its support for decentralisation. This was an especially strong feature of the EBRD municipal model.

The Bank's efforts in the municipal sector contributed to major environmental improvements. Many cities and towns saw higher-quality water and more reliable supplies, with far less wastage from water losses. The application of EU standards to wastewater treatment plants prevented further discharges of raw sewerage into local rivers and reduced pollution, improving health. Disposal of solid waste came under better control and district heating supplies were managed more efficiently, saving costs and carbon usage, while urban transport advances led to less polluting buses and more reliable timetables.

In short, by the late 2000s, thanks in part to decentralisation, the range and quality of local services in many cities had moved closer to their counterparts in western Europe. The EBRD had made a significant contribution to these developments and to this dimension of transition.

Chapter 8

Environment Matters

Introduction

Thirty years ago, the EBRD's regions were home to some of the most energy-intensive and polluting industries in the world. Hushed-up environmental and nuclear catastrophes—most notably the Chernobyl disaster of 1986—spurred some of the first popular protests against the authorities in the USSR. It was clear to the Bank's founders that the economies of the post-communist countries would need to be rebuilt in a sustainable way.

From the outset the EBRD was charged with promoting environmentally friendly economies, long before "sustainability" became a watchword for development organisations. Many of its early investments had dual objectives in targeting desirable environmental results: modernising industries often meant replacing old equipment with new machinery, which allowed the Bank to introduce improvements in energy efficiency. Moving away from heavy state subsidies for fossil fuels gave companies and households better incentives to save energy.

The Bank also helped countries gradually shift away from coal-powered and nuclear energy generation. This costly process felt frustratingly slow to some environmental activists; however, the EBRD successfully pioneered energy efficiency programmes, enabled the closure of unsafe nuclear facilities and supported some of the earliest renewable energy projects. This work progressed over the decades to become a broader Green Economy Transition programme, which is explored in the next volume. This chapter describes the genesis of the EBRD's green philosophy.

1. A Role for the EBRD

The 1980s had brought an increasing awareness of the impact of industrialisation on the environment. As concerns grew, the UN took a higher profile in its dealings on the environment and international consensus emerged over some pressing issues. The Vienna Protocol of 1985[1], regulating substances that harmed the ozone layer, was one of the first examples of voluntary international action to protect the global environment. The Bruntland Report of 1987[2] offered the first definition of sustainable development: a "development that meets the needs of the present without compromising the ability of future generations to meet their own needs". Environmental NGOs started questioning the environmental impact of several large-scale investments in developing countries and their consequences for local populations, air pollution, water contamination, indigenous peoples, wildlife and the quality of the environment. IFIs, notably the World Bank, came under increasing scrutiny. It was in this context that the EBRD's environmental mandate was conceived.

The Bank focused on ensuring that the impact of each investment was subject to proper environmental assessment and monitoring. This meant careful due diligence, especially on projects where environmental concerns were high, and the development of effective mitigation strategies to deal with any consequences.

The pursuit of sustainable development was also an important goal. This raised questions over what types of activities the EBRD should engage in and which activities it should avoid, and thus went beyond simply making sure individual projects did not affect the environment or local communities inappropriately.

The environmental inheritance in the EBRD region was dire. Eastern Europe and Central Asia faced multiple environmental disasters, from pollution in the Baltic Sea and the Danube River Basin to the erosion of the Aral Sea and contaminated water supplies. It was clear that rectifying the deficiencies would take years of painstaking work and substantial investment.

As the EBRD began its operations, governments were preparing for the June 1992 UN Conference on Environment and Development (UNCED)

---

1 https://treaties.un.org/pages/ViewDetails.aspx?src=TREATY&mtdsg_no=XXVII-2&chapter=27&lang=en.
2 http://www.un-documents.net/wced-ocf.htm.

in Rio de Janeiro, better known as the Earth Summit. With the Cold War over there was hope that a truly global approach to environmental problems might be possible.

The event was crucial in raising awareness and building cooperation on a global environmental agenda.[3] Representing the EBRD in Rio, Attali gave his view of the situation facing the region:

> The legacy of the totalitarian societies in Eastern Europe is catastrophic. In 50 years they have destroyed irreplaceable resources and created untold sources of pollution that will threaten the planet for centuries to come … If we were to single out one region of the world where all the environmental mistakes of our age have been committed, it would surely be Eastern Europe.
>
> It is no longer a Cold War but a Green War that is being waged … with two major deadly weapons: the nuclear power stations … each is a time bomb that could go off at any moment; [and] the civilian and military industries that produce hazardous waste, contaminating the soil and polluting the air.[4]

By way of a remedy, he called for an "environmental transition" based on greater transparency, use of market mechanisms, international cooperation ("solidarity") and additional funding.

As a new IFI on the doorstep, with a mandate to match, the EBRD was ideally placed to help clean up the former Eastern Bloc. At the time, however, it was unclear how to shape a Bank geared towards both developing the private sector, where the pursuit of profit was the ultimate objective, and cleaning up the environment.

Today, there is plenty of evidence—including the EBRD's own track record—that green business can be good business, and that environmentally sustainable investment is not only possible but profitable. At the time of the Bank's creation, however, there was no precedent for an organisation made up mostly of investment bankers having the capacity or wherewithal to tackle environmental problems while its core staff were also creating a

---

3   The Conference gave birth to the Climate Change Convention, the precursor to the Kyoto Protocol and later Paris Agreement.
4   Statement by the President of the EBRD at the United Nations Conference on Environment and Development (The Earth Summit), Rio de Janeiro, 10 June 1992.

functioning private sector from scratch. How could such activities be profitable enough to justify committing resources, even supposing governments laden with debt and facing poor fiscal prospects were able to lend financial support for environmental improvements?

Despite these challenges, it proved possible to make a considerable number of environmental improvements under the Bank's guidance and operations. One of the notable attributes of the EBRD was its ability to mould bankers into multitasking operators capable of pursuing other objectives alongside the profitability of projects. Another aspect that emerged, particularly in relation to climate change activities, was the Bank's success in developing profitable segments of sectors incorporating environmental enhancements through the adoption of innovative approaches and supportive investments. The EBRD found a way of making its environmental operations commercially feasible and in so doing created new markets and products that demonstrated the value of environmentally friendly business activities well in advance of many other market participants.

2. Addressing the Environmental Legacy

The collapse of the centrally planned economies and subsequent difficulties in establishing functioning economic and political systems exacerbated an already poor environmental landscape. The prevalence of obsolete technologies, lack of pollution-abatement equipment, poor use of resources and weak environmental management did not help matters. Nor did the fact that there was little regulation of hazardous materials such as asbestos, or of soil and groundwater contamination. Water-quality standards excluded pollutants such as chlorinated solvents. Polluters frequently escaped penalties.[5] Environmental disasters such as Chernobyl were treated as state secrets and there was little or no public participation in decision-making processes. There was an urgent need to review unsustainable industrial practices. Serious fiscal constraints and political volatility in many countries added to the complexity of the task.

---

5   See 'Fostering Economic Transition and Sustainable Development on CEE and the CIS', paper for Euro 2000, D. Prasek, Head of Operational Support, Environment Department, EBRD, October 2002, Aalborg, Denmark. The author is grateful to Dr Prasek for being able to draw on some of his unpublished notes for this and the following section of this chapter.

Decades of poor maintenance and protection of the environment had led to an accumulation of issues to resolve. Investment in modern, clean technology had been inadequate, as had incentives to ensure environmental risks and degradation were minimised. This was true across the energy and natural resources sectors. The focus of central planning systems on output targets meant the predominant attitude of managers and workers had been to disregard the environmental consequences of production, whether in relation to the impact of oil and gas extraction in the pristine natural landscape of Siberia or at nuclear plants and waste dumps near more densely populated urban areas.[6]

The EBRD, with a clear remit to improve the environment and support sustainable development, was able to foster change. It had finance ready to invest in the region, a mission to improve standards and clean up sources of pollution and other environmental damage, and experts able to advise on best practices and their implementation.

Approach to environmental issues

As the first IFI to be given a proactive environmental mandate, the EBRD embedded this into its core activities from the start. These spanned the industrial spectrum as well as infrastructure, where environmental problems abounded. It was natural therefore to apply the Bank's environmental requirements to its operations.

Environmental due diligence

The EBRD required that environmental due diligence be carried out on all projects under preparation. This was conducted at the same time as financial due diligence to reduce the burden on clients. Environmental audits provided a comprehensive assessment of the state of industrial premises and operations, compliance or otherwise with regulations, and potential risks and liabilities. In most cases Environmental Action Plans (EAPs) were introduced to bring companies' operations up to a better standard. The standards re-

---

6   For example, the Metsamor plant was located just over 20 miles from Yerevan, the capital of Armenia, and was built in an earthquake zone. After the devastating Spitak earthquake nearby in 1988, the plant was closed, although only until 1995. It still provides 40 per cent of Armenia's energy needs. BBC, Daryl Mersom, 27 May 2019, https://www.bbc.com/worklife/article/20190527-the-city-in-the-shadow-of-an-ageing-nuclear-reactor.

quired were clarified in a comprehensive paper on the Bank's Environmental Policy and Environmental Procedures agreed in 1996.[7] This ensured that operations met both national standards and those set by the EU at the time. In areas where EU standards did not yet exist, the fallback was national or World Bank standards.

A team of specialists, the Environmental Appraisal Unit (EAU), provided advice and support to project operation leaders (who were typically bankers), went with them on visits to industrial sites and participated in discussions with clients. OpsCom remained the place where projects were examined holistically, including for environmental concerns. In more serious cases, specific issues were referred to senior management and the President. According to a review of the EBRD's environmental practices and performance by the Evaluation Department in 2001, environmental procedures were "practical and efficiently incorporated in the Bank's project cycle" and "effective in safeguarding the establishment of environmental objectives and the covenanting of loans".[8]

Environmental management systems

The EBRD provided technical assistance to its client companies alongside financing. It was realised early on that significant support to enterprises in the Bank's regions of operations would be needed in the sphere of environmental management. Here capacity was generally weak, with little history of implementation of modern management practices and even less of including environmental concerns within them. Responsibility for environmental matters was usually seen as a niche area and left to poorly trained line managers, with little senior management oversight. Operating budgets and capital expenditure programmes did not routinely include environmental concerns and finance officers did not understand the importance of environmental reporting and monitoring.

To help remedy the situation, the Bank used technical cooperation funds alongside its investments to supply experts, such as senior environmental managers from counterpart industries in OECD countries, to work with clients. Training programmes and materials to spread knowledge of good

---

7 'Environmental Policy', 19 November 1996.
8 'Special Study: Evaluation of Environmental Performance of EBRD, Volume 1', April 2001.

practices, including for local environmental consultants, supplemented these efforts as did practical support to operationalise EAPs and meet the Bank's standards. A separate EBRD programme called Turnaround Management (TAM), which from 1994 had deployed retired senior executives to work as part-time advisors for (mainly) manufacturing companies in eastern Europe and the former Soviet Union, was extended to include an environmental component.

The need to comply with higher standards and reduce environmental risks led to greater interest among the EBRD's clients in adopting effective environmental management systems. Here the EU's Environmental Management and Audit Scheme (EMAS) and, after it was finalised in 1996 by the International Organisation for Standardization (ISO), the international environmental standard ISO 14001 were key to assisting the implementation of higher standards and compliance among the companies the Bank dealt with. Environmental management system (EMS) programmes were usually based on ISO 14001 (and later the more tightly energy-focused ISO 50001), which drove improvements in environmental risk management and performance. Companies with EMS certification found it easier to promote their products in export markets while increased transparency of environmental, health and safety reporting raised public awareness of these issues. This led to greater permanency of higher environmental standards and environmental sustainability.

Financial institutions

During the 1990s, the development of the EBRD's business with SMEs expanded significantly with the use of credit lines via financial intermediaries under the wholesale approach (see Chapter 5). To fulfil its environmental remit there was a need to be sure that the Bank's financial institution partners understood its environmental requirements. Financial institutions were given training in environmental due diligence procedures and annual environmental reporting to the Bank[9], and had to adhere to its environmental exclusion list. The Bank developed a multilingual manual on environmental risk management for financial institutions and provided a series of training workshops

---

9   A PED review in 1999, 'Special Study of the Bank's Environmental Due Diligence of Financial Institutions', declared that this arrangement was "very useful".

on environment, health and safety for financial institutions and local consultants in Estonia, the Czech Republic, Hungary, Poland, Slovenia and Russia.

As the EBRD's portfolio expanded, the due diligence burden grew, prompting an A/B/C categorisation of environmental importance.[10] The poor state of municipal and industrial infrastructure and significant environmental, health and safety concerns meant a large number of projects—around two-fifths according to the Evaluation Study (and half by value of proposed investment)—were regarded as "environmentally sensitive" during the 1990s.[11] Technical cooperation projects on environmental activities connected to investments were also numerous. Nonetheless, the Study concluded that in its first 10 years the Bank had "done well in respect of environmental performance and impact in projects with a substantial environmental dimension".[12]

3. Environmental Improvements in Industrial Projects

The involvement of the Bank in many projects where environmental issues presented serious concerns offered multiple opportunities to make a significant impact. These included the introduction of more energy-efficient plant and equipment through new capital investments, safer working conditions and innovative approaches led by the Bank, as well as the decommissioning and upgrading of old and unsafe nuclear facilities. (Nuclear facilities are explored in the next chapter.)

Zarafshan-Newmont Joint Venture, Uzbekistan

An example of how the EBRD, together with foreign and local sponsors, could turn around an uneconomic situation towards profitability while securing a radical improvement in the health and safety of workers and environmental conditions was a project started in 1993 in Uzbekistan.

Zarafshan, a small town located in the Kyzylkum desert some 400 miles west of Tashkent, had been purpose-built to supply materials and labour to

---

10 See current EBRD categorisation checklist for partner financial institutions. https://www.ebrd.com/downloads/about/sustainability/ebrd-risk-english.pdf.
11 'Special Study', Volume 1, 2001, p. viii.
12 'Special Study', Volume 1, 2001, p. 81.

the nearby Muruntau gold mine—the largest gold mine in the former USSR and one of the largest in the world. The mine had been in operation since the 1960s[13] and had amassed a vast stockpile of some 300 million tonnes of ore with low levels of gold whose recovery was regarded as uneconomic.

Engineers from Newmont, a large US-based gold producer, surmised that modern heap leaching technology, which they operated successfully in their own mines in the Nevada desert, could extract gold from the ore much more efficiently than the methods then being used. This led to a joint venture between Newmont and the Uzbek state[14] to extract the gold. The EBRD became involved to help finance the operation and facilitate the process. An A/B loan of US$ 105 million (half of which was the EBRD A loan) was provided in 1993, and extended to US$ 135 million in 1995. The project was the first major FDI, as well as syndication, in Uzbekistan.

Working conditions were poor at the open-pit mine where annual temperatures ranged from 45° C in summer to -30° C in winter in a windy, dusty environment. Particulate emissions were high, made worse by polluting trucks and other machines and from the difficulty in controlling dust from the crushing process. Care was needed too in the use of chemicals (especially cyanide compounds) and their storage and disposal. In agreement with the EBRD, whose environmental assessments provided the foundations for a series of improvements and their monitoring, Newmont committed to apply the strict environmental standards they deployed in their Nevada operations.

Although it took a long time to bring about the environmental changes, which was helped by a further project in 2000, the joint venture delivered the highest standards. These were in line with US Environmental Protection Policy (as Newmont sought), as well as the EBRD's performance requirements and the applicable laws and regulations in Uzbekistan. A later independent evaluation noted "workers' health and safety has improved significantly and continues to be a high priority at the Joint Venture" and concluded that the environmental performance was "excellent" and the extent of environmental improvement "substantial".[15]

---

13 According to the CIA, it made use of forced labourers in earlier times. 'Forced Labour Camps and Prisons in the USSR', CIA/BGI GR 73-1, p.6, December 1972. https://www.cia.gov/library/readingroom/docs/CIA-RDP84-00825R000300020001-8.pdf
14 Specifically, the State Committee for Geology and Mineral Resources (Goskomgeologia) and Navoi, a former part of the USSR Ministry of Machine Building transferred to the Uzbek state.
15 'Zarafshan-Newmont Joint Venture Third Facility', Evaluation Department, March 2006.

The overall operation was a success with extracted gold exceeding targets and a strong financial performance. At the time, it was seen as a "win-win" for all sides. However, in due course a dispute over tax payments led to the seizure of assets by Uzbekistan in 2006. This was settled the following year with a US$ 80 million payment to Newmont by the Uzbekistan government.[16] Full control of the operation was left in Uzbek hands.

Ispat Karmet Steel Works, Kazakhstan

One of the world's largest integrated steel complexes, the Karaganda Metallurgical Kombinat (Karmet) made use of central Kazakhstan's rich high-grade coal deposits and iron-ore from the north. It was the country's only coal-and-steel complex and one of its biggest enterprises, accounting for around 5 per cent of GDP and 10 per cent of all non-oil exports. Production of ingot steel fell by more than half between the break-up of the Soviet Union and privatisation in 1995.

The new owners, JSC Ispat Karmet, requested the EBRD's help to finance US$ 633 million of planned capital investments. The aim was to restore capacity and improve efficiency in the steel and coal divisions, including environmental improvements. In 1997, they agreed a substantial package including an A-loan of US$ 100 million from the Bank and a B-loan of $50 million from participant banks. The IFC approved parallel syndicated financing of US$ 115 million for the project.[17]

After an initial appraisal by the EBRD, a series of assessments and audits revealed a host of environmental issues, including the prevalence of high dust, ammonia, sulphur dioxide and nitrous oxide emissions, as well as a lack of safety culture. Three environmental action plans were agreed with the company covering the iron and steel plant, power generation and the coal mines. Each was designed to achieve compliance with domestic, EU and World Bank environmental standards. According to the evaluation team reviewing the project: "the resulting undertakings went far beyond the original [privatisation] environmental agreement between Ispat and the government."

---

16 'Gold miner Newmont resolves dispute with Uzbekistan', Reuters, 23 July 2007.
17 The onset of an economic downturn from the 1997 Asian financial crisis and the impact of the Russian crisis the following year altered the subsequent financing arrangements.

The team assigned a "good" rating to the environmental performance of the project and rated the extent of environmental change as "substantial".

The operation safeguarded dust and other air emission abatement and health and safety (H&S) improvements. Air quality improvement in the sanitary zone concerned dust in particular [and can be expected to] reduce dust emissions by about 80 per cent by 2002. Improvements in the mining division were assessed as outstanding, while the main H&S improvements included significantly reduced accident rates and acid fumes from pickling. There was also notable improvement in EH&S risk management. Effluent treatment at the steel plant reached discharges well below regulatory limits and those in the mining division were also compliant.[18]

Slovalco Aluminium Smelter Project, Slovak Republic

Another industrial project of local and national environmental importance in which the EBRD was involved early on was the completion of an aluminium smelter project in the Slovak Republic. The Zavod Slovenskeho Narodneho Povstania (ZSNP) aluminium complex had originally been built to serve strategic military needs. A new smelter had been commissioned in the 1980s, but work was halted in mid-1993 due to a lack of funds from state banks. In 1994, the EBRD granted senior loan financing of US$ 110 million and equity financing of US$ 15 million alongside Hydro Aluminium (HAL) of Norway to prepare the company for privatisation through corporate restructuring.[19] It was one of the Bank's largest private-sector operations at the time.

The 2001 Evaluation Special Study described the situation at the start of the EBRD's engagement:

The environmental, health and safety situation in the Ziar basin near the facilities was highly unsatisfactory and air quality was classified in the lowest category, class 5, because of high fluorine, PAH[20], SO_2, NOx and dust concentrations...[21]

---

18 'Ispat Karmet Steel Works', Project Evaluation Department, September 2000.
19 https://www.ebrd.com/what-we-do/sectors-and-topics/the-new-europe/the-real-economy.html.
20 Polyaromatic hydrocarbons.
21 'Special Study', Volume 1, 2001, p. 17.

ZSNP established a subsidiary, Slovalco, to complete the smelter as a modern, state-of-the-art facility and close down the old, polluting units. The EBRD's financing required the company to include a significant environmental remedial programme. The focal point of the project became environmental improvements and clean-up.

A public debate emerged at this time on aluminium-industry pollution and smelter energy use. At the EBRD's insistence, ZSNP publicly addressed these concerns. (In 1997, the Bank's continuing promotion of open communication between the authorities, stakeholders and the public led to the formation of Slovakia's first citizen-based monitoring and advisory group.)

An Environmental Action Agreement required inefficient and polluting units (primarily the two old smelters and the alumina and anode plants) to be closed down prior to the first loan disbursement and for the coal-fired heating to be converted to gas. Environmental improvements and clean-up responsibilities including for the red mud pile (the biggest waste site in the country) were defined in the loan under an Environmental Remediation Agreement between ZSNP, Slovalco and the National Property Fund, with the Slovak government as the ultimate guarantor of ZSNP's obligations.

The overall environmental benefits of the project were significant. Heavily polluting facilities such as the old smelters were closed or refurbished, resulting in a marked improvement in the catchment air quality, reaching an acceptable level (class 3). Black ash, which had previously been present everywhere near the plant, disappeared. The closure of the sinter alumina plant reduced dust emissions and burner gases from the calcination process. Fluoride and other air emissions (including tar from PAH compounds, nitrous oxide, dust and sulphur dioxide) dropped dramatically, despite a 50 per cent increase in aluminium production, as did the volume of water use and waste. Caustic bleeding and the leaking of other pollutants from the red mud pile into the surrounding soil and groundwater, drinking water wells and River Hron were brought under control by the introduction of bentonite and hydraulic walls. An analysis by the project evaluation team noted:

> ... [the] considerable environmental remediation progress, not only in terms of closed old polluting units but also in areas like facilities for haz-

ardous waste, protection of groundwater, reduction of air emissions and preventive action against damage from past red mud disposal.[22]

The Special Study concluded:

> The improvement of [the] environment in Ziar basin near ZSNP has been substantial. The extent of environmental change from highly unsatisfactory to good environmental performance has been 'Outstanding'.
>
> The opinion of the authorities [was] that EBRD's role ... had a very positive impact in the local environment and in ... promoting good relations between authorities, ZSNP and Slovalco.[23]

4. Tackling Cross-Border Pollution

In some cases, pollution from the former Eastern Bloc affected multiple countries and needed addressing in a comprehensive way. Two areas deeply affected were the Danube River Basin and the Baltic Sea, especially the Gulf of Finland near St. Petersburg.

The Danube River Basin

The Danube is the second-longest river in Europe (after the Volga) and flows through 10 countries—more than any other river in the world—before draining into the Black Sea. The Danube Delta is Europe's second-largest wetland (also after the Volga Delta), of which the greatest part lies in Romania[24], where the Razim-Sinoe lagoon is a World Heritage Site. The remainder is in Ukraine. Including its tributaries, the Danube spans 13 countries in total, of which 11 were among the EBRD's original countries of operations.[25] The river's path also includes several capital cities, notably Vienna, Prague,

---

22 'ZSNP/Slovalco Aluminium Works', Project Evaluation Department, January 1997.
23 'Special Study', Volume 1, p. 23; Volume 2, p. 60.
24 An area of approximately 5,500 square kilometres.
25 These were the Czech Republic, the Slovak Republic, Hungary, Slovenia, Croatia, Bosnia and Herzegovina, Serbia, Romania, Bulgaria, Moldova and Ukraine. Other countries were Germany and Austria. The co-operation process also included five further countries—Albania, North Macedonia, Poland, Italy and Switzerland—bringing the total number of countries involved to 18, plus the EU.

Budapest and Belgrade, while Ljubljana, Zagreb, Bucharest and Chisinau are located on major tributaries.

In the face of increasing degradation of water quality, efforts had been made by the countries most concerned to improve the situation as far back as the mid-1980s. The collapse of communism accelerated these efforts, with the European Commission taking overall responsibility for coordinating an Environmental Programme for the Danube River Basin in 1992. Cooperation was formalised by the signing of the Convention on Cooperation and Protection and Sustainable Use of the Danube River in 1994. The Danube River Protection Convention aimed to improve the use and management of surface and ground waters and control and reduce pollution from the loads of nutrients and hazardous substances discharged into the Black Sea. An International Commission established in 1998 sought to bring in international organisations as well as business groups and NGOs and led to various Action Plans and joint programmes.[26]

A Danube Black Sea Task Force (DABLAS) was set up in 2001 as a platform of cooperation involving all actors, including the EBRD. Among its activities was the drawing up of a list of prioritised projects for the rehabilitation of waters in the region. For the period 1999 to 2004, this comprised more than 350 projects in EBRD countries with total investment of just under €4 billion. More than half were municipal projects and around 30 per cent involved industrial and agribusiness areas. An updated plan covering municipal wastewater projects from 2001 to 2005 identified 224 priority projects worth close to €4.5 billion. Aside from national contributions, the EU was the largest source of funding including through the Instrument for Structural Funds for Pre-Accession (ISPA).

The EBRD addressed pollution via its project activities throughout the region. In this context, however, its efforts were focused on the water and wastewater infrastructure sector and were concentrated in Romania. More than 1,000 kilometres of the Danube flows through Romania, which contains the majority of the Danube Delta and a large portion of the proximate Black Sea coast. In total, Romania accounts for 30 per cent of the Danube River Basin and more than one-quarter of its population.

The state of water quality in Romania was particularly poor. An estimate in 2002 suggested that well over one-half of Romania's rivers remained below

---

26   https://www.icpdr.org/main/icpdr/short-history

"good" quality due to sewage and industrial and agribusiness pollution. Similarly, more than 50 per cent of groundwater exceeded recommended limits for noxious and other compounds.[27] Supply systems and distribution networks were of poor quality and used asbestos, cement and lead without sufficient care. Three-quarters of pipes needed replacing and a third were made of iron, while up-to-date systems of cleaning were few and far between.[28] Analysis of the main sources of wastewater in 2004 showed that almost 71 per cent of wastewater coming from the main pollution sources was discharged into the natural receiving waters, especially rivers, either untreated or insufficiently treated.[29]

The EBRD's approach towards municipal water and wastewater treatment differed from that of other actors in the region in that it focused on the governance of municipal finance and municipal entities and on the commercialisation of municipal water utilities. It strove to follow the "user pays" principle and to bring utilities closer towards full cost recovery and financial sustainability. On the environmental front, it was one of the leading international organisations active in the Danube River Basin.

The Bank began investing in water and wastewater treatment projects in the region in the mid-1990s. In Romania, it helped municipalities understand how to begin to address their needs and how to adopt measures in line with the many EU Directives relating to the water and wastewater sector, as well as environmental standards more generally. It was also able to provide finance blended with EU funds as the accession process accelerated. The MUDP (see Chapter 7) in five cities that started in 1995 was followed by a regional water and environment programme the following year, an extension of the MUDP to a further 10 cities and a municipal environmental loan facility financed in parallel by the EU's IPSA, as well as a clutch of other projects. By the mid-2000s, the EBRD had invested almost €400 million in improving Romania's water and wastewater sector with total financing amounting to well over €1 billion.

By helping local water utilities to become operationally and financially viable, which in turn enabled them to borrow commercially, the EBRD was instrumental in transforming the sector. According to Volume 2 of the Evaluation Department Special Study on the Danube River Basin:

---

27 Measures of nitrates, ammonia, phosphates and dissolved oxygen.
28 'Special Study: Assessment of the Bank's Contribution towards Environmental Quality Improvements to the Danube Basin' Vol 2, Evaluation Department, November 2008.
29 'Special Study', Vol 2, p. 16.

[The EBRD] broke new ground and [had] a profound and enduring impact on the subsequent development of the sector [helping] to improve basic living conditions for a significant proportion of the urban population and to realise significant environmental benefits including:
- A reduction in the pollution entering the River Danube, through the upgrading of wastewater treatment facilities.
- Improved water resource use by creating incentives at the household level (water metering and public information campaigns) and through efficient distribution (water supply network upgrading to reduce leakages).
- Human health gains as a result of improved sanitation.
- Energy efficiency gains through financing of energy-efficient pumping and other equipment.[30]

Overall, the 224 projects in the DABLAS database affected 22 million inhabitants. EBRD-financed projects amounted to 15 per cent of the total but affected a higher proportion of the population (five million people), thanks to major projects in Brno, Bucharest, Maribor, Zagreb and Sofia. These projects also accounted for around 25 per cent of the total estimated pollution reduction from the DABLAS portfolio according to estimates cited by the Evaluation Department.[31]

St. Petersburg and the Baltic Sea

Increasing concerns over the impact of industrial and other human activities on the marine environment led to the signing of the Helsinki Convention by the Baltic Sea countries in 1974.[32] A new convention was signed in 1992 to incorporate coastal countries that were previously part of central and eastern Europe, including the USSR. The convention aimed to reduce pollution in the Baltic Sea and protect the marine environment. The government of Finland had also established bilateral relationships with the City of St. Petersburg, which the Helsinki Commission (HELCOM)—the intergovernmental organisation governing the convention—identified as one of the ma-

---

30 'Special Study: Assessment of the Bank's Contribution towards Environmental Quality Improvements to the Danube Basin' Vol 2, pp. 35–37, Evaluation Department, November 2008.
31 'Special Study: Assessment of the Bank's Contributions towards Environmental Quality Improvements in Danube River Basin', Volume 1, Evaluation Department, November 2008.
32 Signatories were Denmark, Finland, the GDR, the Federal Republic of Germany, Poland and the USSR.

jor sources of pollution into the Gulf of Finland. This context encouraged the EBRD to seek projects which could assist with the reduction of pollution in the Neva River and Neva Bay which drained into it.

Although the geographic area of the EBRD's environmental interest related to HELCOM was subsequently extended to include the Barents Sea, the main target of its activities was St. Petersburg. The Bank had been working with the city from the earliest days and a Resident Office was opened there in 1995. As the second-largest city in Russia with a population of close to five million, and a gateway to western Europe, it was an obvious choice for a determined effort to tackle environmental issues.

A focus of the Bank's activities in St. Petersburg soon became municipal and environmental infrastructure. As well as improvements to the functioning of the City, the other main goal was to revamp the municipal utility Vodokanal. The second-largest water and wastewater company in Europe, Vodokanal was created in 1992 and fully owned by the City.

The EBRD, along with a number of donors, began working with Vodokanal in 1994.[33] As elsewhere in the Bank's region, St. Petersburg's water and wastewater systems suffered from a lack of maintenance and investment and were in a dilapidated state. Leakages, an unfinished water-treatment plant, the need for sewage collectors along the Neva River and upgrades to sewerage works were among a host of requirements that fell within Vodokanal's responsibilities. The company had not shaken off the command-and-control methods of the past, which badly needed replacing with modern management. Tariff and payment systems were also malfunctioning.

Immediate change was not possible. St. Petersburg had a long history of poor financial management and an unsustainable fiscal position, while Vodokanal was a large and politically sensitive institution. In 1996, it employed around 9,000 people, five times more than comparable western utilities. It was not until 1997 that the EBRD managed to gain approval for the first projects to improve St. Petersburg's municipal and environmental situation. These operations had a shaky start and went through various restructurings owing to the City's ongoing financial difficulties. Nonetheless, they marked the beginning of a change that over the following years achieved significant operational and environmental progress.

---

33 Donors included DfID (UK), SIDA (Sweden), TACIS (EU) DEPA (Denmark), and French and German Environment Ministries.

The first operation, the St. Petersburg Municipal Support Project[34], offered the city an A/B loan of up to US$ 100 million (of which US$ 50 million was for EBRD's own account), as well as assigning US$ 20 million for the purchase of Eurobonds due to be issued by the city as Russia's first municipal Eurobond issue. The Bank aimed to assist the restructuring of the city's finances, which were in a parlous state. Revenues had dropped by almost 50 per cent in the three years to 1996 and capital expenditure had fallen by 28 per cent in the preceding year alone.

The EBRD hoped to achieve a comprehensive overhaul of St. Petersburg's municipal financing and had been working towards this with the city over the previous two years. The core objective—in line with the Bank's municipal policy—was to improve St. Petersburg's financial standing by cutting costs and improving revenues. This would facilitate non-sovereign borrowing (where the EBRD was willing and able to assist) and help the municipality access international capital markets. The city's ownership of Vodokanal and its key role in tariff-setting processes meant that progress on cleaning up the environment could not easily proceed without addressing the broader issue of St. Petersburg's financial circumstances.

This proved controversial. There were concerns that the project was tantamount to policy-based lending since without a direct link to an investment programme the loan appeared to underwrite the city's finances. Nonetheless, the expectation had always been that the Bank's intervention would lead to support for specific investments. To remedy the situation, the intended programme for water and environmental service improvements—the St. Petersburg Water and Environmental Improvement Programme[35]—was swiftly lined up and agreed with the Board.

Regardless of the issue of direct versus indirect linkage of financing to specific programmes, the Board's assessment of the high-risk nature of the planned investment proved prophetic. The project was severely affected by the onset of Russia's domestic debt crisis the following year, while the water and environmental services programme was slow in delivering the major investments in pollution control that had been envisaged at the start. However, the 1997 operation did succeed in establishing a good working relationship between the EBRD and Vodokanal. Subsequently, the EBRD was able

---

34 'St. Petersburg Municipal Support Project', 15 April 1997.
35 'St. Petersburg Water and Environmental Services Improvement Programme', 12 May 1997.

to support wide-ranging reforms in Vodokanal's management structure, cost controls and long-term funding as well as specific projects under its investment programme. Furthermore, as the first non-sovereign loan in Russia, it helped demonstrate the concept of non-sovereign guarantees for water and wastewater projects, which would be applicable in Russia and ETCs.[36]

The series of loans to Vodokanal and the city that followed had a more direct impact on the environment and discharges into the Gulf of Finland. Among them were:

St. Petersburg Toxic Waste Emergency Clean-up Programme[37], a project with the city to stabilise a hazardous waste site at Krasny Bor and replace it with an alternative waste treatment facility, as well as reducing illegal dumping and the contamination of sources of drinking water (aquifers and surface water). The operation also aimed at improving the institutional framework for hazardous waste collection and disposal.

St. Petersburg South West Wastewater Treatment Plant[38], an operation with Vodokanal via a special-purpose vehicle (SPV) to complete a half-built treatment plant on which construction work had been halted in 1991 when funding disappeared as the Soviet Union broke up. The plant was designed to take an average daily sewage flow for a population of 700,000 and was one of the largest of its kind in Europe. The level of untreated wastewater entering the Gulf of Finland from St. Petersburg was significantly reduced. Financial performance also improved with the achievement of full cost recovery.

St. Petersburg Flood Protection Barrier[39], a project to complete an unfinished (again due to lack of funding) 25-kilometre barrier to protect St. Petersburg from destructive tidal-surge floods and prevent the flushing of untreated or partially treated industrial and municipal effluents, toxic materials and nuclear waste into the water-supply network of the City and the Neva water system.

St. Petersburg Northern Wastewater Treatment Plant Incinerator[40], a further project with Vodokanal to construct a sludge incinerator under a de-

---

36 See 'St. Petersburg Water and Environmental Services Improvement Programme', Project Evaluation Department, 11 April 2005.
37 https://www.ebrd.com/work-with-us/projects/psd/st-petersburg-toxic-waste-emergency-cleanup-programme.html.
38 https://www.ebrd.com/work-with-us/projects/psd/st-petersburg-southwest-waste-water-treatment-plant.html.
39 https://www.ebrd.com/work-with-us/projects/psd/st-petersburg-flood-protection-barrier.html.
40 https://www.ebrd.com/work-with-us/projects/psd/st-petersburg-northern-waste-water-treatment-plant-incinerat.html.

sign-build contract together with a publicly tendered PPP for operation and maintenance. The first such project in Russia, this was designed to provide a sustainable solution to sludge management (in place of disposal to landfill), cut the level of polluting effluent into the Baltic Sea and protect underground drinking-water reservoirs. The amount of disposed material was cut by 95 per cent through the plant's operation.

St. Petersburg Vodokanal Neva Discharges Closure[41], a project originally designed to finance the construction of the Okhta Tunnel. As a result of the Russian financial crisis, it was restructured and became focused instead on the Northern Tunnel Collector and upgrade of the Northern Waste Water Treatment Plant. The environmental benefits were nonetheless similar to the original plan, with the closing of 57 direct discharge sewers bringing a further increase (of almost 10 per cent) in municipal wastewater generated by the city of St. Petersburg being treated in biological wastewater treatment plants. The project yielded a significant reduction in discharge of pollution loads, especially phosphorus, the most decisive pollutant affecting water quality in the Gulf of Finland. As a result, there was a significant decrease in phytoplankton biomass in the southern coast of Neva Bay and, to a lesser degree, in the rest of the Gulf of Finland.

The Northern Dimension Environmental Partnership (NDEP)

In several of these projects the NIB played an important role as co-lender. The nature of the operations also required significant donor resources and the EBRD was able to draw on development funds including the EU's TACIS and finance from organisations concerned with the Baltic Sea area.[42] Of particular significance was the role of grants from the Northern Dimension Environmental Partnership (NDEP), which the EBRD helped to set up along with the NIB in 2001.

The Northern Dimension was an EU initiative developed in 1999 to strengthen dialogue and cooperation between its member states, the Nordic countries, the Baltic States and Russia. The four founding partners were the EU, Norway, Iceland and Russia. One of its objectives was "to

---

41 https://www.ebrd.com/news/2013/ebrd-hails-success-of-st.-petersburg-clean-river-project.html.
42 Finance came from the Nordic Environmental Finance Corporation (NEFCO), Swedfund International, the Finnish Fund for Industrial Cooperation (Finnfund), Finnish Ministry of Environment, SIDA among others as well as co-finance from the EIB in some cases.

help build a safe, clean and accessible environment for the people of the region"[43] and an Action Plan for the Northern Dimension was agreed at the Feira European Council in June 2000. In March the following year, the NIB invited interested IFIs[44] to a regional meeting in Helsinki attended by the President of the EBRD, Jean Lemierre, at which, according to internal records: "The EBRD proposed that a Northern Dimension Environmental Partnership (NDEP) be established to strengthen and coordinate financing of important environmental projects with cross-border effects in the Northern Dimension Area. The proposal was adopted by all participants."

The view was that DFI finance and grants should be coordinated not only to tackle cross-border pollution in a less disjointed way, but also to leverage activities to meet the scale of the problem given the historical legacy, limited availability of local finance and inadequate management capacity. The area to be covered was from north-western Russia to Iceland, including Kaliningrad but also the Barents and White Seas. Two funding windows were proposed: one for the environment dealing with water, wastewater treatment and improvements in the energy efficiency of district heating systems, the other to manage nuclear waste. The EBRD was asked to chair a Steering Group of core IFIs, the European Commission and Russia. The NDEP proposal was endorsed by Heads of State at the European Council in Goteborg, Sweden in June 2001.

A priority list of 13 environmental projects (including three of those mentioned above[45]), amounting to more than €1 billion in value, was drawn up by the EBRD and the NIB for the first Steering Group meeting in September that year. Rules on issues such as the blending of loans with grants, local financing and leadership roles were also agreed. At least €250 million in technical assistance and grant support was thought to be needed to mitigate risks and externalities and improve governance, in order to ensure that the projects (including nuclear-waste proposals) were successful. This led to the creation of the NDEP Support Fund. A pledging conference was hosted by the European Commission in Brussels in early 2002. After receiving Board approval in January 2002, the EBRD took on the role

---

43   NDEP, https://ndep.org/about/overview/history/, accessed 2019.
44   The EIB, EBRD, World Bank, IFC, Council of Europe Development Bank (CEB), NEFCO, European Commission and NIB were represented.
45   St. Petersburg's South West Waste Water Treatment Plant, Flood Protection Barrier and Northern Waste Water Treatment Plant.

of managing the Fund, which was governed by an Assembly of Contributors[46], and it became operational that July once five contributors (including Russia) had pledged at least €100 million.

5. Two Controversial Cases: Sakhalin II and BTC

Environmental issues were the area of the EBRD's activities which attracted most attention from NGOs and civil society organisations (CSOs). As the number of operations grew, particularly in sectors such as natural resources and power and energy, western NGOs also became more vocal. At the same time, after decades of repression, local communities began to find their voice. The EBRD decided to conduct larger and more frequent public consultations to ensure that all stakeholders, and especially those whose livelihoods were directly affected, would be heard. These issues were also closely followed by the Bank's Board.

All of the EBRD's projects were subject to some degree of public disclosure and most passed through their lifecycle without much debate with NGOs or CSOs on their environmental footprint. Nonetheless, the nature of the Bank's work sometimes attracted controversy.

Sakhalin II

In 1997 the EBRD provided a US$ 116 million loan[47] to Sakhalin Energy Investment Company, a consortium of US, UK and Japanese oil, trading and construction companies[48] formed to develop the Piltun-Astokhskoye and Lunskoye offshore oil and gas fields under a Production Sharing Agreement (PSA) with the Russian Government. The EBRD loan, co-financed by parallel loans from OPIC and JEXIM[49], was to help fund Phase

---

46 There are currently 13 contributors: the EU, Russia, France, Canada, Sweden, UK, Germany, Finland, Norway, Denmark, the Netherlands, Belarus and Belgium. France, Canada, the UK, Netherlands and Belgium contribute to the Nuclear window; Russia, Sweden and Belarus to the Environmental window; others contribute to both windows.
47 https://www.ebrd.com/work-with-us/projects/psd/sakhalin-ii-phase-1-oil-project.html.
48 The original shareholders were subsidiaries of Marathon/USX, McDermott, Mitsui, Shell and Mitsubishi.
49 OPIC was the US Overseas Private Investment Corporation. From the end of 2019 it became the US Development Finance Corporation (DFI). JEXIM was the Japanese Export-Import Bank before it merged to become JBIC (Japanese Bank for International Cooperation) in 1999.

I of the US$ 1 billion project to purchase, refurbish and install onsite a Canadian mobile offshore oil drilling unit (to be transported from the Beaufort Sea north of Alaska), and extract crude oil for export from the Astokh feature, an oil and gas accumulation some 2,000 metres below the sea bed in the Piltun-Astokhskoye field.

From the Bank's point of view, supporting the first oil and gas project in Russia under a PSA had considerable scope for a demonstration effect, namely to show international and Russian oil and gas companies that PSAs could be successfully developed and financed in Russia. The hope was that this would lead to the introduction of reliable and effective legislation covering production-sharing and encourage the large upstream oil and gas investments that were needed to exploit Russia's vast natural resources and support its economic development. The project was also seen as offering an opportunity to press for strict environmental conditionality and set precedents in the region and beyond.

The project's location was in the Sea of Okhotsk in shallow waters on the north-east shelf of Sakhalin Island and close to the shore (20 kilometres away). The area is one of high seismic activity[50] and extreme climatic conditions with high seas, ice, tsunamis and typhoons. The risk of oil spills from Russia's first offshore oil production attracted attention from the start. Additional issues highlighted by environmentalists concerned the impact of the project on the livelihoods (mainly fishing) of the indigenous population and the danger posed to Western Gray whales, an endangered species whose summer feeding grounds were in the area.

The company, at the insistence and with the help of the EBRD and other lenders, conducted a wide range of detailed assessments, modelled oil-spill scenarios, prepared response plans, and launched community programmes and several public consultations. The project went to the EBRD Board twice since Directors wanted to see the results of revised modelling and public consultations before approving the project.

International NGOs led by CEE Bankwatch, Greenpeace and Pacific Environment continued to campaign against the project. A local NGO, Sakhalin Environment Watch, also raised a series of issues. The NGOs wrote two

---

50 The Okhotsk Plate covers Sakhalin Island and the boundary between the Okhotsk Plate and the Pacific Plate is a subduction zone. A major earthquake occurred in Sakhalin in 1995 (moment magnitude greater than 7) and the area is a source of megathrust quakes, including among the largest on record (the Kamchatka earthquakes of 1737 and 1952).

joint letters to the EBRD's President stating their concerns over fish stocks and the potential impact of changes on local Nivkh people, oil-spill risks and the danger to the gray whale population.[51] The Bank did not agree with the criticisms, but continued to hold dialogues with representatives of these organisations, including dedicated sessions at Annual Meetings.

The Phase I project began to produce oil in 1999, transporting crude by tanker in the summer months when the sea was not frozen. An extension to the project (Phase II) to develop the Lunskoye field, involving two new offshore platforms and pipelines to bring oil and gas onshore to a liquified natural gas (LNG) terminal 800 kilometres away, began to be discussed with the EBRD in 2002. The Bank undertook a long period of due diligence designed to elicit answers to questions on project decisions and impact assessments of all aspects of the proposals. It was only in December 2005 that the EBRD's Board felt the answers were adequate and there were sufficient mitigation features in place to allow the project to go to public consultation.

Phase II remained controversial for essentially the same reasons as Phase I, notably the whale issue (the new platforms were also located near their summer feeding grounds) and further impacts on Sakhalin's indigenous Nivkh people. In response to criticisms, the company had already developed a Sakhalin Island Minorities Development Plan. The experience of Phase I also led to a number of improvements in public disclosure and consultation arrangements with NGOs and local populations. Public consultations took place in London, Moscow, Sapporo and three locations on Sakhalin Island. A summary of the Environmental Impact Assessment was provided in Russian and English and copies were made available on the island.

Acting as the arbiter of international standards was important but mediating between the company, the Russian authorities, local peoples, campaigners and protestors was a difficult task for the EBRD and absorbed an increasingly large amount of senior management time.

Matters came to a head in September 2006 when the consortium was forced to sell a majority stake to Gazprom, the dominant state-owned Russian energy company. By December, Gazprom owned 50 per cent plus one share. This represented a material change to the original project approved by the Board, and a significant change in direction, and presented an opportu-

---

51 Letters dated from 10 December 2001 and November 2003.

nity for the EBRD to withdraw. On 11 January 2007, the Bank announced it would no longer participate in the project as state ownership had undermined the transition arguments for proceeding. It concluded, however, that from an environmental and social perspective there had been some success from the five years of consultation.

> Through its engagement in the development of the project, the EBRD has helped to introduce commitments to consultation, transparency and treatment of indigenous people. The EBRD has worked with Sakhalin Energy on many enhancements during the construction phase: Sakhalin Energy rerouted pipelines to accommodate the rare Western Gray whale that feeds in the region; a panel of recognised whale experts was established to monitor and advise on operations; significant improvements were introduced to the strategy for on-land pipeline construction, especially the environmentally sensitive crossings of some 1000 rivers; and Sakhalin Energy adopted a standard-setting plan for treatment of indigenous peoples as well as transparency and consultation.[52]

Baku-Tbilisi-Ceyhan (BTC) pipeline

A high-profile project which the EBRD began to look at in 2001 also attracted strong NGO and CSO interest. The largest cross-border infrastructure initiative globally at the time, the Baku-Tbilisi-Ceyhan (BTC) pipeline was a US$ 3.6 billion project to construct a 1,760-kilometre pipeline to carry crude oil from the landlocked Caspian Sea to the Mediterranean port of Ceyhan in Turkey. The Bank saw its participation as an opportunity to play a unique role in fostering regional cooperation between Azerbaijan, Georgia and Turkey, while at the same time ensuring high international environmental and developmental standards were met.

Other potential benefits were widespread. BP estimated that transit fees and royalties accruing to Azerbaijan, Georgia and Turkey would reach US$ 150 billion between 2005 and 2024. The project was also of regional and global significance since it provided a new strategic route for oil exports (particularly to EU countries) from the Caspian, bypassing Russian pipe-

---

52 'EBRD no longer considers current financing package for Sakhalin II', EBRD Press Release, 11 January 2007.

lines and the Middle East and helping to avoid further pressures on supplies through the Bosporus. At the same time, its overland route required navigating environmentally, geologically and politically sensitive areas.

The Board approved a US$ 250 million A/B loan (US$ 125 million for the EBRD's own account and the rest syndicated to commercial banks) to BTC Co. in November 2003. The IFC approved an identical loan. The main companies involved were BP and AzBTC[53], which held 30.1 per cent and 25 per cent of BTC Co. respectively, with the remainder owned by a group of nine oil majors and traders.

As lead sponsor, BP was well aware of the sensitivities of laying a long pipeline through such a complex region and difficult terrain. The company took every opportunity to prepare the route carefully, consult affected parties and offer solutions where appropriate. Environmental and human rights critics remained vigilant and vocal throughout nonetheless, pointing to alleged abuses of land and civil rights in Azerbaijan and Turkey, employment and gender issues, earthquake and oil-spill risks, risks to natural parks and aquifers (especially in the important Borjomi-Kharagauli national park in Georgia) and risks to the export of Borjomi mineral water.[54]

As the project progressed, a vast amount of discussion took place. Advice was given and many assessments, responses and plans were made to address concerns, complaints and grievances.[55] Among them were Environmental and Social Impact Assessments, Public Consultation and Disclosure Plans, Oil Spill Response Plans, Resettlement Action Plans, Right-of-Way Reinstatement Plans and Environmental and Social Action Plans. In addition, the sponsors spent US$ 30 million on various community investments along the pipeline corridor under a Community Investment Programme that involved NGOs and a broader Regional Development Initiative to contribute to sustainable development was supported by the sponsors, the EBRD and the IFC. Over 38 volumes of environmental and social information in five languages were disclosed to the public, amounting to more than 11,000 pages. They stood five metres high when stacked!

---

53   The name reflected the Azeri interest in BTC. It was owned 70 per cent by the Azerbaijan Republic and 30 per cent SOCAR.
54   For example, see 'BTC Pipeline—an IFI Recipe for Increasing Poverty', M. Kochladze, N. Gujaraidze, K. Gujaraidze and V. Titvinidze, CEE Bankwatch and Oxfam GB, Tbilisi, 2005.
55   The EBRD's Independent Recourse Mechanism was also available to deal with complaints, as was the IFC's Compliance Advisor Ombudsman.

The project was successfully completed in 2006 and the target capacity of one million barrels a day was reached in 2007. Both the EBRD and the IFC assessed that the project fully achieved its environmental objectives and had benefited considerably from the extensive consultation process.

[The project] introduced world class standards in all aspects of crude oil production and transportation. The preparation, construction and operation of the BTC project set new global best-practice standards for future pipeline projects.[56]

---

56 'Baku-Tbilisi-Ceyhan Pipeline Project', April 2008, p.4. See also 'Lessons of Experience: Baku-Tbilisi-Ceyhan Pipeline Project', IFC, WBG, September 2006, No. 2.

Chapter 9
Nuclear Safety

1. Nuclear Power Issues

When it came to nuclear power, concerns about tensions between the EBRD's commercial and environmental remits did not apply. Investments in new facilities in the sector were excluded from the Bank's remit from the very beginning. Instead, nuclear safety and the clean-up of former nuclear facilities were paramount in the context of eastern Europe and public concerns over legacy issues. Nuclear plants in several countries were in an unsafe condition and posed a threat not only to the population and environment, but also to economic transition due to the enormous costs involved in bringing them into line with international safety standards.

The EBRD became heavily involved in tackling nuclear safety in its region of operations. In this sector, its activities were driven by environmental considerations rather than a profit-based approach. A host of international donors also joined forces with the Bank to finance nuclear safety funds and activities.

Many of the EBRD's shareholders were worried about the nuclear legacy of the communist period. For the USA and other NATO members, the major concern was how to deal with the management of nuclear weapons as the Soviet Union broke up. For many in Europe, the primary issue was the safety of nuclear power plants. Popular antagonism towards nuclear power remained strong in some shareholder countries, notably Austria and Germany.

The Chernobyl catastrophe in Ukraine in 1986 had brought home to people in both halves of Europe the enormous risks associated with poorly designed and mismanaged ageing Soviet-era nuclear facilities. While Chernobyl was the largest nuclear accident, it was not the first. The industry had suffered high-profile accidents before, including Three Mile Island in

1979[1] in the USA. In 1991, official information that had been suppressed for years emerged on the earlier Soviet Kyshtym disaster of 1957,[2] which added to the popular angst over nuclear power.

The proximity of dangerous nuclear power plants to much of mainland Europe could not be ignored. Yet at the same time, many countries in the former Eastern Bloc depended heavily on nuclear power for electricity production.

Energy supply was an issue in its own right, especially for countries reliant on imported energy, most of which came from Russia. A lack of reliable capacity to supply energy needs was a political problem. Continuing use of nuclear power plants provided one solution. To meet rising demand there was even a readiness to build new nuclear plants, often based on old technology, which was more affordable than plants with the latest specifications. The choice between interrupted electricity and frequent blackouts (and disrupted industrial production) on the one hand and running risks with unsafe nuclear power plants on the other was a genuine dilemma. In many countries, the politics pointed to supplying adequate and reliable power so continuing to use existing nuclear reactors looked attractive.

From the EBRD's point of view, the immediate concern was the safety of existing nuclear plants; in parallel, countries would develop alternative sources of energy supply. International expertise would be essential to make this work, as well as safety upgrades to nuclear power plants and investment in non-nuclear power generation. It was here that the EBRD was well-placed to help.

2. Tackling the Soviet Legacy

International Action

Not all of the newly independent countries among the EBRD's countries of operations had nuclear-power plants and related facilities but the total was nonetheless substantial.[3] One estimate of installed nuclear capacity in

---

1 At the Three Mile Island Nuclear Generating Station (TMI-2) near Harrisburg, Pennsylvania on 28 March 1979, classified as category five on a seven-point International Nuclear Event Scale. The Chernobyl accident was a category seven event, as was the more recent Fukushima Daiichi case in 2011.
2 https://www.britannica.com/event/Kyshtym-disaster
3 The only nuclear-power plant in former Yugoslavia was at Krsko in Slovenia.

1991 in CEE suggested it amounted to more than 40 Gigawatts or 12 per cent of total electricity generation (and 13 per cent of the world's nuclear capacity).[4] Close to half (19 Gigawatts) was supplied by high-risk reactors. These were the RBMK and VVER 440/230 types.[5] International specialists considered that upgrades to bring them to acceptable levels of safety would be uneconomic. Nuclear power plants in Armenia, Lithuania and the North West and Centre power regions of Russia (the area of highest population density)[6] were solely of this type while in Bulgaria and Slovakia around half were.

It was obvious that successful reform of the nuclear energy sector, including safety improvements and the environmental rehabilitation of the nuclear industry, would involve many facets: the safety of operating reactors; the closure of high-risk reactors; strengthening of the energy regulatory system, and in particular nuclear regulators and waste management administration; and the safe and secure management of spent nuclear fuel and waste.

Given the difficult economic environment the former communist countries faced at the time, an early and full clean-up of the nuclear legacy in the region would require substantial support from the West. Intensive work on the issue had been put in train by the G7 and the EC as the Soviet Union began to collapse. Knowing this, Attali appealed to delegates at the Rio Earth Summit to develop a plan.

A few weeks later, at the G7 Heads Summit in Munich, agreement was reached to seek the shutdown of Soviet-designed high-risk reactors.[7] The communiqué stated:

> ... the safety of Soviet-design nuclear power plants gives us cause for great concern ... We offer the States concerned our support within the framework of a multilateral programme of action ... and support the setting up

---

4   As a share of electricity generation nuclear power was particularly significant in Hungary (48 per cent), Bulgaria (34 per cent) and the Czech and Slovak Republics (29 per cent). Source: B. A. Semenov, P. Dastidar and L. L. Bennett, IAEA Bulletin, 1/1993.
5   Other VVER types were judged capable of being made safe with sufficient upgrades. 'Progress Report on Nuclear Safety', EBRD, 1992.
6   These units supplied some 17 per cent of electricity for these regions where some three quarters of the Russian population lived. See 'Nuclear Safety and Electric Power in Armenia, Bulgaria, Lithuania, Russia and Slovakia', a joint World Bank, International Energy Agency and EBRD Report, June 1993.
7   The full text of the communiqué section 'Safety of Nuclear Power Plants in the New Independent States of the Former Soviet Union and in Central and Eastern Europe' is available at http://www.g8.utoronto.ca/summit/1992munich/communique/.

of a supplementary multilateral mechanism ... to address immediate operational safety and technical safety improvement measures...

It concluded that the international fund to be set up to deal with the issue should be coordinated with and assisted by the G24 and the EBRD, with a steering group of donors overseeing the fund administration.

Attali reported to the Board the same day (8 July 1992) that he would contact the Chair of the G7 Deputies to establish the fund. Five days later, after consulting Horst Köhler—at the time the German Sherpa and G7D Chair—the Board was presented with a worked-up proposal for a Multilateral Nuclear Safety Fund to be established within the EBRD as a cooperation fund[8] under a steering committee of national donors and the European Commission. Further work was needed, as was the agreement of the G7. This was achieved early the following year.

The Nuclear Safety Account

By March 1993 the rules of the fund, now known as the Nuclear Safety Account (NSA), had been agreed. It was to be managed by the EBRD[9] on behalf of 14 donor countries and the EC, collectively known as the Assembly of Contributors. Commitments from donors enabled it to begin work in April, with more than US$ 100 million of financing secured by May that year.[10] Priority was given to those reactors that presented the highest levels of risk and where cost-effective safety improvements could be made. These were the design-deficient RBMK and VVER 440/230 reactors[11], where there was a lack of containment and insufficient control, fire protection or capacity of emergency core-cooling systems. Other serious weaknesses in-

---

8 Under Article 20. Paragraph 1 (viii).
9 Under the arrangements, the EBRD acted as the secretariat of the NSA and liaised with the European Commission in its capacity as the G24 secretariat.
10 The Rules required a minimum of ECU 60 million to have been committed before the NSA could become operational.
11 RBMK reactors were water-cooled, graphite-moderated "channel-type" reactors whose technology and safety features were not well understood by western experts at the time of the collapse of the Soviet Union, compared with the VVER pressurised water reactors. The latter comprised three types, of which the 230/440 model was considered too dangerous to be kept in operation (not economically upgradable to acceptable safety levels). Ten were in operation at the time. More modern VVER types, the 213/440 model (14 in operation) and VVER 320/1000 (18 in operation) were regarded as upgradeable over time. The RBMK reactors, one of which was involved in the Chernobyl accident, were not considered upgradeable to adequate international standards.

cluded cracks in the piping of RBMK reactors. Recognising that it would not be possible to close plants immediately, the NSA provided funding for emergency upgrades to address the worst risks. The hope was that, in the meantime, plans could be made for alternative energy sources and that the countries would profit from knowledge-transfer and adopt safety standards similar to those in the West.

Ahead of the G7 Tokyo Summit in 1993, a joint World Bank, International Energy Agency (IEA) and EBRD report looked into alternatives to the continuing use of unsafe nuclear reactors. The EBRD explored the options going forward, principally to evaluate the pros and cons of more rapid closure of high-risk plants. A fast route, leading to closure of higher-risk plants within three to five years, suggested an investment cost of more than US$20 billion by 2000 (of which the greatest part would come from an increase in conventional-power capacity to compensate for the loss of nuclear power). Some countries, facing large import bills from a switch to gas-fired technology (and increased dependence on Russian gas supplies), did not favour the scenario. Others, including Russia, believed the risks associated with their reactors were not excessive and that old, highly polluting thermal plants should be closed first. The alternative, a much slower closure programme over 15 to 20 years, involved greater risks and an even greater cost. Although there was no formal recommendation, the joint study leant towards the faster strategy to address nuclear-safety risks.

The Tokyo Summit endorsed the work and recommended a country by country approach to nuclear safety and power sector development under a framework of coordinated multilateral action led by the World Bank, the IEA, the EBRD and the EIB.

A follow-up report to the G7 Naples Summit a year later showed that slow progress was being made with "no chance" of achieving the fastest path described in the earlier report and very little likelihood of success for an intermediate scenario.

There were three main reasons for the slow response. Macroeconomic and energy-sector reforms, including on nuclear safety, were falling behind in most of the countries concerned. Other hindering factors included the disruption of energy supplies in areas affected by regional conflict, a lack of political will towards reform and weak nuclear regulatory agencies. There were also difficulties in agreeing sector strategies and investment programmes and in preparing projects effectively. Additional technical studies were often commissioned. Finally, uncertainties over the availability of finance and the level of available concessionality affected planning.

Despite the difficulties of reforming the electricity and power sectors, the early years of the NSA were successful. By the end of 1996, pledges to the account of almost ECU 260 million had been made by the EU and 14 donor countries and the EBRD had made some progress in deploying the funds.

An ECU 24 million project to start the closure of Kozloduy Units 1 to 4 in Bulgaria (four VVER 440/230 reactors) had been signed in 1993 and was underway, while an ECU 33 million project in Lithuania to tackle safety at the Ignalina nuclear power plant (involving two RBMK reactors) was signed in 1994. Ignalina was a particularly sensitive plant as it accounted for around 90 per cent of Lithuania's electricity production. Agreements amounting to ECU 75 million related to nuclear power plants in St. Petersburg (four RBMK reactors) and Novovoronezh and Kola (four VVER 230/440 reactors) were reached with Russia in 1995.

The emergency safety upgrades were delivered quickly. The programmes also helped recipients adopt western safety methodological approaches such as plant-specific in-depth safety assessments, which had important long-term effects in improving nuclear safety.

Originally, both the timetable for the NSA (1993–1996) and the range of projects it could cover were limited in scope. The fund's initial agreements did not contain firm closure commitments but rather an understanding that plants should not be operated beyond certain technical trigger points. It was hoped that safety and economic assessments would convince recipients that it would be in their interests to close plants sooner rather than later. It was many years, however, before those reactor units were actually shut down. One of the early lessons from the NSA experience was that it would take massive assistance programmes to achieve plant closures. Nevertheless, the programme did lay the ground for the closure of reactors in Ignalina, Kozloduy 1-4, Bohunice V1 [12] and Chernobyl 1-3.

In due course, closure commitments of first-generation, Soviet-designed nuclear power plants were achieved in EU accession negotiations with Bulgaria, Lithuania and the Slovak Republic. In turn, the EU committed to assist with decommissioning programmes and energy sector projects. At the request of the European Commission and a number of European countries,

---

12   In the Slovak Republic.

in 2001 the EBRD set up support funds for each of the three countries to finance infrastructure decommissioning as well as a wide range of energy projects such as renewables, conventional power supply and grid modifications. The aim was to decommission old reactors and make changes to countries' energy sectors to accommodate the closure of nuclear capacity.

The long and difficult process of dealing with the safety of nuclear power plants was in retrospect unsurprising given the size of the problem, the differences in approach to nuclear issues between the East and West and the specific local issues raised by shutting down significant sources of electricity generation. The EBRD was able to help by channelling funds and providing expert independent advice through the NSA (which was renewed every three years for the subsequent period), as well as addressing the pressing safety issues and laying the groundwork for the eventual closures of these plants. This was supplemented by large investments by the Bank in non-nuclear power generation capacity in the region. Although some countries decided to extend the lives of nuclear power plants, the EBRD was never a party to such a decision, supporting only safety upgrades of existing units.

3. Managing the Consequences of a Nuclear Disaster: Chernobyl

The most significant nuclear power legacy was of course Chernobyl. The exclusion zone around the site and the neighbouring town of Pripyat was a constant reminder of the implications of nuclear failure.[13] The EBRD recognised that dealing with Chernobyl would remain a huge burden for Ukraine. At the time of the Bank's launch in 1991, however, Ukraine was still part of the Soviet Union so financing was restricted under the AEB. It was also not clear that the authorities were seeking to shut down the remaining reactors.

With the NSA in place, however, the Bank was in a position to play a role in this critical nuclear safety legacy case. De Larosière, realising the opportunity and the importance of Chernobyl for the international community,

---

13 It is perhaps ironic that Chernobyl was called the 'Vladimir Ilyich Lenin Nuclear Power Plant'. Some contend that the meltdown and its consequences were a factor that contributed to the ultimate collapse of the Soviet Union itself.

acted early in his tenure as President to address the issue. Writing in June 1994 to G7 Governors ahead of the Naples Heads' Summit, which was due to review progress on nuclear safety, he put forward a proposal.

> I am convinced that the Nuclear Safety Account can play ... a major role in promoting and implementing strategies decided by its Assembly and the G7 ... Other safety measures need to be considered urgently ... the closure of Chernobyl ... deserve[s] Western assistance ... The most recent decisions taken in Ukraine (to continue operation at Chernobyl) ... go in the wrong direction ... It seems to me to be absolutely crucial that the G7 ... announce their willingness to support Ukraine with the appropriate level of concessional funds in order to speed up Chernobyl's closure.

The G7 Heads agreed at Naples to develop a plan to close the Chernobyl nuclear power plant as a priority. This was to be done in the context of developing a comprehensive energy reform plan for Ukraine. The Heads pledged to provide up to US$ 200 million in grants, including a replenishment of the NSA for this purpose, and to allow loans by IFIs. This led to an NSA programme for Ukraine focused initially on short-term safety and security projects at Chernobyl's Unit 3, the last reactor operating by the time of the programme, with the aim of shutting it down.[14]

It was clear that dealing with the consequences of Chernobyl would be an enormous undertaking requiring the closing of operations, the decommissioning of facilities and the conversion of the site into an environmentally less dangerous area. There was also the need to develop an effective independent energy strategy for Ukraine, a task made more challenging by the appalling economic situation in the country, where output had fallen by more than 50 per cent over the previous five years. This prompted the suggestion of a conference on Partnership on Economic Transformation in Ukraine to take place before the next Heads meeting in Canada in 1995.

The Ukrainian overall power system was in very poor shape, frequently coming close to complete shutdown.[15] Ukrainian citizens experienced regular blackouts and reform of the energy sector had become a political priority. The targeted Chernobyl reactors, which continued to work after the

---

14 Unit 2 closed after a fire in 1991; Unit 1 closed in 1996.
15 See The Bulletin of the Atomic Scientists, May/June 1996.

meltdown of the fourth reactor in 1986, supplied some 5 to 7 per cent of Ukraine's total electricity.[16] Local policymakers were concerned that closing them for safety reasons would mean increased reliance on inefficient low-grade coal and gas-fired power plants, which were themselves suffering from decades of poor maintenance and dependent on expensive supplies from Russia or Turkmenistan.[17]

The communiqué by G7 Heads at the Halifax Summit on 16 June 1995 returned to the nuclear safety issue and the replenishment of the NSA in particular. This time the G7 recognised more fully the need to support Ukraine in developing its energy strategy, an area where the EBRD was already closely engaged with the World Bank. The G7 statement read:

> Recognizing the economic and social burden that the closure of Chernobyl will place on Ukraine, we [will continue] efforts to mobilize international support for appropriate energy production, energy efficiency and nuclear safety projects for Ukraine … We call upon the World Bank and the EBRD to continue their cooperation with Ukraine in devising a realistic long-term energy strategy, based on the results of the EBRD-funded least-cost investment study, and to increase their financial contribution in support of appropriate energy sector reform and investment.

In April 1995, under pressure from the international community, Ukraine's newly elected President, Leonid Kuchma, had pledged to close the remaining Chernobyl reactors by 2000 subject to the proviso that sufficient funds be made available. It took further effort and protracted negotiations, culminating in a Memorandum of Understanding agreed in Ottawa between the G7, the European Commission and Ukraine in December 1995, before closure of Chernobyl's legacy reactors by 2000 became a concrete proposal with a comprehensive programme of cooperation laid out along with an agreed action plan. This allowed the EBRD to start working actively with donors and Ukraine to establish a mechanism to finance the remediation plan.

---

16   Ibid.
17   Nur Nigmatullin, the acting Chairman of the State Committee for Utilisation of Atomic Energy, was quoted as saying to the G7 in December 1995: "Of course we want Chernobyl shut down … But you must understand that in the midst of our current economic crisis we cannot do so quickly, inexpensively, and as simply as your governments would like to believe." Cited in The Bulletin of the Atomic Scientists above.

It was not until November 1996 that an ECU 118 million project for the Chernobyl nuclear power plant was signed under the NSA, allowing for the construction of a Liquid Radioactive Waste Treatment Plant (LRTP) to handle 35,000 cubic metres of low and intermediate-level radioactive liquid waste. In addition to funding difficulties, the delay in reaching an agreement was due to ongoing discussions between Ukraine and the EC about integrating the former into the European electricity network.

Consideration was also given to the decommissioning of the Chernobyl units once they had been closed. Improving safety at the site required the decommissioning of the original fuel-storage facilities, which meant moving the spent fuel into a safer environment. Again, the NSA was seen as the best mechanism to achieve this. To facilitate the decommissioning an Interim Spent Fuel Facility (ISF-2) was set up to process, dry and cut more than 21,000 fuel assemblies from the Chernobyl Units 1 to 3, which were then to be placed in double-walled canisters and stored in concrete modules on site. The spent fuel would be stored safely and securely for a minimum period of 100 years. Once all fuel was transferred to the new ISF-2 facility, the existing fuel-storage facilities could be decommissioned.

In parallel, the LRTP was created to retrieve the highly active liquids from their storage tanks, process them into a solid state and move them into containers for long-term storage. Both facilities were financed by the NSA, with €235 million provided by the EBRD alone for ISF-2.

The 1986 Chernobyl accident destroyed Reactor 4. At the time of the explosion, it held 192 tonnes of uranium nuclear fuel. According to estimates, less than 5 per cent was released after the explosion. After extinguishing the fire, covering the reactor core became the most important task to prevent the further expulsion of radioactive materials. Between May and November 1986, a steel and concrete structure—the so-called sarcophagus—was built around the destroyed reactor building to act as a radiation shield.

The shelter had been designed as an emergency measure with a lifespan of 20-30 years. The main challenge in Chernobyl was thus finding a long-term solution for the temporary building that would stabilise the shelter, protect workers from high radiation levels, prevent the release of contaminated material and allow the orderly deconstruction of the remains of the destroyed reactor and the removal of its fuel-containing materials.

A major summit between the G7 and Russia in Moscow in April 1997 on nuclear safety and security reaffirmed the commitment by all sides to deal carefully with the nuclear safety legacy, and Chernobyl in particular. The commitment by Kuchma to close the whole Chernobyl plant by 2000[18] was welcomed again two months later by G7 Heads and then by the EC at their Summit in Lyon.

In Denver in June 1997, the G7 Heads committed to further key work on the Chernobyl legacy. The communiqué stated:

> To date, projects have been agreed totaling over $1 billion … We agreed on the importance of securing the environmental safety of the sarcophagus covering the remains of the destroyed Chernobyl reactor. This task is inevitably beyond the resources of Ukraine alone. This is a major challenge for the international community. We have decided to add to the commitments we undertook in the MOU with Ukraine. We endorse the setting up of a multilateral funding mechanism and have agreed that the G-7 will contribute $300 million over the lifetime of the project…

As a result of the Summit the G7, the European Commission and other donors invited the EBRD to set up a Chernobyl Shelter Fund and manage the "Chernobyl Unit 4 Shelter Implementation Plan". The plan provided a step-by-step strategy for decisions required to develop a programme to make the accident site safe.

The Chernobyl Shelter Fund, the Shelter Implementation Plan (SIP) and the New Safe Confinement project began in 1997. It was managed for the next 20 years by the EBRD on behalf of 45 donors and other contributors and was a remarkable success story. It produced one of the world's most significant engineering feats and was undertaken in a highly contaminated area. The exercise required extreme care in the handling of nuclear materials and protecting workers from radiation and was conducted in a country beset with serious financial and administrative problems.

The first phase of the SIP, which was sponsored by the USA and the EC under its TACIS programme, was prepared by Ukrainian and international experts in 1997. It focused on conceptual solutions to define the engineering work needed for confinement and stabilisation and on a strategy for fuel-containing materials in the shelter. Critical early stabilisation work inside

---

18 The last reactor in Chernobyl was closed down in 2000, as per Kuchma's commitment. https://www.newscientist.com/article/dn257-chernobyl-closes/

and outside the structure took place amid high radiation and the risk of collapse and required very careful planning and implementation. The Chernobyl Shelter Fund became operational in December 1997 with contribution agreements totalling ECU 263 million.

In February 1998, a Framework Agreement between Ukraine and the EBRD was ratified by the Rada (the Ukrainian parliament), which allowed four grant agreements to be drawn up with Energoatom and the Nuclear Regulatory Authority of Ukraine for ECU 154 million as the first phase of the SIP. Major contracts were awarded in the following months based on open tendering rules in line with the Bank's procurement policies. The resulting consortia comprised a mix of international and Ukrainian companies. A joint Ukraine-EBRD committee dealt with the policy issues needed for project implementation.

The two decades of EBRD work on Chernobyl gave rise to a plethora of press reports and films by the world's most prominent media channels. Some bankers achieved moments of TV fame unparalleled in the world of international development. Progress has also been documented on the Bank's own website.[19]

The New Safe Confinement—the largest movable land structure in the world—was moved into its final position in 2017.[20] The arch-shaped structure stands 108 metres high and 162 metres long and has a span of 257 metres. It has an expected lifetime of a minimum of 100 years.

To minimise the risk of workers' exposure to radiation, it was assembled in the vicinity of the site and then slid 327 metres on pads using hydraulic pistons into position above the Unit 4 reactor site in November 2016. After connecting various sub-systems and fully testing its operations, it was declared complete on 26 April 2019, exactly 33 years after the original accident.

The keys from the New Safe Confinement were symbolically handed over to the authorities of Ukraine in July 2019. It cost €1.5 billion and was financed by 45 donor countries and institutions. The EBRD served as the fund manager and largest contributor, providing €715 million in total to Chernobyl projects.

---

19 https://www.ebrd.com/what-we-do/sectors/nuclear-safety/chernobyl-overview.html.
20 https://www.ebrd.com/news/2017/works-at-chernobyl-new-safe-confinement-nearing-completion.html.

4. Other Nuclear Safety Interventions

K2R4

A prerequisite for Ukraine joining the European Energy Community[21] was that two Soviet-designed VVER 1000 reactors be brought up to internationally acceptable safety standards. The two reactors, Khmelnytsky 2 and Rivne 4 (known as K2R4), were to undergo a safety upgrade through loan finance rather than grants. The Chair of the G7, President Jacques Chirac, wrote to de Larosière in January 1996 to request that the EBRD consider financing the K2R4 project, along with the EC and the World Bank. The total package proposed was well over US $1 billion. De Larosière had doubts about the economics of the proposal but accepted the suggestion in principle.[22]

The Board considered a loan for safety upgrades to K2R4 soon after, and again in 2000, but the project turned out to be both technically challenging and controversial with civil society. It underwent a transformation in 2004[23] and was completed by 2009.

As a condition of providing support for K2R4, the EBRD required Ukraine to assess the safety of its other 15 nuclear units. This led to a comprehensive safety upgrade programme, which was later updated to take account of post-Fukushima stress-testing. The Bank provided a €300 million loan to support this programme, matched by another €300 million from Euratom. The programme, scheduled for completion in 2017, is still ongoing.[24]

International Decommissioning Funds

The EBRD also managed international funds for the decommissioning of Soviet-era reactors in Bulgaria, Lithuania and the Slovak Republic, follow-

---

21 Ukraine ultimately acceded to the European Energy Community Treaty in 2011.
22 De Larosière commented: "French President Jacques Chirac, along with Larry Summers, who was then American Treasury Secretary, [were] trying to influence me. I told them that the EBRD could consider looking at the project and even financing it, provided that the financial risk was borne by the G7. At the time the matter went no further…" *50 Years of Financial Crises*, p. 185.
23 https://www.ebrd.com/work-with-us/projects/psd/k2r4-poststartup-safety-and-modernisation-programme.html.
24 https://www.ebrd.com/cs/Satellite?c=Content&cid=1395236708545&pagename=EBRD-FR%2FContent%2FHublet.

ing those countries' decision to close down these facilities as part of their progress towards EU accession.

In Bulgaria, the Kozloduy International Decommissioning Support Fund (KIDSF) was established in June 2001 as an assistance programme of the European Commission and other European contributors to help the Bulgarian government cope with the early closure and decommissioning of four (out of six) VVER-type reactors of the Kozloduy power plant. Units 1 and 2 were shut down in 2002 and Units 3 and 4 in 2006.

In Lithuania, the Ignalina International Decommissioning Support Fund (IIDSF) was set up in 2001 at the EBRD by the European Commission and 14 European governments for the decommissioning of the country's only nuclear power plant with two RBMK 1500 reactors. Unit 1 of the Ignalina plant was closed at the end of 2004 and Unit 2 at the end of 2009. The process led to a spent-fuel storage facility starting operation in September 2016 and a radioactive-waste facility followed in 2017.[25]

In the Slovak Republic, the European Commission together with eight European governments established the Bohunice International Decommissioning Support Fund (BIDSF) at the EBRD in 2001. The fund financed projects to support the decommissioning of Units 1 and 2 of the plant in a safe, secure and cost-effective manner and to introduce new measures in the Slovak energy sector to minimise the impact of the closure through improvements in the efficiency of energy supply and use.[26]

Barents Sea

In the Barents Sea a major environmental challenge was presented by the threat of pollution from old nuclear submarines and poorly stored nuclear waste. Spent nuclear fuel and radioactive waste generated through the operation of Russia's Northern Fleet were distributed among various military bases along the coast of the Barents Sea and were present on its surface and sea bed. The heaviest concentrations were in Andreeva Bay, just 45 kilometres from the Norwegian border, where radioactivity was estimated to reach several million Curies, a concentration level of the same order of magnitude as at Chernobyl.[27]

---

25   A photo gallery on EBRD.com is at https://www.ebrd.com/ignalina-photo-gallery.
26   Read more about Bohunice at https://www.ebrd.com/what-we-do/sectors/nuclear-safety/bohunice.html.
27   Referred to in 'Northern Dimension Environmental Partnership Support Fund', p. 65, 2002.

In 2003 the Nuclear Window was established within the NDEP[28] to deliver environmental improvements and a reduction of risks associated with the nuclear legacy in north-west Russia. The focus areas of concern were Andreeva Bay,[29] Lepse and Soviet-era Papa-class nuclear-powered vessels and submarine reactors.

The Nuclear Window complemented Russian and bilaterally funded programmes aimed at the decommissioning of nuclear-powered vessels, the provision of safe and secure infrastructure for nuclear materials and the safe removal of spent nuclear fuel from the region. This dimension of the NDEP has continued to this day, illustrating the scale of the challenge in cleaning up sources of nuclear pollution and making waters safe in the Northern Dimension Area. Contributors have so far provided €165 million to the Nuclear Window.

Uranium Mining in Central Asia

Central Asia served as an important source of uranium in the Soviet Union and remains so today, with Kazakhstan being the world's leading exporter of the metal. In the late Soviet era, uranium ore was also imported from other countries for processing. A large amount of radioactively contaminated material was placed in mining waste dumps and tailing sites but very little remediation was done prior to or after closure of the mining and milling operations.

An Environmental Remediation Account for Central Asia (ERA) was established in 2015[30] at the initiative of the European Commission and became operational in 2016. The aim of the account was to pool donor funds to assist the Kyrgyz Republic, Tajikistan and Uzbekistan to clean up some of the most dangerous sites left by uranium production in these countries.

---

28   Read more about NDEP Nuclear Window at https://www.ebrd.com/what-we-do/sectors/nuclear-safety/nuclear-window.html
29   Breakthrough in clean-up of Russia's Andreeva Bay. EBRD press release, 26 November 2019. https://www.ebrd.com/news/2019/breakthrough-in-cleanup-of-andreeva-bay.html
30   https://www.ebrd.com/news/2017/progress-with-environmental-remediation-of-uranium-legacy-in-central-asia.html

Conclusion

The rigorous pursuit of high environmental and social standards brought new ideas and a better understanding of their importance to a region where neglect, inefficiency and cover-up had been the norm in such matters. Careful project preparation conducted with thorough due diligence enabled the EBRD to provide sound advice on environmental and social issues to a wide range of companies, large and small. This was especially important in the most polluting sectors.

The introduction of new finance and expert assistance and learning-by-doing helped clients improve conditions for workers, safeguard local and indigenous populations and bring about a cleaner environment, supporting the transition towards more sustainable economies.

There is no parallel elsewhere to the EBRD's interventions on nuclear safety. The threats posed in the earlier period from Chernobyl-type risks were brought under control through the international efforts—by west and east—orchestrated under the aegis of the Bank. At the site of the Chernobyl plant itself, contaminated material is finally housed safely under the massive physical structure financed with the EBRD's help.

The EBRD's role in cleaning up the Soviet environmental legacy, which was established early on, formed a unique dimension of its support to the transition of countries of operations. The importance of the environment to the EBRD's business, however, championed enthusiastically by senior management throughout, provided a solid basis for the next stage in the Bank's "green" journey. We return to this theme in the next volume.

Chapter 10
Embedding Impact in the Business Model

Introduction

By the mid-1990s, the stars had begun to move in the EBRD's favour. The triumvirate at the top were in many ways the ideal combination to stabilise the Bank and set it on a path for success. De Larosière, the internationally respected grand-homme of international finance, a man of great foresight and an astute manager; Ron Freeman, an investment banker with a strong pedigree who understood continental European concerns as well as Anglo-Saxon foibles; and Nick Stern, a well-connected and respected professor of economics with strategic vision who was able to combine theory with practice and get ideas across effectively to a wide range of audiences. Improvements in the economic circumstances of most countries in the region from now on also meant that the timing for a concerted effort to expand and influence the path of transition was auspicious.

As the Bank moved forward, a new methodology to define and measure transition impact was devised over several years, which helped everyone in the institution understand and explain to clients how the EBRD differed from commercial banks. The methodology allowed the Bank to present its activities—from projects and country and sector strategies to strategic and business plans—to shareholders and others in an intellectually consistent and coherent way, and provided a unity of purpose to staff and external observers alike.

1. Defining and Operationalising the Bank's Purpose: Transition Impact

The banking side of the EBRD, reorganised under a tough but respected taskmaster with free rein to drive the business forward at pace, was clear on its remit. The wider organisation needed a similar clarity of purpose. It was here that Stern had a great impact.

Now almost three years old, the EBRD did not yet have a coherent organising philosophy within which to develop and focus its activities. The transition mandate had always been the guiding principle but was not embedded within the Bank in a systematic way. Board project documents did refer to transition impact—mentioning, for example, potential benefits of an operation to market development—but there was no means of assessing it. To the extent that economic tests of validity were used in project analysis, they focused sometimes on the costs of protection[1] but mostly on more general economic rates of return (in line with other development organisations), although often only in a cursory way. The Project Evaluation Department (PED) took a similar economic return approach to *ex post* evaluations.[2]

While such exercises were useful up to a point, they failed to address the dynamic nature of the context—notably that the EBRD was trying to put markets in place rather than adding incrementally to them—and were expensive to carry out when done properly. Methodological improvements were needed to deal with the particular situation of the transition economies and the Bank's operations.

This was a task Stern was eminently well-placed to carry out. In doing so, he was supported early on by a number of EBRD colleagues: Hans Peter Lankes, a recent Harvard PhD graduate, who took on the task of defining how projects should be assessed, and Robin Burgess and Mark Schankerman who were hired to provide more theoretical underpinnings to Stern's thinking. Like Stern, Schankerman was a professor of economics at the LSE and was seconded to the EBRD as Director of Policy Studies. Burgess was a recent Oxford doctoral graduate interested in development econom-

---

[1] For some big corporate investments at the time such as in Hungary and the CSFR, especially in the automobile sector, this was an important aspect to consider. The EBRD always paid close attention to protection issues, in line with its focus on supporting effective market competition.
[2] See for example, 'Project Evaluation: The Bank's Policy Approach', 3 February 1992.

ics who joined the Bank as a consultant. In a paper on 'Investment Projects and the Transition Process' they set out a new and radically different approach to project appraisal which emphasised the broader, dynamic impact of investments rather than relying on the comparative static analysis adopted by others.[3]

Stern was an expert in public-sector economics and had already written prominently on many aspects of cost-benefit analysis.[4] However, in the context of the rapidly changing economic systems and structures of countries moving from central planning to market economies, he realised that the limitations of cost-benefit analysis were severe and reduced its value as a decision-making tool. For example, two similar new road projects might have the same effects in reducing journey times and improving safety (which could be costed on suitable assumptions), but if one, say, was designed as a public-private partnership, it might result in capacity building and demonstration effects going beyond quicker and safer access to yield valuable efficiencies in future infrastructure investments. Similarly, if it opened up linkages between an isolated region and a port with international access, over time it could draw in previously cut-off businesses, expand markets and improve growth to generate higher returns than envisaged in a simple model. Cost-benefit analyses tended to shy away from such issues because of the uncertainties involved and the difficulties in producing reliable quantitative estimates of their value. Ignoring these dynamic effects in the transition context would, however, be potentially misleading as to the absolute and relative benefits of different projects.

In the Lankes, Burgess, Schankerman and Stern view of the world it was the systemic impact of projects that mattered, not simply their immediate financial or even economic returns (as conventionally measured). This was especially important for an international institution such as the EBRD which sought to play a role in influencing outcomes beyond the companies and financial institutions in which it invested. The provision of finance alongside other investors was important, but choosing to support projects that had impact beyond the investment itself was even more so. Hence, the idea was to concentrate on the effects of projects "which may induce important reac-

---

3   R. Burgess, M. Schankerman and N. Stern, 'Investment Projects and the Transition Process', Mimeo, EBRD, 1995.
4   See for example J. Dreze and N. Stern, 'The Theory of Cost-Benefit Analysis', in A.J. Auerbach and M. Feldstein (eds.), *Handbook of Public Economics*, Vol. 2, Elsevier, 1987, Chapter 14.

tions outside the boundaries of the project but which may not easily be captured by the comparison of equilibriums 'with and without the project'".[5]

It was also relevant from another angle. The amount of capital available for the EBRD to deploy fell far short of the needs of the region. Careful project selection was essential to maximise the Bank's impact.

The underlying basis for this viewpoint had its origins in central Europe. The Austrian School, dominated by the ideas of Ludwig von Mises and his pupil Frederich von Hayek and later, from a different perspective, those of Joseph Schumpeter, was a key influence. The important aspects that underpinned their thinking were born of the uncertainties associated with the social, economic and political upheavals of the first half of the 20th century: the shocks imparted by two World Wars and the Great Depression. There were parallels in the collapse of central planning and efforts to replace it with market capitalism.

Von Mises and von Hayek emphasised the dynamic aspects of change, with "markets as a process", and the learning and discovery that takes place through competitive mechanisms and in particular through competitive prices. Competitive market interactions between the myriad independent actors dispersed information and knowledge which could be mobilised to drive economies. In Schumpeter's view, this provided the vehicle for the discovery and innovation of new products and processes which would overtake the status quo ("creative destruction"). The market was seen as a dynamic and creative phenomenon.

This suggested an alternative approach to the appraisal of projects in the transition context, one based on the nature and dynamic aspects of markets. It could take account of backward and forward linkages (effectively supply chains), which influenced the scale and pace of development and the behaviours of markets, driving participants to keep up with competitors and develop skills and innovations to surpass them. A key addition by the EBRD's economists, compared with their Austrian antecedents, was the inclusion of institutions and policies that could influence markets. In the fluid world of transition, the rule of law, level of openness and transparency, and strength and fairness of regulation were important influences on market outcomes and could not be ignored.

---

5   R. Burgess et al., cited in J. Carbajo, 'Assessing the contribution of investment projects to building a market economy: beyond cost-benefit analysis?', in M. Florio (ed.), *Cost Benefit Analysis and Incentives in Evaluation*, Edward Elgar, 2007, Chapter 4.

The team began to build, over a series of iterations, an analytical system which suited the Bank's needs. Starting with a set of indicators of transition progress presented to the Board in 1994 and progressing to a project-level approach after considerable discussion with the banking and evaluation departments, the main elements of the new "transition impact" methodology emerged gradually over several years. The effort to move from the intuitive notion of transition impact of earlier times towards a more structured approach was welcomed by Directors.

The starting point was a thorough assessment of the state of transition in the EBRD's countries of operations in a new publication, the *Transition Report*, issued by the Bank in November 1994. This was the first of what became an annual and much admired series, each of which was the sole responsibility of the Chief Economist.[6] The *Transition Report 1994*, produced by the Office of the Chief Economist (OCE) under the editorial direction of Kasper Bartholdy,[7] was almost 200 pages long and mirrored the World Bank's flagship *World Development Report*. It covered many aspects of transition, from the macroeconomic situation of the region and its individual countries to the pace of institutional change, FDI and trade-policy reform. It was a remarkable achievement for such a small office.

A key consideration, set out at the start of the publication, was the meaning of transition and its measurement. Written by Stern and his predecessor, Flemming, it explained:

> Transition is not only an intermediate goal contributing to economic development ... The market economy, in contrast to central planning, gives, in principle, the individual the right to basic choices over aspects of his or her life ... The right to these choices may be seen as a basic liberty ... Thus the transition is also an end in itself ...[8]
>
> The transition concerns institutional change. It is the institutional arrangements for the allocation and generation of goods and resources, and the ownership incentive and reward structures that institutions embody, that characterise the differences between a market and a command economy.[9]

---

6 Although all interested parties are consulted, *Transition Reports* do not necessarily represent the views of the EBRD's senior management or those of its shareholders.
7 Flemming helped lead the editorial team in which Andrew Tyrie also played a substantial role.
8 *Transition Report 1994*, p. 3, EBRD, 1994.
9 Ibid., p. 4.

Citing the contrasts between Japan, Germany and the USA, however, Stern and Flemming cautioned:

> ... it must be remembered that there are many varieties of market economy which may be viewed as the 'end point' or 'target' of the transition ... [there] is not a simple, linear, one-dimensional progression to a 'standard' market economy.[10]

The key elements of a market economy in their characterisation were: enterprises and households making decisions over production and consumption in response to incentive structures embodied in markets; markets themselves, which were the means by which goods and resources were exchanged; and financial institutions, which allowed the channelling of savings, investments and payments and supported financial discipline.

The state was seen as playing an important role, albeit a very different one from under a command economy, namely as the source of legal and regulatory structures concerning the behaviour of enterprises and financial institutions, property rights, contracts and market functioning, as well as the provider of public goods, taxation, safety nets and protection against poverty.[11]

2. A Set of Transition Indicators

This thinking led to a first set of transition indicators designed to measure the state of transition in the EBRD's countries of operations. Over the course of 1995, they were refined and published in that year's *Transition Report*. Four categories were used to represent the components of the market economy described above: enterprises, markets and trade, financial institutions and legal reform. Each category was sub-divided into discrete dimensions of transition, from large-scale privatisation to price liberalisation, banking reform and effectiveness of legal rules on investment. A classification system was then applied to each indicator to express the extent to which progress had been made against a hypothetical yardstick of the standards expected to be seen in an advanced industrial economy. Scores ranged from 1,

---

10   Ibid., p. 4.
11   Ibid., p. 4.

indicating little or no progress, to 4*, representing the level of an advanced industrial nation. Table 10.1 below shows the structure of the indicators as they appeared in the *Transition Report* 1995.

Table 10.1 Transition Indicators, 1995[12]

Country	Enterprises	Markets and Trade	Financial Institutions	Legal Reform	Average Score	Level of Advancement
Albania	2.7	2.7	1.5	2.0	2.2	B
Armenia	2.3	2.3	1.5	2.0	2.0	B
Azerbaijan	1.3	2.0	1.5	1.0	1.5	C
Belarus	2.0	2.3	2.0	2.0	2.1	B
Bulgaria	2.3	3.0	2.0	3.0	2.6	B
Croatia	3.2	2.7	2.5	3.0	2.9	B
Czech Rep.	3.8	3.5	3.0	4.0	3.6	A
Estonia	3.7	3.3	2.5	3.0	3.1	A
FYR Macedonia	2.7	2.7	2.0	2.0	2.4	B
Georgia	2.3	2.0	1.5	2.0	2.0	B
Hungary	3.8	3.5	3.0	4.0	3.6	A
Kazakhstan	1.7	2.7	2.0	2.0	2.1	B
Kyrgyzstan	3.3	3.0	2.0	2.0	2.6	B
Latvia	2.7	3.0	2.5	2.0	2.6	B
Lithuania	3.0	3.0	2.5	2.0	2.6	B
Moldova	2.7	3.0	2.0	2.0	2.4	B
Poland	3.5	3.5	3.0	4.0	3.5	A
Romania	2.3	2.8	2.5	2.0	2.4	B
Russian Fed.	3.0	2.7	2.0	2.0	2.4	B
Slovak Rep.	3.5	3.5	3.0	3.0	3.3	A
Slovenia	3.5	3.2	3.0	3.0	3.2	A
Tajikistan	1.7	2.0	1.0	1.0	1.4	C
Turkmenistan	1.0	1.3	1.0	1.0	1.1	C
Uzbekistan	2.7	2.3	2.0	2.0	2.3	B

12 For simplified presentation purposes sub-indicators have been aggregated and averaged; similarly for the overall average score. Level of Advancement categories: A, average score 3 and above; B, between 2 and 3; C, score less than 2. 4* cases were treated as having a value of 4.5. There were 12 such scores out of a total of 225. For a more complete picture, see *Transition Report* 1995, Table 2.1, p. 11.

The application of the system to the EBRD's countries of operations provided a helpful picture of the region's progress and highlighted the considerable differences between countries. Some, like Turkmenistan, scored mostly '1' across the set of indicators, while more advanced economies such as Hungary and the Czech Republic scored in a range between '3' and '4*'. The system provided a set of development indicators from a transition perspective and a means of calibrating progress against increasingly objective evidence. Intellectually, it was very appealing and offered the prospect of a regular snapshot, as well as opportunities for academic researchers and others to assess and track progress across central and eastern Europe, Russia and beyond. But there was a desire internally to see if the approach could be applied more directly to the Bank's operations and to the strategies that were developed for each of the EBRD's countries of operations.

To spearhead the effort of applying transition impact criteria more widely to Bank activities, an interdepartmental working group consisting of the OCE, Banking and PED was formed early in 1995. This followed a successful Board retreat where the transition indicators had been discussed as a response to questions about the Bank's overall impact on transition. The aim of the group was to take forward the qualitative aspects of the transition indicators presented in the *Transition Report* and turn them into a checklist that could assist operations staff in focusing on the key dimensions of transition impact in project selection, design and appraisal. If successful, the set of criteria developed could be used to examine the transition impact of EBRD projects at each stage of their development, from first appraisal to the portfolio and their evaluation post-completion.

In order to gauge the usefulness of the idea, Stern proposed to apply the draft project-level indicators of transition impact to the stock of signed projects, which then stood at around 200. To help with the exercise, Professor Paul Hare of Heriot-Watt University, Edinburgh, was employed as a consultant. One of the reasons for inviting his participation was that the project had an underlying research purpose, namely to determine the extent to which the "contribution to transition" criteria differed from conventional financial and economic return indicators. Bankers from eight teams were also invited to score some of their own projects using 14 indicators, three of which related to enterprises, three to financial institutions and eight to markets and trade, with some overlaps. The scoring range for each indicator was from '-1' (negative effect) to '3' (very significant positive effect).

At a workshop at the EBRD in 1995, Hare and Tanya Normak (an economist in OCE) presented preliminary ideas on the transition impact criteria and their research proposal. It was followed by a presentation of their findings at an EBRD research conference in April 1996.[13] Based on an econometric analysis of the Bank's projects using the 14 transition indicators and other project features, the paper concluded:

> that the set of transition indicators is both conceptually and statistically coherent, that there is little evidence to suggest that one or other indicator or subset of indicators can usefully be replaced by a single, composite or synthetic indicator, and that these indicators do not merely replicate information already contained in standard project-based financial indicators [FRR and ERR]. Hence the measures of 'contribution to transition' proposed … could usefully be incorporated in the Bank's project appraisal procedures.[14]

This provided valuable support for the approach. A follow-up report on implementation issues[15] considered the questions of aggregating indicators and the responsibility for the assessment of transition impact. The first question arose in part because the PED, which had adopted the indicators in its work, had gone further in its analysis by aggregating individual scores into a single numeric measure. Views differed on the value of a single measure of transition impact. The Hare and Normak paper concluded:

> It would seem preferable to use project-level indicators as a checklist of issues needing to be explored from an early stage of project design rather than to reduce them to a single numeric benchmark, especially if the latter was merely summarising a set of not very carefully analysed 'impressions' about the project.[16]

The authors did, however, recognise that differences in thinking about implementation could be overcome by seeing the matter as the start of a process of discussion amongst the relevant departments.

---

13 'Estimating the Transition Impact of EBRD Projects", by Hare and Normak, internal paper presented to an EBRD research conference, London, 26 and 27 April 1996, EBRD.
14 Ibid., p. 20.
15 'Estimating the Transition Impact of EBRD Projects: Implementation Issues', by Hare and Normak, internal memo, July 1996, EBRD.
16 Ibid., p. 5.

On the issue of the responsibility for assessing the transition impact of projects, they advocated avoiding increasing the burden on the appraisal process. "The main responsibility must obviously lie with the department that already analyses projects and guides them through the selection and appraisal process, namely Banking."[17]

The involvement of OCE, though in an advisory capacity, was seen as important, as was the contribution *ex post* of PED. This meant a heavy reliance on quantifiable (or testable) indicators of transition for which bankers could be subsequently held accountable. It also placed a premium on learning. The economists had to be willing and able to explain the transition impact system to bankers and train them on its attributes and interpretation.

3. The Introduction of a Formal "Transition Impact" Measurement System

By 1997, the system of project-level indicators had been tested and improved with the help of the working group and the many bankers involved. Reactions among the bankers had been broadly positive. Project leaders found the indicators and the economists' advice on their interpretation of projects helpful for document write-ups for Board approval. Shareholders were also interested to hear management's answers to the question of measurement of development impact, a matter that pervaded debate in other MDBs. This too encouraged the EBRD to identify its impact better. As a way of satisfying this demand a summary paper on the conclusions of the work of the previous years and the latest interpretation of the system was prepared.

Stern and Lankes presented their paper to the Board as a formal introduction of the new conceptual framework at the FOPC in February 1997.[18] Here, the rejection of cost-benefit analysis for project appraisal at the EBRD was made explicit.

> Cost-benefit analysis is not well-equipped to handle two sets of issues which are central to the transition process: radical structural change and learning of market-oriented methods and behaviour. The reason is that the

---

17 Ibid., p. 5.
18 'Transition Impact of Projects', 10 February 1997.

approach ... requires an explicit model of economic structures and behaviour [and] such changes often pose insuperable challenges to the model. The transition, however, is concerned precisely with changing structures and behaviour. Thus the spotlight in the analysis of transition falls precisely where cost-benefit analysis is weakest. Transition focuses on *processes* rather than outcomes ... the particular problem for the EBRD in this context is that the kind of effects that cost-benefit analysis conventionally leaves out are, in fact, central to the impact of the project on the transition. And further ... the value of the processes may go beyond simply the material outcomes they produce.[19]

The process of evaluating the project-level indicators had allowed Stern and Lankes to identify three broad dimensions that described the process of transition to a market economy: the creation, expansion and improvement of markets; the establishment and strengthening of institutions, laws and policies that support markets (including private ownership); and the adoption of behaviour patterns and skills with a market perspective. They argued that the transition impact of projects and related activities could be assessed in a qualitative fashion by way of "checkable stories" based on this approach, which was further broken down into seven components to form a final transition checklist, as shown in Table 10.2 below.

Table 10.2. Project Transition Checklist, from 1997 onwards

1. Contributions to the structure and extent of markets	1.1 Greater competition in the project sector
	1.2 Expansion of competitive market interactions in other sectors
2. Contributions to the institutions and policies that support markets	2.1 More widespread private ownership and entrepreneurship
	2.2 Institutions, laws and policies that promote market functioning and efficiency
3. Contributions to market-based behaviour patterns, skills and innovation	3.1 Transfer and dispersion of skills
	3.2 Demonstration of new replicable behaviours and activities
	3.3 Setting standards for corporate governance and business conduct

---

19 Ibid., pp. 3–4

The methodology introduced in the Stern-Lankes paper was a landmark among DFIs. No other institution paid such attention to the wider, systemic effects of their interventions on market processes, preferring instead to focus on the direct impact of the project itself (and some indirect outcomes like job creation). To a large degree, the approach reflected the unique circumstances facing the EBRD and its region of operations, where markets were only just forming and the focus was on the private sector rather than the large public-sector projects pursued by most DFIs. But it had a more universal applicability to private-sector development.

A further reason for the EBRD approach was the sheer number of projects the Bank pursued, mostly of small size, compared with other institutions. This, as well as the large number of equity and corporate finance deals, made sophisticated numerical calculations of costs and benefits difficult to assess for every project and of limited value, especially with a very small team of economists and limited resources for hiring consultants.

In the case of larger projects such as public-sector infrastructure, economic rates of return were calculated along with an assessment of transition impact. Stern-Lankes noted:

> The close conceptual relationship between economic rate of return, transition impact and environmental impact implies that the three should always be viewed in conjunction when assessing the benefits of a project in relation to the transition.[20]

They also recognised that transition impact was a function of time and context. In other words, some impacts—demonstration effects for example—may require time to take full effect, while a project in a more advanced country may have a much weaker impact on the transition than a similar one in a country at an earlier stage of the transition process. Nonetheless, in the authors' view:

> A qualitative assessment of the strength of a project's contribution to market expansion and learning can be made in a way which is systematically structured to inform the appraisal process [through the use of the checklist].[21]

---

20 Ibid., p. 4.
21 Ibid., p. 6.

Now there was not only financial leverage to take into account in project assessment (the ability of the EBRD to provide finance on its own account and leverage other sources of funds, including through the mobilisation of co-financing), but also transition impact (the project's ability to drive additional investment and change in the economy as market enhancements occurred). Talk of the Bank's multiplier effect, which had so far been described in terms of total project finance catalysed by EBRD investment, now extended to the notion of a transition impact multiplier. In principle, the latter could be seen through progress in the country and sector context.

The new approach was complemented by a paper which applied the analytical tools to an assessment of transition impact trends in the portfolio.[22] This covered countries at different stages of transition and an analysis of projects in the Russian portfolio (127 at the time), measured against the seven transition checklist criteria (as shown in Table 10.2).[23] The analysis showed advanced transition economies tended to be dominated by direct corporate and private infrastructure investments, and early transition countries mainly by public infrastructure and sovereign lines of credit. Private-sector projects focused on "greater competition" and demonstration effects such as "new products and processes", whereas state projects showed higher frequencies of achieving "greater competition in other sectors" and "improved market efficiency via institutions, laws and policies".

This was the first time the Board was presented with an attempt at providing comprehensive information on *ex ante*, *ex post* and "on-the-go" assessments of transition impact. Complementing the OCE work on each project's likely impact on transition was the Evaluation Department's perspective on *ex post* and "on-the-go" contributions of projects in the portfolio though their evaluations of operations nearing or beyond completion.[24] Banking teams completed the picture by providing commentary and examples of transition impacts relevant to their particular sector under each of the checklist criteria.[25]

---

22 'Transition Impact: Assessment of Trends in the Portfolio and Pipeline', 14 March 1997.
23 The two most prominent transition impact criteria were identified for each project and then aggregated to show the dispersion of the criteria among private and state projects, respectively.
24 Given the relatively early stage of many projects in the portfolio in 1996, the sample was small and weighted towards "in flight" projects.
25 Sectors covered included financial institutions, property, early stage equity, transport, telecommunications, natural resources, power and energy, energy efficiency, municipal and environmental infrastructure, and agribusiness.

It had taken a considerable effort to prepare the material—the original request from FOPC for some analysis had been made almost 12 months earlier—and it was something of a "pick'n'mix" collection of insights drawn from project documents, evaluations and observations based on bankers' experiences. Nonetheless, the Board, through the FOPC, which had been closely involved throughout and had pushed for clarity of purpose from the start, thanked management for the "significant amount of work which had gone into the preparation of the paper".

The episode had demonstrated three important lessons. Internally, there was a clear recognition of the importance of conducting a proper assessment of the contributions of projects to the transition process. Second, the exercise had shown a genuine willingness to collaborate between key Bank departments to achieve this goal and reach a consensus of interpretation as far as possible. Third, the extensive discussions helped to foster a corporate culture based on a mutual understanding of the twin purposes of the EBRD: to pursue commercial deals but also those which had a clear impact on moving the transition process forward.

4. Strengthening Risk Analysis in Parallel

Like most commercial banks the EBRD considered the financial risks surrounding its investments. This was particularly challenging given the many unknowns in the region. Early efforts to improve the assessment of project-level transition impact were matched by a similar strengthening of the evaluation of financial risks associated with projects. Hitherto, while working level credit analysis was good, the system was structurally weak, with an optional and consultative process on credit matters and no dedicated process to make specific recommendations. Fortunately, there had been good protection from the strong skills of Freeman in identifying key weaknesses and risks in the projects coming to OpsCom.

During the interregnum between Attali's departure and de Larosière's arrival at the EBRD, Noreen Doyle, an American banker who had been recruited from Bankers Trust and was in charge of the Bank's loan syndication activities, approached Freeman, then acting President, with a proposal to improve risk assessment and give it a more formal role in the project-appraisal procedure akin to that used in commercial banks.

Doyle had some influence not only as a serious banker respected by Freeman but also as one of the three people managing OpsCom.[26] Freeman accepted her suggestion. According to Doyle, he asked her to become Head of Credit, and to establish the Credit Department in the Finance vice presidency in order to avoid any conflict of interest. This meant credit risk assessment would no longer be "an optional stop for the bankers" but a truly independent function able to input advice to bankers on the structuring and design of projects.[27] In this respect, the economists and credit analysts became aligned, each with a different perspective.

Doyle moved across to Finance, taking loan syndications with her, and began by setting up a credit review process in line with commercial practice. The new arrangements were soon up and running. A first step was to develop for the EBRD's countries of operations a set of country risk ratings—which did not then exist—in line with the general approach adopted by credit rating agencies, such as Standard and Poor's.[28] It was followed by the creation of a group to analyse credit risks faced within the growing portfolio, and was complemented in 1996 with a workout segment that was becoming a more urgent need.

Under Doyle's leadership several experienced and tough-minded risk experts with backgrounds in commercial banks, big corporates and IFIs were able to challenge many aspects of bankers' deals and make 'yes/no' recommendations. Bob Harada, a Chase Manhattan US executive with a wealth of financial analytical skills, who had been involved from the beginning, managed the credit analysis side while Mike Williams, a deceptively soft-spoken Brit, joined a little later to deal with the portfolio. The Anglo-American group was completed by the appointment of David Klingensmith, another American from Chase, this time with experience of Asian developing country markets. All were heavily committed to establishing the credentials of the new credit risk department and helping bankers improve the quality of their deals from a risk management perspective. Freeman and Doyle also realised that for the process to work well it would need to be open and collegiate throughout, a doctrine that Freeman had established in OpsCom

---

26   The others making up the OpsCom Secretariat were Gavin Anderson and Jean-Francois Maquet, both senior advisers in the FVP's front office.
27   Conversation with Noreen Doyle, March 2020.
28   Credit rating agencies provided country risk ratings for the larger advanced countries, such as the Czech Republic and Hungary, in due course.

and which Doyle carried through when she later took on the FVP role and Chair of OpsCom, and which has continued since. The new arrangements provided a solid base for ensuring that the EBRD followed its principle of "sound banking" to the letter.

The strengthening of the financial risk process was an important parallel effort to advances in the assessment of transition impact during this time. Collectively, the improvements helped to embed a balanced business model in the EBRD, while the key personalities involved ensured the corporate culture reflected the substance in an open and supportive way that could deliver transition impact while maintaining financial sustainability.[29]

5. Operationalising the Transition Impact System: Introducing Ratings

Having won support for the Stern-Lankes approach on transition impact, the next step was to apply the methodology more formally to the EBRD's operations. This was not a simple matter and went beyond debates by academic economists over erudite theories of impact measurement. It trod on evaluation turf but, far more important, it impacted the Banking Department directly. If the economists got their way, they would be able to define what was a "good" project and what was not. If a formal rating system was introduced, bankers might find their hard-fought deals sacrificed on the altar of transition impact as decided by economists in their conclave.

Stern well understood the risks. Since his arrival he had carefully built up the language of transition by making sure the transition context was always present in documents going to the Board, whether on projects or on policy. An articulate and smooth operator as well as a powerful intellect, he had already taken a prominent role in the Executive Committee and had the full confidence of the President. Nonetheless, keeping the Banking Department onside still represented a major task.

The trick was not to push too hard or too quickly. Stern was in any case not keen on a formal rating system believing that institutional learning takes

---

29 No similar formal process to test for additionality was developed at the time, although it featured in project documents and was challenged by economists in OpsCom when the need arose. It became a more relevant criterion as countries progressed along the transition path and featured prominently in the debate on graduation. See Chapter 12.

time and persistence. Achieving a deep understanding of the importance of transition impact and building that into the corporate culture could not be done overnight. In this context, a formal rating system ran the risk of putting an undue focus on the score and could distract attention from the underlying substance behind the assessment. Just as cost-benefit analysis could be overplayed in the transition context, it was also important not to take the transition impact analysis beyond its limits. Besides, there was much for the EBRD to do in the region, so ruthless prioritising of projects was not yet called for. What was needed was a clear understanding of what the Bank was trying to achieve through its projects and other work from a public purpose perspective.

It was a fair concern that a summary characterisation of transition impact or a label might imply over-precision. There were risks in trying to compare the incomparable and measure the immeasurable. A project's impact depended heavily on the context and many qualitative factors that were difficult to compare across sectors and countries. On the other hand, a summary overview of a project's impact might be more acceptable if risks to the delivery of that impact were added to the picture. This could help to pin down the degree of uncertainty over the assessment of the likely outcomes. Recognition could be given, for example, that the impact on transition of the Bank's interventions was likely to be greater where reforms were underway than in cases where they were not. Conceptually, the system thus evolved to consider both the potential impact of a project on transition (using the checklist) and the risks associated with the delivery of the specific impacts identified.

On the Banking side, there had been a general awareness for some time that there was no real coherence in describing how projects were aligned with the EBRD's mandate and that more discipline was needed. The indicators helped and the idea that transition impact should fit into a consistent and verifiable framework (described at the time as "checkable stories") was regarded as useful.

Some felt that the use of a summary label for a project's impact could be helpful depending on how it might be used. Aggregating the indicators to provide an overall assessment was a way of cutting through the many dimensions behind a project and would force those involved to think through their case and justify their position. A more prominent focus, which a summary rating would surely bring in the view of some OpsCom members, could help pose the right questions and elicit more clarity from bankers.

Senior managers were aware that a labelling or rating system might lead to disputes. On the other hand, it would flush out disagreements and OpsCom was there to resolve any problems. It was particularly important for management to resolve these issues before projects went to Directors for approval. There should be no risk of public disagreement in the Boardroom. For this reason, a move towards ratings had some management value. If some sort of ordinal ranking was introduced with fairly wide boundaries and undue weight was not placed on it—then, the thinking went, why not?

Moving in the direction of an overall classification system based on the indicators was hard to resist. Transition indicators were already being used to justify projects, so a rating was not a huge step to take. There were reasons too why a rating system could prove useful from a Banking perspective. For one thing, it could make it easier to allocate resources to more difficult transition regions, which management was under constant pressure from the Board to do. These areas were labour-intensive and less attractive to bankers since they were time-consuming to travel to, often involved small deals and were more troublesome when it came to conducting business. Recognition of the higher transition impact potential (albeit with higher risks) in these areas would encourage bankers and be a useful signal to the Board of the seriousness of the EBRD's intent when pursuing such projects, especially when combined with a mantra of seeking to pursue transition with full vigour.

Ratings also helped to indicate the quality of projects and thus added a different dimension from volume, again something Directors were keen to understand better and for the Bank to improve upon. From the Bank's perspective, ratings also helped—seemingly paradoxically—in central Europe. While weaker transition impact projects were at risk of criticism here (although often saved by lower financial risks and more attractive returns), projects classified above average ("good" or "excellent") offered a way to demonstrate that transition "gaps" remained even in more advanced countries and that the Bank's investments could make a difference.

Although in its initial form the transition impact methodology had eschewed making comparisons between projects in favour of qualitative assessments and "checkable stories", the Board also saw value in pushing further towards ratings, including as a means of holding management to account for the Bank's contribution to the transition process. The heavy concentration of EBRD business volume in central European countries which were more advanced than other EBRD regions had begun to draw adverse attention from Directors. Some form of differentiation between projects thus had advantages for those Directors advocating that the Bank shift resources away from central Europe towards more difficult activities and countries where transition was weakest. Further yardsticks to help prioritise activities were seen as useful and a project rating system fitted the bill.

Around the time these matters were being discussed, Freeman left the EBRD to return to Salomon Brothers. His successor, Charles Frank, took over as FVP in September 1997 and became acting President following de Larosière's departure in January 1998. His arrival coincided with the emerging conclusions of the Zero Base Budgeting (ZBB) exercise designed to look at the Bank's operational model, simplify its systems and processes and raise productivity.[30] The initiative had begun during Freeman's tenure as FVP but he had not taken much notice. Frank was more familiar with and interested in business management systems than his predecessor and saw scope to speed up decision-making and strengthen the operational mechanics. A project transition impact classification and rating system fitted this general philosophy, so in 1998 the economists tested with Banking, informally at first, a light classification system for concept reviews which involved summary categories on transition impact potential and risks to that impact.[31]

As part of the process the OpsCom system was tightened further, including dividing the agendas between important or difficult projects and the rest.[32] Members were encouraged early on under Frank's chairing of OpsCom to concentrate on their own specialisms. There was a push to make project documents more succinct and tighter procedures were developed, whereby the key non-Banking parties around the table—the credit analysts, economists, lawyers and Treasury/syndications representatives—would submit fully articulated notes of their positions on bankers' project proposals ahead of the OpsCom meeting. Frank took issue with the lawyers having a say in approving projects as opposed to simply fulfilling a compliance function in relation to the Articles. Freeman had been very happy to have lawyers present at OpsCom to discuss transactions (partly due to his own legal

---

30 'Zero Base Budgeting Initiative', 29 January 1997.
31 Labels of "high", "medium" and "low" transition impact were used at this stage.
32 This was an A/B list in which only A projects were fully discussed with the relevant banking team in front of the Committee. 'President's briefing to the Board of Directors on Zero Base Budgeting', 18 September 1997.

training), but Frank came from GE Capital where, as was normal in such investment banks, external counsel were hired by bankers to assist with their transactions. A battle over the role of EBRD's legal staff in the Bank's operations ensued, which was eventually settled with the General Counsel and his representatives remaining active participants at OpsCom, and they remained in charge of all instructions of outside counsel.

Further changes to EBRD procedures were on the cards when Horst Köhler, a former State Secretary at the German Federal Finance Ministry and a G7 deputy, arrived as President of the EBRD in September 1998. Like his predecessor, he began by asking staff to review the Bank's operational priorities. This was all the more necessary since Köhler's arrival coincided with the Russian debt crisis (see Chapter 11).

Stern was once again in the driving seat but this time with less freedom of manoeuvre and it was not long before his interest turned to finding a new role outside the Bank.[33]

Following a discussion at a Board retreat in January 1999, the review of priorities was issued as a short paper.[34] It reaffirmed much of the previous approach, including strengthening local presence and encouraging start-ups and SMEs, but laid a new emphasis on a strategic approach to portfolio management. This recognised the need to balance transition impact, financial returns and risk, and led to a tightening of procedures all round.

As part of the response to the portfolio-management approach, Stern announced in May that OCE would in future formally provide its ratings of transition impact potential and risks in its notes to OpsCom.[35] He explained that transition impact potential would be defined through reference to the checklist categories and the sector-relevant versions. Ratings were to be based on an ordinal scale with broad categories ranging from "unsatisfactory" to "excellent".[36] A similar approach applied to risks, with a range from "excessive" to "low".[37] Here risks to transition impact depended both on the

---

[33] Stern first moved to an economic consultancy in 1999 before becoming Chief Economist at the World Bank in 2000.
[34] 'Moving Transition Forward: Refocused Operational Priorities for the Medium Term', 19 February 1999.
[35] 'Transition Impact Rating of Projects', memo by Stern to the Operations Committee, 24 May 1999.
[36] The Evaluation Department had been using a classification system, albeit a different one, for some time for completed projects (unsuccessful to generally successful) so the introduction of a similar one for ex ante assessments was not altogether alien.
[37] The categories used for transition impact potential were "unsatisfactory", "marginal", "satisfactory", "good", "excellent" and for risks were "negligible", "low", "medium", "high" and "excessive".

likelihood that the transition impact potential would not be realised and on the risk of negative impact deriving from certain attributes of a project (inappropriate subsidies or protection for example). Stern pointed out that, while financial risks could be relevant to transition impact results, transition impact risks were generally separate and different in nature, pertaining to whether the impact argued for—such as higher standards, demonstration effects and so on—would likely occur.

From then on, assessment was made using ratings and the transition impact methodology (that is, based on the checklist and transition context), with typically two of the seven criteria to describe the impact of the project. Once OpsCom had become familiar and happy with the system, it was extended to project documents presented to the Board from mid-2000. This gave Directors a basis of comparison and a view of management's thinking on the (relative) transition value of the operation.

6. Tensions Build

Early misgivings on a "hard" rating system by the well-respected Chief Economist were tempered by a feeling that greater clarity of purpose to projects under a rating system was a reasonable objective. Banking had thus not viewed the introduction of a project classification system and ratings as a source of internal complications. They knew in any case that "satisfactory" projects would still go to the Board for approval and were highly unlikely to be rejected there. Lower-classified projects ("unsatisfactory" or "marginal") rarely made it as far as OpsCom.

Over time the pattern changed. The increased prominence of transition impact in projects and its calibration throughout each stage of their development meant the economists' role in OpsCom became much more significant. Originally, the Chief Economist had not been a member of the Committee but this changed after Stern's arrival. From now on, OCE representatives were a focal point for opinions on transition impact value.

Although "satisfactory" projects were eligible for presentation to the Board, they inevitably invited increased scrutiny and questions from Directors as to whether they really were up to the mark or whether some fudge had been applied to get them "over the line". Team directors and operation leaders who faced Board scrutiny naturally preferred to avoid such questioning if possible, so these pressures fed back through the system to debates with economists over the transition merits of the project. OpsCom was the place where the most serious disagreements were resolved (except in the most strategically significant disputed cases where ExCom was needed). Hence the Chief Economist and representatives from OCE had a critical influence in steering the direction of the EBRD's operations.

Other factors strengthened this development. Turnover in the Board was rapid so earlier discussions were quickly forgotten, while changing personalities here, in OCE and elsewhere led to different emphases. A big influence was the progress of some countries, which led to a more serious questioning of the validity of projects' incremental impact and additionality. The rapid build-up of new projects, several of which repeated earlier transactions—either the same type of project or with the same client—also caused controversy. And in this context some in OCE were keener than their predecessors to exert greater control over projects coming to the Board for approval.

The issue of what new *systemic* impact projects provided became more difficult to explain for the more advanced countries, particularly in repeat projects. Such operations were increasingly common and the ratings provided by the economists often fell below bankers' expectations. As bankers saw it, their operations fostered the transition process in various ways, mainly by helping a client to make competitive changes in difficult circumstances where reasonable financing terms were unavailable and local entrepreneurs still few and far between. Meanwhile, the economists wanted to see innovative products and processes introduced and path-breaking market improvements from changed behaviours and strengthened institutions. A wedge began to appear between the two perspectives, made worse by the fact that bankers used to writing their own scripts were subject to an *ex ante* independent assessment of their efforts (and not simply one *ex post* from the Evaluation Department).

The new Chief Economist, Willem Buiter, an eminent Dutch-born Cambridge professor of international macroeconomics, participated regularly in OpsCom following his arrival at the EBRD in 2000. Buiter was a formidable intellectual economist and combative character, unique in style, insightful and highly entertaining. He was regarded as something of a maverick.[38] His views on projects were often very direct or amusing. In one in-

---

38 Indeed, after leaving the EBRD he wrote a blog for the *Financial Times* entitled 'Maverecon'.

stance, according to EBRD economists present at the OpsCom meeting, he questioned a "nice" project, likening it to a "nice" chocolate pudding which nonetheless did not have any transition impact. Such metaphors clashed with bankers' views on projects. The economists, however, were pleased that OCE's position was represented with exceptional clarity and in a "no nonsense" demeanour.

When Lankes left the Bank for the IMF later in 2000, several months after Köhler's rapid departure to become the new IMF Managing Director, José Carbajo became the OCE director in charge of project assessment and submissions to OpsCom. As part of the work that had been set in train across the Bank on the portfolio approach, he developed a transition impact monitoring system (TIMS)[39] with Buiter's support to cover the transition dimensions of the stock of projects.[40]

It was now possible to trace the path of a project's transition impact performance from beginning to end. The rating at the start, based on the context, the project's contribution and specific performance benchmarks—say, "good" potential with "high" risks to delivery—could now be tracked through to a final result. If, say, after two years the project was on track, the transition risk rating might be adjusted down to "medium", while if at the end some but not all objectives were met, the final impact rating might be recorded as "satisfactory". (Risks at this stage would be "negligible".) This meant it was possible to see both the position of transition impact ratings for new projects and how the existing stock of projects was faring, thus providing an overview of the whole of the EBRD's activities under this dimension. There was now a metric for transition impact that could be discussed in a similar vein to profitability and risk, as targeted under the strategic approach to portfolio management.

It was not long before a further change was made that had a significant effect on behaviours and interactions between bankers and economists. This was the introduction of a corporate scorecard[41] in 2001, which included among a number of targets a category for transition impact based on project scores. Initially, two-thirds of projects were required to be rated "good" or better. The target became more precise in due course—although

---

39 Kjetl Tvedt, an economist in OCE, was also closely involved.
40 A full account of the system can be found in J. Carbajo and Z. Kominek, 'Managing for Results: A decade of project-level impact assessment at the EBRD', EBRD, 2010.
41 Thinking along the lines of a scorecard had been under consideration for a while. See Chapter 12.

never so tight that the EBRD was unable to meet it—and was integrated into bankers' individual objectives and incentives. Over time, various refinements were made to the scoring system, including the addition of a risk-based version, expected transition impact, and a related target for progress in the portfolio. The principle of targeting transition impact as a core component of the Bank's performance (with a high weighting in the scorecard), and that of its bankers, has survived to the present day.

There still remained the question of how to achieve a suitable balance between transition impact, financial returns and risks as envisaged under the strategic approach to portfolio management. The potential conflict between transition impact, as espoused by economists, and financial returns, as sought by bankers, and risk, as focused on by credit officers, needed addressing.

This was the job of OpsCom. The balance between financial risk and return was resolved very much in the same way as in commercial credit committees, namely through a process of negotiation to find a suitable tolerance level. On transition impact and returns, the picture was a little different. In most private-sector projects, there was little conflict between the objectives: restructuring a company to become profitable, for example, normally went hand-in-hand with strengthening its competitiveness or improving its corporate governance (both of which were acceptable from a risk perspective).

The exceptions were when subsidies, protection or exploiting monopolistic aspects of markets came into play and profitability (or the reduction of financial risk) was achieved by supporting market distortions. In public-sector projects there would typically be alignment over tariff-setting improvements and similar conditions, but not when state market power was abused, where there was a lack of reform or when profits were made from supporting an unreformed state entity.

Of course, at the margin a little more push for transition impact (for example, via an extra covenant) might be traded for a little less risk-adjusted financial return (the client might argue for reduced pricing). But the reality of most projects is that discrete elements apply and negotiations take place over many aspects, so such fine trade-offs were difficult to find. Where they were more likely to be found was at the early selection stage when projects chosen for their best commercial profile need not match those selected on transition grounds.

As the transition impact rating system bedded in, the competitive nature of private-sector bankers inevitably began to permeate the system.

"Excellent" ratings were sought from the arbiters of transition impact, the economists, while "satisfactory" ones were often disputed. The independent role of the Chief Economist meant the view on transition impact, like a legal opinion, could be challenged. Once a judgement was given, however, it could not be overturned. The "creative tension" between bankers seeking sign-off on their deals and economists eager to ensure they served the transition process well and were additional meant focused debates took place on nearly every project.

The practical needs and detailed project and local knowledge of the bankers became pitted against the wider, more conceptual perspective and methodologically consistent approach of the economists. Some bankers cynically complained that the economists were the "high priests of transition" while the economists saw the bankers as volume and deal-driven to the exclusion of anything else. The truth was different, as less excitable observers acknowledged.

Bankers realised that the nature of the EBRD meant it was different from a purely commercial organisation and that they could not ignore the mandate. Close involvement with the sector economists on projects was the simplest way of understanding the transition dimensions better and getting help and buy-in. The economists for their part accepted that being based in EBRD's London headquarters limited their understanding of requirements on the ground, the reality of trying to persuade clients to accept transition-related covenants (clients had far less understanding or patience on such matters than even the bankers), and the true difficulties of overcoming local constraints and making progress with the authorities.

Gradually, the economists became more embedded with Banking teams. The process of discussion of projects from their initiation to final review between the two departments, and its evolution and learning by doing, helped to form a real understanding of the nuts and bolts of transition impact and the ways in which the Bank could influence the process. As a result, a "transition impact culture" was fostered within the institution—something that became apparent to new recruits within moments of their arrival.

The Board offered its own view on the transition impact judgement in projects and more often than not took the Chief Economist's decision on this dimension as the correct interpretation—although this did not prevent Directors arguing with the ratings given to particular projects.

7. A Coherent Business Model for a Private Sector-Driven Public Institution

Both the OpsCom exposure and that at the Board meant the language and sources of transition quickly became assimilated into bankers' thinking. The consensus-driven nature of the OpsCom and Board discussions helped to avoid undue stand-offs and led to a better internal understanding of transition impact than might have been expected (notwithstanding many lively discussions and hotly contested arguments). For new bankers, used to difficult discussions at credit committees over the pricing and structure of their projects, it was a shock to be confronted with a similar committee questioning the value of their deal on the basis of whether it added anything from the transition impact point of view. They had to learn fast, and by and large did.

The establishment of "transition impact" as a core feature of the Bank and its activities took some time to become firmly embedded in the institution. Like many aspects of the EBRD's persona, it evolved through a competitive process within a collaborative context as the Bank grew and matured and sought to place itself among its IFI peers. The EBRD's methodological approach reflected the fact that the Bank was serving a different purpose: establishing the transition to functioning markets as a commercially oriented bank with limited donor funds, as opposed to improving social outcomes with donor support, guarantees and repeated capital replenishments.

The debate about transition impact was largely an internal matter (although discussed in publications such as the *Transition Report*). Nonetheless, its operationalisation was of significance, not only to the EBRD in driving it forward in a more focused and relevant way, but also because the institutional mechanism for incorporating this alternative currency to financial returns carried wider implications, including for other organisations seeking to achieve multiple targets. The Bank found an effective way of squaring the two key purposes of the institution and embedding them on an equal footing in the conduct of its operations: on the one hand optimising its resources to deliver its mandate on transition, while on the other ensuring it remained a financially sustainable enterprise. Assessment of transition impact implicitly provided a means to measure the rate of return to the public purse—its development capital—while profits after provisions could help to deliver an adequate rate of return on its financial capital.

Part III

Holding Course

Chapter 11

Russian Crisis

1. Events

On 17 August 1998, the Russian authorities announced a devaluation of the rouble, default on domestic debt obligations and a moratorium on the servicing of some hard-currency debt. A substantial acceleration of inflation, a breakdown in the payments system and a run on deposits followed. The stock market fell sharply, bond yields rose and financial markets became inoperative. Confidence in Russia's economy, markets and outlook suffered a severe blow. The macroeconomic situation was in danger of spiralling out of control, but the most immediate problem was the prospect of a collapse of the banking system.

As a major investor in Russia, and an advocate of reform, the EBRD was badly affected. Along with other IFIs active in Russia—principally the IMF, World Bank and IFC—and the European Commission, the EBRD set to work to find a solution. The IMF had only a month earlier approved new financing of more than US$ 11 billion for Russia as part of an international bailout package, along with an additional US$ 4 billion from the World Bank, and had already disbursed a first tranche of US$ 4.8 billion.[1]

Like many financial crises before and after, including the global financial meltdown 10 years later, the proximate cause—in this case heavy short-term government borrowing and a loss of investor confidence in the Russian government's repayment capacity and ability to defend a fixed exchange rate—was not the real reason for the failure. There had been inadequate structural

---

[1] US$ 0.8 billion was subsequently withheld after the Duma failed to pass critical reform measures. *International Trade Reporter*, 29 July 1998, p. 1328 cited in 'The Russian Financial Crisis of 1998', Congressional Research Service, 18 February 1999.

reform in Russia, which both the EBRD and the IMF had made efforts to address, but in the run-up to the crash of 1998 the full extent of the problem was masked by market buoyancy. The real picture only really became clear to investors, including the EBRD, in the aftermath.

2. Background to the Crisis

In the early years of Yeltsin's presidency, high levels of inflation were fuelled by a substantial expansion of credit by the Central Bank of Russia (CBR), which in turn financed the federal government's persistently high budget deficit and supported inefficient enterprises. The situation was exacerbated by a widespread belief that credit expansion was needed to stimulate output following a sharp decline in production,[2] as well as by an ongoing conflict between reformers seeking tight fiscal policies and their political opponents, and by interest groups and weak enterprises obtaining credits and subsidies.

A stabilisation programme in 1995, backed by an IMF stand-by arrangement (SBA) of around US$ 6.5 billion, brought the fiscal deficit down from more than 10 per cent of GDP to around 5 per cent. Monetary financing of the deficit was replaced by borrowing on international capital markets and via a newly created treasury bill market. Demand for this market's products—short-term rouble notes (GKOs), and longer-dated bonds (OFZs)—began to grow. The fiscal improvement resulted in upward nominal exchange rate pressure. Fearing a loss of competitiveness and possible sharp reversals in the rouble, the authorities introduced an exchange-rate band.

Although in 1995 the government maintained its commitment to tight fiscal constraints, with budget deficits within prescribed parameters, it remained short of money. Revenues were below projections, partly because enterprises with connections to the political elite received exemptions from tax payments. The hard-pressed government delayed expenditures by allowing pension and wage arrears to build up and by failing to pay bills for goods and services. Compounding the problem, taxpayers, many of whom were owed money by the government, then withheld tax payments while well-connected enterprises reduced their tax liabilities through exemptions and informal arrangements.

---

2   John Odling-Smee, 'The MF and Russia in the 1990s', IMF Working Paper WP/04/155 2004, p. 7 and p. 35.

A shortfall in revenues was also a factor behind the government's decision in late 1995 to launch a loans-for-shares scheme, whereby banks controlled by oligarchs made loans to the government using the security of undervalued state assets and subsequently took possession of the assets when the government failed to repay the loans. These transactions, and the support given by the oligarch beneficiaries for Yeltsin's campaign to be re-elected President in June 1996, extended the influence of a wealthy few on the banking sector, the economy and Russian public life. A non-transparent economy increasingly based on collusion, corruption and asset-stripping was poorly placed to handle the subsequent crisis.

On the face of it, prospects improved in 1996 following Yeltsin's re-election. The monthly rate of inflation dropped to low single figures and the fall in output was finally slowing. (Output rose for the first time in eight years in 1997.) Nevertheless the fiscal situation was not healthy. Spending commitments had increased in the run-up to the election and interest rates had to be raised to keep the exchange rate within its band, adding to government interest payments. Revenues also suffered from the erosion of tax discipline as government payment arrears built up, reaching 3 per cent of GDP by the end of the year, and as politically influential oligarchs and those who had helped with Yeltsin's re-election withheld tax payments. Significant intergovernmental transfers, subsidies and devolution of revenue to regional governments made matters worse.

Investors had been reassured, however, by international financial arrangements made in the run-up to the 1996 election: the approval of a three-year IMF Extended Financing Facility for Russia of more than US$ 10 billion in March 1996 and an agreement with Paris Club creditors on Soviet debt a month later.[3] They were also comforted, after the election, by Yeltsin's appointment of well-known reformers Anatoly Chubais to run the Presidential Administration office and later Boris Nemtsov as first deputy prime minister. Combined with an improving economic outlook, this encouraged financial markets to believe a turning point had been reached in Russia's transition similar to those seen in central European countries a few years earlier. The world had also been experiencing a boom in financial markets on the back of deregulation and emerging markets, including Russia, had been caught up in the exuberance.

---

3 The Paris Club group of creditors reached an agreement on the treatment of US$ 40 billion former Soviet Union debt on 29 April 1996.

In the year following Yeltsin's election the dollar-denominated RTS stock index, which had been established in September 1995, more than tripled in value.[4] The euphoria was also seen in the Russian domestic government bond market, where yields fell sharply and whose market value rose from around 3.5 per cent of GDP to 8.2 per cent during the course of 1996. In November, the government issued its first US$ 1 billion eurobond. Encouraged by the easing of capital controls, foreign investors snapped up both foreign currency and rouble-denominated Russian debt. By the end of 1997, foreigners held an estimated 33 per cent of the stock of GKOs and OFZs.[5] Towards the end of the year the stock of GKOs and OFZs exceeded rouble deposits in the banking system. Both of these indicators should have been a warning sign.

Global investors' enthusiasm for emerging markets came to a halt, however, in the second half of 1997 following widespread devaluations and falls in stock market indices in Asia and subsequent sharp declines in output. Fears of contagion to other markets spread rapidly and prompted a flight to quality. Russia was caught up in the mayhem as nervous investors reassessed the scale of fiscal risks, the weaknesses in the banking system and the diminishing prospects of structural reform. The shock to financial confidence around the world also hit commodity prices. Oil prices, which formed the backbone of the Russian economy, crashed between 1997 and 1998[6], adding to Russia's woes. In March 1998, veteran Prime Minister Victor Chernomyrdin was replaced by 35-year-old Sergei Kiriyenko, a reformer who had less clout in the conservative administration.

One of the first casualties of investors' loss of confidence was the Russian stock market. The RTS index fell from a high of 672 on 6 October 1997 to a low of 39 exactly a year later. By May 1998, yields on GKOs had risen to over 50 per cent, more than double the level seen in 1997, and were on a steep upward trajectory, while the central bank's refinancing rate hit 150 per cent later that month. Foreign banks became increasingly reluctant to refinance maturing loans to Russian banks. With their substantial share and treasury bill portfolios plunging in value, local banks were forced to make

---

4   The RTS index rose from sound 150 in July 1996 to just above 500 in July 1997.
5   Annex 1.1 on The Russian Crisis by Rory MacFarquhar from *Transition Report* 1998.
6   See Robert Mabro, 'The Oil Price Crisis of 1998'. Oxford Institute for Energy Studies, 1998. https://www.oxfordenergy.org/wpcms/wp-content/uploads/2010/11/SP10-TheOilPriceCrisisof1998-RMabro-1998. The price of West Texas Intermediate (WTI) fell from a high of US$ 39.0 per barrel in January 1997 to US$ 17.6 per barrel by November 1998.

margin calls. The government struggled to find buyers for weekly auctions of around US$ 1 billion in treasury bills, while foreign reserves diminished rapidly as capital flight accelerated. Wage and payment arrears increased and rising interest rates began to hit enterprises and production.

By July 1998, an emergency package of new loans worth around US$ 17 billion had been agreed with the IMF and the World Bank, with additional funding provided by Japan. Despite the rapid deployment of US$ 4.8 billion of IMF funds to bolster foreign exchange reserves, however, the situation continued to deteriorate. In late August, the CBR announced it had spent almost US$ 9 billion of reserves to protect the exchange rate, and almost US$ 2 billion in the first two weeks of August alone.[7] Several banks were close to default and the CBR pumped liquidity into the system to keep them afloat, but the funds quickly found their way onto the currency markets.[8]

The crunch came on 17 August, when the government announced drastic measures to try to stabilise the situation. The existing exchange rate regime was replaced with a floating rate within an expanded corridor from 6.0 to 9.5 roubles to the dollar.[9] All GKOs and OFZs maturing in 1998 and 1999 were to be restructured, and a 90-day moratorium was imposed on payments by commercial banks to foreign creditors. Within two days of the default, the rouble had fallen by well over 10 per cent and the stock market by even more. On 2 September, the government moved to a fully floating exchange rate and by the end of the month the rouble had lost more than 60 per cent of its value against the dollar.

3. Tokobank: a Case Study

Like the markets, the EBRD had been slow to appreciate the extent of the problems building in the Russian economy. Its country portfolio had been growing rapidly, rising more than threefold between 1994 and 1997 to close to €2.5 billion. Annual business volume peaked in 1996 at €840 million, but even in 1997 reached €730 million. The pace of equity investment was also maintained during this period, including purchases of stakes in banks. A sig-

---

7 Congressional Research Service, 1999, p. 4.
8 Annex 1.1, Transition Report 1998.
9 From its previous corridor of 5.27 to 7.13 roubles to the dollar.

nificant investment in Avtobank in early 1997 was followed by a subscription to a capital increase in October. The following month, the Bank continued to pursue a stake in Inkombank, then Russia's second largest private bank, even though the principal strategic western investor had dropped out.[10]

The EBRD also had a significant holding in Tokobank, in which it had invested in 1994. The transaction was the first major foreign equity investment in a Russian bank and was aimed at supporting the development of the sector. The Bank had initially discussed providing a credit line to Tokobank, but in 1993 proposed instead to take an equity stake of 10–15 per cent. The purchase took place the following year as part of the Financial Institutions Development Programme (FIDP), an initiative launched by the EBRD and World Bank to strengthen a core group of Russian commercial banks.

With relatively few commercially-oriented banks with scalable lending capacity and plausible management in Russia at the time, Tokobank was a logical target. It was the country's fourteenth-largest bank by total assets, relatively new but growing fast and well-capitalised. It was also widely recognised for the strength of its senior management team, most of whom were in their forties, professionally trained abroad and professed commitment to achieving Western banking standards.

Behind the veneer, however, were some less attractive features. The bank was a predominantly wholesale foreign-currency operation whose rouble business was limited and weak. It provided short-term loans and foreign currency services mostly to medium and large-sized companies in the energy sector. Loan portfolio concentration and related-party lending were high. Eleven borrowers accounted for around 80 per cent of Tokobank's foreign-currency loans while 46 per cent of total lending was to the bank's own shareholders, who received preferential pricing on their loans. Capitalisation was strong, with equity amounting to 37.5 per cent of end-1993 assets, but strong competition for deposits led to an increasing reliance on the interbank market and medium-sized banks for funding.

In the nascent Russian banking system, Tokobank's financial situation was not unusual. Nonetheless, when the project came to the Board in September 1994, questions were raised over the size of the equity investment and the fact that Tokobank had paid a dividend the previous year despite making a

---

10 The hope was to find a new strategic investor that the EBRD could support so the investment was scaled back with a larger amount made contingent on this outcome.

loss. These concerns were mitigated by the proposed exit arrangements, which included a put option. The equity participation was approved by the Board.

Despite Tokobank's accreditation under the FIDP and rapid growth in its loan book over the next two years, its financial situation was weak when the EBRD extended a credit line to it in late 1996. The bank was still heavily dependent on foreign-currency lending and funding from the interbank market. It was loss-making, in part because of the impact of substantial taxes, and continued to conduct much of its business with related parties.

In 1997, Tokobank's finances deteriorated further. Oil prices had been falling since the start of the year and metals prices followed from the summer onwards, putting pressure on the earnings of the bank's main clients. Funding foreign-currency activity via the interbank market became more difficult as rising concerns over Russian debt prompted foreign banks to pull back from the market. By February 1998, Russian banks were refusing to lend to Tokobank and the CBR put it into temporary administration. An investigation of Tokobank's books uncovered "a tangle of insider loans, fictive collaterals and suspicious transfers of funds to offshore accounts". [11] By July, known bad loans and trading losses topped US$ 500 million. The EBRD now decided to exercise a put option and exit Tokobank.

The EBRD's response to the evolving situation was being watched closely in Russia and elsewhere. There were also concerns that if the Bank chose to exit at a time of stress, its ability to play a catalytic role in support of other banks in the future would be damaged. There were suggestions too that corporate governance principles had been compromised by other investors not being informed of the existence of the put option.

The strongest feelings stirred up were over the proposition that the EBRD had been secretive about writing the put option in in the first place. According to one account:

> The concealment of the put option by the EBRD left many investors dismayed. One Moscow banker bitterly said of the EBRD, 'First the EBRD gave its stamp of approval but it didn't do its homework. Then it tried to escape from the sinking ship, letting the others drown.'[12]

---

11   Thane Gustafson, *Capitalism Russian-Style*, Cambridge University Press, 2004, p. 94.
12   Filippo Ippolito, 'The Banking Sector in Russia', Bank of Finland Institute for Economies in Transition, *BOFIT* no. 12, December 2002.

This was unfair. The Share Purchase Agreement, which included the put option, had been approved at an Extraordinary General Meeting of Tokobank. Major shareholders were aware the put option was under consideration and that the Bank was working with the CBR to find a strategic investor to rescue the bank. The EBRD's advice was that, in the absence of such an investor, an orderly and transparent liquidation would be the best solution. OpsCom decided in February to exercise the put but held off in May in response to a request from the CBR. The decision was reconfirmed in July should the rescue attempt fail.

Attempts to find a buyer failed and the CBR revoked Tokobank's licence just before the banking crisis in August. At this point, the EBRD intended to play an active role in the liquidation process as a creditor. The first meeting of the Creditors' Committee took place in October but hopes of an equitable resolution were quickly dashed.

The foreign creditors, who were owed more than US$ 300 million, expected to hold a majority of seats on the Creditors' Committee and to select the liquidator. When it came to the vote on the composition of the committee, however, their ballots were declared invalid and four of the seven seats went to a group of Russian companies holding only 20 per cent of Tokobank's debt. Among the creditors voting were five offshore companies affiliated with Mikhail Zhivilo, the President of ZAO Metal Investment Co, which alleged claims of more than US $200 million against Tokobank. These were disputed by the bank's former management and foreign creditors. The liquidator selected had also worked for Mr Zhivilo. Although a Moscow arbitration court later ruled the claims invalid, the committee and the liquidator were left unchanged. Some foreign members of the committee—Dresdner Bank, Bank Austria and the IFC—subsequently boycotted meetings because their Russian co-members blocked discussion of the offshore companies.

In April 1999, Andrew Higgins reported in *The Wall Street Journal*:

> Almost half a year later, a few [creditors] still hope, but many have given up. Instead of an orderly liquidation, the test case has become a brawl in which some of the West's premier financial institutions have been muscled aside by a cluster of Russian companies linked to a 32-year-old Moscow metals trader. The battle has featured bogus credit claims, murky offshore companies and menacing phone calls. One thing it hasn't had much of is money.

The EBRD recovered nothing from either the put option or its loan to Tokobank and its stakes were entirely written off in 1999. David Hexter, who as EBRD's head of financial institutions bore the brunt of the onslaught on the Russian banking portfolio, described the Tokobank experience as "not a happy episode for sure". The Bank also had to write off its equity investment in Inkombank, the third-largest retail bank in Russia, which had its licence revoked by the CBR in October 1998. In the case of the Bank's other large equity investment, in Avtobank, a mostly wholesale bank, provisions were made when it became illiquid following the debt moratorium on government securities. However, it was a large, systemically important bank and not insolvent and after restructuring continued to operate.

4. The Consequences for the EBRD

Investments in the banking sector were not the EBRD's only concern in Russia in 1998. When the crisis erupted in August, it became apparent that all the Bank's projects were potentially in jeopardy. Not only was the banking sector in crisis but the payments system had broken down, disrupting money flows between entities. An immediate full-scale stress-test of the Russia portfolio by the Banking and Credit Departments was put in hand. Clients were contacted to get a better understanding of their situation and a preliminary review of sensitive projects was available by early September.

At the end of August, the EBRD's Russian portfolio stood at close to ECU 3 billion or around 27 per cent of the total. Disbursements were just over half this level, although a similar percentage of the total. About one-fifth of signed projects by value were sovereign and presumed safe, while almost another one-fifth had been classified as impaired prior to the crisis. More than 40 per cent of the non-sovereign portfolio, amounting to nearly ECU 1 billion, was with banks. Apart from the financial sector, the biggest exposures were in the oil and gas and automotive sectors (Sakhalin Oil, KomiArctic Oil, Unified Gas, Kamaz and GAZ, amounting to over ECU 400 million).

When the news broke, on August 17, most people were away on summer vacation. Fortunately, key staff in the EBRD's Moscow office were not. There was a lot at stake for the Bank, not only the threat to its own portfolio but also, as lender of record, to B loan commitments of close to

US$ 1 billion. Lawyers and others in the Resident Office, who had been working closely with the authorities on withholding tax issues, immediately contacted their counterparts in the CBR and relevant ministries to explain the consequences facing the Bank and associated investors. The quick action resulted in a formal confirmation two days later, signed by the first deputy minister of finance and central bank governor, that the EBRD and commercial participants in its loans would be exempt from the moratorium on foreign debt repayments. In effect, this affirmed the EBRD's preferred creditor status and a recognition by Russia of its role as a member of the institution. According to Doyle, "This [action] was critical to our survival … we were only seven years old. If the Russians had defaulted on us we would have been the development bank that failed." Some days later, a similar statement was issued in relation to the World Bank and IFC.

As the crisis unfolded, the Bank advised that it would suspend further disbursements to its clients pending clarification of the situation. The swiftly issued exemption suggested the EBRD would be expected to continue making disbursements to Russian clients. But in a series of letters and visits by senior officials to Moscow during the following month—including Horst Köhler, who took over as President in September—the Bank pointed out that the breakdown in the payments system meant many clients were unable to access funds held in illiquid banks, in order to make scheduled payments to the Bank (of which some US$ 300 million was due within six months), and there was no guarantee that any disbursements by the Bank would reach the intended beneficiaries.

A further consequence of the financial problems in Russia was the risk of contagion to neighbouring countries of operations, either directly through trade and financial relationships or through a global economic slowdown. This would also have a negative impact on the EBRD's projects, although it would be mitigated by the fact that most of the portfolio in these countries was under sovereign guarantee. Economic analysis conducted by the Bank showed that Belarus and Moldova were most exposed to the trade channel, and that the impact could be severe, while Latvia was most at risk from its exposure to Russian assets (GKOs represented more than 10 per cent of banking system assets). Resident Offices were surveyed for their views and generally concurred with the assessment, adding Ukraine to the list of countries most likely to suffer due to a parallel sharp hryvnia devaluation and drying up of liquidity.

The immediate impact on the Bank's financial position was severe. Steven Kaempfer, the EBRD's Vice President Finance, announced at a press conference on 9 September that additional provisions of ECU 180 million would be taken in the third quarter, raising provisioning for Russia to ECU 330 million or almost half the total for the Bank. He estimated that the EBRD would show a loss of ECU 150 million for the year. Fortunately, the Treasury Department had sold its holdings of GKOs in advance of the crisis. Nevertheless, eventual total losses in 1998 amounted to ECU 261 million on the back of provisioning of ECU 553 million, which reduced the Bank's reserves to a negative ECU 160 million.

With ECU 5 billion of members' equity and ECU 20 billion of authorised capital, there was no threat to the viability of the Bank. Nor, despite the poor results, did the rating agencies downgrade the EBRD's triple-A borrower status. Nonetheless, the situation was worrisome and the Bank took steps to address the issues.

5. Efforts to Assist

The Russian financial crisis coincided with an interregnum between de Larosière's departure in January and Köhler's arrival on 1 September. During that time, the Bank was in effect run by the banking department, dominated by the financial institutions group, which had grown rapidly in the previous years to account for more than one third of the portfolio. The new President's first task was to formulate a strategic response to the Russian financial crisis.

Köhler was in many respects well qualified for the Presidency. A former head of the German Federal Ministry of Finance, he had served as a G7 Deputy and Sherpa and played a central role in supervising the Treuhandanstalt, the institution responsible for privatising assets in the GDR. He was also the first President with direct ties to the former communist bloc, having been born in Poland and lived in his early years near Leipzig in Eastern Germany.

One week after his arrival, with the Russian crisis uppermost in everyone's mind, Köhler emphasised the need for careful risk management but noted there was no need to retreat from activities in Russia since the EBRD, through its long-term investment strategy, could contribute to stabilising confidence in the country. The approach was broadly accepted, along with concerns to maintain support to SMEs and to continue to coordinate closely with the Russian authorities and the G7, the IMF, the World Bank and the European Commission.

Bi-weekly Board meetings over the following two months considered the ramifications of the crisis on Russia, the EBRD and its region of operations. There was relief that a government had been formed and confidence that the authorities were moving in the right direction, even if there was likely to be more state intervention going forward. However, progress in tackling insolvencies and the restructuring of the banking sector was slow and the legal framework for business remained inadequate. A contraction of the economy of 4–6 per cent was now expected.[13] Many foreign banks were reducing their presence and in some cases considering withdrawal.

The EBRD's response to the crisis was to provide emergency support to existing clients in the form of working capital, technical assistance and trade finance[14] during the period when the payments system was impaired. Even when this was normalised, however, the operating environment remained challenging. The drop in collateral values and an increase in compulsory foreign exchange surrender requirements deterred investment. There was little the Bank could do to reinvigorate foreign investors' appetite for Russia. The EBRD's investments in Russia, which had been running at around ECU 54 million per month before the crisis, dropped abruptly to just over ECU 16 million and remained at that level until the end of 1999.[15] Activities were focused on managing the RVFs, where 11 small deals averaging ECU 1.6 million apiece were signed in the last five months of 1998 and a further eight in the first half of 1999.

The Bank made major efforts to maintain loans to small businesses. At the time of the crisis, the RSBF involved 13 partner banks covering 23 regions, 6,500 sub-loans and a US$ 100 million portfolio. With these banks insolvent or under threat of failure, the first task was to assign sub-loan portfolios to a safer home. This was achieved by converting the Russian Project

---

13   The outturn for GDP was a fall of 5.3 per cent. The EBRD's forecast at the time was a fall of 5.0 per cent, *Transition Report* 1998.
14   The Ministry of Finance agreed to divert some of the FIDP funds for a US$ 50 million trade-facilitation project deploying revolving short-term credits to selected Russian banks on a non-recourse or sovereign-guaranteed basis.
15   Business volume in Russia in 1998 totalled ECU 541 million, with ECU 74 million signed between mid-August and the end of the year. The total for 1999 was ECU 64 million with ECU 99 million signed by the end of June.

Finance Bank (RPFB), which had been set up by the EBRD in 1992 and in which it had a 35 per cent stake, into the Small Business Credit Bank (KMB) and assigning the portfolios to this bank. The original Russian shareholders of the RPFB were bought out and replaced with international investors— the Soros Economic Development Fund, DEG and Triodos Bank—while the EBRD retained its 35 per cent stake. Credit advisers focused on recoveries from the assigned portfolios and the amounts obtained were collected by KMB. At the same time, RSBF-trained staff from the failed banks were hired by KMB to support new lending. The EBRD also worked with the largest bank, Sberbank, which survived the crisis thanks to its state ownership, universal coverage and market dominance. Subsequent lending— which typically consisted of much smaller, micro-level loans than before the crisis—was largely shared between these two banks. Three surviving regional banks were also involved, although on a very small scale.

New lending more or less stopped while the programme was being re-established but began to pick up slowly through 1999, gathering speed from the summer onwards. However, the EBRD encountered serious problems in recovering loans it had accelerated at some major RSBF partner banks and, in some cases, the related sub-loan portfolios.

In the case of the RSBF, the assigned sub-loan portfolio quality proved to be high, with sub-borrowers showing greater responsibility than many of their larger or less carefully screened peers. By March 2001, the Bank estimated that the repayment rate for the RSBF was close to 99 per cent, with losses amounting to just US$ 5 million out of a total of US$ 564 million disbursed to sub-borrowers.[16] The same could not be said of the six main partner banks involved. By the same juncture, recoveries amounted to just under 50 per cent,[17] leading to a loss of US$ 37 million on borrowed funds.

During this episode, the CBR took little action in the first few months of the crisis and had no clear policy on insolvent banks. The opaque nature of its decision-making processes made it difficult to assess default risks at partner banks. It had failed to stem the practice of asset-stripping via "bridge" banks that had begun even before the crisis. The transfer of valuable assets abroad or to other legal entities took place on a vast scale under its stewardship. In many cases, entire branches of insolvent banks, includ-

---

16 The Bank had originally expected recoveries of 50 per cent.
17 In the case of one bank the recovery rate was 100 per cent.

ing their customers and employees, were taken over by a new entity run by the former management of bankrupt banks. A number of dubious practices were also used against the EBRD during the work-out process. One instance, which led to a series of court cases and appeals, involved a US$ 13.4 million sub-loan via SBS-Agro to Runicom, a subsidiary of Sibneft, where the borrower claimed that the amount had already been repaid. These court proceedings were eventually settled in 2018.

At a higher level, efforts were made by the Bank together with the IMF and World Bank to provide advice to the CBR and Russian ministry of finance on restructuring the banking sector. A joint paper advocated a move towards a banking system based on a core group of competitive private banks. The IMF and World Bank were also instrumental in setting up the Agency for Restructuring Credit Organisations (ARCO)[18, 19], which was created in 1999 to restructure Russia's banks.

Other hurdles included bureaucratic delays, the need for improved legislation (particularly an effective law on the bankruptcy of banks) and poor protection of the interests of depositors and creditors. Nonetheless, the Bank worked with the European Commission to provide technical assistance to the CBR programme on bank restructuring, including support for resolution teams in individual banks and for upgrading regional central banks. It also engaged with the authorities on legislative improvements, again in full coordination with the European Commission, IMF and World Bank.

6. Implications for Business Plans

Following a Board workshop in November 1998, the EBRD set out its near-term plans in Russia which fed into preparations for a new country strategy.[20] The crisis had clearly dampened earlier enthusiasm for Russian projects and instilled a significant degree of caution.

---

18   ARCO began operations in late March 1999, helping banks requesting assistance on a volunteer basis, and obtained legal powers to impose restructurings on banks from mid-July 1999. See 'Restructuring the Russian Banking System', by Marina Chekurova, Chapter 9 in 'Financial Transition in Europe and Central Asia: Challenges of the New Decade', L. Bokros, A. Flemming and C. Votava, World Bank, 2001.
19   The Inter-Agency Coordinating Committee for Banking Sector Development in Russia (ICC) was also important in the aftermath of the crisis.
20   This was eventually issued in 2000 and emphasised the need to restore confidence and credibility in the Russian economy, which the Bank's projects and policy dialogue would support.

The uncertainties over the economic and financial outlook at the time made it easy to decide to reduce activities in Russia substantially. An emphasis was placed on selectivity and "quality projects". Only transactions meeting very high standards for transition (including the integrity of clients) and sound banking were to be considered.

The Bank resolved to pay more attention to the systemic stability and effective regulation of the banking system when evaluating and monitoring financial sector projects. The balance between risk and return was re-evaluated, resulting in a shift towards more and better security, shorter maturities, and more demanding conditions and covenants. Greater attention was to be given to projects earning foreign exchange and those replacing imports or mainly dependent on domestic inputs.

Developing effective economic governance at the regional level and supporting reform-minded regions was also identified as a priority. Suggested ways to achieve this included the development of municipal and environmental infrastructure designed to encourage decentralisation of the financing and provision of local services and commercialisation of local utilities.

The revised approach was supplemented by a joint working group with the European Commission to enhance coordination initiatives in areas including: institutional strengthening of the CBR (covering supervision, accounting, licencing and bankruptcy) and two systemically important commercial banks; trade and working capital finance; and improvements to the investment climate (covering insolvency, standards of corporate governance, bankruptcy and capital markets).

7. Lessons Learned

Although the EBRD suffered a serious financial blow as a result of the 1998 financial crisis in Russia, it was not long-lasting and the Bank returned to profit the following year. Similarly, the Russian economy confounded expectations and rebounded strongly and quickly. GDP rose by 6.4 per cent in 1999, the current account moved sharply into surplus and foreign exchange reserves were rebuilt. The strong macroeconomic performance reflected the impact of the large (40 per cent) real rouble depreciation in the fourth quarter of 1998, which stimulated import-substitution, but also a recovery in world oil prices. By early 1999, imports were around half their pre-crisis level and non-oil exports were growing strongly. The fiscal position was also transformed and moved towards overall balance, showing a primary surplus in 1999.

The Russian authorities failed, however, to take advantage of the situation to advance structural reforms, especially in the moribund banking sector. Partly this reflected the fact that the financial sector was not truly critical to the basic functioning of an economy that largely operated on a system of barter, arrears and various forms of non-intermediated finance.[21] Financial intermediation in Russia remained very low by international standards,[22] which muted the impact of the crisis, and the distorted structure of an economy dominated by natural resources and industrial oligopolies meant normal bank financing of investment was limited. Many banks effectively acted as managers of the treasury operations of their large corporate shareholders, offering a ready source of liquidity and loans when required. Intermediation services to the general public and especially to the real economy via SMEs was small. The EBRD had believed it could help redress the balance by supporting the modernisation of financial institutions and lending to the real economy via the RSBF.

The Bank devoted its next *Transition Report* to a thorough analysis of the financial sector in transition[23] and a Board workshop in January 1999 also looked at some of the lessons. The most important was that, while the Bank had been aware of the weakness of institutions throughout its involvement and in its investments in Russia, it had insufficiently considered the deeper implications of the risks and had underestimated the probabilities of downside scenarios. Underpinning these lessons was the realisation that poor corporate governance (particularly in relation to the rights of minority shareholders, creditors and depositors), inadequate regulation and supervision, inadequate laws on bankruptcy and insolvency and an inability to rely on the effective application of the rule of law needed much closer attention in less-developed transition economies such as Russia.

While the EBRD had rightly moved since 1993 from being an institution focused on public-sector operations and foreign-sponsored projects in

---

21 Estimates of barter ranged from 50 per cent of sales of medium-sized enterprises to 75 per cent of large companies. See 'Have Car, Need Briefs? In Russia Barter is back', by Ellen Barry, *New York Times*, 7 February 2009.
22 Domestic credit by banks to GDP was less than 30 per cent compared with around 100 per cent in more developed economies, *Transition Report* 1998, p. 93. Deposits to GDP were around 10 per cent, again very low, F. Ippolito (2002).
23 *Transition Report* 1998, EBRD.

central Europe to one with a wider portfolio of projects across the whole region and a predominantly private-sector orientation, including an emphasis on financial institutions and local companies, its focus on the specifics of projects meant it failed to put sufficient stress on institution-building or the investment climate and the systemic risks they entailed.

These ideas were echoed in 2001 by Nick Stern, EBRD's former Chief Economist, in a lecture on the first decade of transition.

> It has ... become clear that the political and economic transitions are intricately intertwined and that political support for reforms is vital for their success. The Russian crisis of 1998 embodies all these lessons. Before the crisis, Russia had developed into an economy of striking contrasts. Banks traded sophisticated financial derivatives but were virtually unable to attract ordinary household deposits. Trading on the stock market reached volumes of over US$ 100 million per day but shareholders were often unable to exercise their most basic rights. Vast financial-industrial groups were created to promote synergies between banks and large-scale enterprises, while an ever-increasing number of firms resorted to barter to stay afloat. The self-styled 'oligarchs' in command of these groups amassed substantial fortunes but left their workers and the state with a mushrooming backlog of wage and tax arrears ... investors in search of quick profits did not think sufficiently carefully about the depth of the underlying structural problems.

Stern concluded:

> Perhaps the most important lesson from the Russian crisis and the first decade of transition has been that free trade and private ownership will not by themselves bring well-functioning markets, and that market-supporting institutions are fundamental ... Markets, if they are to function well, need a state with the strength to regulate responsibly, tax effectively and provide its people with basic services, including the rule of law. This much should have been obvious to us all.[24]

---

24 Nick Stern, 'Challenges for the Next Decade of Transition', paper presented at an IMF Conference, 1–3 February 1999. Reproduced in O. Havrylyshyn and S.M. Nsouli (eds.), *A Decade of Transition: Achievements and Challenges*, IMF, Washington D.C, 2001.

Chapter 12

Recovery, Growth, and Graduation

Introduction

The impact of the 1998 Russian crisis on the EBRD had been swift and dramatic. The slow but steady build-up of operational capacity and business volume orchestrated under de Larosière's leadership had run into problems. Barely had the first signs of positive returns on shareholders' equity emerged than the Bank faced a significant loss. It was a rude awakening and a formidable challenge for de Larosière's successor, Horst Köhler, who arrived at the Bank just two weeks after the crisis broke.

The immediate prospect for business with Russia and many other countries of operations strongly affected by the crisis was grim. Real output in Russia fell by more than 6 per cent in the third quarter of 1998 alone, leaving it almost 10 per cent lower that at the end of 1997. While the retreat of commercial finance from the region had increased the need for support for transition, the EBRD could not ignore the principles of sound banking. The priority for Köhler was therefore to stabilise the Bank and take stock of the situation.

1. Revitalising the Contours of the Bank: 'Moving Transition Forward'

When the 1998 crisis hit, Russia accounted for more than one-quarter of the Bank's portfolio of more than €10 billion. While below Russia's share of GDP in the EBRD's region, this indicated the scale of the problem facing the Bank. Russia had contributed significantly to the net loss of €261 million in 1998. The Board and the new President agreed to hold off on new project approvals in Russia and review the Bank's strategy.

A series of discussions with the Board took place, including a retreat in January 1999, which resulted in a new paper outlining the path ahead, entitled 'Moving Transition Forward: Operational Priorities for the Medium Term'.[1] In looking back over the previous period there were many positive achievements that could be acknowledged: the support for the private sector, liberalisation and privatisation, reaching local enterprises, providing equity, a portfolio of more than €10 billion, and operations and Resident Offices in each of the 26 countries of operations. The paper summarised how the Bank saw itself:

> The Operational Priorities of 1994 have stood the test of time and the Bank has delivered on them ... [The Bank] is recognised in the region and beyond as a strong and credible partner and catalyst for the transition process...
>
> For the region as a whole the achievements in economic and political transition have been remarkable. New democratic regimes have shown resilience ... In most countries, well over half the output is generated in the private sector. The prospect of a return to a command economy is now remote. But the experience of countries has differed strongly. Those that have shown sustained and effective commitment to reform are seeing the returns in terms of growth, investment and new enterprises, whereas those that have been unwilling or unable to develop this commitment have been more vulnerable to setback and crisis, as occurred in 1998 in parts of the region.

At the same time the lessons from this experience could not be ignored:

> The transition will inevitably be a complex, demanding and lengthy process ... a key lesson is that the transition requires greater attention and commitment to creating strong institutions ... and underpinned by an acceptable social framework.

Nor could the Russia episode be airbrushed out of the picture:

> With hindsight the probabilities of adverse scenarios were underestimated. And the Bank should have examined more rigorously how it could

---

[1] 'Moving Transition Forward: Operational Priorities for the Medium Term', 22 March 1999.

have used its influence and its project activities to help overcome the institutional problems which were a major factor in generating the crisis.[2]

The paper highlighted the importance of focusing on project quality throughout the Bank's work and paying closer attention to the quality of its project partners. Also highlighted was the need to take a more balanced approach to its project portfolio. In particular, projects were to be managed to pursue transition impact while balancing risks, returns and costs. Operational priorities among products, sectors and country activities had to be chosen in such a way as to safeguard the financial viability of the EBRD; only a financially stable Bank was able to foster transition successfully. The Bank needed a quality asset-earning base and to manage its portfolio through the full project cycle.

The operational priorities were not fundamentally different from those in the strategy formulated by de Larosière five years earlier. They emphasised the importance of the financial sector (with an increased focus on sound regulation), SMEs, restructuring of large industrial enterprises for demonstration effects, equity, use of the full range of financial structures for infrastructure (private, sovereign, non-sovereign and PPPs), and the need for a sound investment climate and strengthened institutions.

Recovery from the Russian crisis

In the event, the Russian economy recovered much faster than expected. The *Transition Report* in 1998[3] had forecast GDP growth of -7.0 per cent for 1999 and the Bank's *Annual Report* published in March 1999 predicted that "capital outflows from countries with weaker fundamentals, such as Romania, Russia and Ukraine, are unlikely to turn around in the near future". Ironically, it was at just this point that conditions were starting to improve. In 1999, GDP in Russia increased by a remarkable 6.4 per cent.

More accurate forecasts would, however, have been unlikely to make much difference to operational activity. Around half of the Bank's industrial projects in Russia were in workout situations, and problematic projects accounted for 30 per cent of its overall portfolio, despite the decent

---

2   Ibid.
3   EBRD *Transition Report* 1998, 'Financial sector in transition', October 1998, p. 68.

performance of sovereign and sub-sovereign loans. The priority was to protect and salvage existing projects, and unwind heavy provisions as far as possible.

A further consequence of the crisis, reflecting a change in demand and investor perceptions, was the large number of cancellations, amounting to more than €900 million in 1998 and 1999. Foreign strategic investors also retreated and the EBRD was more wary than ever of joining forces with new or unknown domestic Russian clients. Project approvals slumped from more than €1 billion in 1997 to around €200 million in 1999. Business volume, measured by new signings, similarly dropped to one-fifth of pre-crisis levels. Annual business investment in Russia in 1999 was €164 million—a mere 7.5 per cent of the Bank's total business, down from 36 per cent and 32.5 per cent, respectively, in 1996 and 1997.

Despite the setbacks and the lowest overall business volume in four years, the EBRD managed to record a small net profit of €43 million in 1999, while the portfolio crept up to close to €11 billion. Almost as soon as prospects started to brighten, Köhler received an invitation to become the IMF's Managing Director. By the spring of 2000, after a tenure of one and a half years, he departed for Washington DC and Frank once again stepped in as acting President. However, this time it was not long before the EBRD's fourth President was ensconced in Exchange Square. Jean Lemierre, previously head of the Trésor and a G7 Deputy, was destined to match the tenures of his predecessors as President put together.

Corporate scorecard

During his brief period in office, Köhler had maintained the austerity regime long in place at the EBRD, as well as backing a zero-base budgeting (ZBB) exercise designed to raise efficiency and productivity that had been launched before his arrival. A further budget consultation was undertaken in 2000, which resulted in the introduction of a corporate scorecard that would allow the Board, as the representatives of shareholders, to hold the President and his senior staff to account for the Bank's performance.

Designed to address concerns about insufficient accountability, the corporate scorecard had been imported from the private sector, where it was used to enable companies to balance short and medium-term corporate objectives[4]. It was hoped the scorecard would provide a focus for performance, align the organisation along key objectives and improve communication with stakeholders. Other IFIs, notably the IFC, were considering similar ideas at the time.

Based on the priorities identified in 'Moving Transition Forward', the corporate scorecard was built around four areas: transition, operational performance, financial performance and organisational performance. The recently introduced rating system for projects, which measured expected transition impact and portfolio transition impact, provided the basis for the first component, along with related policy, legal and investment climate work. Standard metrics of annual business volume, disbursements and level of impaired assets covered the operational dimension. Overall profit/loss was the measure for financial performance while a range of organisational indicators—client satisfaction, employee motivation, process efficiency or specific organisational process targets—was suggested for the last area.

The corporate scorecard was applied in the 2001 budget-setting exercise and formally introduced for the first time that year. It has remained a feature of the EBRD's budgeting and incentive system ever since, with the staff bonus pool depending on performance against the targets set in the scorecard. Specific targets have changed over time but not the basic structure of the four categories.

2. The Second Capital Resources Review, 2001–2005

Agreeing the operational priorities for the forthcoming period was a prelude to the bigger exercise of the next capital review, to cover the period 2001 to 2005, which was due to be agreed by Governors at the EBRD 2001 Annual Meeting. Apart from a failure to build reserves, owing to the 1998 crisis, the track record of the previous period was respectable. The Bank's portfolio had doubled between 1995 and 2000 to just over €12 billion,[5] while operat-

---

4 'Business schools had moved in this direction, influenced by the seminal publication 'The Balanced Scorecard: Translating Strategy into Action' by Robert S. Kaplan and David P. Norton, Harvard Business School Press, 1996. As a performance management tool it fitted the needs of the Bank well.
5 This was just over €1 billion lower than projected and at the bottom of the 10 per cent range set, mainly due to a slowing in the level of new business volume between 1998 and 2000 and a rise in cancellations and repayments in 1998 and 1999.

ing assets had grown in line with projections. As a proportion of the portfolio they now stood at 62 per cent, compared with just 25 per cent at the end of 1994, bringing the EBRD more in line with its sister IFIs. This was described as the Bank having "reached a mature portfolio stage ... within a period of less than ten years".[6]

A transition impact retrospective exercise showed the EBRD had been more effective in achieving transition goals where the environment was receptive to market-oriented change. A country and sector analysis found that it had been particularly successful, after taking into account the limitations of local operating environments, in Bulgaria and Romania but also in Poland, Croatia, Kazakhstan and Bosnia and Herzegovina. It also showed that, by the end of 2000, the EBRD was associated with almost US$ 12 billion of FDI in the region, close to 10 per cent of cumulative FDI into transition economies between 1991 and 2000. The biggest shares were in southeastern Europe and southern CIS, where the EBRD was associated with nearly 20 per cent and 15 per cent of cumulative FDI, respectively.

Geographically, there had been a proportionate shift away from advanced transition countries. In central Europe and the Baltics, investment continued to grow from a high level, albeit slowly, while the extent of the shift away from advanced countries was moderated by the tailing off of activities in Russia towards the end of the decade. The share of business activity going to early and intermediate transition countries increased markedly. Equity investments in these markets had risen to 23 per cent of the total by 2000 from 15 per cent in 1994. On the cost side, general administration expenses had declined in real terms, including three years of zero nominal budget growth. Aside from equity valuations and provisions, net income from interest, fees and dividends was growing respectably as the portfolio expanded.

This backdrop presented a solid base for the next five years. Business volume had been growing on average at 4–5 per cent a year. The resources review anticipated a modest ramp-up in the pace of activity to 5–6 per cent a year, leading to annual business volume of €3.4 billion by 2005, up from €2.7 billion in 2000. Within the total, however, there were some sharp contrasts. Little increase in annual volume in advanced countries was expected, while in early and intermediate countries it was forecast to rise by a

---

6   'Report of the Board of Directors to the Board of Governors on the Capital Resources Review', 22 February 2001.

one-quarter and almost double in Russia, albeit from a low base.[7] The shift in composition implied the Bank's portfolio was heading east. By 2005, it was anticipated that two-thirds of the portfolio would consist of projects in early and intermediate countries plus Russia, in contrast to one-half 10 years earlier.

The rapid rise in the overall portfolio, which crossed the pre-capital increase statutory capital limit of €10 billion in 1998, justified the earlier increase of the Bank's capital. Projections to 2005 also showed a healthy rise in capital utilisation, but not one that breached the 90 per cent prudential trigger limit. Headroom of 17 per cent at the end of the period, even allowing for higher risk scenarios, implied the Bank could continue to grow its business without recourse to shareholders for a further capital call.

The return to profitability was factored in, with a small build-up of reserves of around €1 billion forecast by 2005.[8] This was well below the 10 per cent level of authorised capital stock (now €20 billion) that under Article 36 of the AEB opened up the possibility of a distribution of net income. The Governors agreed to the plan at their meeting in London in May 2001.

3. South and East: Membership Issues in the Western Balkans and Mongolia

Western Balkans

Under Lemierre's leadership, the EBRD sought to move towards the less advanced countries in the eastern part of its region, from Ukraine and Belarus to Georgia, Armenia and Azerbaijan in the Caucasus and Central Asia. One region where it had been especially difficult to develop operations so far was in the south: the Western Balkans.

Following the break-up of the Socialist Federal Republic of Yugoslavia in 1991, the region descended into crisis and war. The largest remnant of the SFRY, the Federal Republic of Yugoslavia (later Serbia and Montenegro), was not recognised by the UN or the IMF, and as such could not become a member of the EBRD. While the Bank was able to work with other

---

7   Even measured against the previous peak years of 1996 and 1997, the projected increase was around 50 per cent.
8   The introduction of IAS39, an updated accounting treatment, meant unrealised equity gains from listed equity investments were incorporated in the figures from 2001 onwards.

successor states, especially Croatia and Slovenia, and helped with the reconstruction of Bosnia and Herzegovina after 1996, the situation on the ground precluded most types of normal business involving central Western Balkan countries until the later part of the 1990s.

Kosovo

The crisis in Kosovo in 1999 further complicated matters, particularly for the three countries of operations most affected by the crisis: Albania, FYR Macedonia[9] and Bosnia and Herzegovina, where a small portfolio of around €300 million had been built up. The EBRD stepped up its engagement with efforts to support the region by the European Commission, EIB, World Bank and IFC. The EBRD contributed extensively to the political discussions taking place in relation to the Western Balkans, including the Stability Pact for South Eastern Europe.

The crisis prompted the EBRD to put forward a Balkan Region Action Plan, as well as one for Kosovo, where the Bank had been one of the first international organisations on the ground after the war ended in June 1999 (a mission was conducted in July). It was also a platform from which to seek donor funds for future investment. The highly risky nature of projects in the region (and limits on exposure) implied an extensive need for grants and concessionary funds to expand activity. A Special Fund, the Balkan Region Action Fund, was advanced as a route towards this goal.

The difficult situation called for unusual measures. Kosovo was still part of the Federal Republic of Yugoslavia (FRY) and thus was not a member of the EBRD at the time. The Bank's lawyers[10] concluded that the Board, through its interpretative powers under Article 57, could in exceptional circumstances authorise the use of cooperation agreements or funds in non-member countries, as long as this was broadly compatible with the Bank's core purposes and functions under Articles 1 and 2. Kosovo's circumstances clearly matched the transition purposes of the Bank, while the political mandate aspects were covered by UN Council Resolution 1244 and the presence of the UN Interim Administration Mission in Kosovo (UNMIK), which held broad powers over the territory.

---

9 From 2019, FYR Macedonia became North Macedonia.
10 The EBRD's General Counsel at the time was Emmanuel Maurice.

The EBRD thus initially had to adopt indirect measures in Kosovo instead of committing its own resources or Special Funds. It managed this by mobilising bilateral funding and extending cross-border projects from nearby countries, namely the Micro-Enterprise Bank of Bosnia and Herzegovina and the Albanian Reconstruction Equity Fund. When FRY succeeded in becoming a member of the EBRD in January 2001,[11] the Bank was able to expand its activities and commit its own resources in Kosovo. A Resident Office was officially opened in Pristina in March 2001.

Federal Republic of Yugoslavia

FRY's membership also prompted a series of activities under another Action Plan, this one being the 'Federal Republic of Yugoslavia—2001 Action Plan'. These included three "quick start" operations: the establishment of a micro enterprise bank to offer trade finance guarantees and lines of credit to private banks; a Yugoslav SME Facility; and a Working Capital Framework Facility for export-oriented companies undertaking corporate governance reforms. A Resident Office was also opened in Belgrade in 2001.

FRY changed its name to Serbia and Montenegro in February 2003. Montenegro subsequently declared independence in June 2006 (following a referendum in May 2006) and became a member in its own right, after a Resolution was passed by the Governors. (The Republic of Serbia became the legal continuation of the State Union of Serbia and Montenegro and remained a recipient member of the EBRD.)

Mongolia

Mongolia became interested in joining the EBRD towards the end of the 1990s but did not broach the subject formally until September 1999, when the Prime Minister wrote to the Chair of the Board of Governors to sound out members' views on a potential application. In anticipation of this

---

11   FRY applied for membership on 15 November 2000 and a draft Directors' report and Resolution to Governors was submitted to the Board on 16 November 2000 with votes by Governors to be received by 13 December. FRY received 9,350 shares (4,675 shares of the original capital stock plus 4,675 from the general capital increase) or 36.52 per cent of the former Socialist Federal Republic of Yugoslavia's shareholding. 'Federal Republic of Yugoslavia—EBRD Membership', 16 November 2000.

request, the Bank had in July considered both the question of membership and Mongolia's status as a possible recipient country.

Membership was relatively straightforward since Mongolia was a member of the IMF and qualified as a non-European country under Article 3, paragraph 1(i). As a wholly new member, there was potentially a question over shares. However, as a small and poor country, Mongolia was expected to be allocated 200 shares, less than 0.01 per cent of the total capital stock, which carried no implications of any consequence for other members and did not affect the EC's overall majority.

Mongolia formally applied to become a member of the EBRD on 30 March 2000, with a request that procedures be completed in time for the Bank's Annual Meeting in Riga. Since the voting period for Governors was 30 days and lead times for circulation of documents to the Board of Directors were typically long, this was a demanding schedule. Nonetheless, there was goodwill to make the effort, and Governors approved the admission of Mongolia as a member on 3 May 2000. Unfortunately, Mongolia was unable to complete domestic legal procedures in time to meet the conditions precedent to membership ahead of the Annual Meeting. A short extension was granted and Mongolia satisfied the conditions to become a member on 9 October 2000.

The issue of recipient status was more complicated. As Mongolia was neither a central and eastern European country nor had it previously been part of a recipient country of the EBRD, it was not eligible as a country of operations under the existing AEB. The expression "Central and Eastern European countries", cited in Articles 1 and 2, was deemed to cover solely the territory of the existing or former socialist republics in central and eastern Europe, including the entire Soviet Union.[12] This was an important ruling since the amendment of Article 1 to include Mongolia in the Bank's region of operations required the unanimous agreement of all members, not simply a qualified majority.

Although Mongolia had not been part of the Soviet Union, it had been a socialist state. It had introduced a multiparty system and a new constitution in 1992 and moved towards a market economy. As a land-locked coun-

---

12   Summary Explanation, attached to the draft Resolution in 'Letter to Governors—Report of the Board of Directors and draft Resolution on the acceptance of Mongolia as a country of operations of the Bank', 19 December 2003.

try in Central Asia bordering Russia, and heavily dependent on it, Mongolia was in many ways a natural fit for the Bank. Directors decided in 2001 that Mongolia was in the sphere of influence of the former Soviet Union and faced similar difficulties to other countries of operations in transition. It was agreed that technical assistance could be provided through a Mongolia Co-operation Fund.

Two years later, on 22 July 2003, the Prime Minister of Mongolia wrote to Lemierre asking for help:

> We believe that the 'EBRD country of operations' status has an important role for overcoming difficulties encountered by our people in their bid for democracy, development of market economy and promotion of private sector.

Although some Directors were concerned with the precedent that a change to the AEB might set and wanted the language to be as narrow as possible, and others worried about the legal procedures, there was no substantive disagreement on admitting Mongolia as a recipient country. By December, the method and language of the change in the AEB had been settled. A simple change was proposed to Article 1, where the geographic reach of the EBRD was described in the paragraph on the Bank's remit. Two sentences were added:

> The purpose of the Bank may also be carried out in Mongolia subject to the same conditions. Accordingly, any reference in this Agreement and its annexes to 'Central and Eastern European countries', 'countries from Central and Eastern Europe', 'recipient country (or countries)' or 'recipient member country (or countries)' shall refer to Mongolia as well.[13]

Mongolia was recommended as a country of operations to the Board of Governors, along with the proposed Resolution language. To proceed to the next stage without a Governors' meeting, votes from at least two-thirds of Governors representing not less than two-thirds of total voting power were required, with a deadline set for 30 January 2004. The subsequent procedure, however, required that all members accept the proposed agreement

---

13 'Letter to Governors', 2003, p. 2.

and take legal steps to deposit an instrument of acceptance executed by a competent person or body with the Bank. This process, involving government and in some cases parliamentary approval, was time-consuming. It took until October 2006 before Mongolia was finally granted recipient status and the EBRD was able to begin ordinary operations there.

4. A Troublesome Trio: Belarus, Turkmenistan and Uzbekistan

The early 2000s saw an acceleration of Bank activity in early and intermediate transition countries. This group comprised the range of countries in Central Asia, eastern Europe, the Caucasus and south-eastern Europe. Overall business volume for this group increased from an average of around €1 billion a year in the late 1990s to €1.5 billion by 2003.

There were multiple reasons for the rise of activity in more challenging markets. Strategically, the EBRD was intensifying its efforts in these regions and was beginning to see some results from its persistence in advocating liberalisation and structural reforms. Rising political stability, supported by the peace process in south-eastern Europe and preparatory efforts in relation to EU accession in Romania and Bulgaria, was a contributing factor, as were improvements in the macroeconomic backdrop. Several ETCs were experiencing double-digit growth rates, while others experienced high and steady growth outside the range of their previous experience. Even Ukraine, after a decade of falling output in which the economy more than halved, finally turned the corner in 2000 with its first year of positive GDP growth in the post-Soviet era.

Against this backdrop, successive Annual Meetings were uplifting affairs. The EBRD was able to point to record business volumes and genuine inroads into areas that shareholders had been pressing the Bank to pursue. "Eastern Europe outperforms global economy in 2001" declared an EBRD press release at the Annual Meeting in Bucharest in 2002.[14] In 2003, another press release noted that the EBRD region "continues to outperform the global economy" and "net capital inflows reached [another high] reflecting

---

14 'Eastern Europe outperforms global economy in 2001', Ben Atkins, EBRD Press Release No. 44, 14 May 2002.

stability and reform in many of the transition countries".[15] The Business Forum for the 2003 Meeting was titled "Coming of Age: opportunities of an evolving region" and introduced a series of panel sessions with the sentence:

> In the thirteen years since their markets opened and democracy was born, the countries of the EBRD region are entering their next phase of development, still growing, but striking out in new directions.[16]

The new decade offered reasons for optimism that the process of "catch up" with western standards and GDP levels might now be spreading outward from advanced transition countries. Nevertheless, not all was rosy across the EBRD's region. Troublesome issues persisted on the political front in a number of countries, notably Belarus, Turkmenistan and Uzbekistan. Questions arose over their compliance with Article 1, particularly in the eyes of human rights organisations and other NGOs and CSOs that monitored political and democratic freedoms in the Bank's countries of operations. These questions went to the heart of the EBRD's political mandate.

Belarus

In the case of Belarus, concerns had been raised through the course of the 1990s over its compliance with Article 1. The Board was required to review operations and compliance with the purposes of the Bank annually (under Article 11, paragraph 2(i)) for each recipient country. A full strategy for Belarus was approved in 1995, but due to increasing concerns over the reform process it was replaced with an interim strategy in 1996. The EBRD argued that the lack of progress limited its ability to find suitable projects and constrained the size of its programme.

The new approach outlined two scenarios, a Base Case and a High Case, with both limited to 12 months before review. The High Case, which would allow the Bank to be more active, was conditional on the Belarusian government adopting more market-oriented policies. At the same time, de Larosière wrote to the Belarusian Prime Minister, Mikhail Chigir, to ex-

---

15 'EBRD region continues to outperform global economy', Jazz Singh, EBRD Press Release No. 48, 22 April 2003.
16 Press briefing pack, Annual Meeting 2003.

plain Directors' concerns about the economic and political situation in Belarus, the very slow pace of reforms, and the frequency with which decrees and proposals inconsistent with market economics were brought forward. He rejected the Prime Minister's request that the EBRD adopt the High Case, but left open the possibility of doing so if the environment became more conducive to investment.

A controversial national referendum on amendments to the Belarusian Constitution in November 1996 led to a substantial redistribution of formal political powers to the Belarusian President, Aleksandr Lukashenko. In parallel, there was a serious deterioration in the protection of basic political freedoms through restrictions on public assembly and trade union activity and control of the media. The reaction of the international community was strongly negative. De Larosière wrote to Lukashenko in January 1997 to register the Bank's concerns. The strategy was then tightened to accommodate three cases: Base, Intermediate and High. The Base Case was restricted solely to those operations which directly promoted the private sector. The High Case was dependent on satisfactory implementation of IMF and World Bank policy conditions and real progress in resolving the political concerns.

Renewed strategies in 1999 and 2001 continued to express serious concerns, which were also set out in a further letter from Lemierre to Lukashenko in 2001. Following the Belarusian presidential elections on 9 September 2001, which were agreed to have been seriously flawed, management held a workshop with the Board to review the situation. Some Directors argued on the basis of the International Limited Election Observation Mission (ILEOM) assessment[17] that the EBRD should remain engaged with Belarus to lend tangible support to grassroots democratisation and that isolation of the country would be counterproductive. Others felt that the Bank's credibility was at stake and the only option was to have recourse to the Governors under Article 8.3. At a further workshop in January 2002, there was agreement that it was essential to follow up Lemierre's letter and that Governors should be informed of the Bank's concerns and approach.

---

17 The ILEOM concluded: "The 2001 presidential election process failed to meet the OSCE commitments for democratic elections…; welcomes and acknowledges the emergence of a pluralist civil society…; [and notes] the isolation of the country is not in the best interest of the Belarus people and is not conducive to strengthening democratic development." Statement of Preliminary Findings and Conclusions, 2001 Presidential Elections in the Republic of Belarus, ILEOM, 10 September 2001, Minsk, p.3.

After receiving advice from the General Counsel on Article 8, it was accepted that the "scenario" approach should continue and a revised strategy was prepared. This proposed a Baseline scenario focused on lines of credit to SMEs, trade finance, and limited direct investments in local and foreign-owned private companies. It included a set of political and economic benchmarks agreed by the international community to determine whether the EBRD would provide any further support on a project-by-project basis. A Regular scenario, under which "normal operations" would resume if sufficient progress was made in demonstrating commitment to democratic principles, replaced the High Case. The President duly wrote to the Governors explaining the rationale for the Bank's scenario approach and seeking their endorsement.

Turkmenistan

Turkmenistan was another difficult case which became more prominent in the early 2000s. De Larosière had written to President Saparmurat Niyazov in 1997 to draw attention to the Board's concerns with the patchy progress of economic and political reforms. In 1999, a strategy was sent to the Board late in the year for discussion in January. It focused on lending to SMEs and microbusinesses, mobilisation of private and foreign investment (including in the oil and gas sector), and the only outstanding public-sector project (the rehabilitation of the general cargo, dry bulk and ferry terminals at Turkmenbashi port on the Caspian Sea). The only other public project, a road operation, had been cancelled due to the failure of the government to raise fuel duties, which were among the lowest in the world.

Almost before the ink was dry, Niyazov used his firm grip on power to announce on 28 December that he would extend his term of office indefinitely. In response, the Board in April adopted a scenario-based country strategy for Turkmenistan, comprising Base, Intermediate and High Cases. The Base Case focused exclusively on private-sector development. A follow-up mission was also arranged to take stock of the situation on the ground and convey the underlying message of the strategy to the government.

An EBRD delegation, led by Frank as FVP and including three Board Directors, visited Ashgabat on 11 to 13 April 2000. Niyazov, however, cancelled the scheduled meeting, prompting Frank to comment: "The President's refusal even to discuss the question of political reform suggests that the Government of Turkmenistan is not committed to one of the basic principles upon which the EBRD was founded."[18] The Directors concluded that the limited strategy was well-judged and appropriate but that the Bank's leverage in Turkmenistan was limited.

The situation was no better a year later when the strategy once more came under review. If anything, it had deteriorated. The Bank had been obliged to stop disbursements of its SME credit line because of the government's increased restrictions on access to foreign exchange. The EBRD decided to focus on managing its existing projects and urged the Turkmen authorities to improve human rights conditions and pluralism and strengthen democratic institutions. It also encouraged improvement of the efficiency of the foreign exchange reserve fund, the removal of unfair restrictions on sub-borrowers of the Bank's SME line on access to foreign exchange, and increased transparency and availability of statistical data.[19] Lemierre wrote once again to Niyazov on 16 July 2001, drawing his attention to Directors' "grave concerns about the state of democracy and the lagging pace of political and economic transition in Turkmenistan".[20] The letter was copied to Governors, decided by the Board with reference to Article 8.3, and was published on the EBRD website under the Public Information Policy.

One year later, there was still no evidence of improvement, and the political and economic benchmarks that had been set had all been failed, save for a small improvement in the availability of economic information. The strategy adopted a graduated response with, as in the case of Belarus, the Baseline, Intermediate and Regular scenarios.[21] The Base Case was seen as the best possible outcome, and Lemierre again wrote to Governors explaining the situation and the Bank's approach.

Uzbekistan

Uzbekistan, like its Central Asian neighbour, suffered from a slow pace of reform. A poor, double-landlocked country, it faced challenges from Islamic extremists in the south and drug-trafficking from Afghanistan in the

---

18 'EBRD registers concern over political and economic developments in Turkmenistan', EBRD Press Release, 19 April 2000.
19 'Strategy for Turkmenistan, Update', 23 July 2001.
20 'Letter to Governors - President's letter to President Niymazov of Turkmenistan', 1 August 2001.
21 'Strategy for Turkmenistan', 12 July 2002.

east, and was beset by weak institutions. Nonetheless, some progress on transition had been made during the 1990s. By the start of 2002, Uzbekistan was the second-biggest recipient of the Bank's investment in Central Asia after Kazakhstan, with country investments amounting to just over €500 million.

A two-year strategy was produced in March 2003, shortly ahead of the EBRD's Annual Meeting in Tashkent. As with Belarus and Turkmenistan, it listed a series of political and economic benchmarks, and was subject to a progress review at 12 months. It did not, however, include a "scenario approach" or rule out projects with the public sector, although it stated that the scope for new investments was limited. The need for intensive policy dialogue with the Uzbek authorities over the future course of political and economic reform was emphasised. The Bank hoped that the Annual Meeting would be a forum for open debate and that, by facilitating a public debate, Uzbek authorities would achieve a better understanding of the costs of their policies for their own people and for Central Asia as a whole.[22]

The strategy drew attention in particular to human rights concerns as reported by various organisations, such as "documented cases of torture in prisons and places of detention, religious persecution of independent Muslims, cases of persecution of human rights defenders … and violations of the freedom of the media". It also referenced reports of the continuation of the Soviet-era practice of compulsory mobilisation of students and schoolchildren to help with the cotton harvest.[23]

Appropriate as it was to document and present the situation as accurately as possible, it appeared to be a confrontational opening gambit to an Annual Meeting where many hundreds of officials, civil society activists and business people from the region and beyond would be gathered. Lemierre and several Governors had, however, been under pressure to justify the decision to hold the meeting in Uzbekistan. As *The Economist* reported, in the run-up to the meeting:

> The EBRD's choice of venue has been heavily criticised [on the basis that] Uzbekistan's government is one of the most repressive in the region, with over 6,500 religious and political prisoners and no opposition or press free-

---

22 'Strategy for Uzbekistan', 14 March 2003.
23 'Strategy for Uzbekistan', 2003, pp. 44–45.

dom to speak of. So the EBRD has been at pains to state that holding the meeting in Tashkent was not an endorsement of the government's policies ... The bank also hoped that holding the meeting in Uzbekistan would result in more openness.[24]

At the Meeting, Uzbek President Islam Karimov took the floor first, as host, to address the assembled company, surrounded by the presidents of neighbouring Central Asian countries: Nursultan Nazarbayev of Kazakhstan, Askar Akayev of the Kyrgyz Republic, Emomali Rahmon of Tajikistan, as well as Edward Schevernazde, President of Georgia. EBRD Governors from many other countries were present. The opening session was broadcast live on local television, a novelty negotiated by the Bank as part of a campaign for greater openness and transparency, and in keeping with its recently upgraded Public Information Policy.

Karimov's speech eulogised reforms undertaken by Uzbekistan and its "renewal of society", the importance of the EBRD and its investments to the country's development, the problems facing the region, especially those caused by war in Afghanistan and terrorism, and the geopolitical significance of resources in Central Asia and the Caucasus. While he spoke of the role of NGOs and CSOs in "countering bureaucratic abuse of power and corruption", he made no mention of human rights.

The Chair of Governors, the UK Development Minister Clare Short, used her opening speech to deliver a strong and critical message on Uzbekistan's record:

> There are particular concerns regarding Uzbekistan about lack of respect for religious freedom, the prevalence of torture and the failure of the judicial system to protect the rights of the citizen ... We are deeply concerned by [the Special Rapporteur's] conclusion that torture is systematic ... Mr President, I urge you to take this report very seriously...[25]

Lemierre, who spoke next, followed suit:

---

24 'Freedom for a day: a breath of fresh air in a repressive land', *The Economist*, 8 May 2003.
25 Opening Statement by Ms Clare Short, Chair of the Board of Governors, Tashkent, 4 May 2003, Proceedings of the Twelfth Annual Meeting of the Board of Governors, p. 21. The UN Special Rapporteur on torture, Theo van Boven, reported to the High Commissioner for Human Rights in February 2003.

We have listened to your statement and to your words, President Karimov, with expectation ... They were strong words, but some of us may have expected words on human rights and on economic progress.[26]

It did not go down well. According to one report at the time:

This amounted to a public scolding of President Karimov's broken promise, and it did not go unnoticed. As Lemierre and Short delivered their critical speeches, President Karimov removed his headphones and demonstratively covered his ears.[27]

At the conclusion of the meeting, Lemierre and Short again supported the EBRD's decision to hold the event in Tashkent and argued that an open, critical dialogue had been useful. Many Governors too were pleased that the Bank and its strategy had challenged Uzbekistan to make more efforts to secure its transition path. Karimov, however, was outraged at what he saw as his humiliation in front of his counterparts from Central Asia and beyond. EBRD business with Uzbekistan subsequently shuddered to a halt. It was not until 2017, almost a decade and a half later, that relations with the EBRD were re-established following Karimov's death the previous year.

5. The Early Transition Countries Initiative

The 2003 Tashkent Annual Meeting had been a bruising experience for the EBRD and especially for Lemierre. The overall message of openness, dialogue, investment and change that had lain behind the event was, however, entirely in keeping with the Bank's philosophy. Its investment approach followed an open and transparent process focused on how to make projects work better for the EBRD and its clients. Likewise, the Board and management discussions were, in the main, about finding a consensus that worked for all. What applied internally was consistently applied externally.

---

26 Opening Statement by Mr Jean Lemierre, President of the EBRD, Tashkent, 4 May 2003, Proceedings of the Twelfth Annual Meeting of the Board of Governors, p. 23.
27 'EBRD Meeting in Tashkent Turns into Scrutiny of Host Government's Abysmal Rights Record', Human Rights Watch, 4-5 May 2003, https://www.hrw.org/legacy/campaigns/uzbekistan.

Ultimately, the EBRD was a very pragmatic investment institution able to look for long-term, sustainable solutions. It had run into trouble in Uzbekistan. But by adopting this approach the Bank had successfully helped most countries move up the transition path. Those that opened up and sought to learn from best practices, reformed their economic, political and governance structures to create a more attractive investment climate, and attracted capital from foreign investors had made the most progress.[28]

After more than a decade of transition, the countries of central Europe were making especially fast progress in converging with their western neighbours. The gap between the region and the less advanced transition countries, however, was growing. One broad grouping—Armenia, Azerbaijan, Georgia, the Kyrgyz Republic, Moldova, Tajikistan and Uzbekistan—were among those having the most trouble in making progress. It was felt that these ETCs needed extra help and attention. They were also the poorest countries of the EBRD region at the time, with a large part of their populations living below the poverty line.

Annual EBRD investments to ETCs began to decline in the early 2000s, from some €200 million excluding oil and gas-related projects in 2000 to around €100 million by 2002, reflecting the difficulty of investment in these countries. They suffered from political and economic instability, slow progress in transition, small domestic markets, underdeveloped local infrastructure, limited access to global export markets, poor governance, weak financial intermediation and low levels of foreign investment. In addition, they had not attracted the same attention from donors as the Western Balkans, where the Stability Pact for South Eastern Europe was helping to garner support.

Concerns with social progress were a preoccupation of some Board members. Surveys had shown increasing unhappiness with the results of transition. Long years of declining output and lost jobs, even when the position was being reversed, had created disappointments and left scars. While some individuals in CIS countries had amassed grotesque fortunes, much of the rest of the population had been left behind. Some Directors were therefore raising the question of whether the Bank should do more to alleviate poverty in ETCs. The

---

28 See for example, 'Progress and patterns in transition', Chapter 2 in 'Ten years of transition', *Transition Report* 1999, EBRD; and 'Progress in transition and the link to growth', Chapter 1 in 'Infrastructure', *Transition Report* 2004, EBRD.

proposed shift to the east brought the issue into a sharper focus as the EBRD began to tread the more conventional development ground of MDBs.

The more challenging climate of countries further east meant an intensive dialogue was needed to improve the conditions for investment, along with considerable capacity-building and work on legal underpinnings by the legal transition team. Some ETCs were heavily indebted and required concessional finance under IMF rules. Donors recognised that additional support would be required for the Bank to tackle these countries' problems effectively and support poverty alleviation. At the same time, the development of low-income countries and poverty reduction were much more readily accessible goals for development departments and their ministers than the concept of transition. This made it easier to drum up donor resources for these countries.

Towards the end of 2003, Michael McCulloch, an experienced senior official at the Department for International Development (DfID) and former UK Director at the EBRD, was invited to conduct an independent review to see what might be done to strengthen the Bank's engagement with ETCs. His conclusion was that the Bank's model should be adapted and supplemented to deal with their particular circumstances. A Bank-wide framework was recommended to provide an umbrella under which various activities—and implicitly increased donor funding and support from other IFIs—could be coordinated.[29] This would draw more attention to their plight and offer a focal point for efforts to improve their situation.

McCulloch's report led to the idea of an initiative specifically for ETCs. The suggestion, and its timing, also provided a valuable counterpoint to the imminent accession to the EU of eight of the EBRD's countries of operations. Building a viable business in poorer countries, even if it took time and extra donor funds, at a time when business in advanced countries was easing off, made sense to some shareholders. With central European countries close to completing the transition phase, there would thus still be a future for the Bank, albeit a different and potentially a more mainstream development one. Some Directors believed that intensified efforts in these countries would not only be justified in themselves but would also help to persuade their governments that the EBRD could be restructured and remain relevant.

In April 2004, at the Annual Meeting in London, the EBRD launched the Early Transition Countries Initiative (ETCI). Its premise was that the

---

29 'A Revised Approach and Action Plan for Early Transition Countries', 17 March 2004.

Bank would take on higher risks and devote more resources and staff in the field to the seven countries[30]—in a context where transition returns for successful projects would be substantial—in exchange for increased availability and predictability of (additional) donor support. To ensure the full support of the Banking Department, the initiative was coordinated via a dedicated ETCI team with an Advisory Board chaired by the FVP, then Noreen Doyle, and a target for the number of ETC deals was set in bankers' annual performance scorecards. A new multi-donor fund was proposed to support the initiative.

The aim of the ETCI was to treble the number of operations (excluding those in the oil and gas sectors) signed annually in the ETCs within three years and to increase the volume of business by at least 50 per cent in that time. As well as microlending programmes and other funding to commercial banks and microfinance institutions, the initiative comprised three facilities: the Direct Investment Facility (DIF), which provided equity-type investments; the Direct Lending Facility, which provided direct loans of up to €4 million to enterprises unable to access finance through the local banking sector; and the Medium-sized Co-Finance Facility (MCFF), which provided co-finance to help local banks fund enterprises requiring larger loans.

After a number of discussions with donors and other IFIs, the ETC Multi-Donor Fund was set up and held its first Assembly meeting on 22 November 2004.[31]

The success of the initiative exceeded expectations. The number of annual projects signed in ETCs quadrupled by the end of 2006 and annual business volume increased to almost €300 million. A review and Board discussion in 2007 concluded that the ETCI (now including Mongolia) was making an impact and helping to alleviate poverty in the ETCs and that it should be continued for a further three years with equally ambitious targets and an added focus on the Asian ETCs. It was also renamed the Emerging Transition Countries Initiative to take account of sensitivities over the use of the term "early". In due course the initiative morphed into a bigger and broader Small Business Initiative (SBI)[32], although the Bank maintained a target for ETC projects in bankers' objectives and the corporate scorecard throughout.

---

30   Thirty professionals were assigned to the initiative in addition to the 24 already working in the area.
31   More about the Early Transition Countries Fund here: https://www.ebrd.com/who-we-are/our-donors/multi-donor-funds.html.
32   The SBI was created in 2013.

6. EU Accession, FDI and Convergence

The prospect of a number of countries of operations joining the EU had been on the EBRD's radar for some time. The Copenhagen European Council of 1993 had agreed that "countries of Central and Eastern Europe that so desire shall become members of the European Union … as soon as an associated country is able to … satisf[y] the economic and political conditions required".

These conditions, known as the Copenhagen political and economic criteria, closely matched the preamble and Article 1 of the EBRD's AEB. The Council conclusions stated:

> Membership requires that the candidate country has achieved stability of institutions guaranteeing democracy, the rule of law, human rights and respect for and protection of minorities, the existence of a functioning market economy as well as the capacity to cope with competitive pressure and market forces within the Union.[33]

For some, this implied that becoming a member state of the EU was tantamount to saying there was no longer any fundamental distinction between West and East among these countries and that the transition towards open market-oriented economies had effectively been accomplished.

The eight central European and Baltic countries plus Bulgaria and Romania applied to become member states of the EU between 1994 (Hungary and Poland) and 1996 (the Czech Republic and Slovenia). Joining required alignment with the EU's *acquis communautaire*. This was an enormous challenge requiring the transposition of some 20,000 legal acts and 80,000 pages of the Official Journal of the European Communities into national legislation. It was clear that the process would be lengthy and far more difficult for some countries than for others.

It was widely assumed that accession would be sequenced as countries with varying degrees of transition progress took differing amounts of time to meet the demanding standards of the *acquis*. European Council members, however, wanted to avoid discriminating between applicants and in

---

33 Copenhagen European Council Conclusions, Section 7, 'Relations with the Countries of Central and Eastern Europe', Part A , 'The Associated Countries', 21–22 June 1993.

their conclusions at Luxembourg in December 1997 included all 10 central and eastern European countries (plus Cyprus and Malta) in the fifth enlargement process.

Membership negotiations for some countries opened in March 1998, following an assessment by the European Commission which concluded that five of the more advanced transition countries—the Czech Republic, Estonia, Hungary, Poland and Slovenia[34]—might be ready to meet the Copenhagen criteria by 2002 or 2003.

Accession negotiations with five transition countries (and Cyprus) began in earnest in Helsinki in December 1999. The European Council also decided to open negotiations with the other five EBRD countries—Bulgaria, Latvia, Lithuania, Romania and Slovakia—and Malta. It also recognised the countries of former Yugoslavia as potential candidates, along with Turkey, although without dates for negotiations or accession.

As an MDB with majority EU ownership and a European character, the EBRD was fully aligned with the process, and its projects and policy work in these countries lent support to those seeking to join the EU. The Bank worked closely with the European Commission, whose substantial financial contribution to technical assistance proved an invaluable complement to the EBRD's investments, and with the EIB in co-financing projects. More financial assistance (for environment and transport) became available from 2000 from the EU's ISPA.

By the start of the new millennium there was strong political momentum within the EU to consolidate the progress being achieved in the integration of central and eastern Europe with its western counterparts. The Nice European Council of December 2000 decided to speed up the negotiation process with the aim of completing it within the following two years. Shortly afterwards, the European Parliament called for the prospective Member States to be allowed to participate in the June 2004 European Parliamentary elections.

In 2001, the Commission proposed that negotiations might be completed by the end of the following year for those that were ready to enable them to participate in the 2004 elections as new Member States. At the Göteborg Council in the summer of 2001, the Commission declared that eight central European and Baltic countries could be ready on time—as well as Cyprus

---

34 Cyprus, at that stage not a recipient of EBRD funds, was also included, making six in all.

and Malta—but that Bulgaria and Romania needed to make further progress. Negotiations were completed for the 10 countries at the Copenhagen Council in December 2002, leading to the Treaty of Accession, which was signed at the foot of the Acropolis in Athens on 16 April 2003 and expected to enter into force one year later.

Quickening progress in the negotiations alerted market investors to the opportunities ahead and the potential returns from investing in countries that would sooner or later join the EU. A wave of FDI and portfolio flows swept into central Europe, principally focused on the most advanced countries. The amounts were significant and the flows, and mood of the times, contributed to growth and rising real incomes. Net private capital flows to accession countries[35] accelerated from an average of around 2 per cent of GDP between 1991 and 1997 to around 6 per cent of GDP between 1998 and 2003, peaking at 7 per cent in 2002. Meanwhile, net FDI doubled to some 4 per cent of GDP, peaking at around 6 per cent in 2000.[36] The increase in FDI was especially marked in the Czech Republic, Poland and to a lesser extent the Slovak Republic.[37]

The process was supported by conditions the EBRD had been promoting throughout the period: privatisations that presented merger and acquisition opportunities; the further opening up of these economies, allowing them to benefit from the globalisation trend that was now in full swing; and an improving regulatory[38] and business-friendly investment climate. In particular, the restructuring of the banking sector was accompanied by a significant involvement of western banks. By 2004, foreign groups owned more than two-thirds of the banking system of accession countries.[39]

7. Expectations Surpassed

The improving economic conditions in the first part of the decade were not confined to central Europe but were spread widely across the EBRD region.

---

35 Including Malta and Cyprus, as well as the 10 EBRD countries of operations.
36 'Financial FDI to the EU Accession Countries', DG-I/MAW/04 78, pp. 6–7, European Central Bank, 19 March 2004.
37 A significant wave of FDI to Hungary occurred earlier, in the first half of the 1990s.
38 See *Transition Report* 2001 for a qualitative assessment of the banking regulatory framework of the eight EBRD first wave EU accession countries.
39 'Financial FDI to the EU Accession Countries', 2004, p. 2.

The millennium began with each of the 26 countries of operations experiencing positive growth, the first time this had happened in the post-communist era. Despite a slowing in global growth in 2001, EBRD countries continued to grow robustly (with the exception of Poland, where growth dipped that year), helped by improving commodity prices and a rapid rise in world trade and FDI as globalisation accelerated. The so-called "convergence play"—investing in accession countries and their financial instruments in the expectation that interest rates would fall towards EU levels and exchange rates appreciate—accelerated the flow of funds towards central Europe, boosting growth and incomes.

Table 12.1 Average Annual GDP Growth EBRD Regions, 2000-2005

Average GDP growth, % pa	2000–2005
Central Europe and the Baltics	4.0
South-eastern Europe	4.8
Eastern Europe and the Caucasus	7.6
Central Asia	9.0
Russia	6.8

Source: EBRD

To begin with, the Bank benefitted from the positive macroeconomic conditions. Annual business volume comfortably exceeded the indicative figures outlined in the second Capital Resources Review (CRR2), with advanced countries initially accounting for the majority of this outperformance but early and intermediate countries catching up by 2005. In 2001, annual business volume exceeded the target by more than €600 million and annual volumes remained well above the planned CRR2 levels in the following years before coming into line towards the end of the period (2005). The benign conditions also helped the Bank to expand investment elsewhere, with annual volumes in Russia, early and intermediate transition countries all better than expected. Early and intermediate countries did especially well, exceeding the target by more than €1 billion in 2005.

The plan had been for the EBRD's annual investments to rise from €2.5 billion in 2001 to just under €3.5 billion by 2005. In the event, they had risen to more than €4.5 billion, a running rate more than 25 per cent above the agreement with Governors. Faster repayments and prepayments towards the end of the period, along with exchange-rate movements, helped keep the portfolio broadly in line with projections. As the next capital resources review approached, however, part of the Board's concern was not that the portfolio was growing nor that the share of advanced countries in the total was excessive—it had in fact fallen sharply to less than 20 per cent by 2005—but that the approach of the Bank's management jarred with the backdrop of EU accession and the notion that the EBRD should step back from some of the most advanced transition countries.

8. Rumblings of Mission Accomplished

The enlargement of the EU on 1 May 2004, including the accession of eight former socialist countries, was celebrated with gala concerts in Berlin, Warsaw and Malta, as well as a gathering of heads of state and government of the now 25 EU member states in Dublin on "enlargement day". The vast majority of the 75 million new EU citizens came from the former communist countries.

In its short existence, the EBRD had made a significant contribution to the achievement of bringing the East and West of Europe together again 65 years after the start of the Second World War. Eight central European and Baltic countries of operations were now EU member states and two more, Bulgaria and Romania, were not far behind in the process (accession took place on 1 January 2007). Success, however, raised the question of the Bank's future role in the region.

The 2004 Annual Meeting in London, which took place a fortnight ahead of "enlargement day", presented an opportunity for Governors to reflect on the situation. British Prime Minister Tony Blair opened the event by pointing towards a future role for the EBRD in the south and east of its region:

> The Bank, as you know, was not set up to exist for ever. It is there to help countries make the transition, to a point where their own domestic institutions and investors and international business provide the basis for their economic growth. The transition is not yet finished in the countries which are about to join the EU. The EBRD will still help them complete this process. But as they gain a new framework of support as EU members, and as

the interest of international investors grows, the EBRD's role should naturally change and fall away over the years to come. Nevertheless, there is still a major role for the Bank in countries further east and south.[40]

The US representative, Samuel Bodman, also addressed the future role of the EBRD. He began with the accession countries:

> These countries deserve our congratulations for their achievements. For the EBRD as well—with its mandate to promote this very type of transition—this is an opportunity to declare victory.
>
> In this context, it is appropriate that the shareholders take a fresh look at the future of this Bank. It has always been our view that transitions are, by definition, fleeting ... Maintaining the status quo may be the easiest path forward, but it is not necessarily the most effective one. In that context, the forthcoming Capital Resources Review in 2006 represents a very good, and much-needed, opportunity for Governors to reassess the Bank's graduation policy. Moving forward, the EBRD should build on its successes in the accession countries by focusing on its poorest countries of operations.[41]

A counter view was presented by the Chair of the Board of Governors, the Prime Minister of Luxembourg Jean-Claude Juncker:

> I do not believe that the transition process is over for the accession countries ... On the contrary, the 'last mile' to a fully functional market economy is usually the hardest, and it takes a specialist institution like the EBRD to accompany our new Member States on that final stretch of the road ... One reason why the future work of the EBRD in the EU accession countries will surely be additional is the greater risk element inherent in some of its future transactions there. This, combined with the push to do more in the least advanced transition countries to the south and the east, will result in an increasingly risky project portfolio that the Bank has to manage.[42]

---

40 'Address by Mr Tony Blair, Prime Minister of the United Kingdom', Annual Meeting, London, 19 April 2004, Proceedings of the Thirteenth Annual Meeting of the Board of Governors, p. 12.
41 'Statement by Mr Samuel Bodman, Head of Delegation for the United States of America', EBRD Annual Meeting, London, 19 April 2004, p. 86.
42 'Opening Statement by Mr Jean-Claude Juncker, Chair of the Board of Governors', EBRD Annual Meeting, London, 19 April 2004, p.13.

The scene was set for a tough dialogue over the future of the Bank as preparations were made for the next capital resources review covering the period 2006 to 2010.

9. The Third Capital Resources Review and Graduation

The pressures facing Lemierre during 2005 as he contemplated the next phase of the EBRD's evolution were immense. To some outsiders—and many insiders, especially bankers—it appeared paradoxical to question the Bank's future direction at this juncture. In conventional terms the EBRD was performing exceptionally well. Its portfolio, operating assets and annual investments were notching up records year after year, transition progress was being made in all EBRD regions, and profits—for so long a weak spot—were on track for another high that year and contributing to growing reserves, which had reached more than €1.75 billion by the end of 2004.

Yet, a number of key shareholders were advocating a significant change in direction. This represented the special nature of the institution as a public-sector body set up to build and support a private sector in countries where it had been absent. By the mid-2000s, markets were in place more or less everywhere in the EBRD region. The issue was how well they worked and whether and where further intervention by a multilateral financial institution such as the Bank was still necessary.

One group—principally the Anglo-Saxon community (the USA, the UK, Canada, Australia and New Zealand), Japan, Switzerland and to some extent the Netherlands—felt the time had come for the EBRD to move on from its core central European geography. By contrast most EU members, including France and the new accession states in central and eastern Europe, believed that much more remained to be done in these countries. The debate became focused around the need for and timing of "graduation" of the advanced countries within this group.

The graduation issue was complicated by the fact that the enlargement process had to an extent accelerated the entry of countries to the EU relative to the originally envisaged conditions. In the cases of Bulgaria and Romania, which became member states later, continuing efforts to align systems with the *acquis* after entry into the EU was explicitly allowed for. Thus, while eight—subsequently 10—of the EBRD's countries of operations had become part of one of the most advanced market-oriented systems in the world, their transition could not be said to be entirely over.

Another point of tension Lemierre faced in deciding business priorities was over Russia. Annual volumes of investment in Russia had grown rapidly between 2001 and 2005. By the end of the period, Russia's share of the portfolio and of annual business volume had recovered to around 25 per cent of the total. Nonetheless, the Russian government believed the figure to be unacceptably low for the EBRD's largest country of operations. At the same time, the rapid increase in business in Russia had raised concerns elsewhere, particularly in the USA where disputes between Russia and Ukraine over gas supplies and pricing were souring perceptions of President Vladimir Putin in Washington. There was also an increasing focus on integrity issues and questions over the pursuit of large deals and high-volume activity in general.

In 2005 and early 2006, much of the Board's time was taken up with trying to find common ground on the issues underpinning the third Capital Resources Review. It took eight discussions at the FOPC of the Board of Directors, other Committee discussions and a Board retreat in 2005, and four more FOPC meetings in 2006 before there was sufficient consensus among Directors to present their conclusions to Governors for the resource decision at the 2006 Annual Meeting.

In the run-up to the middle of the decade, annual EBRD investment volume had accelerated from around €2.5 billion to more than €4 billion. Management, and Banking in particular, were ready to accommodate a similar increase for the rest of the decade towards an investment rate of €6 billion a year. Acceleration of business in advanced transition countries in the run-up to accession was expected to drop, however, now that these countries were EU members. The preference among several important shareholders was to hold annual volume steady at just under €4 billion while adjusting the balance within it. This would prudently make room for more resource and risk-intensive activities and would further transition while being consistent with continuing administrative restraint and efficiency improvements. The portfolio was expected to rise steadily to reach €22 billion by 2010.

Within the total, the share of advanced countries was expected to diminish sharply, to 13 per cent in portfolio terms and 6 per cent by annual volume (falling below 10 per cent in 2008) by 2010. The countries concerned were not happy with this decline or with the proposed closure of some Resident Offices and the consolidation of the management of local offices in the Baltics through a regional hub based in Warsaw. Nonetheless, they accepted the proposals. A significant expansion of regionally based professional staff in south-eastern Europe, the Caucasus, Russia and Central Asia matched the rebalancing effort.

Russia, on the other hand, argued strongly for a better deal than was originally on offer. By December 2005, when the first full draft of the Review was circulated to Directors, annual volume in Russia was projected to rise from €1.2 billion in 2006 to €1.3 billion by 2010, or 36 per cent of the total.[43] By the time the final document went to Governors, the projection for 2010 had risen to €1.6 billion (41 per cent of the total).

The most contentious issue, however, concerned the idea of graduation of some advanced countries of operations. Agreement was finally reached that the eight new EU member states would graduate by 2010, after which the Bank would stop doing new business in those countries.[44]

At the 2006 Annual Meeting in London, a number of Governors commented on graduation. Hilary Benn, Secretary of State at DfID, led the way on behalf of the UK government: "The EBRD anticipates reduced business in these eight [EU] countries over the next five years and it is right that this is so. We expect these countries to graduate from EBRD help."

Gerrit Zalm, the Dutch Deputy Prime Minister and Chair of the Board of Governors echoed these sentiments:

> Where do these successes leave us? With a job well done, and with the task of refocusing the institution. We are moving away from those countries where the job is largely, though perhaps not yet wholly, finished.

Clay Lowery from the US Treasury put forward the strongly held US view:

> With the new CRR strategy, the Bank's management has the necessary policy guidance and tools to complete the task assigned to it 15 years ago. ... It can lead the way in showing that countries can be successful and grad-

---

43 'Capital Resources Review 3', 14 December 2005, p. 93, p. 112.
44 'Report of the Board of Directors to the Board of Governors on the Capital Resources Review 3', 11 May 2006.

uate. ... And it can lead the way in showing that development institutions can be transitional and can be successful, and ultimately can put themselves out of business.

Lemierre commented:

Graduation is a marvellous mark of success. For the eight countries concerned, it is the success of transition, reflecting historic achievements in their economic and political transformation. And for the Bank, it marks the success of the model—the proof that transition works and the EBRD does what it says it will do: withdraw when we are no longer needed.

10. A Graduate Emerges: the Case of the Czech Republic

The 2006 Annual Meeting also saw the Czech Republic take the first clear step by a country of operations towards graduation. Zdenek Tuma, Governor of the Czech central bank and alternate EBRD Governor for the Czech Republic, confirmed that his government had given approval for discussions to begin with the Bank's management on the graduation of his country from EBRD operations. He suggested a target date of October 2007, when the next country strategy for the Czech Republic was due.

Taking pole position on the graduation starting grid among countries of operations was a politically astute move and came at a time when investor interest in central European countries was close to a peak. It sent a strong signal that the Czech Republic had made it across the transition divide and helped give the impression that it was the strongest of the pack. This was not without foundation. GDP per capita was, along with Slovenia, ahead of the other EU-8 by some margin and the Czech Republic was similarly advanced on many social indicators such as life expectancy, infant mortality and PISA[45] scores. There was no doubt about the progress the Czech Republic had made since the beginning of the transition process and that it was as advanced in democratic and economic terms as many other EU members. The proposal that it should graduate was welcomed by the Czech Republic's fellow Governors.

---

45 The OECD's Programme for International Student Assessment (PISA).

Estonia, Hungary and Slovenia also stated in 2006 that they expected to graduate before the end of the decade. None, however, followed the Czech Republic's example in setting an explicit date for graduation. Despite a repeat of the sentiment by Hungary in relation to its new country strategy in 2008, no further step was in fact taken by these countries, or any other, to activate the formal process of graduation.[46]

Following a decision by the Czech Council of Ministers, the country's Minister of Finance, Miroslav Kalousek, wrote to Lemierre on 19 March 2007 "to convey the desire that EBRD operations in the Czech Republic be considered to have 'graduated'". Once a country had formally expressed its desire to graduate, approval was needed by the Board based on a review of a recipient country's progress on decentralisation, demonopolisation and privatisation.

The review, which was conducted over the summer of 2007, was relatively straightforward and consistent with the 1996 Policy on Graduation. It concluded that the Czech Republic had made significant progress in transition and was one of the most open and competitive economies in the region, as well as in the EU as a whole. A detailed analysis of sector transition challenges based on the Bank's indicator system showed few remaining gaps. Just five out of 39 sector and institutional areas showed a "medium" gap (in transport infrastructure and some aspects of energy efficiency). The rest were assessed as "small" or "negligible". The review found that the structure of the Czech economy was "approaching that of an advanced market economy" with most sectors having reached standards found in mature market economies.

The paper recommending graduation of the Czech Republic was presented to Directors on 23 October. It proposed that, effective 31 December 2007, the EBRD's operations in the Czech Republic be considered to have graduated and that the Bank should no longer consider or approve new operations in the country after that date. The Board strongly supported the proposal and congratulated the Czech government and people on their transition achievements.

---

46 The subsequent period of the EBRD's history is covered in Volume 2.

11. Rapid Growth Attracts Foreign Investors

The EBRD's countries of operations had been growing fast for more than five years by the time the Governors signed off in 2006 on the new strategy period to 2010. The carefully calibrated compromises and restrictions agreed, however, were soon to be confronted by unforeseen trends and events.

At the start of the period, macroeconomic conditions across the EBRD's region went into overdrive, even when compared with the recent past. Growth in every sub-region accelerated in 2006 and 2007, reaching double-digit rates in eastern Europe and the Caucasus (see Table 12.2). Per capita figures were even higher.

Table 12.2 Average Annual GDP Growth EBRD regions, 2000-2007

GDP growth, average % pa	CEB	SEE	EEC	Russia	CA
2000-2005	4.0	4.8	7.6	6.8	9.0
2006-2007	6.3	6.1	11.7	8.3	9.4

SOURCE: EBRD

In areas where financial systems remained weak, and where foreign and some domestic investors were less willing to venture without the added comfort of the EBRD's clout and status, the Bank was able to do good business. Annual investment volume outside advanced transition countries jumped by €1.25 billion, an increase of more than one-third, between 2004-5 and 2006-7. The biggest contribution was made by Russia, with a rise of more than €0.75 billion, or 70 per cent, while for eastern Europe and the Caucasus the figure increased by more than 50 per cent.

In line with the strategy, there was a marked contrast in central Europe and the Baltics, where average business volumes dropped by some €370 million or almost 30 per cent. With stock markets booming across the world, vast flows of funds were making their way into the nascent central European financial markets, driving down interest rates and providing substantial liquidity to local banks and the many subsidiaries of foreign banks, allowing them to finance smaller enterprises and seek better returns from riskier ventures.

In these countries, the additionality of the EBRD was rapidly being eroded as the private sector began to thrive and commercial banks in the region extended their reach and increased lending dramatically. The Bank's special status as a hand to hold when venturing into uncharted waters was becoming less valuable in many of the more advanced transition countries. Bankers eager to find deals in countries such as the Czech Republic, Hungary and Poland were effectively being priced out of the market. In the Baltics, business ground to a halt, with less than €500,000 invested in Estonia and Latvia in total in 2006 and 2007. The share of advanced transition EU countries in annual business volume fell far more steeply than planned in CRR3, hitting a low of under 4 per cent by the end of 2007. The pace of decline reflected new market realities, as much as a strategic decision on the part of the Bank's management.

12. 'Supernormal' Profits and the Call for a Dividend Distribution

Full financial results for 2005 arrived just ahead of the EBRD 2006 Annual Meeting. At €1.5 billion, net profit was more than €1 billion higher than in 2003 and 2004. The return on members' equity for the CRR2 period increased to 7.1 per cent. The impressive result reflected the Bank's rapidly expanding portfolio—which now stood at close to €17 billion—as well as healthy margins and a very low level of impairments. The rise in stock market valuations had also boosted the equity portfolio and allowed some sales of earlier investments at a significant profit.

Many shareholders were pleased that the EBRD was easily outperforming its targets and making enough profit at last to build up its reserves. Reserves and retained earnings increased in 2005 by €3 billion. However, as was pointed out at the time by many Board members and the President, the EBRD was not a commercial bank but a transition bank. It needed earnings to be able to cover future risk-taking activities without recourse to shareholders for more capital. Given that the new strategy called for greater risk-taking in the form of investments in less advanced transition countries, the "super-normal" returns provided a welcome base.

Article 36, paragraph 1, which dealt with the allocation of net income, provided for the possibility of a dividend distribution, as well as allocation to surplus or other purposes. However, it also stated: "no distribution [other than to surplus or other purposes] shall be made until the general reserve amounts to at least ten (10) per cent of the authorized capital stock." This threshold was €2 billion. The Bank had not until this point been in a position to invoke this clause of the AEB. By the end of 2005, however, unrestricted general reserves had reached €1.7 billion and CRR3 projections indicated the threshold would likely be exceeded the following year. This raised the question of whether a dividend should be paid to shareholders.

The debate over a possible dividend payment, which began in 2006, was long and divisive. The problem was accentuated towards the end of the year as it became clear that profits for 2006 were going to be strong. By the spring of 2007, the EBRD was again reporting the highest profits in its history—a staggering €2.4 billion for 2006, a 60 per cent increase on the previous year. Unrestricted reserves were by now well above the distribution threshold at €3.4 billion and were fast moving towards what had been seen as a suitable CRR3 end point of €4.2 billion by 2010. Another good year could result in this objective being met and leaving room for other options, provided the Bank did not expand its portfolio or take on additional risks that might threaten the limits of capital utilisation agreed under the CRR3.

The Vice President for Finance, Manfred Scheppers, and the Director, Corporate Strategy, Josué Tanaka, had anticipated this situation and presented a paper on reserves and the allocation of income to the FOPC in January 2007.[47] Based on preliminary figures, they showed that unrestricted general reserves for 2006 would be €1.4 billion above the threshold. They also anticipated a further increase to €1.8 billion by the end of 2007. A big contribution to the positive picture came from equity gains, following some spectacularly profitable exits in 2006[48]. Impairments also reached a record low.

Scheppers and Tanaka noted that the positive results had been driven by the EU accession process as global institutional investors began to include new member states in their target portfolios and local pension funds stepped up investment in their domestic markets. They argued that realisation of such large equity gains could not be repeated, especially as the stock of holdings in central Europe was falling and being replaced by holdings of less liquid and more volatile assets in Russia and south-eastern Europe. The

---

47 'Capital Adequacy, Reserves and Allocation of Net Income', 17 January 2007.
48 Banca Comercială Română accounted for half the increase. In general, the EBRD benefitted from positive valuations and profitable sales of investments it had made early on in the transition process and on which it had worked with clients to improve during the subsequent period. It was in many respects a one-off event.

risk environment that had reduced impairments also seemed unusually benign. Some Directors agreed that the situation and profits of the Bank in 2006 had been exceptional and were unlikely to be sustained.

The paper also reviewed the Bank's capital adequacy and financial viability under a simulated shock event three and a half times greater than the 1998 crisis (assessed as 0.01 per cent probability), timed for the end of 2008. The analysis under a Risk Capital Model for CRR3 showed this could result in losses of €4.6 billion, for which the Bank had sufficient capital (paid in and reserves) to meet capital adequacy and financial viability requirements. Scheppers and Tanaka suggested, however, that a proper economic capital assessment—a framework the Bank did not have at the time but was working on—implied this might be optimistic, even taking into account additional profit above the assumed CRR3 projected level for 2006. A cyclical return to a weaker credit environment, increased concentration in riskier countries (the Russian portfolio had grown faster than expected, for example), and a host of other factors were cited as reasons why the Bank should continue to take a prudent perspective and allocate the additional income to reserves "to buffer the impact of a potential future shock, to protect the paid-in capital provided by its shareholders, to maintain its AAA status and to address effectively the potential impact of the range of uncertainties".[49]

Their recommendation was for a full allocation to reserves. They added, however: "taking account of the exceptional magnitude of realised profits in 2005 and 2006, the Bank could consider … whether funds equivalent to the notional interest to be generated from the reserves could be allocated [under 'other purposes'] … to an EBRD technical cooperation programme." The idea was for a fund of €50 million be set up with Board oversight to support directly some specific technical cooperation activities, such as TAM-BAS[50] and legal transition or nuclear decommissioning work, to catalyse additional donor funds and support activities where donor funds were lacking.[51] Internalising the funding of technical cooperation would be a first for the EBRD, although it had been introduced by the IFC a couple of years earlier.

---

49 'Capital Adequacy', p. 15.
50 Turnaround Management and Business Advisory Services. https://www.ebrd.com/downloads/research/factsheets/tambas.pdf.
51 See 'Capital Adequacy,' pp. 19–20.

The presentation of the paper to the FOPC on 25 January led to a lively but inconclusive discussion, with some Directors supporting management's arguments and others calling for more justification of the size of the proposed allocation to reserves. It started a discussion that occupied the Board and management for much of the next year, as every aspect of allocating income beyond reserves came under scrutiny in an effort to reach a consensus.

Four FOPC meetings, three management papers on the topic and two executive Board sessions between January and April ahead of the EBRD 2007 Annual Meeting led to a holding position to allocate the 2006 surplus income to reserves. It was also agreed to consider fully all the options and parameters for the allocation of 2007 net income in time for the 2008 Governors' Resolution on the issue. Not all Directors were happy with the outcome. Some argued strongly for a full discussion of a dividend option and this was reflected in Statements by their Governors and Heads of Delegation at the Annual Meeting.

The Governors passed Resolution 108 at the 2007 Annual Meeting in Kazan, which allocated net income to surplus after provisions and possible future net losses. The Heads of Delegation for the USA and Australia/New Zealand voted against the proposal and made their dissatisfaction with the decision clear in their Governors' statements.

The Polish Governor, Slawomir Skrzypek, also voted against the Resolution but for wholly different reasons. His statement argued for "the remainder of the net income for 2006 [to be allocated] to activities in early transition countries".

In his closing remarks to the Meeting, Lemierre summed up the debate:

> The main view favours the mission-based allocation of income ... capital and technical assistance ... based on prudence, taking risks, but also capacity to increase the delivery of the mission. Some are in favour of a dividend and some are not ... we must work through the debate.

Ten papers were prepared for subsequent FOPC discussions, covering topics including operational updates, capital adequacy, use of investment grants, support for Banking and nuclear safety (under the "other purposes" category of Article 36), and an external review of distribution practices. Board papers on wider, related questions of the interpretation of the gearing ratio and a new strategic operations framework were also issued and discussed before a conclusion was reached.

Among the more influential papers was a report by Deloitte which looked at other MDB, DFI and commercial practices on dividend payments. This made clear that development institutions reinvested earnings to provide support for their mandates, whereas entities nearer the commercial end of the spectrum were more likely to consider a distribution. The hybrid nature of the EBRD left the question open. But it was clear that for public-sector institutions, repayment to shareholders—as opposed to allocations to mandate-related funds, such as for technical assistance—was rarely done (and only on an exceptional, one-off basis).

In context, a distribution to shareholders would not be a return *on* capital but a return *of* capital. Many Directors agreed that this would be seen as a negative signal of a withdrawal of shareholder support for the institution and countries of operations. Another consideration was the mismatch between shareholder ownership and the perceived contribution of shareholders representing significant donors or countries of operations where the profits were being generated.

A Board retreat was called for 4-5 December to try to resolve the outstanding issues ahead of the 2008 Annual Meeting in Kyiv. By then, more concrete proposals for an allocation of funds to support transition purposes through technical assistance, and the governance process, had been worked out to the satisfaction of many Directors, including those concerned that such funds might result in donor displacement. An additional proposal to help fill a gap in the Chernobyl nuclear containment funds had also been made. This was especially attractive to the G8 and the EU, which had been the main source of funds and were being pressed for commitments. However, perhaps the most critical factor as the debate moved into the new year was market volatility and growing awareness that financial conditions were weakening globally. The case for prudence began to look unassailable.

The final discussion of the Board of Directors' Report to Governors took place on 15 April 2008. Profits for 2007 were once again very strong at €1.9 billion. After adjustments, that left an allocation of €1.1 billion to net income. The proposed Resolution 112 for Governors presented a threefold allocation of this net income: €115 million for a Shareholder Special Fund (SSF); €135 million for nuclear safety activities (Chernobyl); and the remaining €830 million to a new Strategic Reserve.

The SSF supported banking activities, with 40 per cent allocated to ETCs. No more than 32 per cent was permitted for incentive payments and investment grants, which were limited to countries eligible for Official Development Assistance (ODA[52]) only (other than co-financing of NDEP projects), in order to broaden the scope and deepen the intensity of the Bank's transition impact. The Chernobyl contribution was split between the ISF-2 (Nuclear Safety Account) and the NSC (Chernobyl Shelter Fund), which had funding shortfalls of €77 million and €58 million respectively, and made a significant contribution to the €300 million required from G8/EU donors.

The Strategic Reserve, created under the Strategic Operations Framework, was to be counted as part of economic capital but would not provide additional headroom for operations unless specifically authorised to be allocated to unrestricted general reserves at a later date. By itself, it thus had no impact on capital utilisation and operational headroom for the Bank, satisfying those who wanted to limit the immediate scope for new activities.

The Report concluded:

> A number of important factors [have been] taken into account in the distribution decision, including the capital position of the Bank in relation to its medium term strategy and related capital requirements, the signalling effect of a distribution across a broad range of stakeholders and the general environment in the financial markets.

It acknowledged that reserves and capital adequacy at the end of 2007—when unrestricted general reserves had reached €4.5 billion—could have permitted a limited distribution but focused on the "special need" to support Ukraine in funding the completion of the new shelter for the Chernobyl nuclear power plant and the implementation of the nuclear spent fuel facility and "without prejudice to a possible determination by the Governors of a distribution to members" in future.

For the great majority of Governors Resolution 112 was a reasonable outcome and it was passed. Three Governors voted against. Belarus and Russia felt that the large allocation to the Strategic Reserve was unnecessarily restrictive, while Australia was in favour of a dividend. Australia also notified the meeting that they intended to withdraw from the Bank from 2010 "in

---

52   As defined by the OECD.

the context of a job well done". Lemierre responded by expressing his sadness that the Bank, as a multilateral institution, would be "losing [Australia's] commitment to the region and [its] expertise at a time when challenges are very great."[53]

As shareholders and staff packed suitcases to leave and reflected on the 2008 Annual Meeting, feelings were mixed: the Bank's mission had been a success, but was it so successful that it had put itself out of business? At least the May sunshine in Kyiv matched Ukraine's economic boom—GDP per capita had reached new heights, now almost double that of 10 years earlier. This was, all the same, still less than 30 per cent of the level of the EBRD's most successful (and only) graduate, the Czech Republic. More graduates might reduce the scale of the Bank's operations ahead but for sure there would be work to do in less advanced transition countries. But as delegates and staff headed home, financial clouds were gathering, adding to the uncertainties ahead.

Conclusion

It was now almost two decades since the fall of the Berlin Wall and more than 17 years since the start of EBRD operations. The Bank had matured along with many countries of operations. But now, the EBRD was itself in transition.

It faced a new direction: a valid but uncertain one. The issues of graduation and dividends had prompted a whirlwind of activity and raised questions about the future of the Bank.

Fifteen years earlier, it had taken a new French President to clean up the debris after the media storm and to put the Bank on an even keel. On this occasion, an experienced French President, at the end of his eight-year tenure, was destined to survive the shareholder storm caused by the EBRD's own success in central Europe and preserve the Bank for the future.

But the Bank was about to face further headwinds in the form of global forces beyond its control. It was to be a major test for the institution. It would be a new German President's turn to take the EBRD on the next stage of its journey.

---

53   Note that Australia did not leave the Bank.

Appendix

1. **Prospective Membership as at 29 May 1990 (signature of the Agreement Establishing the European Bank for Reconstruction and Development in Paris)**

   42 prospective members (including eight recipient countries)

   Members
   1. Australia
   2. Austria
   3. Belgium
   4. Canada
   5. Cyprus
   6. Denmark
   7. Egypt
   8. Finland
   9. France
   10. Federal Republic of Germany
   11. Greece
   12. Iceland
   13. Ireland
   14. Israel
   15. Italy
   16. Japan
   17. Korea, Republic of
   18. Liechtenstein
   19. Luxembourg

20. Malta
21. Mexico
22. Morocco
23. Netherlands
24. New Zealand
25. Norway
26. Portugal
27. Spain
28. Sweden
29. Switzerland
30. Turkey
31. United Kingdom
32. USA
33. EEC
34. EIB

Members and recipient countries

35. Bulgaria (Recipient)
36. Czech and Slovak Federal Republic (Recipient)
37. German Democratic Republic (Recipient)
38. Hungary (Recipient)
39. Poland (Recipient)
40. Romania (Recipient)
41. USSR (Recipient)
42. Yugoslavia (Recipient)

II. **Membership as at 15 April 1991 (Inaugural Annual Meeting)**

40 members (including seven recipient countries)

Members

1. Australia (30 March 1991)
2. Austria (28 March 1991)
3. Belgium (10 April 1991)
4. Canada (28 March 1991)
5. Cyprus (28 March 1991)

Appendix

6. Denmark (28 March 1991)
7. Egypt (28 March 1991- recipient country since 2015)
8. Finland (28 March 1991)
9. France (28 March 1991)
10. Germany (GDR and FRG merged after unification) (28 March 1991)
11. Greece (29 March 1991)
12. Iceland (29 May 1991)
13. Ireland (28 March 1991)
14. Israel (28 March 1991)
15. Italy (28 March 1991)
16. Japan (2 April 1991)
17. Republic of Korea (28 March 1991)
18. Liechtenstein (28 March 1991)
19. Luxembourg (28 March 1991)
20. Malta (28 March 1991)
21. Mexico (28 March 1991)
22. Morocco (28 March 1991 – recipient country since 2013)
23. Netherlands (28 March 1991)
24. Norway (28 March 1991)
25. Portugal (5 April 1991)
26. Spain (28 March 1991)
27. Sweden (28 March 1991)
28. Switzerland (28 March 1991)
29. Turkey (28 March 1991 – recipient country since 2008)
30. United Kingdom (28 March 1991)
31. USA (28 March 1991)
32. EEC (28 March 1991)
33. EIB (28 March 1991)

Members and recipient countries

34. Bulgaria (28 March 1991)
35. Czech and Slovak Federal Republic (on or before 28 March 1991)
36. Hungary (28 March 1991)
37. Poland (28 March 1991)
38. Romania (28 March 1991)
39. USSR (on or before 28 March 1991)
40. Yugoslavia (on or before 28 March 1991)

III. Members joining between 16 April 1991 and 31 December 1992

Members

1. New Zealand (19 August 1991)

Members and recipient countries

2. Albania (18 December 1991)
3. Estonia (28 February 1992)
4. Latvia (18 March 1992)
5. Lithuania (5 March 1992)
6. Armenia (7 December 1992)
7. Azerbaijan (25 September 1992)
8. Belarus (10 June 1992)
9. Georgia (4 September 1992)
10. Kazakhstan (27 July 1992)
11. Kyrgyz Republic (5 June 1992)
12. Moldova (5 May 1992)
13. Russian Federation (replacing USSR as of 9 April 1992)
14. Slovenia (23 December 1992 – following the fact that Yugoslavia ceased to be a member on 9 October 1992)
15. Tajikistan (16 October 1992)
16. Turkmenistan (1 June 1992)
17. Ukraine (13 August 1992)
18. Uzbekistan (30 April 1992)

Number of members at the end of 1992: 57.

IV. Members joining between 1 January 1993 and 31 December 1995

1. Croatia (15 April 1993, following the fact that Yugoslavia ceased to be a member on 9 October 1992)
2. Former Yugoslav Republic of Macedonia (referred to as North Macedonia since 14 February 2019)
3. Czech Republic (1 January 1993) and Slovak Republic (1 January 1993) replacing Czechoslovakia/CSFR

At the end of 1993, and until the end of 1995 the total number of members stood at 59 and the number of countries of operations had risen to 25.

v. Members joining after 1 January 1996

1. Bosnia Herzegovina (17 June 1996) (60th member)
2. Mongolia (9 October 2000) (61st member)
3. Federal Republic of Yugoslavia (19 January 2001 and referred to as Serbia and Montenegro between 2003 and 2006) (62nd member)
4. Montenegro (3 June 2006) (63rd member)
5. Tunisia (29 December 2011) (64th member)
6. Jordan (29 December 2011) (65th member)
7. Kosovo (17 December 2012) (66th member)
8. China (15 January 2016) (67th member)
9. Lebanon (15 July 2017) (68th member)
10. India (11 July 2018) (69th member)
11. San Marino (7 June 2019) (70th member)
12. Libya (16 July 2019) (71st member)

Index

A

ABN Amro 140
accountability of EBRD 44–5
activities of EBRD 35–6
additionality principle 43, 66, 125–7, 345
administration expenses 45, 121, 316
Advisory Councils 90–1
affordability (of municipal development) 203–4
Afghanistan 326, 328
Agence Française de Développement (AfD) 217
Agency for Restructuring Credit Organisations (ARCO) 306
Aghion, Philippe 51
Agnelli, Gianni 70
Agreement Establishing the Bank (AEB) (1990)
    agreement 45, 69
    and capital review 122, 123
    for Central and Eastern European countries 320–1, 323, 333
    and dissolution of Soviet Union 102
    and distribution of net income 317, 345–6
    and graduation 125, 128
    limited equity commitment 124
    political mandate 89
    preparation for 29–30, 33
    private-to-public financing ratio 116
    signing of 6, 37–40, 47, 49
Akayev, Askar 328
Albania
    commitments to 103
    historical context 8
    interest in membership 33, 69
    and Kosovo crisis 318
    membership 100–1
    municipal development 200
    Resident Office 118
    transition indicators 271
Albanian Reconstruction Equity Fund 319
Allianz 179
Alma-Ata Protocols 99
Alpha Capital 160
Alternates (Directors') 67, 71
Amato, Giuliano 107
Ameritech 172
Andreotti, Giulio 57
Anglo-Suisse 85
Annual Meetings
    (1992) 104–5, 156–7
    (1993) 106
    (1994) 115
    (1995) 122–3
    (1996) 124, 125
    (2000) 320
    (2001) 315
    (2002) 322
    (2003) 327–9
    (2004) 331, 337
    (2006) 340, 342–3, 345
    (2007) 348
    (2008) 349, 351
Annual Reports 76, 313
AOOT Bolshevik 161
appointments to EBRD 47–8, 56–7, 60–1, 67, 71
Armenia 92, 99, 102, 205, 251, 271, 330

Arrow, Kenneth 51, 70
Asian Development Bank (ADB) 21, 44, 45, 66, 217
Assembly of Contributors 242, 252
Attali, Jacques
   appointments 47–8, 51, 57, 67
   concerns about 58–9, 62, 106–7
   and creation of the EBRD 26–8, 29, 46
   and environmental issues 223
   and G7 Summit (Paris) 15–17
   and inauguration of EBRD 70
   and location of EBRD 37, 61, 106–7
   and nuclear safety 105, 251–2
   and preparations for EBRD 47–9, 55
   as President of EBRD 38, 58–9, 62, 71
   resignation 107
   and the Soviet Union 34, 48–9, 92, 94, 96–7, 99–100
   vision for EBRD 31, 39, 46, 108
   vision for Europe 6, 18–23, 43–4, 92
   and Yugoslavia 103
Audit Committee 106, 107
Audit Report (1993) 107
Australia 39, 41, 339, 348, 350–1
Austria 10, 23, 40
Austrian School 268
AV Rt 165, 172
Avtobank 298, 301
AzBTC 246
Azerbaijan 99, 102, 200, 205, 245–6, 271, 330

B

Baker, James 16, 33, 50
Baku-Tbilisi-Ceyhan (BTC) pipeline 245–7
Balcerowicz, Leszek 30, 107, 151, 163
Balcerowicz Plan 10, 152
Balkan Region Action Fund/Plan 318
Baltic Sea 222, 236–40
Baltic States 92, 97, 101, 147, 198, 205, 210
Banca Comercială Română (BCR) 177–8, 197
Banca Commerciale Italiana (BCI) 180
Banca Intesa 180
Banco Santander 83
Bancorex 177
Bank Austria 300
"Bank for Europe" 6, 19–24, 25, 62
Bank Handlowy 179
Bank of America 140
Bank of Poznań (WBK) 82–3

Bank Pekao 178–9
Bank Zachodni 83
bankers
   appointments 60, 67, 75, 80–1
   disagreements with economists 284–9
   reorganisation 110–13
Banking Department
   consolidated 111, 118
   dual system 75, 81, 106–7
   Early Transition Countries Initiative (ETCI) 331–2
   and Resident Offices 120
   and Russian crisis 301
   and transition impact 274, 280–3, 285
banking sector
   privatisations 156, 177–81
   in Russia 136
   and Russian crisis 304, 306, 308
'Bank's Policy Approach to Privatisation Advice, The' 154
Barents Sea 262–3
Baring Vostok 149
Barr Pharmaceuticals 167
Bartholdy, Kasper 269
Baudon, Thierry 60, 81
Bechtel 215
Belarus
   Belovezha Accords 99
   challenges of 323–5
   district heating 210
   local self-government 187
   recipient country 102
   and Russian crisis 302
   and the Strategic Reserve 350
   transition indicators 271
   water services and wastewater treatment 205
Belgium 38, 40
Belovezha Accords 99
Benn, Hilary 341
Berlin Wall 11, 24, 29, 351
Berlinwasser International 215
Berther Pochy 106
"Big Bang" financial deregulation 7
Blair, Tony 337
Board Consultation Visits (BCVs) 90, 92
Board of Directors
   balance of power 58–9
   first meeting 61, 68, 71–2, 75
   formally elected 71

resident 36
and risk 87
role 47, 53–4, 86
and transition impact 289, 290
Board of Governors
appointments 44
first roundtable discussion 156–7
on transition 338, 341
voting power 32
Bodman, Samuel 338
Bohunice International Decommissioning Support Fund (BIDSF) 262
Bolshevik Biscuit Factory 160–2
"Bolshevik conservatives" 93
Bosnia and Herzegovina 104, 316, 318
Boudier, Marc 22
BP 245–6
Brady, Nicholas 70
branches *see* Resident Offices
Brazil 69
Bretton Woods institutions 32
Brezhnev doctrine 5, 9
Bruno, Michael 113
Bruntland Report (1987) 222
BTC Co. 246
Budapest Stock Exchange (BSE) 165
budget for the EBRD 71, 121, 314–15
Bufi, Ylli 100
build-operate-transfer (BOT) model 82
Buiter, Willem 286–7
Bulgaria
accession to EU 333, 334, 335, 337, 339
and Albania 101
beneficiary country 6
changes 11
commitments to 103
country of operation 75
country strategy 90
municipal development 200
nuclear safety 251, 254, 261–2
privatisations 148, 168–9
ratification of Treaty 47
rationing 79
Resident Office 118
as shareholders 40
substandard loans in banking system 156
transition impact 316
water services and wastewater treatment 204–5

Bundesbank 20, 25, 62
Burgess, Robin 266–7
Bush, George 15, 17–18, 27, 50, 93
Business Advisory Council 91
Business Advisory Panel 56
business challenges 75–9
business model of EBRD 265
business plan of EBRD 62–6, 67
Bydgoszcz Water Revenue Bond Project (2005) 216

C

Camdessus, Michel 70, 98, 206
Canada 31, 39, 41, 339
capital markets 216
capital of EBRD 31, 78, 120–4, 125, 128
Capital Resources Review (CRR)
first 123, 125
second 315–17, 336
third 338, 339–42, 345–7
car ownership 206–7
Carbajo, José 287
Carli, Guido 71
Ceausescu, Nicolae 12
CEE Bankwatch 243
Central Asia 222, 263
Central Bank of Russia (CBR)
expansion of credit 294
and the FIDP 137
and Inkombank 301
and Russian crisis 297, 302, 305–6, 307
and Tokobank 299–301
Central Committee of the Communist Party of the Soviet Union (CPSU) 97
Central Europe Agency Line 84
Central Europe and the Baltics (CEB) 316, 336, 344
Československá Obchodní Banka (CSOB) 179–80
Chairman of the Board 113
Chalker, Lynda 67
challenges for EBRD 74–5
Cheney, Dick 50
Chernobyl disaster 221, 224, 249, 255–60, 264, 349–50
Chernobyl Shelter Fund 259–60
"Chernobyl Unit 4 Shelter Implementation Plan" (SIP) 259
Chernomyrdin, Victor 296

361

Chief Economist *see* Office of the Chief Economist (OCE)
Chigir, Mikhail 323–4
China 10, 14
Chirac, Jacques 261
Christophersen, Henning 107
Chubais, Anatoly 143, 159, 175, 295
CIS-7 205
Civic Forum (CSFR) 11
civil society organisations (CSOs) 242, 245, 323, 328
Clinton, Bill 138
coal-powered energy 221
co-financing
    by IFIs 216–17
    with NIB 240–1
    options 80, 87, 334
    in Poland 82–3
    reliance on 65–6
    and Sakhalin II 242
Cold War 5, 23, 34
collective decision-making 7
"Coming of Age: opportunities of an evolving region" Business Forum 323
commercial finance 216, 217, 218–20
Commonwealth of Independent States (CIS) 79, 99, 123, 173, 205–6, 209, 316, 330
communications challenges 78
communism, collapse of 27, 43
Communist Party (Albania) 100
Communist Party (China) 14
Communist Party (GDR) 10
Communist Party (Soviet Union) 5, 9, 34, 93
Community Investment Programme 246
Conservative Party (UK) 105
context for creation of EBRD 5–12
Convention on Cooperation and Protection and Sustainable Use of the Danube River (1994) 234
"convergence play" 336
corporate scorecard 287–8, 314–15
CORUSS group 98
cost controls 109, 117, 125
Council for Mutual Economic Assistance (Comecon) 50, 76, 99, 141, 167–8
Council of Europe 22, 31, 186
countries of operations 73–4, 75, 117
Country Programmes VIce Presidency 67, 68
Country Programmes Vice Presidency 57

country risk ratings 279
country teams 111, 118
country-led approach 110
"creative destruction" 268
"creative tension" 289
credibility of EBRD 129
credit analysis 278
Credit Department 278–80, 301
credit rating 86–7
Creditors' Committee 300
criticism of EBRD 107
Croatia
    independence declaration 103
    membership 104
    municipal development 202
    privatisations 167–8, 180–1
    transition impact 316
    transition indicators 271
    water services and wastewater treatment 198
currency denomination 34
Cyprus 40, 334
Czech and Slovak Federative Republic (CSFR)
    approval of country strategy 90
    beneficiary country 6
    commitments to 103
    demonstrations 11
    dissolution 179
    first projects 84–5, 103
    large state enterprises 77
    loss of federal status 102
    and market economy 123
    small-asset privatisation 153
    transit through 10
    visit from Attali 49
Czech Council of Ministers 343
Czech Republic
    accession to EU 333, 334
    car ownership 206
    district heating 210
    environmental issues 228
    FDI 335
    graduation 342–3, 351
    local self-government 187
    PPPs 215
    privatisations 173–4, 179–80
    projects 114
    public transport 207

Resident Office 118
transition 126
transition indicators 271, 272
water services and wastewater treatment 205
Czechoslovakia 40, 74, 75, 161
Czechoslovakia Investment Corporation (CIC) 84–5

D

DAB 180
Daimler AG 171
Danone 161
Danube Black Sea Task Force (DABLAS) 234, 236
Danube River Basin 222, 233–6
Danube River Protection Convention 234
De Benedetti Group 83
de Larosière, Jacques
   background 109
   departure 283, 303
   and nuclear safety 255–6, 261
   operational priorities 313
   as President of EBRD 107–9
   reorganisation 110–13
   successful approach 115, 265
   successful strategy 128–9
   tough budgetary approach 110, 121–2
de Selliers, Guy 60, 67
de Their, Bret 61
decentralisation *see also* municipal development 185–6, 187–91, 198, 218–20
"Declaration on East-West relations" 16
DEG 305
Deloitte 349
Delors, Jacques 16–17, 20, 24
Delors Commission 19
Denmark 40
depository banks 116–17
design, build and operate (DBO) arrangements 213
d'Estaing, Valéry Giscard 21
Deutsche Telecom 172
Development Banking department 67, 75, 81
Development Finance Institutions (DFIs) 112, 217, 241, 276, 349
devolution 187–91
Dexia 213, 217
digital telecommunications 85

district-heating enterprises (DHEs) 82–3, 210–11, 215, 220
dividend distribution 345–9
dollars 34
Doyle, Noreen 278–80, 302, 332
Dresdner Bank 300
due diligence 222, 225–6, 227–8, 244

E

early transition countries (ETCs)
   challenges of 322–31
   more support needed 331–2
   municipal development 200–1
   and SSF 350
   water services and wastewater treatment 205
Early Transition Countries Initiative (ETCI) 331–2
Earth Summit
   (1992) Rio de Janeiro 222–3
   (2002) Johannesburg 206
Economic Advisory Council 71, 90–1
Economic and Financial Affairs Council (ECOFIN) 28
Economic and Monetary Union (EMU) 19–20, 24, 25
economic challenges 76–7
economic growth 344–5
economic indicators 79
Economics Advisory Committee 53
'Economics of Transition' conference 91
Economics of Transition (journal) 91
economies
   1980s eastern 8–12
   1980s western 6–8
   of EBRD region 335–7
economists, disagreements with bankers 284–9
EDF 174
Edison 215
Egis 165–6
Egypt 33, 39, 41
Emerging Transition Countries Initiative 332
"End of History" 12, 13–14
ENEL 176
Energoatom 260
energy efficiency 78, 221
energy sector 173–6, 250
enterprise challenges 77

363

Environment Advisory Council 91
Environment and Social Advisory Council 91
Environmental Action Agreement 232
Environmental Action Plans (EAPs) 225, 227
Environmental and Social Action Plans 246
Environmental and Social Impact Assessments 246
Environmental Appraisal Unit (EAU) 226
environmental department 112
Environmental Impact Assessment, Sakhalin II 244
environmental issues
    addressing the legacy 224–8
    attention to in projects 84–5
    bank's approach to 225
    challenges 78–9
    controversial cases 242–7
    "environmental transition" 223
    in industrial projects 228–33
    matters 221
    and municipal development 218–20
    policy approach 87–9
    rehabilitation 80
    risk management 227
    role for the bank 36, 222–4
    sound management practices 71–2
    standards 225–6
    sustainability 43, 78, 223
Environmental Management and Audit Scheme (EMAS) 227
environmental management systems (EMS) 226–7
Environmental Policy and Environmental Procedures (1996) 226
Environmental Programme for the Danube River Basin (1992) 334
Environmental Remediation Account (ERA) 263
Environmental Remediation Agreement 232
E.ON 174, 176
Erste Bank of Austria 178
Estonia
    accession to EU 334
    commitments to 103
    declares independence 97
    district heating 210
    environmental issues 228
    graduation expectations 343
    investment volume 345
    membership 101
    municipal development 192
    transition 126
    transition indicators 271
    water services and wastewater treatment 198
Euratom 261
Eurofed 62
Europe 8, 18–19, 20, 155
"European Bank" 62
European Central Bank (ECB) 20, 37, 62
European Charter of Local Self-Government 174, 186
European Coal and Steel Community 22
European Commission
    and break-up of USSR 98
    co-financing 334
    coordination of assistance 16–17
    and environmental management 234
    and EU accession 334
    and IMF meetings 62
    and Kosovo crisis 318
    membership 36
    and NDEP 241
    and nuclear safety 252, 254, 257, 259, 262, 263
    and Russian crisis 293, 306–7
    as shareholders 25, 31–2, 38, 39
European Community (EC)
    and AEB 29
    and break-up of USSR 97–8
    closer union 19, 20
    integration 5–6
    and nuclear safety 251–2, 258–9, 261
    as shareholders 25, 31–3, 36, 40, 44
    and Soviet Union 98
    and TACIS programmes 159, 162, 259
    view on Soviet membership 32–3, 39
    and Yugoslavia 103
European Council
    (1989) (Strasbourg) 5, 20, 24–7
    (1989) Paris special 24
    (1993) Copenhagen 333
    (1997) Luxembourg 333–4
    (2000) Feira 241
    (2000) Nice 334
    (2001) Goteborg 241, 334

(2002) Copenhagen 335
European Economic Community (EEC) 40, 344
European Energy Community 261
European Environment Agency 37
European Investment Bank (EIB)
  co-financing 66, 217, 334
  as an IFI 19, 21, 22, 28
  and Kosovo crisis 318
  loan from 48
  membership 36
  and nuclear safety 253
  and privatisations 172
  and risk 87
  as shareholders 25, 31, 38, 40
European Parliament 22, 334
European Trade Marks Office 37
European Union (EU)
  accession to 208, 254, 331, 332–5, 337
  acquis communautaire 333, 339
  as donor to RVF 145
  environmental standards 226
  as funding source 349–50
  and NDEP 240
  pre-accession and post-accession grants 215
  and solid waste management 208–9
  standards for waste water 220
  and TACIS programmes 240
European Venture Capital Association 147
Evaluation Department
  on environmental procedures 226
  on the MUDP 196–7
  on municipal development 218
  perspective 277
  on privatisation projects 166, 174
  on privatisations 176
  report 2010 176
Evaluation Department Special Study on the Danube RIver Basin (2008) 235–6
Evaluation Special Study (2001) 228, 231
Evaluation Study (2002) 137
ExCom 286
Executive Committee 55, 69, 280
expenses *see* administration expenses
Extended Financing Facility for Russia (IMF) 295
"extended producer responsibility" 209
External Affairs 69

F

Federal Republic of Germany 11, 38, 39, 40
Federal Republic of Yugoslavia (FRY) 104, 317, 318–19
federation for each republic 97
Fedorov, Boris 96
financial and operational improvement programmes (FOPIPs) 198, 211
Financial and Operations Policies Committee (FOPC) 135, 274, 278, 340
financial deregulation 7
financial institutions 80, 134–42, 227–8
Financial Institutions Development Programme (FIDP) 136–7, 298–9
financial intermediaries 65, 116–17, 119, 133
financial results 345–51
financial risk analysis 278–80
financial sustainability 121
Finland 23, 40, 236–7, 239, 240
First Vice President (FVP) 111–12
Fitoussi, Jean-Paul 51
Flemming, John 48–9, 51, 92, 98, 113, 269–70
foreign direct investment (FDI) 73, 80, 126, 168, 191, 229, 316, 335–6
foreign joint ventures 115
Former Yugoslav Republic of Macedonia 104, 187
Fortum of Finland 176
Four Powers 18, 26
France
  donor to RVF 145
  and EBRD's initial capital 31
  and European unity 14, 19
  financing EBRD 48
  and IMF quotas 37, 38
  one of Four Powers 18, 26
  and proposal for EBRD 14–17, 25, 26–9
  public transport 207
  ratification of Treaty 47
  as shareholders 31, 40
  special European Council meeting (1989) 24
  and USSR 34
  view on 'Bank for Europe' 20
Frank, Charles 283–4, 314, 325–6
Frank Knight and Rutley 61
Freeman, Ron 67, 107, 111–13, 120, 265, 278–80, 283–4

Fukuyama, Francis 13–14
FYR Macedonia 140, 200, 271, 318

G

G7
   and EBRD negotiations 26, 29, 38
   and environmental issues 36
   and the FIDP 136
   funding RSBF 138–9
   Memorandum of Understanding 257
   and nuclear safety 251–2, 258–9
   as shareholders 39
   Soviet Study 53
   wary of Soviet Union 50
G7 Deputies 98, 107, 252
G7 Directors 96
G7 Economic Summit 92, 93–5
G7 Heads Summit
   (1989) Paris 14–17
   (1990) Houston 49–50
   (1991) London, 92–5
   (1992) Munich 105, 251–2
   (1993) Tokyo 138, 253
   (1994) Naples 253, 256
   (1995) Halifax 257
   (1997) Denver 259
G8 349–50
G24 16, 31, 105, 252
Gaidar, Yegor 143, 159
Garofano, Giuseppe 57, 67
Gates, Bob 50
GAZ 301
Gazprom 175, 244
GE Capital 284
General Counsel 102, 284, 325
Genscher, Hans-Dietrich 10
Georgia 92, 102, 200, 205, 245–6, 271, 330
Gerashchenko, Viktor 30, 34–5, 102
"Gerashchenko letter" 33
German Democratic Republic (GDR) 6, 10–11, 17, 39, 41, 101
Germany
   borders 10, 23
   country of operation 75
   donor to RVF 145
   and EBRD's initial capital 31
   and IMF quotas 37
   interpretation of events 14
   and proposal for EBRD 25
   public transport 207
   ratification of Treaty 47
   reunification 14, 17–18, 24–6, 29, 32, 39, 59
   as shareholders 31
Gibson, Paul 106
GKI 143
GKOs (short-term rouble notes) 296, 297, 302–3
glasnost 5, 9
Goodman, Dick 60
Gorbachev, Mikhail
   agreement on Germany 39
   announces federation 97
   and dissolution of Soviet Union 98–9
   EBRD support for 92
   facing challenges 50
   and market reforms 5, 94–5
   and political and economic reforms 9
   political pressure on 92–4
   resignation 97, 99
   role in G7 summit 16
   tensions with Yeltsin 93
   view on German reunification 17–18, 26, 32
   visit from Attali 48–9
Gosbank 52
Gosplan 52
Gostomel 153
governance of EBRD 43–4, 47, 72
Governors' Resolution 348–51
"gradualist approach" 152–3
graduation 125–8, 339–41
Greece 23, 40
Green Economy Transition programme 221
Greenpeace 243
gross domestic product (GDP) 7, 8, 76, 79
gross national product (GNP) 8
Group Pekao 178–9
guidelines for EBRD 79–80
"Guidelines for Stabilisation of the Economy and the Transition to a Market System" 93
Gulf of Finland 233, 237, 239, 240
Gutfreund, John 70

H

Harada, Bob 279
Hare, Paul 51, 272–4
Havel, Vaclav 11, 61, 71

Hayek, Friederich von 268
Headquarters Agreement 45, 63
health and safety (H&S) 81, 208, 227–9, 231
heating, district 210–11
Helsinki Commission (HELCOM) 236–7
Helsinki Convention (1974) 236
Herrhausen, Alfred 21
Hexter, David 301
Higgins, Andrew 300
historical context 5–12
Host Country Agreements 118
HTC 172–3
human rights 89, 246, 323, 326, 327, 328–9
Hungary
    accession to EU 333, 334
    aid to 15–16
    beneficiary country 6
    car ownership 206
    commitments to 103
    country of operation 75
    country strategy 90
    demands for reform 10
    district heating 211
    and environmental issues 228
    first projects 83–4
    graduation expectations 343
    joint ventures 9
    large state enterprises 77
    loan finance 21
    local self-government 186–7
    and market economy 123
    membership of Council of Europe 186–7
    opening of border with Austria 10
    PPPs 215
    privatisations 165–6, 172–4
    projects 114, 120
    ratification of Treaty 47
    Resident Office 118
    as shareholders 41
    small-asset privatisation 153
    trade risks 100
    transition 126
    transition indicators 271, 272
    US aid to 27
    visit from Attali 49
    water services and wastewater treatment 205
    and World Bank 19
Hydro Aluminium (HAL) 231

I

Iceland 40, 240–1
ideological issues 12–14
IGC 24, 25
Ignalina International Decommissioning Support Fund (IIDSF) 262
Ignalina nuclear power plant 254
impact of EBRD 267–8
inauguration of EBRD 69–72
incentive systems 54
income growth 7
India 69
industrial projects 228–33
industrial sectors 164–71
industrialization 222
inflation 79, 294–5
infrastructure 80, 114–15, 214
ING 84
initial public offerings (IPOs) 154, 163, 164, 165–6, 167, 178–9, 181
Inkombank 298, 301
institutional culture of EBRD 64
'Institutional Priorities and Medium-Term Scenarios' 115
institution-building plan (IBP) 178
Instrument for Structural Funds for Pre-Accession (ISPA) 234–5, 334
Inter-American Development Bank 44
interest rates 7
Intergovernmental Conference (IGC) 20
Interim Spent Fuel Facility (ISF-2) 258, 350
International Bank for Reconstruction and Development (IBRD) 26, 82
International Commission 234
international decommissioning funds 261–2
International Energy Agency (IEA) 253
International Finance Corporation (IFC)
    co-financing 65, 217, 246–7
    and corporate scorecard 315
    finance from 230
    and Kosovo crisis 318
    legal texts from 21
    not visible in area 114
    and privatisations 172, 177–8, 180
    and Russian crisis 293, 300, 302
    staff experience from 66
    technical cooperation programmes 347
    and Tokobank 300
    use of experience of 56

international financial institutions (IFIs)
   co-financing 87, 98, 217, 331–2
   criticism of 44
   EBRD as 27–9
   and environmental protection 87, 222, 223, 225
   and inauguration of EBRD 70
   and infrastructure projects 115
   legal texts from 45
   and nuclear safety 256
   objective 31
   proposal for new 13, 19, 35, 46, 74
   and Russian crisis 293
   sovereign lending 211
International Limited Election Observation Mission (LL-EOM) assessment 324
International Maritime Organisation (IMO) 70
International Monetary Fund (IMF)
   country programmes model 110
   EBRD meetings 49, 98
   and inauguration of EBRD 70
   and privatisations 178
   quotas review 37–8
   and Russian crisis 293–4, 295, 297, 306
   Soviet Study 50, 92
   and the Soviet Union 32, 95, 98
   stand-by-arrangement (SBA) 294
   World Bank meetings 21, 37–8, 62
International Organisation for Standardization (ISO) 227
international standard banks (ISBs) 136
International Water Limited 215
Intesa Sanpaolo 181
IntesaBCI (IBCI) 180–1
Investiční Banka 84
investment
   in economies of regions 73
   opportunities 63–4
   prohibited 80
   volume 340–1, 344–5
Investment Committee 55–6
investment criteria of EBRD 43
'Investment Projects and the Transition Process' 267
Ireland 25, 40
Iron Curtain 8, 9, 11, 30
Ispat Karmet Steel Works (Kazakhstan) 230–1

Israel 33, 40
Italy 23, 40, 145

J

Japan
   and activities of EBRD 35
   and currency denomination 34
   dominance 19
   donor to RVF 145
   and European issues 27–8, 31
   and graduation 339
   and IMF quotas 37, 38
   military conversion 155
   privatisation funding 162
   reluctance to finance Soviet Union 50
   and Russian crisis 297
   as shareholders 31, 39, 41
   and the Soviet Union 97
   view on Soviet membership 32–3
Jaruzelski, General Wojciech 10
Jay, Sylvia 47–8
JEXIM 242
joint ventures 115
JSC Ispat Karmet 230
Juncker, Jean-Claude 338

K

Kaempfer, Steven 303
Kalousek, Miroslav 343
Kamaz International Management Company (KIMCO) 170–1, 301
Karaganda Metallurgical Kombinat (Karmet) 230
Karimov, Islam 328–9
Kaunas, Lithuania 213
Kazakhstan 99, 102, 147–8, 230–1, 263, 271, 316, 327
KBC 180
Kershaw, Ian 12
KfW 217
Kiev Dairy No. 2 153
Kiriyenko, Sergei 296
Kispo 153
KKR 170
Klaus, Vaclav 30
Klingensmith, David 279
Kohl, Helmut 11, 15, 17–18, 24, 25–6, 32
Köhler, Horst 119, 252, 284, 287, 302, 303–4, 311, 314

Kok, Wim 70
Kołodziński, Pawel 83
Komercijalna Banka 140
KomiArctic Oil 301
Kornai, Janos 70
Kosovo 103, 318–19
Kosovo crisis 318–19
Kozloduy International Decommissioning Support Fund (KIDSF) 262
Kraft Foods 161
Kuchma, Leonid 162, 257, 259
Kyiv, Ukraine 118
Kyrgyz Republic 99, 102, 205, 263, 330
Kyrgyzstan 271

L

landfill 209
Landfill Directive (1999) 209
Lankes, Hans Peter 266, 267, 274–8, 287
large state enterprises 77, 78, 156
large-scale privatisations and restructurings 164–81
Latin America 13
Latvia
  accession to EU 334
  commitments to 103
  declares independence 97
  district heating 210
  investment volume 345
  membership 101
  and Russian crisis 302
  transition indicators 271
le Blanc, Bart 60–1, 96
Le Cacheux, Jacques 51
Le Lorier, Anne 59
Legal Indicator Survey 215–16
legislative programmes 76
Lemierre, Jean 241, 314, 326, 327–9, 339–40, 342, 348, 351
lending capacity 73
Lending Committee 55–6
liberal democracy 7–8, 12–14
liberalisation 152–7
Liechtenstein 33, 40
Lipton, David 151
Liquid Radioactive Waste Treatment Plant (LRTP) 258
liquified natural gas (LNG) 244

Lithuania
  accession to EU 334
  commitments to 103
  decommissioning of reactors 261–2
  membership 101
  nuclear safety 251, 254, 262
  transition indicators 271
  urban transport 213
  water services and wastewater treatment 205
Ljungh, Anders 60
loans-for-shares scheme 295
local currency finance 216–17
local self-government 186–91
local services 185–6
localisation 117–20
location of EBRD 37–9, 48, 61, 105–6
London, UK 7, 37, 38–9, 48, 61, 105
London Stock Exchange 84, 167
losses 74
Lowery, Clay 341
Lubbers, Ruud 25, 26, 29
Lukashenko, Aleksandr 324
Luxembourg 40

M

Macedonia 104
MagyarCom 172
Major, John 62, 70, 94–5
Malta 40, 69, 334, 335
"manageable growth" 124
manufacturing sector 170–1
market economics 6, 12–14, 270
market reform 7–8
"markets as a process" 268
"Marshall Plan" effort 31
"marshrutkas" 207
Mass Privatisation Programme (MPP) 159–62
Matav, the Hungarian Telecommunications Company (HTC) 172–3
McCulloch, Michael 331
McKinsey 68
medium-sized and large enterprises 153
membership of EBRD 74, 317–22
Memorandum of Understanding 175, 257
Merchant Banking department 75, 81
Merchant Banking Vice Presidency 68
Mexico 33, 39, 41, 124
micro and small enterprises (MSEs) 139

Micro-Enterprise Bank of Bosnia and Herzegovina 319
military conversion 155
Millennium Challenge Corporation 217
Millennium Development Goals (MDGs) 206
Ministry of Power and Electrification (Minenergo) 175
Mises, Ludwig von 268
mission accomplished for EBRD 337–9
Mitterrand, François 5, 17–22, 24–7, 29, 30, 70, 138
Miyazawa, Kiichi 138
Mladenov, Petar 11
"Modernisation and Development Bank for Eastern Europe" 24
Moldova
   abstaining from referendum on Soviet Union 92
   and CIS 99
   declares independence 97
   district heating 211
   as ETC 330
   municipal development 200
   recipient country 102
   road accident rates 206
   and Russian crisis 302
   transition indicators 271
   water services and wastewater treatment 205, 206
Mongolia 319–22, 332
Mongolia Cooperation Fund 321
Montague, Adrian 60
Montenegro 104, 202, 319
Morocco 33, 39, 41, 124
Moscow City 158–9
Moscow City Municipality privatisation programme 97
Moscow State Property Agency (MKI) 158
'Moving Transition Forward: Operational Priorities for the Medium Term' 312–13, 315
Mulford, David 30, 34
mulilateral interests 23
Multi-Donor Fund 332
multilateral development banks (MDBs) 206, 274, 331
multilateral fund for nuclear safety 105
Multilateral Nuclear Safety Fund *see* Nuclear Safety Account (NSA)

multiparty democracy 6
multi-product facilities 117
municipal and environment infrastructure (MEI) 192, 195, 200–1, 207, 211, 215–16
municipal development
   affordability 203–4
   bank's approach to 218–20
   core sectors 204–11
   district heating 210–11
   in less advanced countries 200–1
   obstacles to progress 190–1
   operations policy paper 189–90
   private-sector participation 213–17
   private-sector solutions 213–16
   projects 198–204
   and PSCs and PSAs 211–13
   role for the bank 80
   Romania 192–8
   small and challenging projects 198–9
   in smaller municipalities 201–2
   solid waste management 208–10
   sovereign lending 199–200
   sub-sovereign lending 199–200
   Tajikistan 202
   urban transport 204, 206–8
   water services and wastewater treatment 204–6
Municipal Development Operations Policy (1992) 189–91
Municipal Environmental Loan Facility (MELF) 201
municipal support agreements (MSAs) 211–12, 218–19
Municipal Utilities Development Programme (MUDP) 192–7, 235

N

Nagy, Imre 10
naming of EBRD 26
National Bank of Romania 177
National Bank of Slovakia (NBS) 179–80
National Environmental Action Plan for Moldova 206
National Investment Funds (NIFs) 163–4
National Property Fund 232
NATO 18, 23, 39
NatWest Securities Ltd 166
Nazarbayev, Nursultan 328
Nemeth, Miklos 10, 60

Nemtsov, Boris 295
Netherlands 38, 40, 339
Neva River 237
New Safe Confinement project 259–60
New Zealand 39, 41, 124, 339, 348
Newburg, Andre 61, 140
Newmont 229–30
Niyazov, Saparmurat 325–6
NMB 84
non-allocated shares 41
non-governmental organisations (NGOs) 89, 91, 222, 242–4, 245, 246, 328
non-performing loan (NPL) 177
non-sovereign lending 211–13
Nordic Investment Bank (NIB) 66, 217, 240–1
Normak, Tanya 273–4
North Macedonia 187
Northern Dimension Environmental Partnership (NDEP) 240–2, 263, 350
North-South divide 110–11
Norway 23, 40, 240
Novo-Ogaryovo process of negotiations 92–3
NSC (Chernobyl Shelter Fund) 350
nuclear capacity 250–1
nuclear energy 221
nuclear legacy 250–5
Nuclear Regulatory Authority of Ukraine 260
nuclear safety 74, 105, 249–50, 261–3, 264
Nuclear Safety Account (NSA) 252–8
Nuclear Window 263

O

objective of EBRD 36
Oder-Neisse line 26
Office of the Chief Economist (OCE) 111, 269, 272, 274, 277, 284–7, 289
Official Development Assistance (ODA) 350
Official Journal of the European Communities 333
OFZs (longer-dated bonds) 296, 297
OGK-5 175–6
OGKs (large generation companies) 175
oil and gas sector 8, 85–6, 169–70
Oil Spill Response Plans 246
Okhta Tunnel 240
OMV 169
operational challenges of EBRD 65
operational policy issues 86–90
operational priorities 113–15, 312–13
operational reality of EBRD 44–5
operations 73–5, 82–6
Operations Committee (OpsCom) 69, 80, 111–12, 278–86, 288, 290, 300
Operations Manual 79–80, 86
OPIC 242
Organisation for Economic Corporation and Development (OECD)
    countries' growth 7
    EBRD meetings 49, 98
    experts from 226
    and the G24 16, 17, 18
    road accident rates 206
    as shareholders 26–8
    Soviet Study 50, 51
    water services and wastewater treatment 205
organisational structure of EBRD 53–6
output 76, 79

P

Pacific Environment 243
packaging sector 83–4
Paris Club 16, 295
Parker Drilling Company 85
Parker Siberia 85–6
Partnership on Economic Transformation conference 256
People's Republic of China 9
perestroika 5, 9
Petőfi Nyomda Rt. 83
Petrom 169–70
pharmaceutical industry 165–8
Phelps, Edmund 51–2, 70
Phibro Energy Inc 85
Phillips and Drew 61
pipelines 245–7
Pissaloux, Pierre 47–8
Pliva 167–8
"pocket banks" 136
Pöhl, Karl Otto 61, 62
Poland
    accession to EU 333, 334
    aid to 15–16
    and Albania 101
    beneficiary country 6
    commitments to 103

371

country of operation 75
country strategy 90
district heating 210, 211
economic growth 336
environmental issues 228
FDI 335
first projects 84
first Resident Office 118
large state enterprises 77
loan finance 21
local self-government 186–7
membership of Council of Europe 186–7
municipal development 217
National Investment Funds (NIFs) 163–4
operations in 82–3
PPPs 204, 215
private sector 63
privatisations 173–4, 178–9
projects 114, 120
reform in 151
and reunification of Germany 26
as shareholders 41, 348
small-asset privatisation 153
substandard loans in banking system 156
trade risks 99, 100
transition 126
transition impact 316
transition indicators 271
urbanisation 206
US aid to 27
visit from Attali 49
water services and wastewater treatment 205
and World Bank 19
Poland/Hungary Assistance for Reconstruction of Economies (PHARE) 17
Polish Mass Privatisation Programme (PMPP) 153–64
Polish Private Equity and Enterprise Funds 149
political challenges of EBRD 76
political conditionality of EBRD 30–1
political freedoms 9–12, 21
political institution 46
political mandate 89–90
pollution 233–47
"portfolio approach" (1999) 204
portfolio value 345–7
Portugal 40

Post-Privatisation Funds (PPFs) 142, 147–8
post-privatisation programmes 141–50
Post-Signature Conferences 49, 53, 57–9, 67, 68–9
Powell, Charles 28
power sector 173–6
preparations for EBRD 29–36, 46–9, 60–1
Presidents 6, 38, 39, 46, 47, 58–9, 71, 106–11, 113
private equity funds 148–50
private equity investment 144–7, 148–50
private sector
  development 46
  enterprise 7
  investment 35, 70–1
  participation 213–17
  priority 114–15
  size 63
  support for 115–17
private-to-public financing ratio 116, 120
Privatisation Advisory Programme, Evaluation Report 162
Privatisation Advisory Programme for the Russian Federation (PAPRF) 159–60
Privatisation Law (Hungary) 166
privatisation programmes 157–64, 182
privatisations
  bank's approach to 153–7, 181–2
  challenges of 77
  historical context 7–8
  industrial sectors 164–71
  large-scale 164–81
  lessons from 181–3
  post-privatisation programmes 141–50
  smaller 76
  supporting 151–3
  in the UK 7
Privredna Banka Zagreb (PBZ) 180–1
procurement 219
Production Sharing Agreements (PSAs) 200, 211–13, 218–19, 242–3
productivity 117
profitability 120–2, 339, 345–9
prohibited investments 80
Project Evaluation Department (PED) 123, 266, 272, 273, 274
Project Support Agreements (PSAs) 195–6, 200, 211–13, 218–19, 242–3
projects 66, 74, 82–5, 111–12

Provisional IRA 105
Public Consultation and Disclosure Plans 246
Public Information Policy 328
public infrastructure projects 114–15
public service contracts (PSCs) 195–6, 200, 202, 208, 211–13, 218
public transport 207–8, 218–19
public-private partnerships (PPPs) 204, 214–15, 219, 240, 313
Putin, Vladimir 340

R

Rahmon, Emomali 328
Raiffeisen Zentralbank Österreich (RZB) 140, 213, 217
RAO UES (Unified Energy System of Russia) 175–6
RBMK reactors 251, 252–3, 254
Reagan, Ronald 7, 8, 9
"Reagan-Thatcher era" 7–8
Regional Development Initiative 246
regional offices 74, 117–20
regional trade 99–100
Regional Venture Funds (RVFs) 142–7, 304
regulated sectors 171–81
Reiniger, Peter 166
reorganisation 110–13, 128–9
Republic of Korea *see* South Korea
Republic of Tatarstan 170–1
reserves allocation 347–8
Resettlement Acton Plans 246
Resident Offices 59, 118–20, 237, 301–2, 319, 341
responses to challenges 79–81
restructuring
    of large enterprises 157
    large state enterprises 78
    large-scale 164–81
    lessons from experience of 182–3
    and privatisation 153–4
    supporting 151–3
Right-of-Way Reinstatement Plans 246
risk analysis 64–5, 86–7, 278–80
risk assessment 278–80
road accident rates 206
Robert Fleming & Co 84
Robinson, Mary 61
Rocard, Michel 24
role of bank 337–9
Romania
    accession to EU 333, 334, 335, 337, 339
    beneficiary country 6
    commitments to 103
    country of operation 75
    country strategy 90
    Danube Delta 233, 234–6
    infrastructure 192–6
    municipal development 192–8, 201, 217
    opposition to communist authorities 12
    privatisations 169–70, 177–8
    projects 114
    public transport 207
    ratification of Treaty 47
    and Russian crisis 313
    as shareholders 41
    transition impact 316
    transition indicators 271
    water services and wastewater treatment 192–6, 202, 205, 213, 234–6
Romanian Munipal Utitlities Development Programme (MUDP) 192–8
Rostropovich, Mstislav 70
RTS stock index 296
Ruding, Onno 29
Runicom 306
Russia
    banks in 136
    Belovezha Accords 99
    disputes over gas supplies 340
    district heating 210
    economic recovery 313–14
    economy following the crisis 307
    energy supply from 250
    environmental issues 228
    exports 141
    investment 336, 340, 341, 344
    local self-government 187, 216
    membership of World Bank 136
    military conversion 155
    municipal development 200
    and NDEP 240–2
    nuclear safety 251, 253–4, 258
    privatisations 175–6
    progress of reforms 143
    projects 114
    recipient country 102
    Resident Office 118

and Sakhalin II 242–3
share of bank's portfolio 311
and the Strategic Reserve 350
urbanisation 206
water services and wastewater treatment 198, 205
Russia Project Finance Bank (RPFB) 305
Russia Small Business Fund (RSBF) 136, 137–9, 304–5, 308
Russian crisis
  background 294–7
  consequences for the EBRD 301–3
  economy following the 307–8
  efforts to assist 303–6
  events 293–4
  impact on EBRD 311
  implications for EBRD 306–7
  lessons learned by EBRD 307–9
  review of strategy following the 311–15
  and Tokobank 298–301
Russian Federation 170–1, 271
Russian Project Finance Bank (RPFB) 304–5
Russian Venture Capital Association (RVCA) 147
Russo, Massimo 98
RWE 174
RZB 217

S

Sachs, Jeffrey 151–2
Sakhalin Energy Investment Company 242–5
Sakhalin Environment Watch 243
Sakhalin II 242–5
Sakhalin Island Minorities Development Plan 244
Sakhalin Oil 301
Santander Bank Polska 83
Sarcinelli, Mario 67, 111
Sberbank 137
SBS-Agro 306
Schabowski, Guenter 11
Schankerman, Mark 266, 267
Scheppers, Manfred 346–7
Schevernazde, Edward 328
Schlüter, Poul 26
Schumann, Robert 22
Schumpeter, Joseph 268
sector teams 110–11
Serbia 104, 200, 201, 319
Servier 166
Shareholder Special Fund (SSF) 349–50
shareholders of EBRD 25, 31–2, 40–1, 73
Sherbank 305
Short, Clare 328–9
Sibneft 306
Sidell, Ron 106
Single European Act (1987) 72
Şişecam 168
Skidmore, Owings and Merrill 106
Skrzypek, Slawomir 348
Slovak Republic
  decommissioning of reactors 261–2
  "extended producer responsibility" 209–10
  FDI 335
  local self-government 187
  nuclear safety 254
  privatisations 174
  transition 126
  transition indicators 271
Slovakia 251, 334
Slovalco Aluminium Smelter Project 231–3
Slovenia
  accession to EU 333, 334
  environmental issues 228
  graduation expectations 343
  independence declaration 103–4
  membership 104
  transition 126
  transition indicators 271
small and medium-sized enterprises (SMEs)
  challenges of 78, 119
  in competitive private sector 63
  development 80, 127, 133, 156, 284, 304
  funds for 116, 139, 148, 227, 325
  in market economy 114
  projects 84–5
  and Russian crisis 308, 313
Small Business Credit Bank (KMB) 305
Small Business Initiative (SBI) 332
small-asset privatisation 153
social level challenges 76
Socialist Federal Republic of Yugoslavia (SFRY) 6, 75, 103–4, 317
Société Générale 217
soda ash plants 168–9
Sodi 168–9
solid waste management 208–10, 219, 220

Solidarity 9, 10
Solvay 168
Soros Economic Development Fund 305
sound banking principle 64
South Korea 27, 33, 39, 41, 69
sovereign lending 199–200
Soviet Constitution 34
Soviet Kyshtym disaster 250
Soviet Study 49–53, 92, 95
Soviet Union
    9+1 Agreement 93
    "500 days" plan 93
    Action Plan 97–8
    allocation of shares 32
    appointment of Gorbachev 5
    approach towards 92–9
    break-up 97, 249
    on brink of disintegration 59
    collapse in trade 76, 141
    collapse of communism 27
    commitment to reform 34
    countries as equal members 72
    country of operation 75
    country strategy 93, 95–7
    deterioration of economy 92
    dissolution 12, 73–4, 99
    economic reforms 9
    economy 49–50
    environmental issues 227
    federation announced 97
    first operations in 85–6
    joint ventures 9
    membership 32–4, 39, 104
    military conversion 155
    mounting concerns 49–50
    nuclear legacy 250–5
    oil production 85
    one of Four Powers 18, 26
    possible inclusion in Europe 6
    and preparatory conference 29–30, 31
    rationing 79
    reform 5
    reluctance to finance 50
    role in G7 summit 16
    as shareholders 25
    Soviet Study 49–53, 92
    stagnation of economy 24
Sovinet 85
Spain 25, 40

Special Association Agreement (IMF) 98
Special Privatisation and Restructuring Programme (SPRP) 143–4
Special Restructuring Facility 157
Special Restructuring Programme (SRP) 104, 142
special-purpose vehicle (SPV) 239
St. Petersburg Flood Protection Barrier 239
St. Petersburg Municipal Support Project 238
St. Petersburg Northern Wastewater Treatment Plant Incinerator 239–40
St. Petersburg, Russia 198, 200, 214, 236–40
St. Petersburg South West Wastewater Treatment Plant 239
St. Petersburg Toxic Waste Emergency Clean-up Programme 239
St. Petersburg Vodokanal Neva Discharges Closure 240
St. Petersburg Water and Environmental Improvement Programme 238–9
Stability Pact for South Eastern Europe 318, 330
staff numbers of EBRD 73, 74–5
Standard and Poor's 86–7, 279
stand-by-arrangement (SBA) 294
State Committee for the Management of State Property (GKI) 159
State Property Fund (of Ukraine) (SPF) 162
state sector enterprise 7, 35
State Statistics Committee 160
Stern, Nick
    as Chief Economist 113, 123
    impact 266–7
    part of ideal combination 265
    transition impact 272, 280, 284–5
    view on Russian crisis 309
    view on transition 269–70
    view on transition impact 274–8
Stern. Ernie 56–7, 62, 67
Stern-Lankes approach 280
Strategic Operations Framework 350
Strategic Reserve 349–50
strategy review of EBRD 311–15
"Stronger Local Presence" 118
subsidiary loan agreement (SLA) 195
sub-sovereign lending 211–13, 218–19
Suez Environment 215
Summers, Larry 51

sustainable development
  definition 222
  importance 221
  pursuit of 222
Swedbank 213
Sweden 40
Switzerland 40, 138–9, 339

T

Tajikistan
  and CIS 99
  as ETC 330
  municipal development 200, 202
  recipient country 102
  transition indicators 271
  uranium mining 263
  water services and wastewater treatment 202, 205
TAM-BAS 347
Tanaka, Josué 346–7
Task Forces 113–15, 116, 118, 137
Taylor, John 128
teams formation 80
Technical Aid to the Commonwealth of Independent States (TACIS) 159, 162, 240, 259
technical cooperation programmes 347
technological innovation 7
telecommunications 172–3
Telecommunications Law (Hungary) 172
TGKs (regional generating companies) 175
Thatcher, Margaret
  and "Bank for Europe" 25, 26
  election 7
  and Gorbachev 9
  ousted 8
  view on German reunification 17–18, 26
  view on international involvement in bank 28
"Thatcher revolution" 7
Three Mile Island (USA) 249–50
Tokobank 298–301
trade
  collapse in 76
  downturn in 141
  links between east and west 8–9
  regional 99–100
Trade Facilitation Programme (TFP) 136, 141–2

trade finance 140–2
trade-facilitation product 140–2
transition
  checklist 275–7
  completion of 125–8
  investment 43
  varying rates of 123–4
transition impact
  debate about 290
  defining and operationalising 266–70
  formal measurement system 274–8
  multiplier 277
  principle 66
  ratings system 280–9
  success of 316
  "transition impact culture" 289
  transition impact monitoring system (TIMS) 287–9
  transition indicators 123, 126–8, 270–4
Transition Reports 123, 269, 270–1, 290, 308, 313
Treaty establishing EBRD 39–41, 46–9, 68, 69
Treaty of Accession 335
Treaty of Rome 5, 20, 72
Trichet, Jean-Claude 21
Triodos Bank 305
Troika 25, 26
Troika Dialog 171
Tuma, Zdenek 342
Turkey 40, 245–6, 334
Turkmenistan 99, 102, 271, 272, 325–6
Turnaround Management (TAM) 227
"two halves of Europe" 18–19

U

Ukraine
  Belovezha Accords 99
  Chernobyl disaster *see* Chernobyl disaster
  declares independence 97, 99
  disputes over gas supplies 340
  economic growth 322, 351
  Memorandum of Understanding 257
  municipal development 200
  nuclear safety 261
  recipient country 102
  Resident Office 118
  and Russian crisis 302, 313

water services and wastewater treatment 205
Ukraine Privatisation Advisory Programme 162–3
Ukrrichflot 162–3
unallocated shares 101
unemployment 76, 79
UniCredit 179
Unified Gas 301
Union of Soviet Socialist Republics (USSR)
    and the Baltic Sea 236–40
    beneficiary country 6
    borrowing limits 38, 50
    country strategy 92–8
    dissolution 98–100
    dissolution implications for EBRD 102–3
    environmental issues 221, 236–40
    membership 31–4, 48
    projects 85–6
    as shareholders 41
Union Treaty (Russian Republic) 93, 96
uniqueness of EBRD 43
United Kingdom (UK)
    and activities of EBRD 35
    co-financing 242
    and creation of the EBRD 27–8, 47
    economic thinking 13
    and the EMU 25
    financial reform 7
    and financing of EBRD 48
    and graduation 339
    and IMF quotas 37–8
    interpretation of events 14
    and location of EBRD 37, 45, 60, 61, 105
    market reform 7
    one of Four Powers 18, 26
    reluctance to finance Soviet Union 50
    schism to political unity 5
    as shareholders 31, 40
    view on Soviet membership 32–3
United Nations (UN) 45, 103, 222, 318
    UN Conference on Environment and Development (UNCED) (1992) (Earth Summit) 222–3
    UN Interim Administration Mission in Kosovo 318
uranium mining 263
urban development 80
urban transport 204, 206–8, 213, 218–19

urbanisation 190, 206
USA
    and activities of EBRD 35
    aid from 15
    concerns about Attali's style 58
    concerns over potential projects 67
    and currency denomination 34
    dominance 19
    donor to RVF 145
    and EBRD's initial capital 31
    economic growth and politics 7–8, 13
    Environmental Protection Policy 229
    financial deregulation 7
    and graduation 339, 341–2
    influence in Europe 23
    interest in nuclear dimension in Europe 23
    interpretation of events 14
    membership 36
    military conversion 155
    one of Four Powers 18, 26
    and political conditionality of EBRD 31
    power in World Bank 44
    reluctance to finance Soviet Union 50
    as shareholders 31, 33, 39, 41
    and Soviet commitment to reform 34
    sponsors of first projects in Soviet Union 85
    troops in West Germany 18, 23, 27
    view of Russia 340
    view on Soviet borrowing 38
    view on Soviet membership 32–3
    voted against Governors' Resolution 348
"user pays" principle 235
utilities 171–2
Uzbekistan 99, 102, 200, 228–30, 263, 271, 326–30

V

Varyeganneftegaz 85
Venezuela 69
Veolia 215, 219
Vienna Protocol (1985) 222
Vnesheconombank (Bank for Foreign Economic Affairs) 52, 217
Vodokanal 237–40
Volcker, Paul 7
voting procedures of EBRD 31, 32
VVER reactors 251, 252, 254, 261

W

Waigel, Theo 62, 71
Warsaw Pact 18, 93
Warsaw Stock Exchange (WSE) 153–64, 178, 179
"Washington Consensus" 12–13
waste management 208–10
water services and wastewater treatment
    Baltic States 198
    Croatia 198
    and the Danube River Basin 234–6
    Estonia 198
    and municipal development 204–6, 219
    municipal projects 201–2
    and NDEP 241
    and PPPs 215
    Romania 192–6, 202
    Russia 198
    St. Petersburg, Russia 198, 237–40
Western Balkans 317–18
White Nights 85
Wibble, Anne 107
Williams, Mike 279
Williamson, John 12–13
World Bank
    advice on privatisation 159
    appointments from 57, 60
    co-financing 65, 82–3, 217
    environmental standards 226
    Financial Institutions Development Programme (FIDP) 136–7, 298–9
    and Kosovo crisis 318
    legal texts from 21
    meeting with EBRD on Soviet Union 98
    meetings with IMF 37–8, 62
    and nuclear safety 253, 261
    and PAPRF 159–60
    possible duplication of effort 68
    power of USA 44
    as primary support 19
    and privatisations 169, 172
    risk 87
    and Russian crisis 293, 297, 302, 306
    and Russian membership of 136
    Soviet Study 50, 51
    special association of Soviet Union 95
    staff experience from 56, 66, 81
World Bank Public Sector Assistance Loan (PSAL2) 178
World Energy Council 210
World Institute for Development Economics Research 151
World Water Forum, Kyoto (2003) 206

Y

Yavlinsky, Grigory 98
Yeltsin, Boris 50, 93, 96, 98, 138, 143, 294, 295–6
yen 34
Yugoslav Republic of Macedonia 103–4
Yugoslavia 6, 8, 41, 74, 102, 103–4

Z

Zagreb 213
Zagreb Stock Exchange 167–8
Zalm, Gerrit 341
Zarafshan-Newmont Joint Venture (Uzbekistan) 228–30
Zavod Slovenskeho Narodneho Povstania (ZSNP) 231–3
zero-base budgeting (ZBB) 125, 283, 314
Zhivilo, Mikhail 300
Zhivkov, Todor 11
ZSE 174

The fall of the Berlin Wall in 1989 was one of the monumental events which led to the EBRD's creation © iStockphoto

The Berlin Wall ©iStockphoto

Aerial view of the destroyed reactor at Chernoby (1986) © EBRD

Since 1998 the EBRD has helped to restore and renovate Georgia's Enguri Dam, the world's second largest arch dam. © EBRD

First meeting of the EBRD Board of Directors elects the Board of Directors and approves the Bank's resolutions (May 1991) © EBRD

The EBRD's new London Headquarters opens at One Exchange Square in March 1993

Jacques Attali, EBRD President (April 1991–June 1993) © EBRD

Jacques Attali (left) and French businessman Antoine Riboud (right)
at the inauguration of the EBRD in London (16 April 1991) © Daniel Simon/Getty Images

Jacques de Larosière, EBRD President
(September 1993–January 1998) © EBRD

Horst Köhler, EBRD President,
(September 1998–April 2000) © EBRD

Jean Lemierre, EBRD President
(July 2000–July 2008) © EBRD

Jacques ATTALI

Paris, 23 May 1990

Dear Prime Minister,

The founding members of the European Bank for Reconstruction and Development have chosen London as the Headquarters of this new international institution. I am absolutely delighted. If I may say so, I am also sure that the arguments you put forward played an essential role in the choice.

As you know, this new institution will have the task of helping the Central and Eastern European countries evolve towards market economies, will help towards the development of a private sector in these countries and will help attract to them both foreign capital and know-how.

To enable the Bank both to start up under the best possible circumstances and to have the closest possible relations with the financial community in London, it should have a Headquarters in the City, worthy of its task. The financial conditions offered by the host country to help it to become established and to start functioning will also play an essential role in its success.

I hope that you will permit me therefore to draw your attention, and that of your government, to these material details, which you yourself mentioned in your brochure advocating London as the site, so that they can be quickly resolved in a satisfactory manner in the interests both of London and of the new institution.

Please accept, Prime Minister, the assurance of my very best regards and of my deepest respect.

Jacques ATTALI

The Rt. Hon. Mrs Margaret THATCHER, F.R.S., M.P.
Prime Minister of the United Kingdom of Great Britain and Northern Ireland

0022A ANNEX A

EUROPEAN BANK FOR RECONSTRUCTION AND DEVELOPMENT

FIRST POST SIGNATURE CONFERENCE 18/19 JULY 1990

AGENDA ITEM 1: PRESENTATION OF THE PRESIDENT DESIGNATE'S TEAM

M PISSALOUX	Cabinet
MRS JAY	Cabinet
MR BAUDON (France)*	Project Finance and Country Programming
MR GOODMAN (USA)	Legal
MR JAHR (FRG)	Information Technology
MR LINCOLN (Ireland)	Personnel
MR MARSHALL (Canada)	Treasury
MR NIEROP (Netherlands)	Legal
MR DE SELLIERS (Belgium)	Corporate Finance
MR STANTON (UK)	Administration and Finance

* Subject to confirmation from the World Bank

25 June 1991

PRESS RELEASE

At its meeting on 25 June 1991, the Board of Directors of the European Bank for Reconstruction and Development approved the Bank's first operation.

This operation is a loan of US$ 50 million (equivalent of about ECU 35 million), made to the Bank of Poznan (WBK), for onlending to several heating enterprises and other enterprises with privatisation potential in Poland involved in the production and sale of heat and steam.

The loan, guaranteed by the Republic of Poland, will have a 15 year maturity, including 5 years of grace.

The objectives of the project supported by the loan are to:

a) Support implementation of a comprehensive heating sector restructuring programme that would improve the regulatory framework and financial structure of the sector entities;

b) Extend the life of existing assets through rehabilitation and introduction of modern technologies, thereby significantly reducing capital expenditures;

c) Encourage energy conservation in the heating sector through appropriate investments and by supporting energy pricing reform, thereby improving the energy-related convertible currency earnings of Poland;

d) Reduce environmental pollution through investments in energy-efficient equipment and systems as well as by supporting a programme to replace small coal-fired boilers by gas-fired boilers.

This operation involves a parallel co-financing by the World Bank.

The first operation of the Bank has thus been approved less than 17 months after the launching of negotiations for the creation of the European Bank.

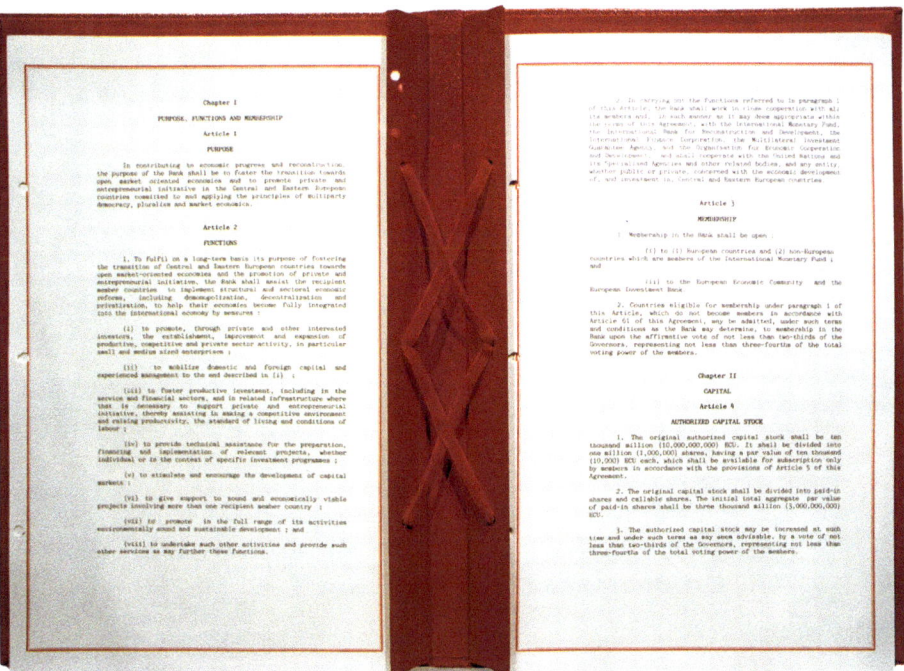

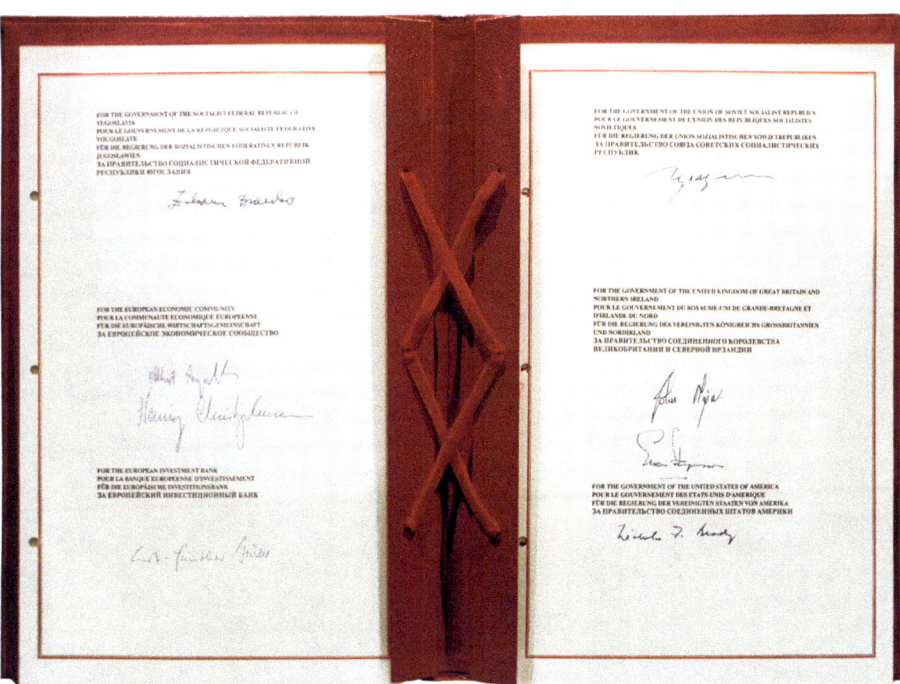

The Agreement Establishing the Bank (AEB). It was signed in Paris on 29 May 1990.
The Agreement entered into force on 28 March 1991 © EBRD

Poster commemorating the 1992 EBRD Annual Meeting in Budapest © EBRD

Poster commemorating the 1993 EBRD Annual Meeting in London © EBRD

Poster commemorating the 1994 EBRD Annual Meeting in St Petersburg © EBRD

Poster commemorating the 1995 EBRD Annual Meeting in London © EBRD

Poster commemorating the 1996 EBRD Annual Meeting in Sofia © EBRD

Poster commemorating the 1997 EBRD Annual Meeting in London © EBRD

Poster commemorating the 1998 EBRD Annual Meeting in Kiev © EBRD

Poster commemorating the 1999 EBRD Annual Meeting in London © EBRD

Ron Freeman, former Head of the Banking Department at the EBRD (1991-1997), visits the Bank as an alumnus in 2014 © EBRD

Nick Stern, former Chief Economist of the EBRD (May 1994-December 1999) visits the Bank as an alumnus in 2016 © EBRD

Ministers and Heads of Delegation pose for a group photograph in Paris at the launch of negotiations to establish the EBRD (January 1990) © EBRD

UK Prime Minister Margaret Thatcher and US President Ronald Reagan walking together through the grounds of the White House, Washington DC (19 November 1985)
© Keystone/Hulton Archive/Getty Images

Russian Politburo member Mikhail Gorbachev during an official visit to London (1984)
©Tom Stoddart/Getty Images

François Mitterrand (President of France) and John Major (UK Prime Minister) at the inauguration of the EBRD. It is attended by Governors representing the 41 initial members of the Bank (16 April 1991) © EBRD

World leaders gather in Paris for the 15th G7 Economic Summit (14-16 July 1989)
© Peter Turnley/Getty Images

François Mitterrand at the Elysée Palace (9 August 1990) © Eric Bouvet/Getty Images

Her Majesty Queen Elizabeth II visits the site of EBRD's Headquarters (at One Exchange Square), while it is still under construction (November 1991) © EBRD

Charles, Prince of Wales at the inauguration of EBRD's Headquarters at One Exchange Square (March 1993) © EBRD

Charles, Prince of Wales signs the plaque marking the inauguration of the EBRD's Headquarters at One Exchange Square (March 1993) © EBRD

*For Product Safety Concerns and Information please contact
our EU representative GPSR@taylorandfrancis.com Taylor & Francis
Verlag GmbH, Kaufingerstraße 24, 80331 München, Germany*